Math Contest Preparation, Problem Solving Strategies, and Math IQ Puzzles

for Grades 4 and 5

顶级

英文奥数, 解题策略, 及 IQ 思唯训练宝典

小学四, 五年级

Frank Ho   Amanda Ho

何数棋谜

Ho Math Chess Learning Centre

Table of Contents

Preface 前言

After over 20 years, 7 days a week of researching on creating math, chess, and puzzles workbooks, Ho Math Chess has made a revolutionary innovation in creating math worksheets. This long, tremendous, and practical teaching experience have helped us develop and create this series of Ultimate Math Contest Preparation, Problem Solving, and Math IQ Puzzles workbooks.

Ho Math Chess worksheets not only will raise students' marks; our worksheets also improve students' brainpower. This is achieved through our proprietary and copyrighted Frankho ChessDoku, Frankho ChessMazes, and various puzzles.

We have come a long way to reach today's progress; it has been hard work for our worksheets research team. We did not know how to answer when our students started to ask us when we will take some time off. We were very moved when our students requested to do our worksheets -- "Can I work on the worksheets which move numbers around?"

Ho Math Chess has shown its marketing strength by its teaching philosophy - fun math and is backed up by its substance that is our unique and world-first math, chess, and puzzles integrated math worksheets.

In the process of producing this grade 4 and 5 workbooks, I noticed that integers operations and algebraic equations had been taught to grade 4 students in China. It is debatable if algebra should be taught so early, especially in North America, when so many students are struggling with basic computations in grade 4, but since this workbook is also aiming to sell in China and Asian countries, so we bring this to meet to the highest international standard. The students using this workbook could be trained to participate in the international math contests, not just a local or any national math contest. Teachers or parents could decide if they want to teach algebra as an option; it is up to you.

Why is it so important to work on word problem-solving?
I give the following of my teaching experience as an example to demonstrate that it is s not enough just to do computations.

Computation Problem	Word problems	Comments
$37 \times 2 =?$ $74 \div 7 = ?$	Each pizza is cut into 7 equal pieces. Each child will eat about 2 pieces of pizza. How many pizzas are needed for a class of 37 children? **11 pizzas**	A grade 4 student had no problem to work out the answers for the Computation Problem. But when these two computation problems are combined to become a word problem, the student got totally confused and was not able to come up with an answer.

Frank Ho
April 2019

How were the Chinese classic model problems written? 中国古算题是如何写的?

Chinese classic word problems are classified according to their models. Around the 4th century, Chinese (孙子算经) was fascinated by the discoveries of various linear models, but these models were not documented from the modern algebra's viewpoint. Today, we learn to appreciate why those class model problems were passed on from generation to generation and even were taught in some of the Chinese math textbooks. These classic model problems present opportunities for students to do enriched math and learn difficult techniques on how to solve advanced word problems. They provide an opportunity to separate the wheat from the chaff.

Model 1, $a \pm x = b \pm x$, Give and Take, 取舍问题, 移多补少

The model of $a \pm x = b \pm x$ provides students with an opportunity to deal with more advanced subtraction word problems when $a \neq b$.

Example

Adam has 18 beads; Bob has 12 beads. How many beads that Adam must give to Bob so that each has the same number of beads?

Method 1, Use the Line Segment Diagram (Students should be taught this method before working on Chinese model problems.)

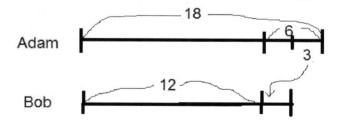

Method 2, Use T-table

The total number of beads does not change. So, the result must be 15 each.

Use a T-table to work backwards.

Bob	Adam
12	18
+3,15	-3, 15

Method 3 Use a given idea as follows.

The amount <u>given</u> = half of the difference 給数= 差数旳一半
Difference = 2 ties of given amount 差数 = 給数的 2 倍
(Use 2 and 0 as an example to figure the above.)

Adam gave Bob 8 apples so that each f them has the same number of apples. What was the original number of a difference?

The original difference I was 16.

Example

Adam has 15 apples, and Bob has 18 apples. Mom bought 7 more apples. How to share the 7 apples such that Adam and Bob, each of them has the same number of apples?

The total of all apples is $15 + 18 + 7 = 40$
If each gets 20, then they have an equal number of apples.
Working backwards, Adam must have 5 more, and Bob must have 2 more.

Example

Container A has 6 apples. Move 1 apple from container A to B, and then each container has the same number of apples. How many apples difference between containers A and B originally?

```
   A │ B
 ─────┼───────
   6  │ 6̸  4
 -1, 5│ +1, 5
      │
      │
```

6 apples difference

Model 2, Sum, Multiplier, Difference problems 和倍差問題

$x + y = a, x - y = b$ **Sum and Differnce** 和差問題

$x + y = a, x = by;\ ay + y + b = c; x : y = a : b, x + y + c$
$\qquad = d$ **Sum and Multiplier** 和倍問題

$x - y = a, x = by$ **Difference and multiple** 差倍問題

The Chinese math contest books use the Line Segment method or formulas to solve the above problems. We have offered different ideas to solve them.

Sum and Multiplier	Sum and Difference	Difference and Multiplier	Sum, Difference, Multiplier	Advanced Sum, Difference, Multiplier
Mrs. Su donated 39 chess books to her grade 1 and grade 2 classes, and grade 2 got twice as many books as the grade 1. How many books did each grade get?	Adam and Bob have 688 apples. Adam has 4 more than Bob. How many apples does each of them have originally?	Ms. Su donated 4 times as many books to grade 2 than grade 1, and the difference was 120. How many books did Ms. Su donate to grade 1 and grade 2?	There are 190 apples in boxes A, B, and C altogether. Box B has 3 times as many as Box C. Box C has 10 more than Box A. How many apples does each box have?	Bag A has 56 kg more than bag B. If 4 kg were eaten in bag B, then the weight of bag A is 4 times of bag B. What are the weights of bag A and bag B?
Method 1 uses the box method by changing "1 time" to "1 box". Assume the grade 1 got 1 box of books, then the grade 2 got 2 boxes. $\frac{39}{2+1}$ $= 13\ chess\ books\ for\ grade\ 1$ $13 \times 2 = 26$ chess books for grade 2	Method 1, Use the Line Segment Diagram. The method uses the formula. Method 3 Convert the same problem to Sum and Multiplier. $\frac{688 - 4}{2} = 342$ apples … Bob Adam 342 + 4 = 346	Method 1 Think the 1 time as one box. $\frac{120}{4-1} = 40$ books … grade 1 Grade = 4 x 40 = 160 books.	$3C = 3(10 + A)$ There are 190 apples in box A, B, and C altogether. Box B has 3 times as many as Box C. Box C has 10 more than Box A. How many apples does each box have? $10 + A$	$56 + B$ $B - 4$ Bag A has 56 kg more than bag B. If 4 kg were eaten in bag B, then the weight of bag A is 4 times of bag B. What are the weights of bag A and bag B? $56 + B = 4\ (B - 5)$ B = **19 kg** …. **bag B** $56 + 19 = $ **75 kg …. bag A**

Model 3 – Surplus and Shortage $ax \pm b = cx \pm d$ 盈亏問題

Use algebra to solve this kind of problem.

Model 4 – Chickens and Rabbits 鸡兔同笼

C +R = a
2C+ 4R = b

Use a diagram for grade 1 and then use the Assumption method for higher grades. Use the Systems of Equations for more complicated problems.

Model 5 – Planting trees 植树問題

Read the grade 3 and 4 workbooks for details on three models.

Why do most Chinese math contest books use formulas to teach student contest problems? 为何中文奥数書教学生用公式解题?

One thing that puzzled me is I found that many Chinese math contest books use formulas to solve many classic Chinese math word problems. This is very contradictory to the pedagogy of school textbooks. This way of using formulas to do math contests is not many Chinese schoolteachers would agree since I have read many reports published on their blogs.

After I taught some Canadian grade 2 to grade 5 students using the conceptual teaching method, I think one reason that Chinese math contest books use formula is to achieve the immediate effect, so everyone in the class can "do" work and move forward together.

Below is a math sheet that I used to experiment on some Canadian students and found that even after I explained with Line Segment Diagram, a method to solve the Sum and Difference problems, some students still could not comprehend. But if I taught them using formulas by simply plugging numbers into each formula, then everyone could do it. So, an after-school learning centre in China, for achieving the purpose that all students could solve the Sum and Difference problems, the formula is a much easier way of teaching them. Some Canadian students could not understand the concept of using the visual Line Segment Diagram on why or how they told me why I did not tell them earlier to just plug in the numbers to get answers after I showed them how to use formulas.

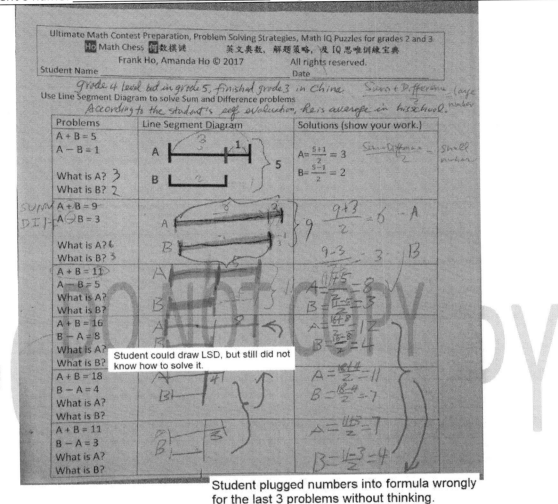

How to choose the right workbook? 如何因材施教的选何数棋谜書?

How to choose the right Ho Math Chess "Ultimate" workbook" for your students or child? It is a difficult question to answer because it really depends on the ability of each child. The simple reason is that there is no unified world math contest curriculum so all countries in the world can agree to. To complicate the condition, the difficulty level of math contests also depends on if the contest is international, national, or regional. The nature of the math contests also is sometimes country dependable. How are we going to create a math contest workbook, so most of the children in the world would like to use it? The solution is to produce a math contest workbook that meets the content of international math contests standards. With the understanding of the above conditions, we used many strategies and raised the bar to a very high level when creating this workbook.

Computation ability

You cannot write a math contest workbook solely based on a student's school's math computation ability. The earlier a student can master the skills of $+ - \times \div$, the better chance that students could work on all kinds of whole number word problems. So, we do not choose a workbook based solely on a student's grade.

Thinking skills

A student's math contestability can be assessed based on computational ability, then by the student's thinking skills. It also depends on if the students could transfer the skills learned from a whole number of different data types such as decimals, fractions etc. Parents should not misjudge a child's math ability only on computational ability. The ability to be able to solve problems and can think in a calculated and logical direction is equally important, if not more important.

Repeated model problems or problem-solving strategies

Some word problem-solving strategies and model problems are mentioned in different grades in this workbook, so what is the difference? If a teacher teaches math contest preparations only model problems, then the student's thinking direction is restricted and framed to one-track mind; the ability to think out of the box is clouded. The same problem-solving strategy or the same model problem may get repeated, but the problems they applied t are more complicated, and the data types also changed.

For example, in grade 1, we may teach students to use a diagram or acting out a method to solve the Chickens and Rabbits problems. The strategy method is to use List or Acting out, which is not superior to the Model Problem Assumption method – a systematic method, but in grade 4, we may teach a student to use algebra to solve the same type of problem and the values of data. The Chickens and Rabbits problem in grade 4 also could get much complicated with inequality. So, these are various reasons, both the same model problems and problem-solving strategies may appear again in different grades.

Why teach both problem strategy and Chinese model problems?

As we have shown that many times that the classic Chinese model problems fascinated Chinese is because many of these problems have linear models, and some of them are complicated, so Chinese have come with ways of solving these problems without using algebra but arithmetic. These methods train students on how to think without resorting to using routine algebraic equations too quickly. The problem-solving strategy sometimes is to use an indirect method to solve the problems without using a few exact steps, such as the strategy of the Trial and Error method. It offers students a chance to explore a problem and to think in a non-restricted way.

With the above background information in mind, a teacher or parent could use the assessment in this workbook to assess a student's ability to choose the appropriate workbook.

How to use this workbook? 如何使用本書?

This 3-in-1 unique workbook was written for the preparation of any international math contests, which usually have higher standards and more difficult problems than the national or regional math contests. Because of the above goal, we have included the algebra in this grade and have computational fractions problems. This inclusion sets us apart from any other math contests workbooks and is a clear dividing line between grade 3 and grade 4 math contest workbooks contents in our published series. Many complicated problems have been recommended to use algebra, although the arithmetic method is often offered as well. The reason of offering the algebraic method is to take away the burden of spending the time to think the arithmetic ways (Many times they are just to interpret the results of algebraic equations.) and cut the chase to formulize thoughts into an equation; thus the computation becomes more or less a routine task.

The grade 4 students start to learn integers and algebra in China, and many word problems could use this technique, but in BC, Canada, students usually learn integers and algebra in grade 6 or 7. Many concepts of fractions are taught to the student even in grade 2 with no computations, but in China, the concept is not taught until grade 5. Because of the curriculum difference, we take the approach of inclusion, not exclusion, so students from many countries could learn many math concepts that are normally taught in their day schools.

The following website offers the contents of electronic math textbooks currently used in China. There are many different regional versions, and you can find them all here. For example, the People Teaching version (人教本) the second semester teaches 4 methods of Chickens and Rabbits (鸡兔同笼) including the List method, Trial and Error method, Oral method and the Assumption method.

www.wsbedu.com

The math curriculum used in BC, Canada can also be found by searching on the internet, so we can make a comparison of math curricula between countries. Most of math contests problems exceed school math curricula and do not really have any standard guidelines to follow. Teachers or parents need to teach according to the student's ability and learning curve when using this workbook. Do not teach from the page by page but choose the suitable pages. This workbook was not written just for the student to practice, but it also was written to guide teachers or coaches on how to solve a problem by offering many alternate solutions. Teachers or coaches must be careful not to confuse students when showing options for solutions.

This workbook makes a turning point of our Ultimate Math Contest series because we start to teach algebra in this workbook. Many classic Chinese word problems could be solved by using algebra. It is also beneficial to train students from grade 1 by using our series of math contest workbooks because of our systematic training method. For example, the Surplus and Shortage problem 盈亏问题 $ax \pm b = cx \pm d$ can be easily solved by using algebra.

The strength of problems in this workbook is rated very high, so students thoroughly study this workbook should be able to prepare for any international math contests. This is because the contents of this workbook are an international standard, and it has been written to a very high standard, and students will get ahead among peers after studying this workbook.

Frank Ho

January 2017

The trend of math contest problems

Look at the Canadian and Chinese math contest problems, and I feel the trend of more arithmetic challenging math problems are moving into the area of using the strategies of pattern, sorting, listing, classifying, combination, arrangements, and number theory. The reason is these types of problems do not have any model problems to follow, nor the student can really rely on previously learned problems to draw similarity and figure it out.

1. Number Pattern

Example 1

What is the unit digit of 2^{2012}?
Observe the following $2^1 = 2, 2^2 = 4, 2^3 = 8, 2^4 = 6, 2^5 = 2, 2^6 = 4\ldots\ldots$, then we know that the exponents of 2 has a cycle of every 4 digits 2, 4, 8, 6. $2012 \div 4$ has the remainder of 0, so its unit digit is 6.

Practice

What is the unit digit of 2^{1995}?

$1995 \,(\text{mod}4) \equiv 3$
The unit digit is 8.

2. Number Pattern using algebra

Example 2

Calculate $\left(1 - \frac{1}{2^2}\right)\left(1 - \frac{1}{3^2}\right)\left(1 - \frac{1}{4^2}\right)\cdots\left(1 - \frac{1}{2011^2}\right)\left(1 - \frac{1}{2012^2}\right)$

$= \left(\frac{3}{2} \times \frac{1}{2}\right)\left(\frac{4}{3} \times \frac{2}{3}\right)\left(\frac{5}{4} \times \frac{3}{4}\right)\left(\frac{6}{5} \times \frac{4}{5}\right)\cdots \cdots \cdots \left(\frac{2011}{2010} \times \frac{2009}{2010}\right)\left(\frac{2012}{2011} \times \frac{2010}{2011}\right)\left(\frac{2013}{2012} \times \frac{2011}{2012}\right)$

The 1st term cancelled with the 4th term.
The 3rd term cancelled with the 6th term
The 5th term cancelled with the 8th term
.....
The $(n - 3)^{th}$ term cancelled with the nth term
The above process will leave with two terms the second and the $(n - 1)^{th}$ term.

$= \frac{1}{2} \times \frac{2013}{2012}$

$= \frac{2013}{4024}$

Practice

Calculate the answer as one single exponent.
$2^0 + 2^1 + 2^2 + 2^3 \ldots + 2^{2012}$

Let T= $2^0 + 2^1 + 2^2 + 2^3 \ldots + 2^{2012}$
2T= $2^1 + 2^2 + 2^3 + 2^4 \ldots + 2^{2013}$
2T-T = $2^{2013} - 1$

3. Graph Pattern

Example

Example Shade the next figure.

The answer is as follows.

The vertex is assigned by  . When we draw the figure, we follow the step that is the vertex is not adjacent to the other 2 shaded triangles.

Practice

Observe the following pattern and find out how many triangles when it is at the nth figure.

The answer is 4n.

4. Number and figure mixed pattern

Example

Replace the ? by a number.

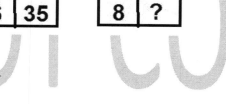

Practice

Replace the ? by a number.

The bottom + 15 = top for the left two. The top + 15 = bottom for the next two. The last one is **53+15=68**

5. Combination of pattern, sorting, listing, classifying, combination, arrangements, and number theory

Select 4 digits from the digits 1, 2, 3, 4, or 5 such that the right digit is larger than the left digit and the bottom digit is larger the top digit, how many selections are there?

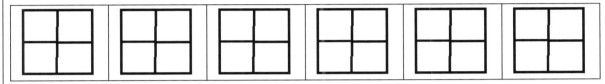

12 13 14 23 24
34 45 25 45 35

What is the remainder of the following fraction?

$$\frac{1^1 + 2^2 + 3^3 + 4^4 + 5^5 + 6^6 + 7^7 + 8^8 + 9^9 + 10^{10}}{3}$$

Hint: Use the divisibility of 3.

Because 3, 6, and 9 are divisible by 3 so $3^3, 6^6, 9^9$ are also divisible by 3.

$4^4 = 4 \times 4 \times 4 \times (3+1)$, $4^3 \times 3$ is divisible by 3. $4 \times 4 \times 4$ has the remainder of 1 when divided by 3.

$5^5 = 5 \times 5 \times 5 \times 5 (3+2)$, $5^4 \times 3$ is divisible by 3. $5 \times 5 \times 5 \times 5 \times 2$ has the remainder of 2 when divided by 3 (The last digit is 0).

$\frac{7^7}{3} = \frac{7^6(6+1)}{3} = \frac{7^6 \times 6 + 7^6}{3} = \frac{7^6 \times 6 + 7^5(6+1)}{3} = \frac{7^6 \times 6 + 7^5 \times 6 + 7^5}{3}$ So if we continue to expand, then we finally will have $\frac{7^6 \times 6 + 7^5 \times 6 + 7^5 + \dots + 7(6+1)}{3}$, so the remainder is 1.

$\frac{8^8}{3} = \frac{\left(2^3\right)^8}{3} = \frac{2^{24}}{3} = \frac{4^{12}}{3} = \frac{4^{11} \times (3+1)}{3}$ So if we continue to expand, then we finally will have $\frac{4^{11} \times 3 + 4^{10} \times 3 + \dots + 4(3+1)}{3}$, so the remainder is 1.

The sum of each remainder $= \frac{1+1+0+1+2+0+1+1+0+1}{3} = \frac{8}{3}$, the remainder is 2.

Modular arithmetic method

There are two modular operations involved.
Modular Exponentiation

If $a_1{}^n \equiv a_2{}^n \ (mod \ m)$ then $a_1 \equiv a_2 (mod \ m)$

Modular addition

If
$a_1 \equiv a_2 (mod \ m)$
$b_1 \equiv b_2 (mod \ m)$
Then $a_1 + b_1 \equiv a_2 + b_2 (mod \ m)$

Mod 3.
$1 \equiv 1, 2 \equiv 2 \ or - 1, 3 \equiv 0, 4 \equiv 1, 5 \equiv 2 \ or - 1, 6 \equiv 0, 7 \equiv 1, 8 \equiv 2 \ or - 1, 9 \equiv 0, 10 \equiv 1$

$1^1 + 2^2 + 3^3 + 4^4 + 5^5 + 6^6 + 7^7 + 8^8 + 9^9 + 10^{10} \ (mod \ 3) \equiv$

$1^1 + (-1)^2 + (0)^3 + (1)^4 + (-1)^5 + (0)^6 + (1)^7 + (-1)^8 + (0)^9 + (1)^{10}$

$\equiv 1+1+0+1+(-1)+0+1+1+0+1 \equiv 5 (mod3) \equiv 2$

Student's name: _____   Assignment date: _____

How many are 3-digit natural numbers and divisible by 11 and the sum of 3 digits is 13?

The divisibility rule for 11 is the difference (including 0) of the sum of the odd-digit numbers, and the sum of the even-digit numbers is divisible by 11.
Is it possible that the difference of sums is 0?

A+B+C=13
Case 1
A-B+C=0
2B=13
A+B=6.5, which is not possible.
Case 2
A-B+C=11
B=1
There are **7** conditions. 319, 913, 418, 814, 517, 715, 616

How many 4-digit natural numbers, which are <5000 and are divisible by 11 and the sum of 4 digits is 13?

Method 1 Sum and difference problem

There are only **11** conditions which will give a difference 11 and sum of 13. 1309, 1903, 3091, 3190, 1408, 1804, 4081, 4180, 1507, 1705, 1606

Method 2 System of equations

Case 1
A+B+C+D=13
A-B+C-D=0
No solutions
Case 2
A+B+C+D=13
A-B+C-D=11
A cannot be 1 or 2 because A=1, C=11 and A = 2, C=10
The solutions are 3190, 3091, 4180, 4081

Case 3
A+B+C+D=13
-A+B-C+D=0
A=1, C=0
The solutions are 1903, 1804, 1705, 1606, 1507, 1408, 1309

Move the last 3-digit of a 6-digit number to the front of the 6-digit number to form a new 6-digit number, then the 7 times of the old 6-digit number is equal to the 6 times of the new 6-digit number. What is the old 6-digit number?

The old number is $\overline{abcxy}$, the new number is $\overline{xyzabc}$.
$7\,\overline{abcxyz}=6\overline{xyzabc}$.

Write two numbers in expanded form.

$$7(1000\overline{abc}+\overline{xyz}) = 6(1000\overline{xyz}+\overline{abc})$$

$$7000\overline{abc}+7\overline{xyz} = 6000\overline{xyz} + 6\overline{abc}$$

$6994\overline{abc}=8993\overline{xyz}$

Use the Euclidean Algorithm (repetitive alternate division method), and we find the GCF, which is 13.

To find GCF of two large numbers, repeatedly use the following fact that
GCF (m, n) = GCF (m−n, n) where m and n are integers

1	6994	5993	5
	5993	5005	
1	1001	988	76
	988	910	
	13		

Both sides divided by 13.
$538\,\overline{abc}=461\overline{xyz}$
$\overline{abc}$ must be 461.
$\overline{xyz}$ must be 538.
The number is 461538.

The sum of two numbers is 80 and their product can divide 4875. What is the difference between these two numbers?

$4875=3 \times 5 \times 5 \times 5 \times 13$
The two numbers are 5×75 and 15×65. The differences are 70 and 50.

Student's name: _____   Assignment date: _____

Student's math ability assessment 学生计算能力评估

Fill in each box with a number. The same shape of box has the same number.

$13 + \square = \bigcirc \times \bigcirc$ 12, 5 x 5

$4 + \square = \triangle \times \triangle$ 12, 4 x 4

Fill in each box with a number. The same shape of box has the same number.

$2 + \square = \bigcirc \times \bigcirc$ 3 x 3

$9 + \square = \triangle \times \triangle$ 4 x 4

Fill in each box with a number. The same shape of box has the same number.

$21 + \square = \bigcirc \times \bigcirc$ 6 x 6

$34 + \square = \triangle \times \triangle$ 7 x 7

Fill in each box with a number. The same shape of box has the same number.

$39 + \square = \bigcirc \times \bigcirc$ 8 x 8

$11 + \square = \triangle \times \triangle$ 6 x 6

Fill in each box with a number. The same shape of box has the same number.

$27 + \square = \bigcirc \times \bigcirc$ 6 x 6

$55 + \square = \triangle \times \triangle$ 8 x 8

Replace each ? with a number.

Standard form	hundreds	tens	ones
685 = 600 + 40 +45	6	4	**45** ?
629	**6,** 629-29 =600 ?	2	9
801	**4,** 801- 310=491 ?	31	91

Replace each ? with a number.

Standard form	hundreds	The fifties	tens	ones
875, 875-250-30=595	**5** ?	5	3	**95** ?
1089 1089-500-9 = 580	**5** ?	10	**8** ?	9
347, 347-150-7=190	**1** ?	3	**9** ?	7

In Christine's class, there are 20 children who are 10 or younger, 8 are old than 10, and 6 are older than 11. How many children altogether are in Christine's class?

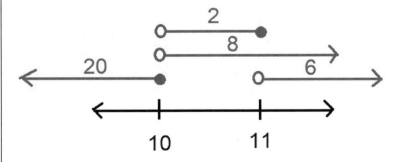

There are 28 children in Christine's class. 20 + 2 + 6 = **28**
There are only 2 children who are over 10 and below 11 years old.

Student's name: _____　Assignment date: _____

Find the pattern to replace each ? by a number.

Series	Sum
1	$1 = 1 \times 1$
1+3	$4 = 2 \times 2$
1+3+5	$9 = 3 \times 3$
. . .	
1+3+5+…+95+97+99	2500 ?

Term	Series	Sum
1	1	1
2	1^2+2^2	5
3	$1^2+2^2+3^2$	14
4	? $1^2+2^2+3^2+4^2$	? 30
5	? $1^2+2^2+3^2+4^2+5^2$	? 55
6	? $1^2+2^2+3^2+4^2+5^2+6^2$	? 91

blank
blank

$$\frac{99 + 1}{2} = 50, \qquad 50 \times 50 = 2500$$

blank　　　　　　blank
blank　　blank
blank　　blank
blank　　blank
blank　　blank
blank　　blank
blank　　blank

Place 1, 2, 3, or 4 in each of 4 boxes such that no boxes have the same order of numbers.

1234	1243	2314	2341
1324	1342	4213	4231
1423	1432	3124	3142
2134	2314	3214	3241
2341	2413	3412	3421
2431	4123	4312	4321

Mixed word problems 混合文字题

A whole number is a perfect square if it can be expressed as the product of two whole equal numbers. How many perfect squares are greater than 0 and less than 1000?

31

If 3 Grogs = 7 Gizmos, then 42 Gizmos = ? Grogs.

18

10 and one half years = _____ months.   **126**

How many digits does the product $1 \times 1 \times 10 \times 10 \times 10 \times 10 \times 10 \times 10 \times 10$ have?   **8**

Jeff makes 3 out of every 5 shots when he plays basketball. Out of 45 shots Jeff tries, he will make _____ shots?   **27**

$1 \times 2 \times 3 \times 4 \times 5 \times 6 \times 7 = 2 \times 60 \times$ _____.   **42**

A carton of 8 one-litre (L) bottles costs $3.19. How much do 128 bottles cost?   **$51.04**

1

Shirley has 2 skirts (pleated and wrap) and 3 blouses (plain, frilly, and print). How many different outfits could Shirley wear?   **6**

The Parking fee is charged as follows:

First hour $1.00
Each additional half-hour or part of a half-hour $0.50

How much does Jeff have to pay if he parked from 10:15 a.m. until 2:30 p.m.?   **$4.50**

14:30 – 11:15 = 3:15 = 7 of half hours = $3.50, $3.50 + $1 = $4.50

Christine's kettle can hold 6 jars of jelly at a time. She made 103 jars of jelly. How many kettlefuls of jelly did she have to cook?   **18**

Part A – Algebra and Chinese classic word problems 代数及中国古算题

Introduction

The elementary math of grade 4 in China starts to introduce algebra with the model of $ax \pm b = c$.

Because of this distinct curriculum difference from North America, we decide to shift our problem-solving technique from arithmetic to algebra and introduce algebra in this workbook.

Should students just use equations to solve all word problems? 用方程式解所有文字题?

From a teacher or a math contest coacher's view, there are many questions begging for answers such as when is the good time to teach algebra to elementary students? Should elementary just use algebra to solve all word problems? What is the advantage of using arithmetic to solve word problems if the algebra can do all?

I have spent some time to explore and did research on the above problems and then discovered something which I liked to share with teachers or coaches. Teachers can pick some examples to teach students to understand when to use arithmetic and when to use algebra. To teach the entire contents of this section to students is perhaps beyond a student's capacity to handle.

When we saw some complicated grade 7 Singapore math word problems and the author suggests readers use the Bar Graph to model (In China it is called Line Segment Diagram.) to solve them and at the same time, we saw some complicated Chickens and Rabbits in China, we begin to feel the need for elementary students to learn simple one-variable equations. Chinese students are taught simple equations in grade 4, so they have a bit advantage when working on some word problems.

Student's name: _____   Assignment date: _____

The following is a similar problem to the one that appeared in the 2012 Kangaroo Math Contest grade 3/4 practice.

When the father was 28 years old, his son was 4 years old. Now the father is two times as old as his son. How old is the father now?		
Algebra	Arithmetic - use proportion	Arithmetic - use pattern

Algebra column:

One-variable equation

$28 + x = 2(4 + x)$
$x = 20$
$28 + 20 =$ **48 ...father**
$4 + 20 = 24$ ... son

Arithmetic - use proportion column:

$$\frac{28+x}{4+x} = \frac{2}{1}$$

Method 1
Use fraction subtraction property, we get

$$\frac{28 + x - 4 - x}{4 + x} = \frac{2 - 1}{1}$$

$$\frac{24}{4 + x} = 1$$

$24 = 4 + x$
$x = 20$
$28 + 20 =$ **48 ...father**
$4 + 20 = 24$ ... son

Method 2

By using the cross-multiplication, it is the same step as the algebra method.

Arithmetic - use pattern column:

father	son
28	4
29	5
30	6
31	7
32	8
33	9
34	10
35	11
36	12
37	13
38	14
39	15
40	16
41	17
42	18
43	19
44	20
45	21
46	22
47	23
48	**24**

Use arithmetic or algebra to solve word problems? 用代数或算術解问题

Many word problems can be easily solved by using algebra and thus, using algebra equations to solve word problems is thought of as a universal method. However, the idea of using algebra equations to solve word problems may not always work because some word problems can be easily solved by using the arithmetic method. It is also true that by using the algebra equation, some word problems can be understood better by students.

If, in most cases, it is much easier to use algebra to solve word problems, then why do we not just learn algebra and forget about using the arithmetic method to solve word problems? In China, the simple algebra equation is introduced to grade 4 elementary students, so we see that some mathematics educators did feel that it perhaps takes away the burden from students when solving word problems by introducing algebra to elementary students in very early years. My own experience tells me that student still benefits by using arithmetic method since the arithmetic method really trains students on "how to think", in contrast, the algebra method becomes very routine and procedural once the equation is set up.

We can explore the relationship between arithmetic and algebra as follows:

1. Problems can be easily solved by using arithmetic than algebra.
2. Problems can be easily solved by using algebra than arithmetic.
3. Problems can be easily solved by either using algebra or arithmetic.

1. Problems can be easily solved by using arithmetic than algebra.

Example 1 - Continuous percents of increases and/or decreases

The Best Thrifty store had a series of discounts on a pair of shoes, so after a 10% increase, followed by a 10% decrease, then followed by a further 15% decrease, Adam bought his shoes for $85. What was the original asking price (ignore all taxes.)?

Arithmetic method	Algebra method
Method 1 - Proportion method Is it easier to use the proportion method? $\frac{85}{100} = \frac{85}{x}$, $x = 100$ price before 15% discount $\frac{90}{100} = \frac{100}{x}$, $x = 111.1$ Price before 10% discount $\frac{110}{100} = \frac{111.1}{x}$, $x = 101$ Price before 10% increase Method 2 – Work backward Division method $85 \div 0.85 = 100$ $100 \div 0.9 = 111.1$ $111.1 \div 1.1 = 101$	Is it easier to use the algebra method? Let x be the original price. $x \times 1.1 \times 0.9 \times 0.85 = 85$ $x = 101$

Example 2 – Simple work problem

It takes 3 days for Adam to paint the house alone and Bob 4 days to paint the same house alone, how many days it will take for both working together?

Arithmetic method	Algebra method
Method – Use unit 1 as the total work amount. $1 \div \left(\frac{1}{3} + \frac{1}{4}\right) = 1\frac{5}{7}$ days	Is it easier to use the algebra method? In contrast, so complicated work problems are easy to solve by using algebra. Let x be the number of days. $x \left(\frac{1}{3} + \frac{1}{4}\right) = 1$ $x = 1\frac{5}{7}$ days

Student's name: _____ Assignment date: _____

Example 3 – Fractions

There are two containers: Container A has 1 L water in it, and the container B is empty.
We like to pour water from the container A into container B first and then from Container B into the container. The detailed procedure is as follows:

Step 1, Pour one half of water from A into B.
Step 2, Pour one-third water from B into A.
Step 3, Pour one-fourth of water from A into B.
Step 4, Pour one-fifth of water from B into A.

Continue the above steps until step 2011, how much water was in the container A right after step 2001?

Arithmetic method		Algebra method
Method – Use unit 1 as the total work amount. 1 (pour $\frac{1}{2}$)$-\frac{1}{2}=\frac{1}{2}$	$0+\frac{1}{2}=\frac{1}{2}$	Is it easier to use the algebra method?
$\frac{1}{2}+(\frac{1}{2}\times\frac{1}{3})=\frac{2}{3}$	$\frac{1}{2}-(\frac{1}{2}\times\frac{1}{3})=\frac{1}{3}$	
$\frac{2}{3}-(\frac{1}{4}\times\frac{2}{3})=\frac{1}{2}$	$\frac{1}{3}+(\frac{1}{4}\times\frac{2}{3})=\frac{1}{2}$	
$\frac{1}{2}+(\frac{1}{5}\times\frac{1}{2})=\frac{3}{5}$	$\frac{1}{2}-(\frac{1}{5}\times\frac{1}{2})=\frac{2}{5}$	
$\frac{3}{5}-(\frac{1}{6}\times\frac{2}{5})=\frac{1}{2}$	$\frac{2}{5}+(\frac{1}{6}\times\frac{2}{5})=\frac{1}{2}$	

After every odd-numbered step, the quantity in each container will always be one half of 1L.
2011 is an odd number, so we know that there will be one half of 1L in container A after the 2011th step.

Example 4 – Proportion

At a Chinese banquet, 52 dishes were served all together. Every 2 guests shared a dish of rice between them; every 3 guests shared a dish of soup among them, and every 4 guests shared a dish of soup. How many guests were at the banquet?

Arithmetic method	Algebra method
Total dish each guest shared was $\frac{1}{2}+\frac{1}{3}+\frac{1}{4}=\frac{13}{12}$	Is it easier to use the algebra method?
The proportion of total dishes each guest used to the number of guests is as follows:	Let x b the number of guests.
$\frac{\frac{13}{12}}{1}=\frac{52}{x}$	$\frac{1}{2}x+\frac{1}{3}x+\frac{1}{4}x=\frac{13}{12}x$
$x=48$ guests	$\frac{13}{12}x=52$
	$x=48$

Student's name: _____   Assignment date: _____

Example 5 – Backward Fractions

Adam gave $\frac{1}{4}$ of his basket of apples to Bob, Cindy got $\frac{1}{3}$ of what was left. Then David took $\frac{1}{5}$ of what was left in the basket. Adam had 45 apples left in the basket. How many apples did he have in the beginning?

Arithmetic	Algebra	Proportion?
Method 1 – Use Multiple steps. $45 \div \frac{4}{5} = \frac{225}{4}$ $\frac{225}{4} \div \frac{2}{3} = \frac{675}{8}$ $\frac{675}{8} \div \frac{3}{4} = 112.5$ Method 2 – Use one statement What fraction was left in the basket eventually? $\frac{4}{5} \times \frac{2}{3} \times \frac{3}{4} = \frac{2}{5}$ $30 \div \frac{4}{5} \div \frac{2}{3} \div \frac{3}{4} = 75$	Is it easier to use the algebra method? $x \times \frac{3}{4} \times \frac{2}{3} \times \frac{4}{5} = 45$ $x = 112.5$	$\frac{4}{5} = \frac{45}{x}, x = \frac{225}{4}$ $\frac{2}{3} = \frac{\frac{225}{4}}{x}, x = \frac{675}{8}$ $\frac{3}{4} = \frac{\frac{675}{8}}{x}, x = 112.5$

Student's name: _____   Assignment date: _____

Practice 1 – Backward Fractions

The school had a carnival and Adam went to four booths. Each time he entered a booth, he had to pay a $0.50 entry fee and a $0.50 exit fee to get out. Adam went to the first booth, spent one half of his money at booth one, and then spent one half of what he had left at the second booth, and then he went to the third booth, and the fourth booth did the same thing. After paying the exit fee at the fourth booth, he had $10 left. How much money did Adam start with?

Arithmetic				Algebra	Proportion?
	Before in	**Before out**	**out**	Is it easier to use the algebra method?	
First booth	$182.50	$91	$90.50		
Second booth	$90.50	$45	$44.50		
Third booth	$44.50	$22	$21.50		
Fourth booth	$21.50	$10.50	$10		

Practice 2 – Backward Fractions

The trend of sale prices of a pair of ABC shoes is as follows:
2011 – This year's sale price has gone up 10% more than last year's sale price.
2010 – This year's sale price had gone up 15% more than last year's sale price.
2009 – This year's sale price had gone up 20% more than last year's sale price.
The sale price for 2008 was $90, what was the sale price of 2010?

Arithmetic	Algebra	Proportion?
One statement $90 \times 1.2 \times 1.15 \times 1.1 = 136.62$	Is it easier to use the algebra method?	Is it easier or more understanding? $\frac{120}{100} = \frac{90}{x}, x = 90 \times 1.2$ $\frac{115}{100} = \frac{x}{90.12}, x = 90 \times 1.2 \times 1.15$ $\frac{110}{100} = \frac{x}{90.12 \times 1.15}, x = 90 \times 1.2 \times 1.15 \times 1.1 = 136.67$

2. Problems can be more easily solved by using algebra than arithmetic

Example 1

Adam can pick 30 apples per minute, and Bob can pick 25 apples per minute. Adam will pick 6 minutes less than Bob if each of them picks from the same apple tree. How many apples are there on the apple tree?

Arithmetic method	Algebra
When solving math word problems, this kind of problem a present headache to students is because it represents inequality. How can an elementary student connect the information to set up an equation such that this problem can be solved? We use the "making the assumption" method to create a contradictory condition, and then after resolving the contradiction, the answer is found. Method 1 – Assume that Adam and Bob use the equal time to pick apples, then which time shall we use? Adam's 30 apples / minute or Bob's time of 25 apples / minute? **Let's assume time used is Adam's 30 apples per minute with 6 minutes left** (this statement creates an untrue and contradictory condition for Bob, so we will have to resolve it.), but the fact the total number of students does not change no matter how the apples are picked, we will use this condition to resolve the contradiction for Bob which does not pick at 30 apples per minute. If Bob picks at 30 minutes per minute, then Bob will be left with 6 minutes, and it means in this 6 minutes, Bob will pick 150 apples less (25 apples times 6 minutes = 150). Now the interesting thing is if we use the different number of apples (150) divided by the number of apples /per minute, we will get Adam's pick time. So, we can find out how much time Adam will use to pick up apples: $\frac{6 \times 25}{30-25} = 30$. The number of apples on the apple tree will be $30 \times 30 = 900$ apples The problem here is how many elementary students can understand this method by assuming Bob's picked time, which is equal to Adam's picked time? Clearly, it is much better explained in the algebra method on the right column, method 2. The difficulty situation stems from the fact that the way to solve this problem is to use "multiplication method" $30x = (x + 6)25$ just like in algebra, and yet, we used "division method": $\frac{6 \times 25}{30-25}$ arithmetic, which comes from the algebra method.	Method 1 Let the number of apples on the tree be x. $$\frac{x}{30} + 60 = \frac{x}{25}$$ The difficulty is how many elementary students can solve the above rational equation? Method 2 Let Adam's apples picked time be x. $30x = (x + 6)25$ $30x = 25x + 6 \times 25$ $(30\text{-}25)\,x = 6 \times 25$ $x = \frac{6 \times 25}{30-25}$ $x = 30$ minutes The number of apples $= 30 \times 30 = 900$ apples Method 2 Let Bob's apples picked time be x. $25x = 30(x - 6)$ $x = 36$

Integers

Example 2 - Ratio

Adam's monthly salary to Betty's monthly salary is in the ratio of 2 to 3. However, in a certain month, the ratio becomes 5 to 7 because Adam had a $58 commission, and Betty had a $27 commission. Find their respective basic salary.

Arithmetic method	Algebra method
	Let Adam's salary be $2x$, and Betty's salary is $3x$. $$\frac{2x + 58}{3x + 27} = \frac{5}{7}$$ $x = 271$ Adam's salary = $2 \times 271 = \$542$ Betty's salary = $3 \times 271 = \$813$

Example 3 – Complicated work problem

It takes Adam and Bob together 36 days to finish building a large fence, and it takes 45 days for Bob and Cathy together to finish building the same fence, and the same fence takes Adam and Cathy together 60 days to finish building. How many days does it take for Adam to work alone to finish building the fence?

Arithmetic method	Algebra method
	A+B=36 B+C=45 C+A=60 2(A+B+C) =141 A+B+C=70.5 A=25.5

3. Problems can be easily solved by either using algebra or arithmetic.

Example 1- Chickens and Rabbits

Company A and Company B together had 540 chess sets stored in the same shared warehouse. After Company A imported 35% of their inventory in the warehouse and company B imported 25% of their inventory in the warehouse. Thereafter, their total inventory in the warehouse was 660 sets. How many chess sets did each company have before importing?

Student's name: _____ Assignment date: _____

Arithmetic method	Algebra method
Assume all chess sets in the warehouse are all company B's inventory. $$\frac{660-540}{0.35-0.25} = \frac{120}{0.05} = 2400$$	Let company A have chess sets $= x$ before importing. Let company B have chess sets $= y$ before importing. So, we can use the System of Equations to solve x and y. $x + y = 400$ $0.35x + 0.25y = 660 - 540 = 120$ $35x + 25y = 12000$ $7x + 5y = 2400$ $2x = 400$ $x = 200$ $y = 200$

Algebra 代数 – 萬能解题之王

In grade 4, only the simple model is introduced, such as $ax \pm b = c$, but we have offered some advanced such as rational calculations for advanced students.

Many advanced word problems appeared in China's Chickens, and Rabbits problems, Surplus and shortage, Travelling problem, Work problem, Age problem, or appeared in Singapore's fraction or ratio problems can all be solved by using algebra instead of drawing the complicated Line Segment Diagrams (Bar charts).

Student's name: _____ Assignment date: _____

Integers 整数的介绍及＋－×÷

Example: Usually, we record +2 as gain 2 points, while -3 as loss 3 points.

1. If + \$4 means make \$4, then _____ means loss \$3.   -3

2. If + 6 means go up 6 m, then _____ means go down 5 m.   -5

3. If + 2 means 2 units to the right, then – 2 means 2 units to the _____. left

4. If + 12 means win 12 games, then _____ means loss 8 games.   -8

5. If + 16^0C means 16^0C above 0^0C, then _____ means 21^0C below 0^0C.   -21

6. If + 15 means 15 stories up, then _____ means 3 stories down.   -3

7. If – 4 means 4 m below sea level, then _____ means 7 m above sea level.   +7

8. If +35 means move forward 35 m, then _____ means move 12 m backwards.   -12

9. If +2 means the year next to next year, then _____ means last year. -1

10. If – 2 means loss 2 points, then _____ means gain 5 points. +5

11. If + 45^0 means turn clockwise 45^0, then _____ means turn anticlockwise 23^0. -23

12. If – 7 means 7 m less, then +13 means _____**13 m more**.

13. If + 100 means put in 100 marbles, then – 45 means _____**take out 45 marbles**.

14. If + \$27 means earn \$27, then – \$21 means _____**lose \$ 2**.

15. If + 14 means go up 14 units, then – 8 means _____**go down 8 units**.

16. If + 48 means 48 turns to the right, then – 32 means _____**32 turns to the left**.

Student's name: _____ Assignment date: _____

Put each letter on the number line.

| $I = -4$ | $H = +3$ | $G = -2$ | $R = -6$ | $T = +7$ |

```
←──┼──┼──┼──┼──┼──┼──┼──┼──┼──┼──┼──┼──┼──┼──┼──→
   -7 -6 -5 -4 -3 -2 -1  0  1  2  3  4  5  6  7  8
```

What do you notice?

The further the number to the right, the _____ the number.   **greater**

The further the number to the left, the _____ the number.   **smaller**

Compare each pair of numbers using < or >.

1. $+7$ __<__ $+24$ 2. 0 __<__ $+15$

3. -5 __<__ $+7$ 4. -13 __>__ -28

5. -4 __>__ -9 6. $+52$ __>__ -87

7. $+20$ __>__ $+8$ 8. -37 __<__ $+21$

9. -18 __<__ 0 10. -29 __>__ -63

Order the following number from least to greatest.

1. $+7, -3, +20, -16, 0$ $-16, -3, 0, +7, +20$

2. $-4, +8, -21, -62, +15$ $-62, -21, -4, +8, +15$

3. $+5, +23, -10, -17, -42$ $-42, -, 17, -10, +5, +23$

4. $+39, -16, -25, +2, +17$ $-25, -16, +2, +17, +39$

5. $-9, -26, +3, +37, +14$ $-26, -9, +3, +14, +37$

6. $-17, -29, -6, +9, -45$ $-45, -29, -17, -6, +9$

7. $-32, -18, -4, -15, -1$ $-32, -18, -15, -4, -1$

8. $+6, -2, -16, -29, -25$ $-29, -25, -16, -2, +6$

Find the net change.

1.   Borrowed $5 and returned $2   -$3 _____

2.   Made $12 and spend $15   -$3 _____

3.   Lost $10 and gained $15   +$5 _____

4.   Went up 5 floors and down 7 floors   -2 _____

5.   Warmed up 6 ^{0}C and cooled down 10 ^{0}C   -4^0 C _____

6.   Went to the left 10 m and to the right 3 m   -7 m _____

7.   Turned 30^0 clockwise and 45^0 counterclockwise   -15° _____

8.   Moved forward 200 m and backward 400 m   -200 m _____

9.   lost 11 games and won 15 games   +4 g _____

Student's name: _____ Assignment date: _____

Addition of integers 加整数

Example:

$(+5) + (+3) = 5 + 3 = +8$ $(-5) + (-3) = -5 - 3 = -8$

$(+5) + (-3) = 5 - 3 = +2$ $(-5) + (+3) = -5 + 3) = -2$

$(+3) + (-5) = 3 - 5 = -2$ $(-3) + (+5) = -3 + 5 = 2$

1. $(+2) + (+5) = $ **7**   2. $(+7) + (+3) = $ **10**

3. $(+4) + (-2) = $ **2**   4. $(+5) + (-5) = $ **0**

5. $(+6) + (+3) = $ **9**   6. $(+3) + (+4) = $ **7**

7. $(+2) + (-2) = $ **0**   8. $(+8) + (-3) = $ **5**

9. $(+10) + (-7) = $ **3**   10. $(+2) + (-7) = $ **-5**

11. $(-3) + (+5) = $ **2**   12. $(-8) + (+5) = $ **-3**

13. $(-8) + (+2) = $ **-6**   14. $(-6) + (+3) = $ **-3**

15. $(-4) + (-6) = $ **-10**   16. $(+5) + (-6) = $ **-1**

17. $(-2) + (-3) = $ **-5**   18. $(+3) + (+4) = $ **7**

19. $(-8) + (-1) = $ **-9**   20. $(-8) + (-2) = $ **-10**

21. $(-14) + (-9) = $ **-23**   22. $(-9) + (-1) = $ **-10**

23. $(-5) + (-4) = $ **-9**   24. $(+4) + (-6) = $ **-2**

25. $(-6) + (+3) = $ **-3**   26. $(+3) + (+2) = $ **5**

27. $(-4) + (+7) = $ **+3**   28. $(+5) + (-6) = $ **-1**

29. $(+15) + (-21) =$ **-6**

30. $(+14) + (-26) =$ **-12**

31. $(+21) + (+28) =$ **+49**

32. $(+31) + (+31) =$ **+62**

33. $(-60) + (-27) =$ **-87**

34. $(-25) + (-74) =$ **-99**

35. $(+27) + (+32) =$ **+59**

36. $(+29) + (+31) =$ **+60**

37. $(+43) + (-16) =$ **+27**

38. $(+28) + (-52) =$ **-24**

39. $(+26) + (+42) =$ **+68**

40. $(+35) + (+42) =$ **+77**

41. $(+31) + (-58) =$ **-27**

42. $(+51) + (-62) =$ **-11**

43. $(+52) + (-52) =$ **0**

44. $(+52) + (-41) =$ **+11**

45. $(-25) + (+26) =$ **+1**

46. $(-62) + (+27) =$ **-35**

47. $(-42) + (+53) =$ **+11**

48. $(-29) + (+29) =$ **0**

49. $(-26) + (-63) =$ **-89**

50. $(+47) + (-37) =$ **+10**

51. $(-16) + (-17) =$ **-33**

52. $(+38) + (+26) =$ **+64**

53. $(-26) + (-27) =$ **-53**

54. $(-28) + (-31) =$ **-59**

55. $(-32) + (-21) =$ **-53**

56. $(-26) + (-52) =$ **-78**

57. $(-18) + (-37) =$ **-55**

58. $(+21) + (-36) =$ **-15**

59. $(-27) + (+41) =$ **+14**

60. $(+17) + (+36) =$ **+53**

61. $(-17) + (+72) =$ **+55**

62. $(+41) + (-14) =$ **+27**

63. $(-15) + (+62) =$ **+47**

64. $(-27) + (-17) =$ **-44**

65. $(+48) + (-25) =$ **+23**

66. $(-17) + (+53) =$ **+36**

67. $(+28) + (+24) =$ **+52**

68. $(+19) + (+24) =$ **+43**

69. $(-20) + (-16) =$ **-36**

70. $(+12) + (-17) =$ **-5**

Student's name: _____ Assignment date: _____

Subtraction of integers 减整数

Example:

$(+5) - (+3) = 5 - 3 = 2$ $(-5) - (-3) = -5 + 3 = -2$

$(+3) - (+5) = 3 - 5 = -2$ $(-3) - (-5) = -3 + 5 = 2$

$(+5) - (-3) = 5 + 3 = +8$ $(-5) - (+3) = -5 + -3 = -8$

1. $(+3) - (+7) =$ **-4**   2. $(+4) - 0 =$ **4**

3. $(-1) - (+4) =$ **-5**   4. $(-3) - (+3) =$ **-6**

5. $(-6) - (-2) =$ **-4**   6. $(-6) - (-6) =$ **0**

7. $(+3) - (-5) =$ **8**   8. $(+3) - (-2) =$ **5**

9. $(-6) - (+3) =$ **-9**   10. $(-8) - (+1) =$ **-9**

11. $(+4) - (+4) =$ **0**   12. $(+6) - (+3) =$ **3**

13. $(+8) - (-4) =$ **12**   14. $(+4) - (-1) =$ **5**

15. $(-5) - (-5) =$ **0**   16. $(-7) - (-1) =$ **-6**

17. $(+8) - (+5) =$ **3**   18. $(+8) - (+3) =$ **5**

19. $(-4) - (+3) =$ **-7**   20. $(-4) - (+2) =$ **-6**

21. $(-8) - (-2) =$ **-6**   22. $(-9) - (-3) =$ **-6**

23. $(+7) - (-8) =$ **15**   24. $(+6) - (-5) =$ **11**

25. $(-4) - (+4) =$ **-8**   26. $(-9) - (+2) =$ **-11**

27. $(+9) - (+2) =$ **7**   28. $(+3) - (+1) =$ **2**

Ho Math Chess 何数棋谜 奥数,解题策略,及 IQ 思唯训练宝典

Student's name: _____ Assignment date: _____

Mixed operations of additions and subtractions 加减整数

1. $(+3) - (+15) =$ **-12**

2. $(+18) + (+30) =$ **48**

3. $(+2) + (-17) =$ **-15**

4. $(+36) - (-5) =$ **41**

5. $(+16) - (+21) =$ **-5**

6. $(+25) + (+2) =$ **27**

7. $(+18) + (-4) =$ **14**

8. $(-8) - (-48) =$ **40**

9. $(+4) - (+17) =$ **-13**

10. $(-25) + (-5) =$ **-30**

11. $(+50) - (-5) =$ **55**

12. $(-22) - (+4) =$ **-26**

13. $(+31) - (+2) =$ **29**

14. $(+72) - (+10) =$ **62**

15. $(-78) - (-30) =$ **-48**

16. $(+18) + (-36) =$ **-18**

17. $(-40) + (-51) =$ **-91**

18. $(+5) + (+35) =$ **40**

19. $(-7) + (+63) =$ **56**

20. $(+50) - (-50) =$ **100**

21. $(-15) - (-50) =$ **35**

22. $(+36) - (+5) =$ **31**

23. $(-2) + (-36) =$ **-38**

24. $(+25) + (-25) =$ **0**

25. $(-37) + (+3) =$ **-34**

26. $(+33) - (+27) =$ **6**

27. $(+42) - (+4) =$ **38**

28. $(+39) + (-5) =$ **34**

29. $(+3) - (-47) =$ **50**

30. $(+29) - (+20) =$ **9**

31. $(+8) - (-38) =$ **46**

32. $(+25) + (-30) =$ **-5**

33. $(+39) - (+25) =$ **14**

34. $(+28) + (+3) =$ **31**

35. $(+53) - (-20) =$ **73**

36. $(+15) - (-30) =$ **45**

Ho Math Chess   何数棋谜 奥数,解题策略,及 IQ 思唯训练宝典

Student's name: _____ Assignment date: _____

Multiplication of integers 乘整数

$(+5) \times (+3) = +15$ $(-5) \times (-3) = +15$

$(-5) \times (+3) = -15$ $(+5) \times (-3) = -15$

1. $(+4) \times (-2) =$ **-8**   2. $(+4) \times (-3) =$ **-12**

3. $(+3) \times (+2) =$ **6**   4. $(+3) \times (+3) =$ **9**

5. $(-2) \times (-7) =$ **14**   6. $(-8) \times (-2) =$ **16**

7. $(+5) \times (+5) =$ **25**   8. $(+6) \times (+7) =$ **42**

9. $(+8) \times (-4) =$ **-32**   10. $(+9) \times (-4) =$ **-36**

11. $(+6) \times (+3) =$ **18**   12. $(+7) \times (+1) =$ **7**

13. $(+2) \times (-7) =$ **-14**   14. $(+6) \times (-6) =$ **-36**

15. $(+1) \times (-3) =$ **-3**   16. $(+9) \times (-4) =$ **-36**

17. $(-9) \times (+2) =$ **-18**   18. $(-4) \times (+1) =$ **-4**

19. $(-7) \times (+6) =$ **-42**   20. $(-7) \times (+7) =$ **-49**

21. $(-7) \times (-8) =$ **56**   22. $(+3) \times (-5) =$ **-15**

23. $(-3) \times (-5) =$ **15**   24. $(+6) \times (+2) =$ **12**

25. $(-8) \times (-2) =$ **16**   26. $(-4) \times (-7) =$ **28**

27. $(-2) \times 0 =$ **0**   28. $(-2) \times (-4) =$ **8**

29. $(-7) \times (-9) =$ **63**   30. $(+7) \times (-2) =$ **-14**

31. $(-2) \times (+7) =$ **-14**   32. $(+5) \times (+7) =$ **35**

Ho Math Chess 何数棋谜 奥数,解题策略,及 IQ 思唯训练宝典

Frank Ho, Amanda Ho © 1995 - 2020

Student's name: _____ Assignment date: _____

Division of integers 除整数

$(+6) \div (+3) = 2$ $(-6) \div (-3) = 2$

$(-6) \div (+3) = -2$ $(+6) \div (-3) = -2$

1. $(+8) \div (-2) =$ **-4**   2. $(+35) \div (-7) =$ **-5**

3. $(+12) \div (+3) =$ **4**   4. $(+27) \div (+3) =$ **9**

5. $(-18) \div (-3) =$ **6**   6. $(-39) \div (-3) =$ **13**

7. $(+63) \div (+7) =$ **9**   8. $(+18) \div (+6) =$ **3**

9. $(+72) \div (-8) =$ **-9**   10. $(+25) \div (-5) =$ **-5**

11. $(+56) \div (+7) =$ **8**   12. $(+64) \div (+4) =$ **16**

13. $(+38) \div (-2) =$ **-19**   14. $(+48) \div (-6) =$ **-8**

15. $(+54) \div (-9) =$ **-6**   16. $(+54) \div (-9) =$ **-6**

17. $(-64) \div (+8) =$ **-8**   18. $(-39) \div (+13) =$ **-3**

19. $(-87) \div (+3) =$ **-29**   20. $(-24) \div (+3) =$ **-8**

21. $\dfrac{-65}{-5} =$ **13**   22. $\dfrac{42}{-7} =$ **-6**

23. $\dfrac{-16}{2} =$ **-8**   24. $\dfrac{+66}{6} =$ **11**

25. $\dfrac{-68}{-4} =$ **17**   26. $\dfrac{-36}{9} =$ **-4**

27. $\dfrac{+72}{-4} =$ **-18**   28. $\dfrac{-32}{-4} =$ **8**

29. $\dfrac{+45}{+5} =$ **9**   30. $\dfrac{+15}{-3} =$ **-5**

31. $\dfrac{+38}{-2} =$ **-19**   32. $\dfrac{+45}{+3} =$ **15**

Integer puzzle 整数谜题

Integer, Expression # 2

Ho Math Chess (何數棋谜　趣味數學)

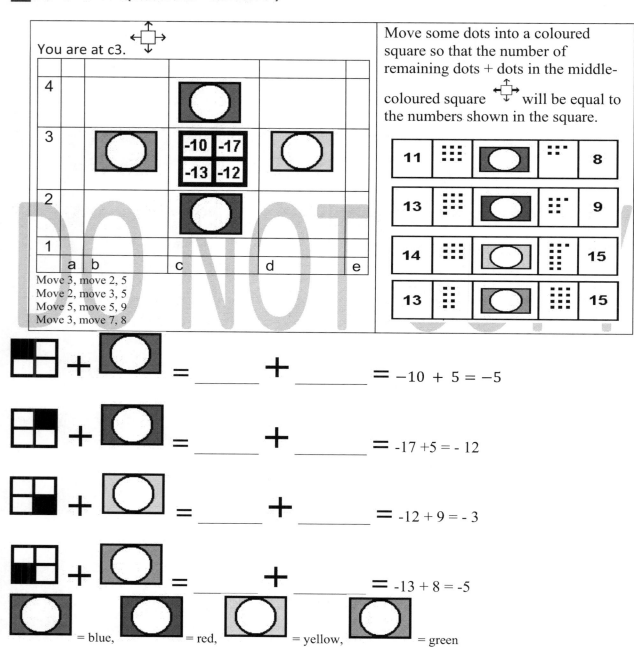

Integer word problems 整数文字题

Integer, Expression # 3

Ho Math Chess (何數棋谜　趣味數學)

Multiplying two integers

Express the results of the following questions by two directed numbers (integers with signs).

If 5 days from the day before yesterday is Thursday, what day is it today?

Wednesday

Veena saves \$2 per day. At the end of 7 days, she will have saved \$14.
$(+2) \times (+7) = +14$
How much would Veena have saved 7 days (-7) ago when compared to today.
$(+2) \times (-7) = -14$
Veena spends \$2 (-2) per day. How much will she have spent after 7 days?
$(-2) \times (+7) = -14$
Veena spends \$2 (-2) per day. How much will she have spent 7 days ago? i.e., how much she was better off than now?
$(-2) \times (-7) = 14$
Suppose you divide two integers. Use examples to illustrate your answers. The quotient is an integer. When the quotient:

1. Less than both integers. $\dfrac{45}{9}$

2. Greater than both integers. Impossible

3. Between the two integers. $\dfrac{45}{5}$

4. Equal to $+1$. $\dfrac{45}{45}$

5. Equal to -1. $\dfrac{45}{-45}$

6. Equal to 0. $\dfrac{0}{45}$

Equations 等式

It makes sense for students to learn some equations before ratio and proportion, so many students got confused about proportions simply because they do not know how to solve the equations of proportion, especially the method of using cross multiplication. The purpose of this section is to give the student the knowledge of using equations to solve proportion and percent problems.

An equation is a mathematical sentence using = sign to connect 2 quantities. The left side of = sign or the right side of the = sign is called an algebraic expression. The expression consists of numbers, operators, or variables (unknown quantity representing by a letter, normally by x). The operators can have brackets (parentheses), exponents, plus, minus, multiplication, or division etc. which are used in elementary school mathematics. To solve an equation is to find all the values of the variables so that both sides are equal.

To solve the equation, quite often, we use the following equation of properties:

The equation does not change when both sides add the same quantity.

The equation does not change when both sides subtract the same quantity.

The equation does not change when both sides multiply the same quantity.

The equation does not change when both sides divided by the same quantity.

Arithmetic operations properties 算式律

The arithmetic operations with real numbers are governed by a few properties, and they are presented below.

Closure for addition, subtraction and multiplication.

For real numbers a and b :

$a + b$ is a unique real number.

$a - b$ is a unique real number.

$a \times b$ is a unique real number.

If 2 real numbers are added, subtracted or multiplied, then the result is always a real number. The result is "enclosed" in the universe of the real number.

For division, it may not be true, such as $\dfrac{8}{0}$.

Commutative property 交换律 for addition and multiplication of 2 numbers

For real numbers a and b .

$a + b = b + a$

$ab = ba$

The results are not changed when the order of 2 numbers is changed.

Which one of the following operations is commutative, and which one is not?

Problems	Commutative or not
To put on soap and wash hands	☐ no
To put on gloves and put on a coat.	☐ yes
To wash hands and eat.	☐ no

Student's name: _____ Assignment date: _____

To wash clothes and dry them.	☐ n
To eat rice and eat chicken.	☐ n
To hang up the phone and say goodbye.	☐ n
To multiply 2 and 3.	☐ y
To mix blue and green paint.	☐ y
The number of different outfits of pairing pants and shirts.	☐ y
The number of ways of choosing food from a menu.	☐ y
To check and checkmate the king.	☐ n
To flip ⠿ around	☐ y
To get an area of a rectangle.	☐ y

Associative property (grouping property) 結合律 for addition and multiplication of 3 numbers

For real numbers a, b, c

$(a + b) + c = a + (b + c)$

$(ab)c = a(bc)$

Use the associative property to make 10 first and then add the third number.

4 6 + 3	4 3 + 6	9 7 + 1	4 8 + 2	7 8 + 3
13	13	17	14	18

Use the associative property to make a nice number (number with trailing zeros) first then multiply the third number.

$12 \times 6 \times 5$ = 360	$11 \times 4 \times 25$ = 1100	$7 \times 25 \times 4$ = 700
$13 \times 2 \times 5$ = 130	$14 \times 2 \times 25$ = 700	$7 \times 15 \times 4$ = 420
$2 \times 7 \times 5 =$ 70	$8 \times 4 \times 25$ = 800	$8 \times 8 \times 25$ = 1600

Student's name: _____   Assignment date: _____

Identity of addition

For real number a
$$a + 0 = 0 + a = a$$
Zero is the additive identity. Any number add a 0, its answer is still the number itself.

Identity of multiplication 乘一不变

For real number a
$$a(1) = (1)a = a$$

One is the multiplication identity. Any number multiplies 1. Its answer is still the number itself.

Identity of quotient 商不变性質

For real number a, b, c, d
$$a \div b = c$$
$$(a \times d) \div (b \times d) = c$$
$$(a \div d) \div (b \div d) = c$$

The quotient will not change if both the dividend and divisor is multiplied or divided by the same number.

Additive inverse 相反数

For any real number a, there exists a unique real number $-a$ such that
$$a + (-a) = a - a = 0$$
The number $-a$ is known as the additive inverse.
a and $-a$ are additive inverse to each other and the opposite of each other.

Multiplicative inverse 倒数

;For any nonzero real number a, there exists a unique real number $\dfrac{1}{a}$ such that

$a\left(\dfrac{1}{a}\right) = \left(\dfrac{1}{a}\right)a = 1$, the number $\dfrac{1}{a}$ is known as the multiplicative inverse or reciprocal of a.

a and $\dfrac{1}{a}$ are multiplicative inverse or reciprocal to each other. Since 1 is the product of $a \times \dfrac{1}{a}$ so to get $\dfrac{\frac{1}{a}}{b}$,

we just must inverse $\dfrac{a}{b}$ to get the answer $\dfrac{b}{a}$.

Student's name: _____   Assignment date: _____

Distributive property 分配律

For real numbers a, b, c

$a(b+c)=ab+ac$	$a(b-c)=ab-ac$	$(a+b)c = ac+bc$	$(a-b)c = ac-bc$

The vertical multiplication is an example of using the associative property.

| $a(b+c)=ab+ac$ | $24 \times 37 = 24 \times (7+30)$ $= 168 + 720 = 888$ Note on the right-hand side. When 3×24, it really means 30×24. | $\begin{array}{r} 2\,4 \\ \times\ \ 3\,7 \\ \hline 1\,6\,8 \\ 7\,2\ \ \\ \hline 8\,8\,8 \end{array}$ | One can see clearly the reason why the product lined up with tens of place value when 3 $\times 24$. |
| $a(c+b)$ $= ac+ab$ | $24 \times 37 = 24 \times (30+7)$ $= 720 + 168 = 888$ Note how 3 and 24 are multiplied first. | $\begin{array}{r} 2\,4 \\ \times\ \ 3\,7 \\ \hline 7\,2\ \ \\ 1\,6\,8 \\ \hline 8\,8\,8 \end{array}$ | |

Number vs. Symbols 数对比符号

Children are familiar with whole numbers, but as soon as the data types change to decimal, fractions, or percent, they get confused very quickly. For the same reason, if the whole number is changed to a symbol, then they also get confused. The following problems are to guide children from whole numbers to symbols.

If A and B are one-digit whole numbers, then find the answers to the following questions.

$$6 = \underline{\quad} \times 3 = (A - B) \times 3$$
2

There are multiple answers for A and B. Find them all by making a T table.

A	B
9	7
8	6
7	5
6	4
5	3
3	2
2	0

= 7 answer

Variable and expression 变数及代数式

In algebra, an unknown quantity or number is represented by a letter such as x, y. An algebraic expression is a mathematical sentence consisting of numbers, operators, or variables with no equal sign.

Fill in _____ with an answer.

Word phrases	Expression	Comments
The product of 10 and a number	$10x$	Do not write the product as $10 \times x$. The number (called coefficient) is placed in front of the variable, and there is an implied × sign between the number and variable. $3x$ means 3 times x.
A number is doubled.	$2x$	Write variable (unknown) X as x or χ since X looks like a multiplication sign. We normally use x, y, z as variables but not always.
One hundred divided by a number	$\dfrac{100}{x}$	Do not write division as $a \div b$. Use $\dfrac{a}{b}$ as a division in algebra since we need to work with LCD in the future.

Variable and expression

Word phrases	Algebraic expression
A number is tripled.	$3x$
4 times x	$4x$
x times 2 (a number is doubled.)	$2x$
x times x (a number is multiplied by itself.)	x^2
one-sixth of a number (a number divided by 6)	$\frac{x}{6}$
When will be Maria's age 7 years from her age now?	$7 + x$
1 times x	x
x times 1	x
2 x times 4	$2x \times 4$
2 times a	$2 \times a$
a times 2	$a \times 2$
thirty-one kilometres less than the distance	$x - 31$
4 times 2 x	$4 \times 2x$
3 minus x	$5 - x$
1 more than a number	$1 + x$
a number decreased by four	$x - 4$

Student's name: _____   Assignment date: _____

Writing algebraic expressions 写代数式

Word Phrase	Algebraic expression
99 subtracted from a number	$x - 99$
a number divided by 23	$\dfrac{23}{4}$
The sum of a number y and 15	$y + 15$
one multiplies a number.	x
the difference between a number and forty	$x - 40$
99 multiplied by a number	$90x$
a number multiplied by 1	x
the product of 2 and 5 and a number	$2 \times 5 \times x$
If x is an odd number, what is the next larger odd number?	$x + 2$
a number divided by 5523	$\dfrac{x}{5523}$
5523 divided by a number	$\dfrac{5523}{x}$
I rode roller coaster x times and the total time is 300 minutes, what is the average time?	$\dfrac{300}{x}$
It took me 30 minutes to finish my grocery shopping, and it included the time of x minutes waiting in the line, what is the time I spent on shopping?	$30 + x$

Student's name: _____ Assignment date: _____

Writing algebraic expressions

Word Phrase	Algebraic expression
Let t be the time taken between school and home round trip. How long did it take for 7 round trips?	$7x$
It took Stanley and Edward 5 hours altogether to finish typing a science project report. How much time did Stanley spend on typing assume Edward typed x hours?	$5 - x$

Writing algebraic expressions

Word Phrase Answers may vary.	Algebraic expression
The sum of a number and 9. Do not write the answer in a direct operation statement such as "a number adds 9."	$x + 9$
	$5 - x$
	$9x + 4$
	$\dfrac{1}{2x}$
	$5a$
a number x multiplied by itself	x^2
	$x^2 + 30$

Ho Math Chess　何数棋谜 奥数,解题策略,及 IQ 思唯训练宝典

Frank Ho, Amanda Ho © 1995 - 2020

Student's name: _____ Assignment date: _____

Writing algebraic expressions

Answers may vary.

_____	$u + \dfrac{u}{4}$
111 less than a number	
_____	$200\,m$
_____	$\dfrac{1}{2x}$
_____	$3x - 1$
_____	x^2
_____	$u - 4u$

Order of operations 先乘除後加减法

When finding the value for an expression (called evaluating), the way to do it is from left to right and use the rule of BEDMAS (bracket, exponent, division, multiplication, addition, subtraction). It means:

Do the bracket first.
Do the exponents second
Then do division or multiplication depending on whichever comes first.
Finally, do addition or subtraction depending on whichever comes first.

For example, $3 + 2 - 4 + (2 + 3) \div 5 \times 2 - 1 + 2^2$
$= 5 - 4 + 5 \div 5 \times 2 - 1 + 4$
$= 1 + 1 \times 2 - 1 + 4$ (5 ÷ 5 must be done before multiplication and been added to others)
$= 1 + 2 - 1 + 4$
$= 3 - 1 + 4$
$= 2 + 4$
$= 6$

Evaluate the following expressions.

Expressions	Value	Comments
$7 - 2 \times 3$	1	
$7 - (2 \times 3)$	1	Are the brackets necessary? ____ yes
$(7 - 2) \times 3$	15	
$2 \times 7 - 3$	11	
$(2 \times 7) - 3$	11	Are the bra no
$2 \times (7 - 3)$	8	
$4 \times 5 + 6 \times 7$	62	

Student's name: _____ Assignment date: _____

Evaluating the mixed expressions 四则计算

Fill in each box by a number. 0.5, 0.5, -2, -2, 5, 5

$x \div 2 = x \times \boxed{}$

$x \times 2 = x \div \boxed{}$

$x - 2 = x + \boxed{}$

$x + 2 = x - \boxed{}$

$x \div 0.2 = x \times \boxed{}$

$x \times 0.2 = x \div \boxed{}$

½, 2, -2, -2, 5, 5

Expressions	Value	Comments
$4 \times (5 + 6) \times 7$	308	
$4 \times (5 + 6 \times 7)$	168	
$(4 \times 5 + 6) \times 7$	182	
$45 \div 5 + 9 \div 3$	12	
$(45 \div 5) + (9 \div 3)$	12	Are brackets necessary? ___ no
$42 \div (5 + 9) \div 3$	1	
$48 \div (5 + 9 \div 3)$	6	
$(45 \div 5 + 9) \div 3$	6	
$1 + 2 + 3 \div 3 - 2 - 1$	1	
$(1 + 2 + 3) \div (3 - 2) - 1$	5	
$1 + 2 + 3 \div (3 - 2) - 1$	5	
$1 + 2 + 3 \div 3 \times 2 - 1$	4	
$1 + 2 + 3 \div 3 \times (2 - 1)$	4	

Order of operations calculation

$24 - 12 \div 2 \div 1 + 2 \times 3 \times 1$

24

$12 \div (8 \div 2 \times 2 + 4 - 2)$

1.2

$3^2 - 4 \times 3 + 4(3^2 - 4)$

17

$25 \div 5 + 4 \div 2 - 2 \div 1$

5

$7 \div 3 + 2 \times 1\frac{1}{2} \div 3\frac{2}{3}$

3 5/33

Student's name: _____ Assignment date: _____

Order of operations 先乘除後加减

$2 + 3 \times 1 - 4 \div 2$ 3
$1\frac{1}{2} \div 2\frac{2}{3} + 2 \div 3$ 1 11/48
$1 \div 3 \div 1 \div \frac{1}{3} - 1\frac{1}{3} \div \frac{1}{3}$ -3
$2 + 3 \times 3 - 1^2 - 1 \div 4$ 9 3/4
$4 \times 2 - 16 \div 8$ 6
$\left(3 + \frac{1}{2}\right) \div \left(2 + \frac{2}{3}\right) - 4\frac{1}{2} \times 2\frac{1}{2}$ -9 15/16

Evaluate the following expressions with unknowns 变数的運算

Evaluate. Use $x = 1$, $y = 2$, $z = 3$	Value	Comments
$1x$	1	$1x$ means x.
$y - x$	1	
$z - x$	2	
$z - x - y$	0	
$4x + 3x + 2x$	9	
$4x + 3x - 2x$	5	
$4x - 3x - 2x$	-1	
$4x - 3x + 2x$	3	
$\dfrac{z}{3} + 9$	10	
$\dfrac{z}{3} + 9 + 2x$	12	
$2x + \dfrac{z}{3} - 1$	2	
$z + 2\dfrac{2}{3}$	5 2/3	
$-z + 2\dfrac{2}{3} + x$	2/3	
$\dfrac{x + y + z}{2} + 3$	6	

Student's name: _____ Assignment date: _____

Write a story for an equation. 文字描写方程式

Equation	Explain your strategy to solve.	Solve	Write a story of the equation. Answers may vary.
$6 = C+5$	Move 5 to the left.	$6 - 5 = C$ $1 = C$	After getting 5 more apples, Charlie has 6 apples.
$C + 2 = 21$	Move 2 to the right.		
$3 + C = 20$			
$10 = C - 1$			
$5 = C - 7$			
$N - 4 = 10$			
$N - 6 = 21$			
$N + 6 = 16$			
$N + 9 = 101$			
$10 - N = 3$			
$19 - N = 5$			
$4 = 18 - N$			

Cross multiplication in cases of (called proportion) 交义相乘

When an equation is in the form of , the cross-multiplication method can be used to get the result. The basic idea is to get the cross product .

Notice a and d , b and c can be exchanged in $\dfrac{a}{b}=\dfrac{c}{d}$ to get the same result. If $\dfrac{a}{b}=\dfrac{c}{d}$, a and d exchanged to get $\dfrac{d}{b}=\dfrac{c}{a}$ or if $\dfrac{a}{b}=\dfrac{c}{d}$, b and c exchanged to get $\dfrac{a}{c}=\dfrac{b}{d}$.

Proportion can be reduced in 2 ways, top with bottom (a,c) and (b,d) such as, for example, $\dfrac{x}{2}=\dfrac{\cancel{6}\,2}{\cancel{3}\,1}$ or left with right numbers such as $(a,b),(c,d)$, for example, $\dfrac{3}{\cancel{4}\,2}=\dfrac{x}{\cancel{2}\,1}$.

The technique of cross multiplication is very important, and it plays a very important role in elementary school math, but unfortunately, some students have ignored its importance when at the elementary schools, later many problems students encountered in high school is because they did not master the technique of cross multiplication. Cross multiplication concept can be used to solve many different types of problems; some of them are as follows:

Proportions in ratio, rate, similarity, scale etc.

I am solving equations in the form of $\dfrac{x}{a}=b$ or $\dfrac{x}{a}=\dfrac{b}{c}$ etc.

This method is extremely important in solving equations taught elementary school. For example, the equations model in elementary school are all in the forms of $\dfrac{x}{a}=b$ or $\dfrac{x}{a}=\dfrac{b}{c}$, so a simple method of using cross multiplication could be used to solve all equation problems. If the model is changed to $\dfrac{x}{a}=\dfrac{b}{c}+dx$ then the cross-multiplication concept will not work for the model $\dfrac{x}{a}=\dfrac{b}{c}+dx$

Rational equations in high school such as $\dfrac{x^2-3x+2}{x-2}=\dfrac{x}{2}$

Cross multiplication could continuously be used in high school

The cross-multiplication technique can also be used in high school. The following two examples are given here to stress the importance of learning the concept of cross multiplication.

Factor $x^2 + 3x - 2$

$$\begin{array}{cc} 1 & -2 \\ & \times \\ 1 & -1 \end{array}$$

Finding equations when the slope and one point are given in high school

$$\frac{y-1}{x-2} = \frac{3}{4}$$

Trigonometric ratios

For example, $\sin 30^0 = \dfrac{1}{2}$, the product concept could be used to get the answer when 2 of them are unknown, and one of them is known, but the concept of cross multiplication still helps in solving trigonometric ratios.

Example

Tina bought 2 pencils for $2.50. At the same price rate, how much would a dozen pencils cost?

Method 1: Use unit-rate

$$\frac{2.50}{2} \times 12 = 2.5 \times 6 = 15 \text{ dollars}$$

Method 2: Use the equivalent ratio

$$\frac{2.50}{2} = \frac{X}{12} \quad (\times 6)$$

$X = 2.50 \times 6 = 15$

Since 12 is a multiple of 2, so it is easier to use multiple factors to figure out X.

Method 3: Use cross multiplication

When the equivalent ratio does not have multiple integral factors, then cross multiplication can be used.

$$\frac{2.50}{2} = \frac{x}{12}$$

$2x = 12 \times 2.5$

$x = 15$

Student's name: _____ Assignment date: _____

Method 1	Method 2
Multiply both sides by LCD	Cross Multiplication
$\dfrac{x}{2} = \dfrac{3}{4}$ Multiply both sides by LCD, which is 4. (The reason the cross multiplication is introduced is that the above concept of multiplying 4 on both sides is difficult for the elementary students to understand: it involves equation property, fraction cancellation, and then numerator $\times$. It takes 3 extra steps to achieve the result of the cross-multiplication.) $4 \times \dfrac{x}{2} = \dfrac{3}{4} \times 4$ $2x = 3$ $x = \dfrac{3}{2}$	$\dfrac{x}{2} = \dfrac{3}{4}$ 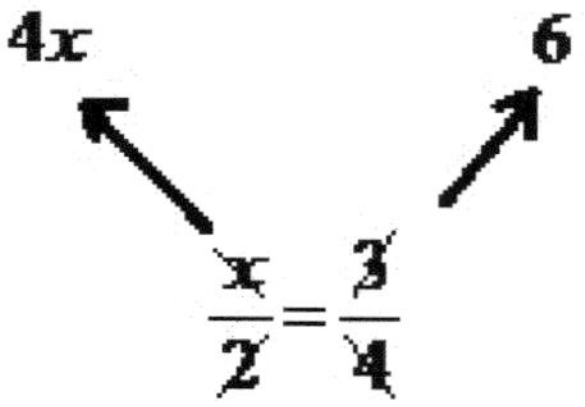 Cross multiply as shown above $4x = 6$ $2x = 3$ $x = \dfrac{3}{2}$
Multiply both sides by LCD is the more accurate and the general method to solve equation problems since it does not require further reducing later, and it can also handle more complicated equation models such as $\dfrac{x}{a} = \dfrac{b}{c} + dx$ etc.	The cross-multiplication method always assumes the LCD is the product of the 2 bottom numbers, and in some cases, it is not true. As we can see that the above cross multiplication assuming the LCD is 8. so, the reducing is required later. However, for the elementary student, the cross multiplication offers the advantage of being easy to operate for an equation model like $\dfrac{x}{a} = \dfrac{b}{c}$.

Student's name: _____ Assignment date: _____

Cross multiplication

After we understand how to cross-multiplication works using LCD in the last section, here 2 ways of cross multiplication is introduced. Do both method 1 and method 2 for the same question.

Method 1: Just blindly do cross multiplication without any analyzing.	**Method 2**: Only do cross multiplication on number × number and leave the side with variable alone and later exchange number and variable to get the answer.
$\dfrac{n}{2} = \dfrac{4}{3}$ $3n = 8$ $n = \dfrac{8}{3}$	$\dfrac{n}{2} = \dfrac{4}{3}$ We still do cross multiplication but only do number × number and leave the variable side alone. We did not do $3 \times n$. So $n = \dfrac{8}{3}$
$\dfrac{x}{2} = \dfrac{4}{5}$	Only multiply 2 and 4 and leave 5 and x alone. Exchange 5 and x to get the answer.

Cross multiplication

Method 1: Just blindly do cross multiplication without any analyzing.	**Method 2**: Only do cross multiplication on number × number and leave the side with variable alone and later exchange number and variable to get the answer.
$\dfrac{y}{3} = \dfrac{5}{7}$	$y = \dfrac{15}{7}$
$\dfrac{3}{2} = \dfrac{x}{5}$	$x = \dfrac{15}{2}$
$\dfrac{7}{2} = \dfrac{a}{13}$	$x = \dfrac{91}{2}$
$\dfrac{9}{2} = \dfrac{y}{9}$	$y = \dfrac{81}{2}$

Cross multiplication in equation 方程式转换成比例

Equation	Ratio
$3A=2B$	A : B = ?　3 : 2
? $4G=5B$	There are 5 boys for every 4 girls. G : B = ?　5 : 4
$4B=7A$	A : B = ?　4 : 7
$\frac{3}{5}A = \frac{2}{3}B$	A : B = $\frac{2}{3} : \frac{3}{5}$ = ?　10 : 9
$\frac{1}{2}A = \frac{2}{3}B$	A : B = ?　4 : 3

Student's name: _____ Assignment date: _____

Equations	Solve	Comments
$x + 1 = 2$	1. Isolate x by leaving x to the left side, but not always. Usually, we move x to the side where it has a positive sign. We normally write the solution as $x =$ a number, so it is a good idea to move x to the left. 2. Move the numbers to the right. There are 2 ways the number can be moved. **Method 1 (adding/subtracting)** $x + 1 = 2$ The first way is to add -1 to both sides so the number 1 on the left side disappears. $x + 1 - 1 = 2 - 1$ $x = 1$ **Method 2 (moving numbers)** Notice that the above, on the left side, the number added -1 is cancelled with the original number 1. So, we can really think it as having moved the number 1 to the right side and changes its sign from $-$ to $+$. So, the $1 - 1$ part on the left side can be omitted. $x + 1 = 2$ $x = 2 - 1$ $x = 1$	**Method 1 (adding/subtracting)** Subtract 1 on both sides so that 1 will be cancelled and x on the left side is isolated. $x + 1 = 2$ $x + 1 - 1 = 2 - 1$ $x + \cancel{1} - \cancel{1} = 2 - 1$ $x = 1$ Method 2 (moving numbers) Note the above the right-hand side 1 is cancelled with -1 anyway, an operation is just like to move 1 to the other side and change its sign whenever the number is moved to the other side. $x + 1 = 2$ $x = 2 - 1$ $x = 1$

Student's name: _____ Assignment date: _____

Fill in answer in ☐ and _____.

Equation	Unknown or variable	Comments
$? + 1 = 3$	$? = 3 - \boxed{} = \boxed{} 2$	Subtract 1 from both sides. $? + 1 - 1 = 3 - 1$ $? = 3 - 1$ It can be thought of as if a number is moved to the right-hand side. Its sign is changed from + to − or vice versa. $? + \; 1 = 3 \; \ominus 1$
$\chi + 1 = 3$	$\chi = 3 - \boxed{} = \boxed{} 2$	$\chi + \; 1 = 3 \; \ominus 1$
$\chi + 2 = 3$	$\chi = 3 - \boxed{} = \boxed{} 1$	
$\chi + 3 = 5$	$\chi = 5 - \boxed{} = \boxed{} 2$	
$\chi + 4 = 7$	$\chi = 7 - \boxed{} = \boxed{} 3$	

Student's name: _____ Assignment date: _____

$5 + x = 9$	$x = 9 - \square$ $= \square\ 4$	Move 5 to the right side.
$x + 6 = 9$	$x = 9 - \square$ $= \square\ 3$	
$7 + x = 9$	$x = 9 - \square$ $= \square\ 2$	
$x + 8 = 9$	$x = 9 - \square$ $= \square\ 1$	
$x + 9 = 9$	$x = 9 - \square$ $= \square\ 0$	
$0 + x = 19$	$x = 19 - \square$ $= \square\ 19$	
$x + 12 = 19$	$x = 19 - \square$ $= \square\ 7$	

Student's name: _____ Assignment date: _____

Equation	Unknown or variable	Comments
$? - 1 = 3$	$? = 3 + \square$ $= \square\ 4$	Add 1 from both sides. $? - 1 + 1 = 3 + 1$ $? = 3 + 1$ It can be thought as if 1 was moved to the right-hand side, and its sign is changed from $-$ to $+$. $? - 1 = 3 \ \boxed{+1}$
$\chi - 1 = 3$	$\chi = 3 + \square$ $= \square\ 4$	$\chi - 1 = 3 \ \boxed{+1}$
$\chi - 2 = 3$	$\chi = 3 + \square$ $= \square\ 5$	
$\chi - 3 = 5$	$\chi = 5 + \square$ $= \square\ 8$	
$- 4 + \chi = 7$	$\chi = 7 + \square$ $= \square$ 11	

$\chi - 5 = 9$	$\chi = 9 + \square$ $= \square\ 14$	Move 5 to the right side.
$-6 + \chi = 9$	$\chi = 9 + \square$ $= \square\ 15$	
$\chi - 7 = 9$	$\chi = 9 + \square$ $= \square\ 16$	
$\chi - 8 = 9$	$\chi = 9 + \square$ $= \square\ 17$	
$-9 + \chi = 9$	$\chi = 9 + \square$ $= \square\ 18$	
$\chi - 10 = 19$	$\chi = 19 + \square$ $= \square\ 29$	
$\chi - 12 = 19$	$\chi = 19 + \square$ $= \square\ 31$	

Equation division 方程除法

$2 \times ? = 6$	$? = \dfrac{6}{\Box}$ $= \Box\, 3$	Divide both sides by 2. $\dfrac{2 \times ?}{2} = \dfrac{6}{2}$ $? = 3$ It can be thought as if 2 were moved to the right-hand side at the bottom position. Use the concept of cross multiplication, and we know when moving a factor of a product, the factor always goes to the denominator of the other side. It can be shown step by step as follows: $\dfrac{2 \times ?}{1} = \dfrac{6}{1}$ $\dfrac{?}{1} = \dfrac{6}{2 \times 1}$ $? = \dfrac{6}{2}$ $2 \times ? = \dfrac{6}{②}$
$2\chi = 8$	$\chi = \dfrac{8}{\Box} = \Box$ 4	The idea of moving comes from the cross multiplication. $\dfrac{2x}{1} = \dfrac{8}{1}$
$\dfrac{3x}{1} = \dfrac{9}{1}$	$\dfrac{\cancel{3}x}{1} = \dfrac{9}{3}$ $= \Box\, 3$	

Without working on enough cross-multiplication exercise, the concept of moving factor seems to be difficult for students to grasp. Alternatively, students could be taught by dividing the same number to both sides of the equation, and the result is x will be isolated anyway after the division, so we do not really need to write an extra step for the division $\dfrac{3x}{3} = \dfrac{9}{3}$. For example, $3x = 9$, both sides divide 3, then $3x$ will become x. so on the left side, we could just write x and on the right side, we write $\dfrac{9}{3}$. The equation becomes $x = \dfrac{9}{3} = 3$.

$3x = 9$	$x = \dfrac{9}{\square} = \square$	3
$\dfrac{3x}{1} = \dfrac{12}{1}$	$\dfrac{3x}{1} = \dfrac{12}{3} = \square$	4
$3x = 12$	$x = \dfrac{12}{\square} = \square$	4
$3x = 15$	$x = \dfrac{15}{\square} = \square$	5
$3 \times x = 18$	$x = \dfrac{18}{\square} = \square$	6
$4x = 16$	$x = \dfrac{16}{\square} = \square$	4
$5 \times x = 20$	$x = \dfrac{20}{\square} = \square$	4
$7x = 28$	$x = \dfrac{28}{\square} = \square$	4
$9x = 36$	$x = \dfrac{36}{\square} = \square$	4

The idea of working on fractional equations (rational equations) is to convert the fractions to whole numbers by multiplying LCD to both sides of the equation. However, with the equation in $\frac{a}{b} = \frac{c}{d}$ form, the exchange of ad and bc could be used to solve the unknown.

$\frac{?}{2} = 6$	$? = 6 \times \square$ $= \square$ 12	Multiply both sides by 2. $? = 2 \times 6 = 12$ It can be thought as if 2 were moved to the right-hand side and then $\frac{?}{2} = 6$ multiply 6. The idea comes from cross multiplication and is demonstrated as follows. $? = 12$ $\frac{?}{2} = \frac{6}{1}$
$\frac{x}{2} = 6$	$x = 6 \times \square$ $= \square \ 12$	$\frac{x}{2} = 6$
$\frac{x}{2} = 8$	$x = 8 \times \square$ $= \square \ 16$	
$\frac{x}{3} = 7$	$x = 7 \times \square$ $= \square \ 21$	

Student's name: _____ Assignment date: _____

Equation division

$\frac{x}{4}=8$	$x= 8 \times \square$ $= \square\ 32$	
$\frac{x}{5}=10$	$x= 10 \times \square$ $= \square\ 50$	
$\frac{x}{6}=12$	$x= 12 \times \square$ $= \square\ 72$	
$\frac{x}{7}=13$	$x= 13 \times \square$ $= \square\ 91$	
$\frac{x}{8}=14$	$x= 14 \times \square$ $= \square\ 112$	
$\frac{x}{9}=11$	$x= 11 \times \square$ $= \square\ 99$	
$\frac{x}{10}=12$	$x= 12 \times \square$ $= \square\ 120$	

Student's name: _____ Assignment date: _____

Solve Equations – addition and subtraction 方程加减法
$x + 4 = 0$ -4
$x - 4 = 0$ 4
$x + 4 = 2$ 2
$x - 4 = 2$ 6
$4 + x = 0$ -4
$4 - x = 0$ 4
$4 + x = 2$ -2
$4 - x = 2$ 2

Student's name: ______________________ Assignment date: ____________________

Solve Equations – addition and subtraction.
$x+4=0$ -4
$x-4=0$ 4
$x+4=6$ 2
$x-4=2$ 6
$4+x=0$ -4
$4-x=0$ 4
$4+x=2$ -2
$4-x=2$ 2

Student's name: _____ Assignment date: _____

Solve Equations – multiplication and division 方程乘除法

$4x = 12$

3

$x \times 4 = 16$

4

$4x + 4 = 2$

-1/2

$6x - 4 = 8$

2

$4 + 2x = 0$

-2

$4 - 8x = 0$

1/2

$4 + 4x = 2$
-1/2

$4 - 4x = 2$

½

Ho Math Chess 何数棋谜 奥数,解题策略,及 IQ 思唯训练宝典

Frank Ho, Amanda Ho © 1995 - 2020

Student's name: _____ Assignment date: _____

Solving word problems using equations 解方程式文字题

Addition word problems using equation 加法解方程式文字题

The number is 27 more than 35. What is the number?

62

The difference of a number and 49 is 137. What is the number?

186

A number minus 45 equals 132. What is the number?

177

Subtraction word problems using equation 减法解方程式文字题

The sum of a number and 37 is 961. What is the number?

924

The difference between 462 and a number is 344. What is the number?

118

A number plus 186 equals 251. What is the number?

65

The number is 18 less than 91. What is the number?

73

Multiplication word problems using equation 乘法解方程式文字题

A number divided by 4 equals 502. What is the number?

2008

How much is 456 multiplied by 12?

5472

How much is 63 times 34?

2142

What is the sum of nine 148's?

1332

Number A is 128 and is twice as much as number B. How much is number B?

64

Division word problems using equation 除法解方程式文字题

9744 divided by 14, what is its quotient?

696

756 divided by a number. Its quotient is 3. What is the number?

252

How many times is 508 of 8?

63.5

A number multiplied by 9. Its product is 1458. What is the number?

162

8 multiplied by a number equals 356. What is the number?

44.5

The product of a number and 12 is 276. What is the number?

23

Number A is 128; number B is twice as number A. How much is number B?

256

Number A is 48 and number B is 12. How many times is number A of number B?

4

Student's name: _____ Assignment date: _____

Techniques in solving linear equations 解方程式技巧

To solve linear equations $(ax + b = 0)$, we rely on the equation properties as follows:

- Add a number to both sides of an equation
- Subtract a number from both sides of an equation.
- Multiply both sides of an equation by a number.
- Divide both sides of an equation by a non-zero number.

Moving variable to the side where the sign will be positive

Move x to the left side	**Move x to the right side**
$3x = 2x + 2$	$2x + 2 = 3x$
$4x = 3x - 2$	$4x - 2 = 2x$
$5x = 2x - 2$	$3x = 5x + 2$
$5x = 2x - 6$	$4x = 5x + 2$
$6x + 2 = 5x$	$7x = 9x - 2$
$9x + 2 = 7x$	$6x = 8x - 2$

2, 2
-2, 1
-2/3, -1
-2, -2
-2, 1
-1, 1

Model 1: Converting decimals to integers

$0.5x + 0.7x + 3 = 0.2x - 4$ Hint: We like to work on integers, not decimals. $\quad =$ $\quad =$ -7
$1.5x + 2.2x + 3 = 1.2x - 42$ $\quad =$ $\quad =$ -18
$3 + 0.3x + 2 + 0.4x = 5 + 0.8x - 6$ $\quad =$ $\quad =$ 60

Student's name: _____ Assignment date: _____

Model 2: Removing brackets by expanding

This model is important in solving complicated word problems of Surplus and Shortage

$2(3 + 5x) = 3(5x - 3)$ Hint: Move x to the side, which gives the positive sign (coefficient) to avoid the negative operation.   =   =   3
$2(3 + 5x) = -3(-5x - 3)$ =   =   -3/5
$2(3 + 5x) + 4x = -3x(-2 - 3)$ =   =   1/8
$3(5x - 3) = 2(7x - 3)$ =   =   3

Model 3: Cancelling the common factors

$$4 \times \frac{x}{2} + \frac{3}{2} \times 6x + \frac{x}{4} \times 8 = \frac{x}{3} \times 9 + \frac{x}{4} \times 8 + \frac{1}{5} \times 25$$

Hint: Cancel the common factors first, if possible.

=

=

5/8

$$\frac{1}{2}(24x - 6) = \frac{1}{4}(16x - 8)$$

Hint: Cancel the common factors first, if possible.

=

=

=

1/8

$$\frac{1}{3}(27x - 9) = \frac{1}{4}(24x - 16)$$

Hint: Cancel the common factors first, if possible.

=

=

-1/3

Student's name: _____ Assignment date: _____

Model 4 Multiplying both sides by LCD

$\frac{1}{2}(5x - 6) = \frac{1}{4}(7x - 8)$

LCD is 4

Multiply both sides by 4

$4 \times \frac{1}{2}(5x - 6) = \frac{1}{4}(7x - 8) \times 4$

$2(5x - 6) = 7x - 8$

4/3

$\frac{x-3}{4} = \frac{2x}{6} - 3$

One method to do this problem is to convert $\frac{2x}{6} - 3$ to an improper fraction and then use cross multiplication, but the cross multiplication is just a shortcut for converting both sides to have the same LCD. In this case, the LCD is 12, but by using cross multiplication, one would get LCD as 24. So, **the universal way to do rational equations is still to convert both sides by multiplying LCD**.

27

$2 + \frac{x-3}{3} = 3 + \frac{2x}{9}$

9

Linear equation 直线方程式

The graph below shows Jaden's bike race speed.

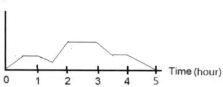

(A) What was Jaden's speed during the first half-hour?
  Blank line   blank line
  Blank line   blank line
Steady increase.

(B) What was Jaden's speed during the second half-hour?
  Blank line   blank line
  Blank line   blank line
Constant speed

(C) During what part of the race was Jaden going the slowest?

  Blank line   blank line
  Blank line   blank line
The hours are between 4 and 5.

(D) At about how long did it take Jaden to finish the race?
4.5 hours
  Blank line   blank line
  Blank line   blank line
(E) The bike racecourse is 90 km, with 10 rest stations in equal distance. How far apart as the distance between each station?

$\frac{90}{11} = 8.27$ km

  Blank line   blank line
  Blank line   blank line

Ho Math Chess 何数棋谜 奥数,解题策略,及 IQ 思唯训练宝典

Student's name: _____ Assignment date: _____

Jaden has a fencing material of 18 m, and he wants to build a rectangular garden. What could be the possible lengths and widths?

1, 8
2, 7
3, 6
4, 5
5, 4

$\Box 432 \div 6$ is about 405 for the quotient. What digit could be in the box?

2

Justin's age is between 20 and 40 years old. Last year his age was a multiple of 4. This year his age was multiple of 5. How old is Justin?

25

Justin's age is between 20 and 40 years old. Last year his age was a multiple of 5. This year his age was multiple of 6. How old is Justin?

36

What is the remainder when 2.75 is divided by 4?
The remainder is 0.03.

Jaiden paid $1.00 for a $0.15 eraser. Show how many ways can he get his change back in 25 cents, 10 cents, and 5 cents?

25 cents	3	2	2	2
10 cents	0	2	1	0
5 cents	0	1	3	5

Student's name: _____ Assignment date: _____

Review of equation 方程複習

If $5 \times x = 120$ and $\frac{x}{y} = 3$, then what is y?

8

Find N if $3 \times (25 + N - 13) = 96$.

$N = 20$

What is x if there are three equations as follows:

$$x - y = 5$$
$$y + z = 4$$
$$z + 1 = 3$$

7

What is n if $0 = 1 \times n \times 1$?

0

What is n if $1 = 1 \times n \times 1$?

1

What is $\square$ if $21 - \square = 54 \div 3$?

3

When a number is added to twice of itself, the result is the difference of the number less than 12, what is the number?

3

Student's name: _____ Assignment date: _____

If ☐6 + 78 = 114, then what value is the missing part ☐?

In this problem ☐6 is a 2-digit number.

3

If $\frac{28}{48} = \frac{\Delta}{12}$, what is the value of Δ?

7

If $1 + 2 \times p = 25$, then $p - 11 = ?$

1

Inequality 不等式

Should inequality concept be included in the elementary school curriculum? It is in the grade 9 curriculum in BC, Canada, but it appears in some Asian countries in the elementary schools' math contest problems.

Solve the following inequalities.

$6x + 7 \geq 7x$
$2 - 4x < 11 - 33$

$6 < x \leq 7$

Student's name: _____ Assignment date: _____

Uncertain equation 不定方程式

The uncertain equation means that the number of variables is more than the number of equations. This kind of problem shows up in China's math contests but never taught in North America elementary day school's regular math curriculum.

Two sizes of string lights set red and blue are used to decorate a 150-m street. There are exactly 2 m between two sets of lights. The red string lights set is 11 m long, and the blue string lights set is 8 m long. A set of string light is connected to each end of the street with no space between each set and the end of the street. How many blue and red sets are connected on the street?

$11R + 8B + 2(R + B - 1) = 150$
$10B = 152 - 13R$
If $R = 4$ then $B = 10$ because $152 - 13$ B must have an ending 0.

4 sets of red light and 10 sets of blue lights.

Line Segment Diagram 萬能解題法 - 线段图法

When teaching word problems, the Line Segment Diagram should be the first method introduced to students.

1. What is the line segment method for solving word problems?

The line segment method is used as a universal method to give elementary students a graphic presentation after analyzing word problems, so they are able to link the relationships between numbers and use the relationships to solve the problem. It may be viewed as a graphic representation (model) of an algebraic equation.

For example, to use the line segment to show 3 + ? = 5.

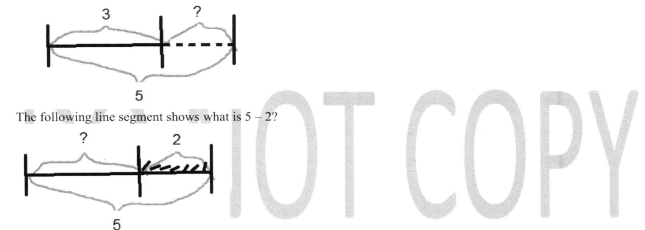

The following line segment shows what is 5 – 2?

2. How is the line segment different from an algebraic method?

Algebra is to set up an equation to solve unknown variables by manipulating the equation in the left or right order (for one equation). The line segment method is to find a solution by analyzing and then equating the relationship between line segments.

3. Can the method of line segment solve al and every elementary math word problem?

The line segment method can solve many types of word problems, but not all and everyone. For example, many data management and statistical problems, patterns, logic problems using charts etc. are not suitable for using line segment methods.

4. Is the algebraic method better and more powerful than the line segment method?

Generally speaking, the algebraic method is more powerful and fast than the algebraic method, but unless you have mastered elementary algebra solving the equation, most elementary students cannot use algebra to solve word problems.

Further, the word problems can train student's thinking skills and increase their brain power, so there are benefits not to use algebraic method elementary math level. There are some problems that can be solved easier by using the line segment method, instead of an algebraic equation. There are a few examples presented here to illustrate the difference.

Example 1

After Frank spent 20 % of his pay on a computer. He spent $\frac{2}{5}$ of the remaining on a DVD. He had $72 left. How much money did he have at first?

Algebraic method	Line segment method

To solve it using algebra, the equation is

$$x - \left(x - \frac{x}{5} \right) \frac{2}{5} = 72$$

Most elementary students cannot solve the above algebraic equation, but they can use the line segments to solve the above word problem.

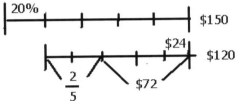

By providing a set of tools to elementary students, elementary students can solve some difficult problems, which sometimes they see these word problems again when they are in secondary schools.

Student's name: _____　Assignment date: _____

Line segment Diagram

Whole numbers Arithmetic using line segment	Algebra using x
Give and take (Building foundation of learning equation - 取捨問題) Caroline has 185 pogs, and Thomas has 79 pogs. How many pogs must Carolina give to Thomas so that both have the same number of pogs? 53 Caroline has 185 pogs, and Thomas has 79 pogs. How many pogs must Carolina give to Thomas so that he would have 40 more pogs than her? 73 (53+20)	
Caroline is 48 years old, and Thomas is 11 years old. In how many years will Caroline be twice as old as Thomas? 48-11=37, 37-11=26	

Chickens and Rabbits problems 鸡兔同笼

A grade-7 girl (in Canada, British Columbia) asked me (Frank) how to solve a Chickens and Rabbits like (2 unknown variables with the power of 1) question, and when I started to introduce a systematic method to her, she lost interest and insisted her teacher only taught the Trial and Error method. There is nothing wrong with the Trial and Error method, especially if this is just a homework exercise, but I must teach students who are interested in math contests a universal method to get the advantage of speed. As my elementary math education was educated in Chinese, so I know the Chickens and Rabbits problems were taught to Chinese, not in the Trial and Error method. So, this sparked my interest in exploring how the Chickens and Rabbits problems are taught in China and Canada and at what grades. Why were Chinese so interested in this kind of word problem in around the 4th century? What is the implication of learning a universal method of solving the Chickens and Rabbits problems?

Chickens and Rabbits problem is one of the most famous Chinese classic word problems and was introduced about 2000 years and was used in old Chinese officials' qualifying examinations. It has since appeared all over the world, and even appears many times in grade 1 math contests, whether in China or other countries. In ancient times, a Chinese use an oral method to answer this type of problem in a few seconds to impress the examiners. But today, the Assumption Method is introduced in most Chinese math contest preparation books. The Assumption Method is simply to transfer one variable from "head" to "leg," so students only must deal with one variable, and the method is very similar to Travelling problems. So, this basically answered why Chinese were so interested in Chickens and Rabbits problems, because they had discovered the way of solving System of Equations using the elimination method 1500 years ago,

We studied the Chinese books on Chickens and Rabbits and some problems appeared in North America math contests and noted the followings:

- 898-Chickens and Rabbits problem is a classic 2-variable problem, so how can Chinese give this kind of problem in grade1 enrichment math books? What method do they teach at such young kids? In ancient times, the Chinese used the oral method and today. They use the diagram to teach young kids, such as grade 1 students.
- The concept of a system of equation method was used in solving the Chickens and Rabbits problem in 4th century China, but their mathematical notations are very different from today's algebraic notations.
- Can the method of solving Chickens and Rabbits be used as a universal method to solve other 2-variable word problems by mastering the method of Chickens and Rabbits problems without using algebra?
- The Assumption Method using the idea of pushing the data to the extreme could be used in solving many other word problems like finding out the combination of coins of coin problems.
- The Assumption Method itself is basically a procedure of Solving Systems of Equations.
- Is the method used in 4th century China to solve the Chickens and Rabbits problems different from the method of Systems of Equations used in modern math? No.

Chickens and Rabbits word problem was first mentioned in a Chinese mathematics book entitled 孙子算经. This mathematics book was published in the 4th century, but the exactly published year is not sure. In that book, there is a math problem as follows:

"今有鸡兔同笼，上有三十五头，下有九十四足，问鸡兔各几何."

用现代话说就是这样:

"今有鸡兔同笼，从上面数有头 35 个，从下面数有脚 94 只，问鸡和免各有多少只？"

The English translation is as follows:

There is a total of 35 chickens and rabbits in a cage with 94 legs altogether. How many chickens and rabbits each of them is there in the cage?

The above problem is a very classic and famous Chickens and Rabbits word problem. The problem is a very good example of 2 variables question which can be handled by using arithmetic. It also can be used to solve other arithmetic problems, which are two variables in nature. Students are encouraged to be familiar with Chickens and Rabbits problems to use its method as a general method to solve a variety of two-variable problems.

We will present the methods of solving it in 5 methods.

Method 1 – Drawing a diagram Method 画图显示法

This method can be used to teach very young children, but it takes time to draw when the number of heads gets larger.

Step 1. Assume all heads are chickens, so draw 35 chickens (or 35 rabbits with 4 legs) with 2 legs. So, the total number of legs is 70.

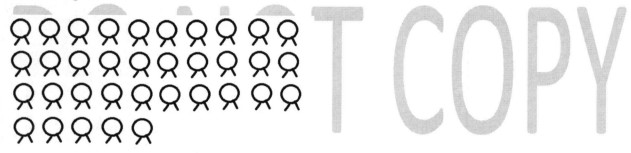

Step 2. But there are 94 legs, so we need 94 – 70 = 24 more legs. This proves our assumption is wrong, and we must change some chickens to rabbits by drawing two more legs on some chickens to get extra 24 legs.

Step 3. How many heads have 4 legs now? 12 heads have 4 legs, so this is the answer for the number of rabbits. 35 – 12 = 23 … number of chickens

This diagram method is the modern way of how Chinese teaches grade 1 kids to solve the Chickens and Rabbits problem, but of course, the numbers used are all small numbers, so they can be drawn easily.

I believe this kind of problem is presented in the grade 1 math book for the purpose of challenging some enriched students in addition to training their brain powers. It challenges young children to see how they handle two variables. This diagram method was not the method used in 4th Chinese math book 孙子算经.

Method 2 - Chinese oral method 中国古心算法 (金鸡獨立兔子舉手)
(Half the number of legs minus the heads = number of rabbits).

There is a total of 35 chickens and rabbits in a cage with 94 legs altogether. How many chickens and rabbits each of them is there in the cage?

The method used in the Chinese book is to have each chicken raise one leg, and each rabbit raises 2 legs. In this case, the number of legs will be reduced to 47 by having 94 divided by 2 (有些書叫抬脚法或鸡飛). It uses the concept of turning all legs to heads to have the same measurement unit (i.e., head) between the number of heads and the number of legs.

Explanation in words

After dividing the number of legs by 2, the problem changes to pure heads problem. The ratio of the number of chickens to their legs is 1 to 1 (each chicken 1 leg), so the number of legs becomes the number of heads for chickens. The number of heads of rabbits to their legs is 1 to 2 (each rabbit 2 legs) so that each rabbit has 2 legs, and it means there are 2 heads if we use the unit of "one head one leg" for both chicken and rabbit. So, we know the difference between the total legs (with one extra leg added for each rabbit) and the total number of heads (each chicken and each rabbit has only one leg.) is the number of rabbits. 47 − 35= 12

Interestingly, the above "half the legs and minus the heads" method is exactly the method of the Systems of Equations method used in modern math. The Chinese's "half the legs and minus the heads" method was used as an oral computation method to get an answer very quickly when tested orally.

Explanation in algebra

$2C + 4R = 94$ ..... (1)

$\frac{(1)}{2} = C + 2R = 47$ .... (2) This can be thought as each chicken has one leg and each rabbit has 2. Each rabbit has one more leg than its head.

$C + R = 35$ ....(3) This can be though as each chicken and each rabbit has only one leg.
(2) – (3)
$R = 12$ ..... rabbit numbers
$C = 23$ .... chicken

It does not matter how the Chinese math contest books and textbook explain the reason for having the legs method - the classic oral method; many students still got confused about why it works. The algebraic method offers insight as to why the oral method works.

The computation procedure can be depicted as follows:

$$\begin{bmatrix} 35 \text{ heads} \\ 94 \text{ legs} \end{bmatrix} \rightarrow \begin{bmatrix} 35 \\ 47 \text{ bottom divided by } 2 \end{bmatrix} \rightarrow \begin{bmatrix} 35 \\ 12 \text{ bottom minus top} \end{bmatrix} \rightarrow \begin{bmatrix} 23 \text{ tom minus bottom} \\ 24 \end{bmatrix}$$

The disadvantage of the oral method

The oral method of halving the number of legs only works for the Chickens and rabbits condition. It can not be used as a general method to solve the variations of the Chickens and Rabbits problem.

Example

Example 1
There are 12 children in Patricia's class, and the boys and girls read 46 books altogether. Each boy read 3 books, and each girl read 5 books. How many books did each boy read and how many books did each girl read?

The oral method of halving the books 46 will not work. What can we do?

Not all similar Chickens and Rabbits problems can use the above "half the legs and minus the heads" method, so the use of the above method is very limited. It is considered as a special case of the system of equations.

Example 2
There are 17 tricycles and bicycles and a total of 41 wheels. How many tricycles and bicycles are there?

Student's name: _____ Assignment date: _____

Chickens and Rabbits problems Chinese oral method practice

Half legs minus heads = number of rabbits

Oral practice	Answers
Total heads = 3 Total legs = 8	Rabbits = 1 Chickens =2
Total heads = 3 Total legs = 10	Rabbits = 2 Chickens =1
Total heads = 4 Total legs = 12	Rabbits = 2 Chickens =2
Total heads = 4 Total legs = 10	Rabbits = 1 Chickens =3
Total heads = 4 Total legs = 14	Rabbits = 3 Chickens =1
Total heads = 5 Total legs = 14	Rabbits = 2 Chickens =3
Total heads = 5 Total legs = 16	Rabbits = 3 Chickens =2

Student's name: _____ Assignment date: _____

Chickens and Rabbits problems Chinese oral method practice

Half legs minus heads = number of rabbits

Oral practice	Answers
Total heads = 6 Total legs = 18	Rabbits = 3 Chickens =3
Total heads = 6 Total legs = 20	Rabbits = 4 Chickens =2
Total heads = 6 Total legs = 16	Rabbits = 2 Chickens =4
Total heads = 6 Total legs = 22	Rabbits = 5 Chickens =1
Total heads = 7 Total legs = 16	Rabbits = 1 Chickens =6
Total heads = 7 Total legs = 18	Rabbits = 2 Chickens =5
Total heads = 7 Total legs = 20	Rabbits = 3 Chickens =4
Total heads = 8 Total legs = 28	Rabbits = 6 Chickens =3
Total heads = 8 Total legs = 18	Rabbits = 1 Chickens =7
Total heads = 8 Total legs = 24	Rabbits = 4 Chickens =4
Total heads = 8 Total legs =16	Rabbits = 0 Chickens =8

Student's name: _____   Assignment date: _____

Method 3 – Using Algebra, Systems of Equations for advanced students 联立方程

There is a total of 35 chickens and rabbits in a cage with 94 legs altogether. How many chickens and rabbits each of them is there in the cage?

The following demonstrates the reason behind the Chinese's oral method to solve the Chickens and Rabbits problem.

R + C = 35 …….. (1)
2C + 4R = 94 ….. (2) (the total number of legs divided by 2)
$\frac{(2)}{2}$ C + 2R = 47 ……….(3)
(3) − (1) R = 47−35 = 12 (Half the legs then minus the heads = rabbits number)
C = 35 − 12 = 23

The following demonstrates the reason behind the Assumption Method of solving the Chickens and Rabbits problem.

Assume all heads are chickens	Assume all heads are rabbits
R + C = 35 …….. (1) 2R + 2C = 70 … ..(2) (Assume all heads are chickens.) 4R + 2C = 94 …….(3) (3) − (2): R = $\frac{94-70}{4-2}$ = 12 --- number of rabbits C = 35 − 12 = 23	R + C = 35 …….. (1) 4R + 4C = 140 … ..(2) (Assume all heads are rabbits.) 4R + 2C = 94 …….(3)(2) − (3): C = $\frac{140-94}{4-2}$ = 23 --- number of chickens C = 35 − 23 = 12

Unless students are already familiar with the concept of Systems of Equations, this method cannot be used, at least for young grades students who will not be able to use this method.

However, for higher grades students, to use this algebraic method will be able to solve all kinds and variations of Chickens and Rabbits problems, the drawback for algebraic method is that if this method is taught too earlier, then students actually do not learn the insights of Chickens and Rabbits too much since it basically just plugs in data into equations.

By doing the arithmetic method, students actually require using more thinking skills than the algebraic method.

Practice

A Big boat can hold 6 people, and a Small boat can hold 4 people. There were 44 people on boats. How many people were on the small boats?

.
B + S = 10 …….. (1)
6B+4S=44 …….. (2)

It is interesting for us to find out that when the above problem is presented to Chinese parents, many of them taught their children the above Systems of Equations method without realizing that this method is not taught to their children until grade 11 in BC, Canada. Most children do not remember how to use the Systems of Equations at all after a few days later. But it also shows how powerful the above the algebraic method is because after 10 to 20 years later, the only method the parents could help children to solve the Chickens and Rabbits problem is the algebraic method.

Method 4 – Using Algebra of one variable equation 一个变数法

If the student has mastered algebra solving technique taught at the beginning of this workbook, then the question of solving Chickens and Rabbits problem becomes much easier.

Let x be the number of chickens.

$2x + 4(35 - x) = 94$

$2x + 140 - 4x = 94$

$-2x + 140 = 94$

$2x = 46$

$X = 23$ ... ... The number of chickens

$35 - 23 = 12$ .... The number of rabbits

The above equation involves the bracket, so it is normally beyond a grade-four student's ability. However, by mastering this technique, many elementary school's word problems can be easily solved.

Method 5 – Using the universal Assumption method 假设法

We recommend this method if the algebraic method is not used.

There is a total of 35 chickens and rabbits in a cage with 94 legs altogether. How many chickens and rabbits each of them is there in the cage?

A universal way without using the system of equations method to solve 2-variable Chickens and Rabbits problem is to assume all heads are in a larger number of legs to exchange for the heads of a smaller number of legs.

$$\text{\# of chicken} = \frac{\text{\# of heads} \times 4 - \text{\# of total legs \#}}{4 - 2}$$

The following way is to assume all heads are in a smaller number of legs to exchange for the heads of a larger number of legs.

$$\text{\# of rabbits} = \frac{\text{\# of total legs} - \text{\# of heads} \times 2}{4 - 2}$$

This method can be used as a universal method to solve any 2-variable problems without using a System of Equations, but more complicated problems will be better off to use a System of Equations.

There are many variations of "chicken and rabbit" problems involving a different number of legs.

Step 1. Assume all heads are chickens, so the total number of legs is 70.

Step 2. But there are 94 legs, so we need 94 − 70 = 24 more legs. This proves our assumption is wrong, and we must change some chickens to rabbits.

Every time when we change one chicken to a rabbit, we increase the legs by 2. So, with 24 legs short, we need 12 rabbits.

At this point, since all the heads are converted to legs, so the 2-variable problem is now converted to a 1-variable problem dealing with only legs.

$\frac{94-70}{4-2} = 12$ heads for rabbits.

Same problem with multiple solutions 同題異解

Example 老小和尚与饅頭

There are 100 senior monks and junior monks in a temple. Each senior monk can eat 3 buns, and 3 juniors together share one bun. How many senior and junior monks each in the temple?

Method 1 – Systems of Equations

$3S + \frac{1}{3}J = 100$

$S + J = 1000$

Method 2 – Use the Assumption method.

$\frac{100 \times 3 - 100}{1 - \frac{1}{3}} = 75 \dots$ junior monks

$100 - 75 = 25$ senior monks

Method 3 - Use ration.

Every 4 buns can be eaten by one senior monk and 3 junior monks.
$\frac{100}{1+3} = 25$ groups of buns

There are 25 senior monks in groups and $25 \times 3 = 75$ junior monks.

Method 4 – Use one variable equation.

Let x be the number of senior monks.

$$3x + \frac{100 - x}{3} = 100$$

$x = 25 \dots$ the number of senior monks.

In comparison to the above methods, the ratio method is much simpler than the other 3 methods. The Systems of Equations method is a general method, but in this example, it is more difficult to operate than the Assumption method and the one-variable equation. If a proportion method can be used, then do not use the one-variable equation. If a one-variable equation can be used, then do not use the Systems of equations method. If the student can not use the one-variable equation, then use the Assumption method.

Is the following problem a Chickens and Rabbits problem? 下列問題是鸡兔問題吗?

To solve the Chickens and Rabbits problems, it is interesting to note that some Chinese parents teach their children the method of Systems of Equations, and some of the Canadian teachers at daytime schools teach children the Guess and Check (Trial and Error) or pattern (List table) method. Many math contest books also suggest the Trial and Error method. We offer many different methods for the same problem.

Example

In Mr. Ho's science lab, there are 3-legged stools and 4-legged chairs. There are 72 legs for all stools and chairs in Mr. Ho's lab, and there are 3 more stools than chairs. How many stools and chairs are in Mr. Ho's lab?

There are no heads mentioned in the above problem, so there is only one variable that is a leg.

Method 1- System of Equations offered by a parent

$3S + 4T = 72$
$S - T = 3$

The grade-4 girl could not really understand it after being taught by her mom.

Method 2 - Use T table

This solution is suggested by a daytime schoolteacher.

4 legs of chair	3 legs of stool
18	21
12	15
9	12

Method 3 - Use ratio

$(S - 3): S = 4 : 3$

$4S = 3S - 9$
$S = 9$
$C = 12$

Student's name: ____________________________ Assignment date: ____________________

Problem

Problem 1

Find the value of each square and circle.

$$\square + \bigcirc = 18$$
$$\square \times 4 + \bigcirc \times 2 = 50$$

Problem 2

There are 36 chickens and rabbits altogether. There are 100 legs altogether. How many rabbits and how many chickens are there, respectively?

14r, 22c

Problem 3

There are 126 chickens and rabbits altogether. Chickens have 126 fewer legs than rabbits. How many rabbits and how many chickens are there, respectively?

63r, 63c

Problem 4

There are 107 chickens and rabbits altogether. Chickens have 284 fewer legs than rabbits. How many rabbits and how many chickens are there, respectively?

c=83, r=24

Problem 5

There are some stools with 3 legs and some chairs with 4 legs in Mr. Ho's science lab. If there are 117 legs with 35 seats in the lab, how many stools and chairs are in Mr. Ho's science lab?

23 stools, 12 chairs

Problem 6

There are 108 legs of all chickens and rabbits. If the total number of chickens is exchanged with the total number of rabbits, then the total number of legs of chicken and rabbits becomes 78. How many rabbits and how many chickens are there, respectively?

r=23, c=8

Once you have mastered the concept of how to solve "chickens and rabbits" problems, then its universal method can be equally applied to many other different word problems using the same concept.

Problem 7

There are 50 questions on the final exam. For each correct answer, 4 points are granted, and for each incorrect or no answer, one point is deducted. Allison got 115 points, how many incorrect answers did she get?

17

Problem 8

There were 290 students in grade class last year. This year there were 13 new students including a 4% increase in female students (out of all female students) and 5% of male students (out of all male students), how many boys in the class and how many girls in the class this year?

male 225, female 156

Problem 9

A total of 19.75 is collected from a parking meter, which takes only dimes and quarters. If 86 coins are collected, how many dimes, and how many quarters are collected?

75 quarters, 11 dimes

Problem 10

In the Provincial Hockey League, a team gets two points for a win, one point for a tie, and no points for a loss. One team lost 5 of their 52 games and ended the season with 84 points. How many games did they win?
37 wins, 10 draws, 5 losses

Problem 11

The total number of heads is missing.

Ho Math Chess class is going on a field trip. There are 25 children in the class. If 7 children can ride in a van and 4 children in each car, what is the least number of vehicles needed so that every seat is taken?

 1 car and 3 vans

Problem 12

The membership in the chess club costs $100 for a family and $55 for an individual. Susan sold $4175 to 62 members. How many family and individual memberships did she sell?

 17 f 45 I

At a math test, 23 problems were given, 5 points were given for each correct answer, and 2 points were deducted for each incorrect answer. Cindy got 38 points for her test. How many incorrect answers did she have?

c=12, l=11

Student's name: _____   Assignment date: _____

Chickens and Rabbits vs. Work vs. Travelling problems 鸡兔, 工作, 行程等問題的比较

Some Work problems or Travelling problems can be transferred into Chickens and Rabbits problems, but the Work problem can be solved by using 1 as the work amount, so the advantage of transferring Work problems into Chickens and Rabbits is not obvious.

Example

It takes Adam 6 hours to finish painting the house and Bob 10 hours alone to finish painting the same house. Adam started to paint the house first and then left. Bob continued painting to finish the entire job. Together they used 7 hours. How many hours did Adam paint?

Method 1 - Conversion of Work Problem into Chicken and Rabbit problem

Let the entire job be 30 hours (total number of legs) since it is the LCM of 10 and 6. The work rate for Adam is $30 \div 6 = 5$ (legs)
The work rate for Bob is $30 \div 10 = 3$ (legs)

The above Work Problem can be transferred to a Chickens and Rabbits problem.

Assume all of 7 heads are 3 legs.

$\frac{30 - 7 \times 3}{5 - 3} = 4.5$ for Adam;'s hours

Method 2 - Use unit 1 as the total work amount

Let x be the hours Adam worked

$$\frac{x}{6} + \frac{1 - \frac{x}{6}}{\frac{1}{10}} = 7$$

$x = 4.5 = $ Adam's work hours

Although students have to work on a bit complicated fraction computation to get the answer but do not have to worry about the conversion to Chickens and Rabbits problem

Method 3 - Use LCM 30 of hours 6 and 10 as the total work amount.

The work rate for Adam is $30 \div 6 = 5$. The work rate for Bob is $30 \div 10 = 3$

Let x be the hours Adam worked.

When using the LCM, a different approach of using the total amount of 30 is used instead of the number of total hours used in Method 2.

$$5x + (7 - x)3 = 30$$

$$x = 4.5 \text{ hours}$$

If the same approach is used as Method 2, then the equation is turned into fraction again, so the advantage of working as a whole number equation is lost.

Method 4 - Use algebra

Let x be the hours Adam worked.

$$x + \frac{30 - 5x}{3} = 7$$

$$3x + (30 - 5x) = 21$$

$$3x + 30 - 5x = 21$$

$$3x - 5x = 21 - 30$$

$$2x = 9$$

$$x = 4.5 \text{ hours}$$

How can a Chickens and Rabbits problem transfer to a Travelling problem? 鸡兔转成行程問題

At this moment, the Chickens and Rabbits problem is transferred to a Travelling problem as follows:

The Chickens have travelled to a distance of 70 legs at a speed of 2 legs/per head but need to reach 94 legs distance. So, the Chickens will turn into Rabbits by speeding up at 4 legs per head.

How many heads are required for some Chickens turning into Rabbits to reach from 70 legs to 94 legs?

$\frac{94-70}{4-2} = 12$ heads for rabbits.

Step 3. $35 - 12 = 23$ … number of chickens

Student's name: _____   Assignment date: _____

Problem

There are 12 heads of chicken and rabbits altogether. Total legs of chickens and rabbits are 32. How many rabbits are there and how many chickens are there?

Assume all 12 heads are chickens as follows; then there are _____ legs. So, we know we need to exchange some chickens to rabbits.

How many chickens need to be exchanged for rabbits?

There are 16 tricycles and bicycles altogether. There are 38 wheels in total. How many tricycles and how many bicycles?

There are 15 of two-cent stamps and five-cent stamps altogether. The total value is 54 cents. How many two cent stamps are there and how many five-cent stamps are there?

A dog breeder sold 6 puppies that were either spotted or black in colour. She sold spotted ones for $45 each and the black ones for $55 each. She collected $290 after selling all her puppies. How many spotted ones did she sell? Are there any other possibilities? Show your work and explain how you know.

$$\frac{6 \times 55 - 290}{55 - 45} = 4 \text{ spotted ones}$$

It is difficult for students to understand that the solution of two linear equations only has one intersection, so there is only one solution. So alternatively, students can provide a T Table to show that there is only one answer.

Spotted ones	Black ones
	6, not possible
	5, not possible since $5 \times 55 = 275$
	4, $5 \times 55 = 220$, $290 - 220 = 70$ not possible
	3, $3 \times 55 = 160$, $290 - 160 = 130$ not possible
	2, $2 \times 55 = 110$, $290 - 110 = 180$ possible
	1, $1 \times 55 = 55$, $290 - 55 = 235$ not possible 1

Student's name: _____   Assignment date: _____

Sarah decided to go on a diet for 27 days, and she made a deal with her mom. Her mom would give Sarah $2 for every day she lost weight, but Sarah would pay her mom $1 for every day she did not lose weight. At the end of 27 days, Sarah got $30. How many days did Sarah lose her weight?

Method 1 - Make a T Table.

Method 2 - Use equation

Let x be the number of days Sarah got $2.00

$2x - (27 - x) = 30$
$-27 + 3x = 30$
$x = 19$ --- days got $2
$27 - 19 = 8$ days of not got lose weight

Method 3 - Use Chickens and Rabbits method

Assume that Sarah lost her weights for 27 days, then she would have got $2 \times 27 = \$54$
She only got $30, so it means that she did not lose weight every day.

$\frac{54 - 30}{2 - (-1)} = 8$ days she did not lose weight

The only problem with the above operation is not many low grades students understand the operation of 2 - (-1). It could be explained as if she did not lose weight, and then she would not get $2 and also have to pay her mom $1, so her real loss is not just $1 but $3.

Amanda has $40 to buy theatre tickets. Box seats are $7 each, and orchestra seats are $5 each. If she buys 8 tickets, then in how many ways that she can buy a different number of seats?

Amanda bought some plants for $70. Hanging plants are $7 each and table plants are $5 each. If she bought one dozen plants, then in how many plants of each kind did she buy?

There are tricycles and bicycles with total wheels of 61 in the Nature Park. There are more tricycles than bicycles. What is the largest possible number of tricycles in the park?

The bike shop has 28 cycles that have either 2 wheels or 3 wheels. Altogether there are 68 wheels. How many cycles have 3 wheels?

Method 1: 28 x 3 = 84, 84 – 68 = 16, 16 / (3-2) = 16. 2 wheelers. 28 – 16 = **12** … 3 wheelers.

Method 2: 28 x 2 = 56, 68 – 56 = **12** … 3 wheelers

Mona had a test of 20 questions, and for each correct answer, she got 5 points, but if she answered wrong, she got two points deducted. Mona answered all questions, and her final marks were 65, how many questions did she answer correctly?

20 x 5 = 100, (100- 65) / (5 + 2) = 5 wrong, 20 – 5 = **15** correct.

Wilson took out 4 black marbles and 3 white marbles each time out of a bag with the number of black marbles was twice the number of white marbles. How many times would have it taken for Wilson to have 18 black marbles and 1 white marble left in the bag?

8 times.

Method 1, b – 4t=18
$\frac{b}{2}$ – 3t = 1, b – 6t=2, 2t = 16, t=8

Method 2, Work backwards using pattern. Try to see if there are 10 times of taking out black and see if it will suit whites, okay?

# of times	8	7	6	5	4	3	2	1	0
Black	18	22	26	30	34	38	42	46	50
White	1	4	7	10	13	16	19	22	25

Systems of Equations using symbols 联立方程用符号

The more complicated problems below just use the method of solving the Systems of Equations.

$\square + \bigcirc = 13$ 6, 7
$\square \times 5 + \bigcirc \times 2 = 44$

$10 \leq \square + \bigcirc \leq 20$ (Answers may vary.) 11, 6
$\square \times 5 + \bigcirc \times 2 = 67$

$10 \leq \square + \bigcirc \leq 20$ (Answers may vary.) 5,7
$\square \times 4 + \bigcirc \times 2 = 34$

$\square + \bigcirc = 11$ 8,3
$\square \times 7 + \bigcirc \times 5 = 71$

$\square + \bigcirc = 18$ 7, 11
$\square \times 4 + \bigcirc \times 2 = 50$

$30 \leq \square + \bigcirc \leq 40$ 8, 30; 17, 13
$\square \times 4 + \bigcirc \times 2 = 94$

2-variable Systems of Equations 2 变数联立方程

Normally the knowledge of Systems of Equations will not be introduced until grade 10 in North America, but it appears in Singapore elementary school. In the following example, one of the equations is introduced by using ratio.

James was paid \$80 daily if he worked all day, and he was paid \$35 if he worked half day. In January, James was paid \$1060 after working 20 days. How many full days did James work in January?

$F+H=20$

$80F+35H=1060$

\$8 full-day, \$12 half-day.

3-variable Systems of Equations 3 变数联立方程

There are apples in three boxes: A, B, and C. Box A has 20% of the total of apples in Boxes A, B, and C. The ratio of the numbers of apples in Box B to the number of apples in Boxes A and C is 2:1. Box B has 24 more apples than the apples in Box C. How many apples in each box?

$A = 0.2(A+B+C)$

$A = 0.2(1.5B) = 0.3B$

$B : (A+C) = 2 : 1$

$B - 24 = C$

$A=9, B=30, C=6$

Correct and incorrect answers 答题数问题

The correct and incorrect problems are a variation of Chickens and Rabbits problem, it deserves special attention is because the incorrect answer has a penalty, so it is a negative integer.

Example

Clara took a test with 20 questions. For each correct answer of each question, she gets 4 points, for a wrong answer, she has one point deducted from her total score. If Clara answered all questions and her score was 10, how many questions did she answer correctly?

Method 1- The Assumption method

$\frac{20 \times 4 - 10}{4 - (-1)} = 14$ ……. Number of wrong answers   Blank   blank

$20 - 14 = 6$ ……. Number of correct answers   Blank   blank
Blank   blank
Method 2 – Algebra with one variable

Let x be the number of correct answers.
$4x - (20 - x) = 10$ Blank
Blank   blank

Problem

10 points for each correct answer, penalty 5 points for each incorrect answer. Andria answered 8 problems with 20 points. How many problems did she answer correctly?

$10x - 5(8 - x) = 20$ Blank
$x = 4$ correct answers   Blank
Blank
Blank
Blank

10 points for each correct answer, penalty 5 points for each incorrect answer. Andria answered 10 problems with 85 points. How many problems did she answer correctly?
8 correct problems   Blank   blank

7 points for each correct answer, penalty 3 points for each incorrect answer. Andria answered 18 problems with 90 points. How many problems did she answer correctly?
15 correct problems   Blank   blank

Student's name: _____   Assignment date: _____

Chickens and Rabbits using systems of equations for advanced students 高级有难度问题

In a group of cows and chickens, the number of total legs was 14 more than twice the number of heads. How many cows were there?

# of chickens = x, # of cows = y
$2x + 4y = 14 + 2(x + y)$
$y = 7$ (cow)

Lollipop is $0.4 per 100 g, and Sour candy is $1.2 per 100 g. Altogether Jimmie bought 2000 grams paid $2 more for Lollipop than Sour candies. How many grams does Jimmie have bought for each candy?

$0.4 per 100g = 40 cents per 100 g = 0.4 per gram, $1.2 per 100 g = 1.2 cents per gram
$0.4 (2000 - s) - 1.2s = 200$ cents
$s = 375$ grams, Lollipop $= 2000 - 375 = 1625$ gram

There are 3 kinds of vehicles, and their information is as follows. Find out the number of each vehicle.

$B + C + T = 20, 2B+4C+4T=40, B + 4C+ 2T = 54$

Number of each vehicle	Vehicle type	Wheels	Seats
? **4**	Bicycle	2	1
? **12**	Car	4	4
? **2**	Truck	4	2
Total	20	40	54

of variables > # of equations 变数数目>方程数目

Celine has 3 kinds of toy vehicles: wagon, bicycles, and tricycles in a total of 28. She counted they have 76 wheels altogether. Find the number of each type of vehicle she has collected.

$x + y + z = 28$
$4x + 2y + 3z = 76$.
$z = 36 - 2y = 2(18-y)$

Tricycle (z)	2	4	6	8	10	12	14	16
Bicycle (y)	17	16	15	14	13	12	11	10
Wagon (x)	9	8	7	6	5	4	3	2

6 wagons, 20 bicycles, 2 tricycles

of variables > # of equations (Test with penalty)
Correct, incorrect, and unanswered 答题数問题

Christine took a test with 20 problems. For each she answered correctly, she gets 1 point and gets one point deducted for each question she answered incorrectly, and she gets no point if she did not answer at all. After the test, Christine got 8 points, how many problems she answered correctly, incorrectly, or did not answer at all?

$X + y + z = 20$ (x correct, y is incorrect, z did not answer.)
$X - y = 8$
$2x + z = 28$, $z = 2(14-x)$

Z (no answer)	0	2	4	6	8	10	12	0
X (correct)	14	13	12	11	10	9	8	14
Y (incorrect)	6	5	4	3	2	1	0	6

Student's name: _____ Assignment date: _____

# of variables > # of equations 变数的数目大於方程的数目

Van has 7 seats, and the car has 4 seats. There are 41 seats altogether. How many cars and how many vans are there?

Method 1
$4c+7v=41$
$c= (41-7v)/4= (40 +1 − 8v+v)/4=10-2v+ (1+v)/4$, so v =3, c=5 since c and v have to be natural numbers. $(1+v)/4$ must be an integer and it must be 3, 7, …etc. but 7 is not reasonable.
V=3, c = 5.
Method 2 Use the Trial and Error method. Try there are 10 cards, 9 cars by making a table.

car	van	Total seats
10 x 4 = 40	One seat left	
9 x 4 = 36	5 seats left	

# of variables > # of equations

Samantha had performed 24 concerts and sang 426 songs altogether. At each concert, she sang one of the 3 songs: 16, 20, or 25. How many concerts she had sung 25 songs, 20 songs and 16 songs??

$x + y + z = 24$
$16 x + 20 y + 25 z = 426$
$4y+9z=42$
$y=(42-9z)/4=10-2z+(2-z)/4$, so z must be 0 or 2. (0 is not reasonable.)

16 songs (x)	16
20 songs (y)	6
25 songs (z)	2

$x + y = 13$

$4x + 2y = 40$

y=6
x=7

$x + y = 21$

$4x + 2y = 68$

x=13, y=8

$x + y = 47$

$4x + 2y = 130$

Blank

x=18, y=29
Blank

One hundred senior and junior monks together ate 100 Chinese buns. Each senior monk ate 3 buns, and every 3 junior monks shared one bun. How many junior monks and how many senior monks are there?

$3(100\text{-}j) + \dfrac{j}{3} = 100$

25b, 75j
Blank   blank

There are 44 chickens and rabbits and altogether 110 legs. How many chickens and how many rabbits are there, respectively?

33 c, 11r
Blank

Blank   blank

There are 22 chickens and rabbits and altogether 62 legs. How many chickens and how many rabbits are there, respectively?

9r, 13c Blank   blank
Blank   blank

Each bus has 6 wheels, and each car has 4 wheels. There are 44 wheels altogether and more buses than cars. How many cars and how many buses are there, respectively?

6 buses and 2 cars

There are 5 more rabbits than chickens and rabbits have 46 more legs than chickens. How many chickens and how many rabbits are there, respectively?

18r, 13c
Blank   blank

There are 2 times as many rabbits as chickens and altogether 110 legs. How many chickens and how many rabbits are there, respectively?

22r, 11c
Blank   blank

There are 22 chickens and rabbits. Rabbits have 34 more legs than chickens. How many chickens and how many rabbits are there, respectively?

13r, 9c
Blank   blank

There are 27 chickens and rabbits altogether, and rabbits have 24 more legs than chickens. How many chickens and how many rabbits are there, respectively?

13r, 14 c
Blank   blank

Exchange 2 rabbits with 2 chickens, then the number of chickens is equal to the number of rabbits, altogether there are 58 legs. How many chickens and how many rabbits are there, respectively?

11r, 7c
Blank   blank

There are six more chickens than rabbits and ten more rabbit legs than chicken legs. How many chickens and how many rabbits are there, respectively?
Blank   blank
11r, 17c

Ho Math Chess 何数棋谜 奥数,解题策略,及 IQ 思唯训练宝典

Student's name: _____   Assignment date: _____

In a group of cows and chickens, the number of legs was 14 more than twice the number of heads. How many cows were there?

Blank   blank

7
Blank   blank

There are 2 types of 50 vehicles, car and bicycles parked in the parking lot and there are
          160
wheels. How many of them are bicycles?

20
Blank   blank

There are 50 adults and children in a concert, and the ticket price for each adult is $10, and for each child is $5. The concert collected tickets fee for a total of $400. How many were adults at the concert?

30
Blank   blank

A dog breeder sold $11120 altogether for 115 puppies that were either spotted or brown in colour. He sold spotted ones for $80 each and browns ones for $120 each. How many browns did he sell?

48 browns
67 spotted
Blank   blank
Blank   blank

Blank   blank

Sum and Difference, Sum and Multiplier, Difference and Multiplier problems 和差, 和倍, 差倍

Most Chinese math contest books have some word problems labelled with Sum and Difference, Sum and Multiplier, or Difference and Multiplier problems as model problems. We have never seen any North America published math contest books using similar classifications as in Chinese math contest books. Being able to read Chinese fluently, we do have the advantage to make a comparison between a Chinese math contest book writing style and the North American math contest writing style. We feel so fortunate that we can combine the advantages of both the East and the West, then came up with an integrated math contest book, which we think is much better than the ones produced either in China or the West.

The Chinese writing style using model problems, which do offer an advantage that is students can identify the problems very quickly and then use these model problems as a base to solve more difficult problems. The following problem demonstrates that it can be solved easily if students are familiar with the Sum and Difference model problem.

Example

Together, Adam, Bob and Cathy have 80 marbles. Adam has 7 marbles more than Bob has. Cathy has 19 marbles. How many marbles does each of them have?

$80 - 19 = 61$, which is the sum of Adam and Bob.
$A + B = 61$
$A - B = 7$.
$Adam = \frac{61+7}{2} = 34$
$Bob = 61 - 34 = 27$

Without practising this kind of model problems, even a good student will get a bit confused on how to solve them systematically. Most of elementary math contest problems deal with two variables so that it makes sense that students master the relationship between two variables.

The Line Segment Diagram method (discussed in this workbook and very extensively in our previous lower grades workbooks) can be used to explain the concepts on how to solve Sum and Difference, Sum and Multiplier, Difference and Multiplier model problems.

Many times, this type of model problem has appeared in Kangaroo Math Contest or requires its knowledge to do a bit more complicated problem.

We have discussed the strategy on how to change this type of Sum and Difference problem to a story to solve it in *Grades 3 and 4 Ultimate Math Contest Preparation, Problem Solving Strategies, and Math IQ Puzzles.*

Advanced Sum and Difference 和差問題

Example

The Sum and Difference problem is not limited to two variables only.

Adam, Bob and Cathy altogether have 150 books. Adam has 13 more books than Bob, and Bob has 7 more books than Cathy. How many books does each of them have?

After the Line Segment Diagram is drawn, then the solution becomes clear.

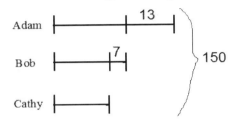

Method 1

$150 - 20 - 7 = 123$
Cathy $= \frac{123}{3} = 41$
$41 + 7 = 48$ ...... Bob
$48 + 13 = 61$ ...... Adam

Method 2

Bob $= \frac{150-13+7}{3} = 48$
Cathy $= 48 - 7 = 41$
Adam $= 48 + 13 = 61$

Method 3

Adam, Bob and Cathy altogether have 150 book. Adam has 13 more books than Bob, Bob has 7 more books than Cathy. How many book does each of them have?

C + 7 + 13   C + 7

C

$C + C + 7 + C + 7 + 13 = 150$
$C = 41$

The difference in the Sum and Difference has different ways of expressing, so to make the Sum and Difference more complicated.

Problem

Adam and Bob have 216 apples, and if Adam gives 26 apples to Bob, then each has the same number of apples. How many apples does each of them have?

$A + B = 216$
$A - B = 52$ ($A - 26 = B + 26$, or the difference = 2 times of the quantity given 26×2)
$A = 134, B = 82$

Adam and Bob have 216 apples, and if Adam gives 26 apples to Bob, then Adam still has 8 more than Bob. How many apples does each of them have?
Difference = 26 x 2 +8 = 60
$A = 78, B = 38$

Adam and Bob have 216 apples, and if Adam gives 26 apples to Bob, then Adam still has 6 less than more than Bob. How many apples does each of them have?
Difference = 26 x 2 – 6 = 46
$A = 134, B = 82$

Adam and Bob have 216 apples, and if Adam eats 8 apples and Bon eats 6 apples, then, as a result, they have an equal number of apples. How many apples does each of them have?
The difference is $A - 8 = B - 6$, $A - B = 8 - 6 = 2$. Assume Adam has 8 and Bob has 6, then if they have an equal number of apples, the difference must be 2.
$A = 109, Bob = 107$

Sum and Difference application
The sum of a 2-digit whole number is 9. The difference of the original 2-digit number and the new number is 9 when its tens digit and ones digit are exchanged.

$A + B = 9$
$10A + B - 10 B - A = 9$
$9A - 9B = 9$
$A - B = 1$
$A = 5, B = 4$

Student's name: _____ Assignment date: _____

1	If the sum of three whole numbers is 48 and A = 28, B − C = 4. what is B, and what is C?

B = 12, C = 8

Blank line   blank line
Blank line   blank line
Blank line   blank line
Blank line   blank line
Blank line   blank line
Blank line   blank line
Blank line   blank line
Blank line   blank line

1	Some string 2205-inch-long was cut into two unequal pieces. One-piece was 57 inches longer than the other. What is the length of the longer one?

$\frac{2205+57}{2} = 1131$ inch

Blank line   blank line
Blank line   blank line
Blank line   blank line
Blank line   blank line
Blank line   blank line
Blank line   blank line
Blank line   blank line
Blank line   blank line

Systems of equations 联立方程

Fill in each box by a number.

□ + △ = ____

□ − △ = ____ ×⟩ 128

33, 31, 64, 2

Fill in each box by a number.

□ + △ = ____

□ − △ = ____ ×⟩ 72

19, 17, 36, 2

□ + △ = ____

□ − △ = ____ ×⟩ 48

8, 4, 12, 4

□ + △ = ____

□ − △ = ____ ×⟩ 9

3, 0, 3, 3

□ + △ = ____

□ − △ = ____ ×⟩ 39

8, 5, 13, 3

□ + △ = ____

□ − △ = ____ ×⟩ 24

5, 1, 6, 4　　　　(7, 5, 12, 2)

□ + △ = ____

□ − △ = ____ ×⟩ 56

9, 5, 14, 4

Frank Ho, Amanda Ho © 1995 - 2020

Student's name: _____ Assignment date: _____

$\square + \triangle = $ _____
$\square - \triangle = $ _____ $\times$ > 1

1, 0, 1, 1

$\square + \triangle = $ _____
$\square - \triangle = $ _____ $\times$ > 111

20, 17, 37, 3

$\square + \triangle = $ _____
$\square - \triangle = $ _____ $\times$ > 55

8, 3, 11, 5

$\square + \triangle = $ _____
$\square - \triangle = $ _____ $\times$ > 65

9, 4, 13, 5

$\square + \triangle = $ _____
$\square - \triangle = $ _____ $\times$ > 143

12, 1, 13, 11

$\square + \triangle = $ _____
$\square - \triangle = $ _____ $\times$ > 267

46, 43, 89, 3

Student's name: _____ Assignment date: _____

Advanced Sum and Multiplier 高級和倍

The straightforward way of solving advanced Sum and Multiplier is to use algebra.

Example

Jennifer bought three sizes of beads, large, middle, small in a total of 826. The number of large beads is 2 times the middle beads; the small beads are 3 times as many as the large beads. How many different sized beads are there?

$L = 2M$

Jennifer bought three sizes of beads, large, middle, small in a total of 828. The number of large beads is 2 times of the middle beads; the small beads is 3 times as many as the large beads. How many of each different sized beads are there?

$S = 3L = 6M$

$L + M + S = 828$
$2M + M + 6M = 828$
$9M = 828, M = 92$
$S = 552$
$L = 184$

Student's name: _____   Assignment date: _____

Problem

Jennifer bought three sizes of beads, large, middle, small in a total of 826. The number of large beads is 5 more than 3 times of the small beads; the middle beads is one more than as many as the small beads. How many of each different sized beads are there?

$$L + M + S = 826 \qquad L = 5 + 3S$$

Jennifer bought three sizes of beads, large, middle, small in a total of 826. The number of large beads is 5 more than 3 times of the small beads; the middle beads is one more than as many as the small beads. How many of each different sized bead?

$$M = 1 + S$$

All Variables are being built on the small beads.

$5 + 3S + 1 + S + S = 826$
$5S = 820$
$S = 164$
$M = 165$
$L = 5 + 164 \times 3 = 497$

Sum and Multiplier and geometry

A rectangle and an octagon share a common side. The perimeter of the rectangle is 36 cm, and its length is twice its width. What is the perimeter of the octagon?

48 cm

Advanced Difference and Multiplier problems 高级差倍問题

It will be easy to solve more complicated Difference and Multiplier problems using algebra.

Example

Adam and Bob have the same weight of apples. Adam sold 7 kg of his apples and Bob sold 21 kg of his apples, then the remaining of Adam's apples is three times Bob's remaining apples. How much does each Andrew and Bob each have originally?

Method 1, algebra

$A - 7 = 3 (A - 21)$
$56 = 2A$
Adam = Bob = 28 kg

Method 2, arithmetic

Bob sold $21 - 7 = 14$ more kg which corresponds $(3 - 1)$ 2 times.
So, Bob's share now is $14 \div 2 = 7$ kg.
$7 + 19$ sold $= 25$ kg originally

The idea of using the difference divided by its corresponding fractional number to get Bob's or Adam's share is not very clear to most students. We recommend students use algebra to solve more complicated Difference and Multiplier problems.

Example

Adam, Bob, and Cathy are triplets. David is 4 years older than Adam. The sum of these four people is 60. How old is each of the triplets?

$\frac{60-4}{4} = 16$ years old

Problem

Andrew has as seven times many as Bob's apples. If each of them gets 5 more apples, then Andrew has four times of Bob's. How many apples does each of them have originally?

$7B+5 = 4 (B + 5)$
$7B + 5 = 4B +20$
$3B = 15$
$B = 5$ …. Bob's apples
40 ….. Andrew's apples

Andrew is 30 less than his father's age. Next year Andrew's father's age is 3 times Andrew's age. How old is Andrew? How old is Andrew's father?

answer

F + 30   F   F + 1 = 3(F+31)

Andrew is 30 less than his father's age. Next year Andrew's father's age is 3 times of Andrew's age. How old is Andrew? How old is Andrew's father?

The above problem could be a Difference and Multiplier problem or an Age problem. If you use algebra, then it does not matter anymore because as long as you know how to set up the equation correctly, the rest is just to solve the equation. The word problem becomes more of a routine job.

Andrew has some apples in one basket and has as many oranges as apples in another basket. If he buys 35 more oranges and 10 more apples, then the number of oranges is 2 times of the apples. How many oranges and apples does he have in the beginning?

$O + 35 = 2(O + 10)$
$O = 15$ oranges $= 15$ apples

Travelling problem, Distance and Speed 行程問題

3 travelling models in the elementary school math

| Model 1, Travelling in opposite directions from the same point. 反向行程 | Distance from A to B = speed1 × time1 + speed2 × time2

Amelie and Karissa start to bicycle towards to each other from two towns that are 45 km apart. They met in 2 hours. What is Amelie's speed if Karissa travels at 5 km per hour?

$5 \times 2 + 5 \times A = 45$
$5A = 35$
$A = 7$ km per hour |
| Model 2, Travelling towards each other. 相向行程 | When to meet? Time = $\dfrac{distance}{speed1+speed2}$

Two women 500 km apart begin driving towards each other at the same time. One of the women travels at 130 km/h and the other at 120 km/h. In how many hours will they meet?

$\dfrac{500}{130 + 120} = 2$ hours |
| Model 3, One travels first, then the other tries to catch up with. 同向或追及行程 | When to catch up? Time = $\dfrac{advanced\ travel\ distance}{fast\ speed-slow\ speed}$

An eastbound freight train travelling at the speed of 75 km per hour is already 70 km from Vancouver when a passenger train leaves Vancouver on the parallel tracks at 100 km per hour at 2 p.m. At what time will the passenger train pass the freight train?

$\dfrac{70}{100 - 75} = 2.8$ hours $= 2$ hours 48 minutes

2 hours 48 minutes + 2 p.m. = **4:48 p.m.** |

The travelling problem becomes very easy if the student masters the elementary algebra skills.

Student's name: _____   Assignment date: _____

Problem

Cindy and Tom both walk from their houses towards each other. Toms' speed is 2 times of Cindy's speed. The distance between their houses is 24 km. What distance will Tom have walked when they meet?

16 km

A car travels 180 km in 4 hours. What is its speed?

s = 45 km/hr

The distance from Vancouver to Beijing is about 8500 km. The speed of a Boeing 777 is 900 km/hr. About how long will the plane in the air if it goes from Vancouver to Beijing?

9 hr 27 min

. A car travels from Vancouver to Banff. It took Andy 4.5 hours for the first 250 miles and 5.5 hours for the rest of 280 miles. What is his average speed?

53

10:23 a.m.

Student's name: _____ Assignment date: _____

Two buses start from the same bus station at the same time. The eastbound bus travels at 20 km/h, and the westbound bus travels at 25 km/h. How long will it take them to be 9 km apart?

x = 12 min

Kathleen drove to downtown at 30 km/h. How fast does she have to go back to average 40 km/h?

x = 60 km/hr

At 8:00 a.m., the Carters left for Portland 525 km away. They drove the first part at 65 km/hr. At 10:30 a.m., they stopped for one hour. Then they complete the trip at an average speed of 70 km/h. Find its average speed and the time they arrive at Portland.

15:41

Dave drove 452 km from Toronto to Ottawa. Part of the trip was on the normal road at 50 km/h, and the rest was on the highway at 70 km/h. If the total travelling time was 8 hours, how many hours were spent on the highway?

normal 15.4 hr   highway 2.6 hr

It takes Michael 30 minutes to go to school by bus. The distance between the school and his home is 8 km. The average speed of the bus is 21 km/h. He walks at 6 km/h. How long did he walk?

1 km

Bobby and Danny are 1000 m apart. It takes 16 minutes to walk towards each other. Bobby walks 2 m/min faster than Danny. How fast does Bobby walk?

32.25 m/min

Jack drives to work at 8:00 a.m. every day. One day he drove at 30 km/h for 4 minutes and found that he would be late for 10 minutes at this speed. He increased his speed to 45 km/h, and he arrived 5 minutes earlier. What is the distance between his place and his work?

22.5 km

Student's name: ______________________ Assignment date: ____________________

City A and City B are 150 km apart. A car leaves City A at 8:00 a.m. The car travels at a speed of 40 km/hr until 9:45 a.m. If the car wants to reach City B by 11:00 a.m., how fast will the car have to go?

64 km/hr

Blank blank
Blank blank
Blank blank
Blank blank
Blank blank
Blank blank

Travelling bridge or tunnel 过桥或隧道问题

$$\frac{train\,length + bridge\,length}{speed} = time\ to\ pass$$

An 800-meter long train travelling at 20 meters per second went into a tunnel. The front of the train emerged the tunnel 90 seconds after the rear of the train entered the tunnel. Find the length of the tunnel in meters.

Hint: Draw a diagram.

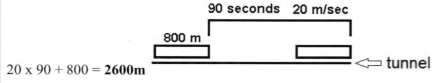

20 x 90 + 800 = **2600m**

A 240-meter-long train travelling at 15 meters per second went into a tunnel. It took 20 seconds for the rear of the train to totally exit the tunnel counting from the time when the front of the train just started to enter the tunnel. Find the length of the tunnel, in meters.

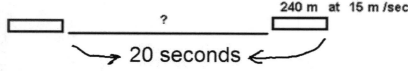

20x15=300, 300 –240 = **60 meters**

A 100-meter-long train travelling at 400 meters per minute went into a 6700-meter tunnel. Find the time it takes for the train to get out of the tunnel totally.

(6700+100)/400=**17 minutes**

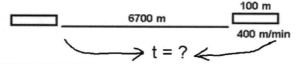

It takes 30 seconds for a 160-meter train to totally pass a 440-meter bridge. What is the train's speed per second?

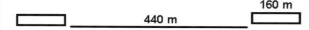

(440+160)/x=30, x=**20 meter per second**

It takes 15 seconds for a 150-meter train to totally pass a 300-meter bridge. What is the train's speed per second?
(300+150)/x=15, x= **30**

Student's name: _____   Assignment date: _____

Other Travelling problems 其他行程问题

The travelling problems appear in many countries in Asia, but they do not show up in North America elementary schools. The following problems appear in grade 5 in China.

Adam travels from Town A to Town B, and Bob travels from Town B to Town A. Adam travels 15 more minutes to arrive in Town B after they meet. What is the distance between Town A and Town B?

Adam walks from home to school at a speed of 65 m/minute. After 16 minutes, her mother tries to catch up to him by bike at a speed of 195 m/ minute to bring his forgotten homework left at home. The distance from home to school is 1800 m. Can Adam's mother catch up with Adam before he reaches his school?

$\frac{65 \times 16}{195 - 65} = 8$ Blank   blank

$65 \times (16+8) = 1560 < 1800$ Blank   blank

So, Adam's mother can catch up to Adam before he reaches school.

Blank   blank
Blank   blank
Blank   blank
Blank   blank

Student's name: _____　Assignment date: _____

Age problems 年齡問題

Grade 3 and above

Iris will be four times as old as Katie will be in 5 years. If Katie is 6 years now, how old will Iris be in 4 years?

Katie = 6 + 5 = 11, Iris = 4 × 11 = 44, 44 - 5 + 4 = 43.

Jack is twice as old as Jill was 4 years ago. If Jack is now 20 years old, how old is Jill now?
This problem requires work backwards, then work forward.

Four years ago, Jack was 20 - 4 = 16, which was twice as old as Jill. Jill was 8 four years ago.
Jill now is 8 + 4 = **12**.

Sophie is 38 years old, and her three sons are 7, 8, and 9 years old. In how many years will Sophie's sons' total age be as old as their mother?

Method 1 – Solve this problem as a travelling problem. Treat the age as distance and age difference as the speed distance.
This is very similar to the travelling catch-up problem.

$$\frac{38 - 7 - 8 - 9(\text{ This is the distance that three sons must catch up. })}{3 - 1 \text{ (speed difference)}} = 7$$

Method 2 – Use algebra
Let x be the number of years
$38 + x = 3x + 7 + 8 + 9$
$x = 7$

It takes 7 years.

Justin's age is between 20 and 40 years old. Last year his age was a multiple of 4; this year, his age is a multiple of 5. How old is Justin this year?

25

Justin's age is between 20 and 40 years old. Last year his age was a multiple of 5; this year, his age is a multiple of 6. How old is Justin this year?

36

Problem

1. Adding 10 to my age, I will be three times as old as I am now. How old am I?

$$10 + x = 3x$$

$$x = 5$$

2. In 11 years, I will be twice as old as I am now. How old am I?

$$I + 11 = 2I$$

$$b = 11$$

3. Jeff is 4 years older than Jill. The sum of their ages is 18. How old is Jeff?

$$Jill = 7 \quad Jeff = 11$$

4. Frank is 3 years younger than 2 times Fred's age. The sum of their ages is 48. How old is Frank?

$$Frank = 31 \quad Fred = 17$$

5. Cindy is 12 years old. Her dad is 40 years old. How many years later, her dad's age will double her age?

$$x = 16$$

6. Tara is 8 years old. Kelly is 12 years old. How many years ago is Kelly twice as old as Tara?

$$x = 4$$

7. In five years, you will be $1\frac{1}{2}$ times as old as you are now. How old are you now?

$$x = 10$$

8. Sunny is 6 years older than Jason. In four years, Sunny will be twice as old as Jason will be then. How old are they now?

$$\text{Sunny} = 8 \quad \text{Jason} = 2$$

9. Garrick is 6 years older than Kirsten. Four years ago, Gerick was three times as old as Kirsten was then. How old are they now?

$$\text{Garrick} = 13 \quad \text{Kirsten} = 7$$

10. "You will be 24 years old when I'll be at your age." Thea said to Ethan. "You were only 9 years old when I was at your age," Ethan said to Thea. How old are they now?

$$Ethan\ldots x \quad difference\ldots 24-x \quad Thea\ldots x-(24-x)$$
$$(2x-24)-(24-x)=9$$
$$x=19$$

11. Andy is 3 times as old as Anna. In 5 years, he will be twice as old as she will be then. How old are they now?

$$\text{Anna} = 5 \quad \text{Andy} = 15$$

12. Eric is 8 years younger than Earnest. In 6 years, Earnest will be twice as old as Eric will be then. How old is each now?

$$\text{Eric} = 2 \quad \text{Earnest} = 10$$

Student's name: _____   Assignment date: _____

Work problems 工作問題

Work problem related to the Travelling problem

Work problem	Travelling problem
Amelie and Karissa are going to paint a 400 m² wall. Amelie paints from the left side of the wall towards the right-hand side at the speed of 25 m²/hour. Karissa paints the opposite way at 15 m²/hour. In how many hours will they finish the painting? $$\frac{400}{25+15} = \textbf{10 hours}$$	Oscar and Aiden walk towards each other at the same time. Oscar walks at 6 km per hour, and Aiden walks at 5 km per hour. When will they meet if they are 55 km away? $$\frac{55}{5+6} = \textbf{5 hours}$$

Example

Leon can make 15 muffins in 1 hour, and Justin can make the same amount of muffin in 2 hours. Together, how long will it take them to make 30 muffins?

Method 1, find the work rate and treat this problem as a Work Problem

$$\frac{30}{\frac{15}{1}+\frac{15}{2}} = 1\frac{1}{3} \text{ hour} = 1 \text{ hour } 20 \text{ minutes}$$

Method 2, use ratio

$$\frac{22.5}{1} = \frac{30}{x}$$
$$= \frac{30}{22.5} = 1 \text{ hour } 20 \text{ minutes}$$

Method 3, Use Fraction Method

$$\frac{22.5}{1} \times 30 = 1 \text{ hour } 20 \text{ minutes}$$

Method 4, Use the Unitary Method

24	1 hour
6	15 minutes
30	75 minutes

If 8 boys paint 8 houses in 8 weeks and 6 girls paint 6 houses in 6 weeks. How many houses will 12 boys and 12 girls paint in 12 weeks?

For a boy: 8 houses $\times \frac{12 \text{ boys}}{8 \text{ boys}} \times \frac{12 \text{ weeks}}{8 \text{ weeks}} = 18$ houses

For a girl: 6 houses $\times \frac{12 \text{ girls}}{6 \text{ girls}} \times \frac{12 \text{ weeks}}{6 \text{ weeks}} = 24$ houses

The answer is $18 + 24 = 44$ houses.

Surplus and Shortage (Excess and Deficit) 盈亏問題

We have mentioned that many Chinese model problems were and are popular because they model problems themselves have built-in linear models such as Planting Tree problem, Sum and Difference, Chicken and Rabbits problems etc. The Surplus and Shortage problem has a built-in four model conditions. The model for the Surplus and Shortage problem is to find x when $ax \pm b = cx \pm d$.

For example, a number of balls are given to a class. where each equation is the number of balls and x is the number of students in the class. If each person gets a balls, then there could be an excess or deficit of b balls, and if each person gets c balls, then there could be an excess or deficit of d balls. To explain the conditions, we make a table with 4 models as follows:

	$cx + d = 3x + 6$	$cx - d = 9x - 8$
$ax + b = 4x + 2$	Surplus, surplus 盈, 盈 $4x + 2 = 3x + 6$ $x = 4$ …. Students 份数 $= \dfrac{大盈 - 小盈}{每份数的差}$	Surplus, shortage 一盈, 一亏 $4x + 2 = 9x - 8$ $x = 2$ …. students 份数 $= \dfrac{盈 + 亏}{每份数的差}$
$ax - b = 7x - 2$	Shortage, surplus 一亏, 一盈 $7x - 2 = 3x + 6$ $x = 2$ …. students 份数 $= \dfrac{盈 + 亏}{每份数的差}$	Shortage, shortage 亏, 亏 $7x - 2 = 9x - 8$ $x = 3$ … students 份数 $= \dfrac{大亏 - 小亏}{每份数的差}$

The Chinese contest book uses the comparison method to compare the left equation with the right equation and figure out the answer. The formulas are listed above in the table. But if the student understands algebra and can solve the equation $ax \pm b = cx \pm d$, then we recommend students use algebra to solve this type of problem. Even more complicated problems could be solved by using algebra.

Example

A number of balls are given to a class. If each person gets 9 balls, then there will be a shortage of 15 balls. If each person gets 4 balls, then there will be an excess of 10 balls. How many balls are there? How many people are there?

$9S - 15 = 4S + 10$

$5S = 25$

$S = 5$ students

$9 \times 5 - 15 =$ **30 balls**

Problem

A number of balls are given to a class. If each person gets 7 balls, then there will be a shortage of 6 balls. If each person gets 5 balls, then there will be an excess of 14 balls. How many balls are there? How many people are there?

students =10, balls = 64

A number of balls are given to a class. If each person gets 4 balls, then there will be a shortage of 8 balls. If each person gets 3 balls, then there will be an excess of 19 balls. How many balls are there? How many people are there?

students = 27, balls = 100

A number of balls are given to a class. If each person gets 8 balls, then there will be a shortage of 49 balls. If each person gets 5 balls, then there will be a shortage of 10 balls. How many balls are there? How many people are there?

students = 13, balls = 55

A number of balls are given to a class. If each person gets 3 balls, then there will be an excess of 38 balls. If each person gets 5 balls, then there will be a shortage of 14 balls. How many balls are there? How many people are there?

students =26, balls = 116

Advanced Surplus and Shortage (Excess and Deficit) 高级盈亏問題

Example

Andrew walked from home to his school at the speed of 110 m and arrived at the school 2 minutes earlier, but if he walked at the speed of 100 m per minute, he would be late for 3 minutes. How far is Andrew's school from his home?

Is this a Travelling problem? Yes, it can be a travelling problem, and the easy way to solve this type of problem is to use algebra.

Method 1

Assume the distance to be x.

$$\frac{x}{110} + 2 = \frac{x}{100} - 2$$

Convert the fraction equation to the whole number equation by multiplying LCD.

$$1100(\frac{x}{110} + 2) = \left(\frac{x}{100} - 2\right)1100$$

$$10x + 2200 = 11x - 2200$$

$$x = 4400$$

Method 2

Assume the time to arrive is x, which is the time in comparison.

$(x + 2)\,120 = (x - 2)90$
$120 \times 2 + 90 \times 2 = (120 - 90)\,x$
$x = \frac{240 + 180}{30}$ The reason of causing the distance to be $240 + 180$ is because the speed difference which is
$120 - 90$.
The time $= x = 14$
The distance is $(14 - 2)120 = 1440$ m

The Chinese math contest book uses the above method 2 without using algebra but using words to explain (as described above.). The algebra is more direct, and the Chinese way is the same as the steps in algebra, so we would recommend students follow the algebra section in this workbook and use algebra to do more complicated problems.

Method 2 has an advantage without using fractions. Many complicated word problems in Chinese math contest books could be easily solved by using algebra, yet the teachers try to teach in arithmetic, so it makes the learning even harder, these complicated math contest problems do not appear in their day school textbooks but are being taught after-school learning centres.

Problem

If each room takes 6 people, then there will be a short of 1 room (6 people), but if each room takes 9 people, then there will be one extra room (9 people) left. How many rooms are there? How many people are there?

$6R + 6 = 9R - 9$ (total people = total people)   Blank line   blank line
   Blank line   blank line
$15 = 3R$ Blank line   blank line
Room = 5   Blank line   blank line
$6R + 6 = 30 + 6 =$ **36 people**   Blank line   blank line
   Blank line   blank line

If 3 sheets of paper are used every day, then there will be an extra day of supplies left. If 5 sheets are used daily, then there will 3 days short of papers. How many sheets are there? How many days expected to be used?

Assume the number of days = x.
$3D + 3 = 5D - 15$ Blank line   blank line
$2D = 18$ Blank line   blank line
$D =$ **9 days**   Blank line   blank line
$3 \times 9 + 3 =$ **30 sheets**   Blank line   blank line
   Blank line   blank line

Nico's class went boating. If each boat added one extra person, then each boat would sit 6 people if one less boat were rented. Then each boat would sit 9 people. How many people were there?

Method 1, algebra
$6(B + 1) = 9(B - 1)$
$B = 5$ boats
   Blank line   blank line
Method 2, Use quantity difference divided by its fractional number
   Blank line   blank line
The quantity difference is $9 + 6 = 15$ which was caused by the difference of sitting $9 - 6 = 3$
15 divided by $3 =$ **5 boats.**   Blank line   blank line
   Blank line   blank line

If each room takes 3 people, then there will be 30 people without rooms. If each room takes 6 people, then there will be 3 people left and 2 extra rooms left. How many rooms are there? How many people are there?
   Blank line   blank line
Assume the number of rooms is R.   Blank line   blank line
$3R + 30 = 6(R - 2) + 3$ Blank line   blank line
$R =$ **13 rooms**   Blank line   blank line
$P =$ **69 people**   Blank line   blank line

If each room takes 6 people, then there will be 15 students without rooms. If all rooms except 2 take 5 students, the remaining 2 rooms will each have only two students. How many rooms are there? How many people are there?

$6R - 15 = 5(R - 2) + 2 \times 2$ (R = the number of rooms)　　Blank line　　blank line

$\qquad = 5R - 10 + 4$　　Blank line　　blank line

$\qquad = 5R - 6$　　Blank line　　blank line

R = 9 rooms　　Blank line　　blank line

$6R - 15 =$ **39 students**　　Blank line　　blank line

Blank line　　blank line
Blank line　　blank line
Blank line　　blank line
Blank line　　blank line
Blank line　　blank line
Blank line　　blank line
Blank line　　blank line
Blank line　　blank line

3
Part B – Word problem solving strategies 文字問題解題策略

Many strategies we talked about in our lower grades workbooks before still apply to grades 4 and 5. These strategies are listed as follows:

A quantity divided by its corresponding fractional number 数量除以分率

Change problem to story 改题为故事

Work backwards 倒算法

Guess and Check (Trial and Error) 測試法

Make a table (t-table) 做 T 表

Draw a picture 畫个图

Make a list 列举法

Write the answer on sentence 边唸边写答案

Mark numbers on geometry figures 在几何图形上标示数

Change data to whole numbers 转换数为正整数

Change data to small numbers 转换数为小正整数

Use a smaller sample 用小樣本

The slight change is perhaps in the area of data types and the multi-step problems. However, there are a few strategies which are our own inventions and were never mentioned in any other workbooks. These few invented strategies are to use t-table in the Give and Take problem; to mark or write values right on the sentence for the word problems, to change the data type to whole numbers from fractions, %, or decimals etc. data types especially when working backwards.

A quantity divided by its corresponding fractional number 数量除以分率

The concept of using a quantity divided by its corresponding fractional number is not being taught or mentioned in the West but more often taught in the Chinese contest book and used many times in solving word problems, although it is not being taught at their day school. A fractional number can be expressed as $\frac{p}{q}$, where p and q are none 0 integers. A fractional number can be a whole number, integers, decimal, %, fraction, or a ratio.

The strategy or method is very important and could be powerful in solving many word problems.

Example 1 To find the rate from the sum.

Andrew bought 3 pens in the morning and 4 same pens in the afternoon. The total cost was $35, what was the average cost per pen?

$$\frac{35}{3+4} = \$7 \text{ per pen}$$

Example 2 To find the rate of the difference.

The concept of finding a rate from the difference is not being emphasized in normal math textbooks or math contest books, but it is very important in solving word problems. The "rate" here does not necessarily mean a unit price. It could mean a group number, a class of students, a bag. It could mean a collection of objects.

Example

Andrew drove 5 hours in the morning and 2 hours in the afternoon. Assume he always drove at the same speed, and he drove 180 km more in the morning than the afternoon. What was his driving speed?

$$\frac{180}{5 - 2} = 60 \text{ km/hour}$$

A number of balls are given to a class. If each person gets 9 balls, then there will be a shortage of 15 balls. If each person gets 4 balls, then there will be an excess of 10 balls. How many people are there?
$9P - 15 = 4P + 10$

The number of people $= \frac{difference\ of\ balls}{difference\ of\ each\ perso's\ balls} = \frac{15+10\ (The\ difference\ of -15\ to\ 10\ is\ 25)}{9-4} = 5$ people

A rate is a group of people in this example.

Example 2 To find the original quantity

Andrew spent \$35 on the Christmas shopping, and it was $\frac{5}{7}$ of his monthly allowance. What was his monthly allowance?

$$35 \div \frac{5}{7} = 49$$

To divide a quantity by a fraction, you will get the whole amount, which is the original amount. This is very different from a normal idea. That is when a quantity divided by a number, and one would get a rate instead of the whole (original) quantity. The reason is the fraction itself has the idea of the whole (the denominator) built-in.

After getting a 10% discount on a Christmas gift, Andrew paid \$150. What was the original sale price?

$$150 \div (1 - 0.1) = 1500 \div 9 = \$166.67$$

Changing a problem to a story 改题意为故事

Basic Chickens and Rabbits problem 基础鸡兔同笼

We talked about the oral method used for the Chickens and Rabbits problem in ancient Chinese government exams in the section of Chickens and Rabbits.

The idea is to change "legs" to "heads" since when the number of legs is divided by 2, it turns the number of chickens from 2 to 1, which is equivalent to one head. It also turns the 4 legs of a rabbit to 2 heads of each rabbit. This again is to change the problem to a story of turning legs to heads, but I feel not too many grade-4 children will understand it.

Student's name: _____ Assignment date: _____

Basic Sum and Difference problem 基礎和差問題

Many times, children get confused on how to work out problems is because the solution and method are completely concentrated on the explanation from the math point of view, so I have found a technique to make children understand better, that is to change the wording of problem to a story.

Example 1

Changing the Sum and Difference problem to a Sharing story problem

A typical Sum and Difference problem	A sharing story
Adam and Bob have 25 pencils. Adam has 3 more pencils than Bob. How many pencils does each of them have?	Another way is to think about how to solve the Sum and Difference problem is to think in a different way as follows:
The typical method of solving this kind of problem is to use the Line Segment Diagram or to use formula.	Adam and Bob want to divide 25 pencils, and Adam wants to have 3 more than Bob. Why not just give 3 pencils to Adam first, then divided the rest equally?
Another way is to think Adam and Bob want to divide 25 pencils, and Adam wants to have 3 more than Bob. Why not just give 3 pencils to Adam first, then divided the rest equally? Most children will understand this way of dividing, especially if the teacher can act on the idea of using a small sample.	Most children will understand this way of dividing, especially if the teacher can act on the idea of using a small sample.
The Chinese math cont4est uses the following formulas: $$\text{large number} = \frac{25+3}{2} = 14$$ $$\text{small number} = \frac{25-3}{2} = 11$$	$25 - 3 = 22$ $\frac{22}{2} = 11 \ldots.$ Bob's share $11 + 3 = 14 \ldots\ldots$ Adam' share.

Example 2

Adam and Bob had 25 pencils. After Adam used 4 pencils and Bob used 3 pencils, Adam still had 2 more pencils than bob. How many pencils did each of them have originally?

Often, the difference is not clear, and it has to be found first

Thinking 1

After Adam used 4 and Bob used 3, then if they had an equal number of pencils, it means Adam had 1 more pencils than Bob. But Adam still had 2 more pencils than Bob, which means Adam had 3 more pencils than Bob in the beginning. So, the difference is 3.

Thinking 2

  Adam   Bob

  - 4   -3
   2   0

Adam had 6 and Bob had 3, so the difference is 3.

large number $= \frac{25+3}{2} = 14$

small number $= \frac{25-3}{2} = 11$

If we can figure out the difference is 3, then the answer will be the same as the last problem.

$25 - 3 = 22$

$\frac{22}{2} = 11$ .... Bob's share

$11 + 3 = 14$ ...... Adam' share.

Student's name: _____   Assignment date: _____

Problem

1	Fernando has 7 more goldfish than Gabriel. Together they have 41 goldfish. How many goldfish does each one of them have?

Fernando has 24.
Gabriel has 17.

2	Fernando and Melissa had 3140 apples altogether. Melissa had 422 more apples than Fernando. How many apples did each one of them have?

Fernando has 1359.
Melissa has 1781.
53

3	There are 65 seats in three classes. There are 21 seats in class 1. Class 2 has 14 more seats than class 3. How many seats are there in class 2?

29

4	The distance from Halifax to Vancouver is 5593 km, and the distance from Halifax to Winnipeg is 1045 km more than the distance from Winnipeg to Vancouver. Find the distance from Halifax to Winnipeg.

A: Halifax to Winnipeg
B: Winnipeg to Vancouver

A + B = 5593
A − B = 1045

Basic Sum and Multiplier problem 基礎和倍問題

Adam and Bob had 570 kg of apples. Adam's apples weigh twice as much as Bob's. How much does each one of them have?

One can use the Line Segment Diagram method, and this method can show the source of the following formulas used.

sum ÷ (Multiplier + 1) = small number
small number × Multiplier = large number

和 ÷(倍数+1) = 小的数
小的数 × 倍数 = 大的数

Think the basic unit as 1 bag (or 1 part or 1 share 一份), so this problem is changed to Adam has as twice as many bags as Bob's.

The following uses the idea of the Corresponding method because the quantity is 570, which corresponds to 3 bags. We always look for a corresponding value to a quantity when working on word problems to find the relationship.

570 kg is the weight of 3 bags, one bag is $\frac{570}{3}$ = 190 kg
What is Bob's weight?
Adam has 190 × 2 = 380 kg

Problem

The length of a rectangle is seven times its width. Find its dimensions if the perimeter is 112 cm.

$\frac{112}{8}$ = 14 ... width
98 ... length

A house and lot are worth $96000. The lot costs seven times the house. What is the value of the lot?
96000÷ 8 × 7=84000

Student's name: _____　Assignment date: _____

Basic Difference and Multiplier problem 基礎差倍問題

Adam had 580 kg of apples more than Bob. Adam's apples weigh three times as much as Bob's. How much does each one of them have?

One can use the Line Segment Diagram method or use this method to show the source of the following formulas used.

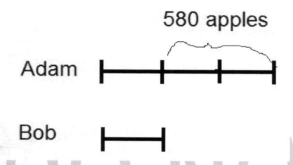

difference ÷ (Multiplier − 1) = small number
small number × Multiplier = large number

差÷(倍数 −1) = 小的数
小的数 × 倍数 = 大的数

Think the basic Multiplier units as 1 bag (or 1 part or 1 share 一份), so this problem is changed to Adam has 2 more bags than Bob's.

The following uses the idea of the Corresponding method because the quantity is 580, which corresponds to 2 bags. We always look for a corresponding value to a quantity when working on word problems to find the relationship.

580 kg is the weight of 2 bags, one bag is $\frac{580}{3-1}$ = 290 kg, which is the weight Bob has.
Adam has 290 × 3= 870 kg

Problem

Fernando had 2146 apples, and he divided them into 2 piles. One pile had 284 more than the other. How many apples did he have in each pile?

1215, 931

Evan has as 3 times as many oranges as Melissa. Altogether they have 56 oranges. How many oranges does Evan have?

M=14
G= 42

Student's name: _____   Assignment date: _____

Mixed Sum, Difference, and Multiplier 和差倍混合题

Black bears have paws; all black and white bears have paws all white. There are some black bears and some white bears, and all the number of black paws and the number of white paws is 248. The number of black bears is 16 more than white bears. How many are white bears and how many black bears there?

$248 \div 4 = 62$ bears altogether

$\frac{62-16}{2} = 46 = 23$ …. White bears

$23 + 16 = 39$ black bears

Black bears have paws all black paws, and white bears have paws all white. There are some black bears and some white bears, and all the number of black paws and the number of white paws is 52. The number of black bears is 3 more than the white bears. How many are white bears and how many black bears there?

$52 \div 4 = 13$

$B + W = 13$

$B - W = 3$

$B = 13, W = 5$

Summary 結論

In summary, whenever a child encounters a problem, the teacher could use the strategy of changing the problem to a story that the student could relate to, especially when the story is something that children could act on it.

Marking or writing directly while reading the problem 直接在图上标示答案或句旁写答案

Marking on figures

Example

Find angle A.

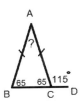
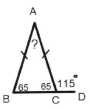

We know the triangle is an isosceles triangle, and each of the two equal angles is 65. So, angle A = 180 − 65 × 2 = 50

Writing information beside sentences

This method does not work on all word problems but will work on some word problems when one variable is directly built on another variable in the form $ax \pm b$.

Example

Adam has two more apples than Bob. Bob has four times of Cathy's apples. Cathy has 10 apples. How many apples does each of them have?

$$40 + 2 = 42$$

$$40$$

Adam has two more apples than Bob. Bob has four times of Cathy's apples. Cathy has 10 apples. How many apples does each of them has?

See the Marking or Writing Method section for more information.

Changing data types to small whole numbers 转换原题成小正整数

I have found that students are most comfortable with small whole numbers because they can "see" the answers but get confused when the data type is changed. Take a look at the following example to see what I am saying.

Example 1

	Change the fraction to a whole number.
Students may get confused when the data type is a fraction. What is $\frac{2}{3}$ of 3?	What is 2 of 3? The student can "see" the answer is 6. At this point, ask the student how did she or he get the answer? If the student did not know, then tell him or her, there are only four operators $+ - \times \div$.
What fraction of 6 is 2? $? \times 6 = 2$	Change the question to $? \times 6 = 12$ The student can "see" the answer is 2, then ask the student how the answer arrived? If the student can answer the step of how to get the answer for the whole number, then remind the student the step of doing the left-side problem is the same.

Student's name: _____   Assignment date: _____

Example 2

Because Trial and Error is a method constantly taught at students' day schools, so some students "refused" to listen and tried to understand if there are any other methods available such as the systematic method. They even used calculators behind my back to get the answers by using the Trial and Error method. So how did I take care of this situation? I remember there was an Age problem, and one student just used the Trial and Error method to come up with a correct answer, so I change the human age problem to a tree age problem. This has convinced this student to learn a systematic method other than the Trial and Error method.

Age problem

Human age problem	Tree age problem
John is 5 years old, and his friend Tom is 13 years old. How many years later will Tom be twice as old as John? John Tom 6 14 7 15 8 16 Three years later. So, when the numbers are small, it is easy for the Trial and Error method, but this may mislead students to think that to always Trial and Error method without using any other methods. The above method can also be called a T-table method.	There are two trees on Tom's farm: pine and fur. The pine tree is 13 years old, and the fur tree is 101 years old. How many years later will the fur tree be twice as old as the pine tree? Method 1 Trial and Error method The answer is 75 years later, but it will take a bit longer to list each year up to 75 years. Method 2 We know that 26 is double of 13. It will take fur $101 - 26 = 75$ years. Method 2 – one-variable equation The difficulty in this method is to come up with an equation. The rest of the work is routine steps to solve the equation. $$101 + x = 2\,(13 + x)$$ We can not apply the "Writing method" directly to this problem. We get $x = 75$ after solving the above equation.

Work backwards and order of operations 倒算法及運算規則

Introduction

Many work backwards problems are introduced in the previous versions of this **Ultimate Math Contest Preparation, Problem Solving Strategies, and Math IQ Puzzles series of** workbooks.

The work backwards problems can be classified into the following categories:

Horizontal calculations involving the order of operations

$$51 - 9 + \boxed{} \div 3 - 9 + 15 = 84$$

$$\underbrace{51 - 9}_{42} + \boxed{} \div 3 - 9 + 15 = 84$$

$\boxed{} \div 3$ is an unknown, so it is to be solved like solving an equation.

$$\boxed{} \div 3 = 84 - 42 + 9 - 15$$
$$= 36$$
$$\boxed{} = 36 \times 3$$
$$= 108$$

Vertical calculation

See problems in the next few pages.

Fraction or % problems

Often, the fraction problems require the use of 1 and the % problems require the use of 100% (still is 1).

The Corresponding method that is to use quantity divided by its corresponding fractional number is the way to get back the original amount. We call this Corresponding method in the grade-3 workbook.

Example
Fernando spent $\frac{2}{5}$ of his money, and he had $1275 left. How much did he have originally?
$2125

Work backwards and making a table 倒算法与列表格

Often, when working on work backwards word problems, we use a table to help get the original amount.

| 1 | Adam, Bob and Cathy have 33 pencils altogether. If Adam gives Cathy 2 pencils, Cathy gives Bob 3 pencils, and Bob gives Adam 4 pencils, then they have an equal number of pencils. How many pencils does each of them have originally? |

| Use a table.

Adam Bob Cathy
11　11　11
13　11　9
13　8　12
9　12　12 | Do addition or subtraction before multiplication or division.
It does not matter how many are given to take from each other, and the final result will be all the same.
$\frac{33}{3} = 11$
Adam: $11 + 2 - 4 = 9$
Bob: $11 - 3 + 4 = 12$
Cathy: $11 - 2 + 3 = 12$ |

| 2 | Adam, Bob and Cathy have 216 pencils altogether. If Adam gives Cathy as many pencils as Cathy has, Cathy gives Bob as many pencils as Bob has, and Bob gives Adam as many pencils as Adam has, then they have an equal number of pencils. How many pencils does each of them have originally? |

	Adam	Bob	Cathy
Last amount	72	72	72
Bob gives to Adam	36	108	72
Cathy to Bob	36	54	126
Adam to Cathy	99	54	63

answer

Problem

$\square + \square = 18$ **9, 9**

$\square + 5 - 7 = \triangle$ 9, 7

$\bigcirc + 6 - 9 = \triangle$ 10, 7

$\square + \square + 1 = 13$ **6, 6**

$\triangle + 5 - 8 = \square$ 9, 6

$\bigcirc + \bigcirc + \bigcirc = \triangle$ 3, 3, 3, 9

$\square + \square + \square = 24$ **8, 8, 8**

$\triangle + 8 - 9 = \square$ 9, 8

$\bigcirc + \bigcirc + 1 = \triangle$ 4, 4, 9

$\bigcirc - 2 = 9$ **11**

$\bigcirc + 4 - 5 = \triangle$ 11, 10

$\square - 2 + 3 = \triangle$ 19, 10

Ho Math Chess 何数棋谜 奥数,解题策略,及 IQ 思唯训练宝典
Frank Ho, Amanda Ho © 1995 - 2020 　　　　All rights reserved.
Student's name: _____ Assignment date: _____

1	$\square \times \square + \bigcirc \times \bigcirc = 85$ The largest whole number is _____.　9 9 x 9 + 2 x 2 = 81
2	$\square \times \square + \bigcirc \times \bigcirc = 61$ The largest whole number is _____.　6, $5^2 + 6^2 = 61$
3	$\square \times \square + \bigcirc \times \bigcirc = 85$ The largest whole number is _____.　7, $7^2 + 6^2 = 85$
4	$\square \times \square + \bigcirc \times \bigcirc = 290$ The largest whole number is _____.　13, $13^2 + 11^2 = 290$
5	$\square \times \square + \bigcirc \times \bigcirc = 296$ The largest whole number is _____.14, $14^2 + 10^2 = 296$
6	$\square \times \square + \bigcirc \times \bigcirc = 369$ The largest whole number is _____.15, $15^2 + 12^2 = 369$

Student's name: _____ Assignment date: _____

Fill in each [   ] by a number.

$6 = $ [   ] $\times 3$ **2**

$7 = $ [   ] $\times 0.1$ **70**

$3 = 6 \times$ [   ]   **½**   **0.5**

$49 = 45 \times$ [   ]   **49/45**

$0.02 = 100 \times$ [   ]   **1/500**   **0.002**

$\frac{7}{2} = 7 \times$ [   ]   **½**

0.5

$\frac{3}{2} = 6 \times$ [   ]   **1/4**

$\frac{5}{3} = 49 \times$ [   ]   **5/147**

Student's name: _____ Assignment date: _____

Fill in each [ ] by a number.

$5 = \boxed{} \times \dfrac{3}{4}$ **20/3**

$0.5 = \dfrac{1}{5} \times \boxed{}$ **5/2**

$0.2 = \dfrac{1}{5} \times \boxed{}$ **1**

$\dfrac{3}{2} \div \dfrac{4}{9} = \dfrac{1}{5} \times \boxed{}$ **135/8   16 7/8**

$\dfrac{3}{2} \times \dfrac{8}{9} = \boxed{} \times \dfrac{2}{3}$ **2**

$1\dfrac{2}{3} \times 2\dfrac{2}{5} = \boxed{} \times 1\dfrac{2}{3}$ $\dfrac{12}{5}$ **=2 2/5**

$\boxed{} \times 1\dfrac{2}{3} = 1\dfrac{2}{7} \div 2\dfrac{2}{3}$ **81/280**

$1\dfrac{2}{3} + 2\dfrac{4}{3} - \left(2\dfrac{1}{2} - \dfrac{2}{3}\right) = 1\dfrac{1}{5} \times \boxed{}$ **95/36**

Student's name: _____   Assignment date: _____

Finding the remaining amount using fractions

1-remaining fraction problem 一个剩馀数问题 using one statement
Using one-step, we think that one statement is important to get the original amount.

What was the original amount?	Spending the following fraction of the original amount	How much was left?
$120	$\frac{1}{2}$	$60 ?
$120	$\frac{1}{3}$	$80 ? $120 \times \frac{2}{3} = 80$ $\frac{2}{3}$ *must be done in your head.*
$120	$\frac{1}{8}$	$105 ?

2-remaining fractions problem 二个剩馀数问题

What is the original amount	Spending the following fraction of the original amount	Spending the following fraction of the remaining amount	How much was left?
$120	$\frac{1}{2}$	$\frac{1}{3}$	$40 ? Use one statement. $120 \times \frac{1}{2} \times \frac{2}{3} = 40$ All the remaining fractions must be done in your head.
$120	$\frac{1}{3}$	$\frac{1}{8}$	$70 ?
$120	$\frac{1}{8}$ 15, 105	$\frac{1}{5}$ 21, 84	$84 ?
$32	$\frac{5}{8}$ 20, 12	$\frac{3}{4}$ 9	$3 ?

Finding the original amount after 2-remaining fractions problem 由剩馀数找原始数问题

Use the line Segment Diagram to find the original number.
The remaining quantity divided by its corresponding fractional number (fraction, %, or ratio) to find the original quantity by using one.

1st spending the following fraction of the original amount	2nd spending the following fraction of the remaining amount	The amount left	What was the original amount?
$\dfrac{1}{2}$	$\dfrac{1}{3}$	$60	$$60 \div \left(1 - \frac{1}{3}\right) \div \left(1 - \frac{1}{2}\right)$$ $$= 60 \times \frac{3}{2} \times \frac{2}{1} = \$180$$

1st spending the following fraction of the original amount	2nd spending the following fraction of the remaining amount	The amount left	What was the original amount?
$\dfrac{1}{2}$	$\dfrac{1}{3}$	$90	$\begin{array}{l}\dfrac{1}{2}\qquad\dfrac{1}{2}\\ \$135 \\[4pt] \dfrac{2}{3}\quad\dfrac{1}{3}\\ \$90\end{array}$ $90 \div \left(1 - \tfrac{1}{3}\right) \div \left(1 - \tfrac{1}{2}\right)$ $= 90 \times \tfrac{3}{2} \times \tfrac{2}{1} = \mathbf{\$270}$
$\dfrac{1}{8}$	$\dfrac{1}{5}$	$280	**$400**
$\dfrac{2}{3}$	$\dfrac{3}{5}$	$120	**$900**

Ho Math Chess 何数棋谜 奥数,解题策略,及 IQ 思唯训练宝典

Student's name: _____   Assignment date: _____

Word Problem

Melissa finished 124 km which is her $\frac{2}{5}$ of her 5-day trip in 3 days. How many km per day must she average for the remainder of the trip?

$$\frac{124 \div \frac{2}{5} - 124}{2} = 93 \text{ km}$$

This problem was created for our students during the class teaching in 2013 around the Halloween time.

Kirsten went to trick and treat on the Halloween night and was awarded many candies. If Kirsten gave half of her candies to Elise, then Elise would have 109 less than Kirsten's original number of candies. Kirsten's remaining number of candies was as many as Elise had after Elise received some candies from Kirsten.

How many candies did Kirsten and Elise each have originally?

208 for Kirsten and 0 for Elise.

Method 1 - Use arithmetic to work backwards

Elise	Kirsten
109	109
0	218

Method 2 - Use algebra to work backwards
Let x be the original candies Kristen has?

$$x - \frac{x}{2} = x - 109$$
$$x = 218$$
Elise = 0

Melody invested in stocks. On the first day, she lost half of her money. On the second day, she gained $400. On the third day, she gained as much as she had at the end of the second day. She had $2600 after the three days. How much did she have at the beginning of the first day?

At the end of the second day, she had $1300.
At the end of the first day, she $1300 - 400 = 900$
At the beginning of the first day, she had **$1800**.

Student's name: _____   Assignment date: _____

3 remaining with extra spending 分数的 3 个剩餘

This kind of remaining problem appears more frequently in Asia, and the Line Segment Diagram can be used to help solve it.

Day 1: Garrick spent half of his money and $100 extra.
Day 2: He spent half of the remaining and $100 more.
Day 3: He spent half of the remaining and has $250 left.
How much money did he have in the beginning?

Day 1: Garrick spent half of his money and $100 extra. (1200+100) x 2 = 2600
Day 2: He spent half of the remainder and $100 more. (500 +100) x 2 = 1200
Day 3: He spent half of the remainder and has $250 left. 350 x 2 =500

Work backwards, and the answer is $2600.

Fraction and rational equation 分数方程式文字问题

This kind of problem involves a rational equation, and it does not appear in North America but frequently appears in Singapore.

Cindy gave $700 to her mother. She then spent $\frac{5}{7}$ of her remaining money and she had $\frac{7}{10}$ of her money left. How much money did Cindy have at first?

It can be easily solved by using algebra. 35000

With 8 weeks remaining, Han has collected 31 more cans than Garrick. If Garrick is to collect more cans than Han, he must average at least how many more cans per week than Han?
12÷ 3= 4

Grade 4 students were covering the gym floor with plywood to get ready for the Fun Fair.

Before class starts, they covered $\frac{1}{4}$ of the gym area. _____

At recess, they covered $\frac{1}{3}$ of the remaining gym floor area. _____

At lunch, they covered $\frac{1}{2}$ of the remaining gym floor area. _____

After school, they covered the last remaining 28 m². _____

How many square metres were covered each time above, and what is the total area of the gym?

The money is divided among 3 brothers. The first brother took one half and $1. The second brother took the remaining one half and $2. The third brother took the remaining $500. What was the original amount?

500 + 2 = 502   502 x 2 = 1004

1004 + 1 = 1005

1005 x 2 = **2010**

Meghan spent one half of her trip budget on room rent, and then she spent $\frac{1}{3}$ of the rest and extra $15 for her food. She then spent $\frac{1}{5}$ of the remaining on the gift and had $16 left. How much did she have in the beginning?

$105

Ho Math Chess 何数棋谜 奥数,解题策略,及 IQ 思唯训练宝典

Student's name: _____ Assignment date: _____

Adding 2 digits

```
    2 □
+ □ □ 8
-------
  2 0 5
```

7, 17

Adding 2 digits

```
  □ □ 2
+   6 □
---------
□ □ 0 1
```

93, 9, 10

Adding 2 digits

```
  5 5 8 □
+ □ □ □ 7
---------
  9 2 0 6
```

9, 361

Adding 2 digits

```
    5 □ 6 □
+   □ 7 □ 8
-----------
  □ 4 3 2 1
```

5, 3, 8, 5, 1

Adding 3 digits

```
  □ 9 □
    □ 8
+   6 7
-------
1 1 0 0
```

9, 5, 3

Adding 3 digits

```
  □ 9 □
    □ 2
+     6
-------
  6 6 0
```

5, 2, 6

Frank Ho, Amanda Ho © 1995 - 2020　　　　　　All rights reserved.

Student's name: _____ Assignment date: _____

$$\begin{array}{r} \Box\Box 3 \\ - \Box\Box \\ \hline 9 \end{array}$$

10, 94

$$\begin{array}{r} \Box\Box 5 \\ - \Box\Box \\ \hline 7 \end{array}$$

10, 98

$$\begin{array}{r} \Box\Box 3 \\ - 19\Box \\ \hline 8 \end{array}$$

20, 5

$$\begin{array}{r} \Box\Box\Box \\ - 245 \\ \hline 7 \end{array}$$

252

$$\begin{array}{r} \Box\Box\Box\Box \\ - 3393 \\ \hline 1088 \end{array}$$

4481

$$\begin{array}{r} \Box\Box\Box\Box \\ - 379 \\ \hline 2734 \end{array}$$

3113

$$\begin{array}{r} 3\Box 7 \\ \times \Box \\ \hline 3\Box 93 \end{array}$$

7, 9, 3

$$\begin{array}{r} \Box\Box 7 \\ \times \Box \\ \hline \Box 588 \end{array}$$

3, 9, 4, 1 or 6, 4, 2, 2

Problem 1

```
        3   7   5
  ×         □   □ ₄₅
      1   □   7   □ ₈₅
    □   □   □   □
                1500
    □   6   8   □   □ ₁₇₅
```

Problem 2

```
        4   □   □ ₈₂
  ×                 8
    3   8   5   6
```

Problem 3

```
            □   □ ₁₃
  ×         7   □ ₉
        □   □   □ ₁₁₇
      □   □
                91
      □   □   2   □ ₁₀₇
```

Problem 4

```
            8   4
  7 )□ □ □ □ □ □
      □ □ □ □
          □ 1
        □ □ □ □
              3
```

591, 56, 3, 28

Problem 5

```
        4   □ □
  7 )□ □ □ □ □ □
      □ □ □ □
          □ □ □ □
      2   8
            □ □
          1   4
              0
```

42
3094
28
14

Tree structure diagram 树形图

The tree structure diagram method is an act on (形象直观法).

Example

Example 1

How many paths are there in the following figure from point A to point B?

Students can use the pencil to mark the paths or use counting on the dots method.

The answer is 3.

Example 2

There are 3 trains going from city A to city B, and there are 3 buses going from city B to city C. If the passengers can take any train or any bus going from city A to city C, then how many ways are the from city A to city C?

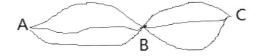

Addition Principle – Different branches (不同源的树枝用加法原理)
From A to B, you use addition because there are different tree branches (top to down direction).

Multiplication Principle – Same source of branches (同源的树枝用乘法原理)

For each branch going from A to B, there are 3 more corresponding branches from B to C, so each branch branches out into 3 different sub-branches. To complete the task, you need to do multiple steps.

The number of total paths is 3 times 3 = 9 because for each branch from A to B, and there are 3 more corresponding different branches. From branch to sub-branches, you use multiplication.

Problem

Three digits 4, 5, and 6 are arranged with no repeated digits, how many different numbers can be arranged?

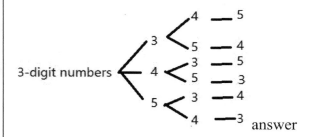

Students can also use the List method.

Johnny threw a die (6 faces with digits 1 to 6 written on each face.) and flipped one coin (head and tail on each side). How many combinations can he get? Use a trees diagram to show your answer

12

Wendy had digits 1, 2, 3, each written on a cardboard in one bag and letters A, B, and C, each written on cardboard in another bag. If he chooses one card from each bag, then how many different combinations of numbers and letters can he get? Use a tree structure to show your answer.

9

Wendy had digits 1, 2, 3, each written on a cardboard in one bag and letters A, B, and C, each written on cardboard in another bag. If he chooses two cards from the numbered bag and one letter from the letter bag, then how many different combinations of numbers and letters can he get? Use a tree structure to show your answer.

9
12A, 13A, 23A
12B, 13B, 23B
12C, 13C, 23C

Student's name: _____ Assignment date: _____

List Method or Box method $a = x + y + \cdots + z; a = bx + cy + dz$ 列表法或填盒子法

Readers are asked to refer the workbook of Ultimate Math Contest Preparation, Problem Solving Strategies, and Math IQ Puzzles for Grades 3 and 4 for details on the List method or Box method. The List method is being used as one strategy for the one-step problem or sometimes used as one method in multi-step problems. For example, the List method is used as one way of finding the Greatest common factor. The Box method is often used as one way of finding the combinations or arrangements.

Many problems involve the following partitioning of sum models:

$a = x + y + \cdots + z$
$a = bx + cy + dz$

Example

Joseph wrote the numbers 1, 2, 3, 4, 5, 6, 7, 8, 9, and 10 each on a piece of cardboard. He then picked some cards and added their sums; all sums are equal to 24. At least how many pieces of cardboards did he pick up?

This problem is to partition the sum of 24 using the model of a= $x + y + \cdots + z$.

$24 = 10 + 9 + 5$

At most, how many pieces of cardboards did he pick up?

$24 = 1 + 2 + 3 + 4 + 5 + 9$

Example

Check the following price list to find out if it is possible for Minnie to spend $1.10 to buy all pencils?
if it is possible for Minnie to spend $0.44 to buy all erasers? What combinations of pencils and erasers can Minnie buy with $1.10?

	Pencil	Eraser	Ruler
Price per item	10 cents	6 cents	5 cents

Because 110 is divisible by 10, so it is possible for Minnie to buy all pencils.
Because 44 is not divisible by 6, so it is not possible to buy all erasers.

What combinations of pencils and erasers can Minnie buy with $1.10?
To have the ones digit to be 0, it needs multiples of 5 of 6 cents.

Price per item	Pencil	Eraser (Start with the largest multiple of 6 cents possible, then drop in increment.)
	10 cents	6 cents
	2	15
	5	10
	8	5
	11	0

1	The pet store sold 24 hamsters, rabbits, and guinea pigs. Rabbits were sold as many as 3 times as hamsters, and the rest were guinea pigs. What combinations are possible?

One can use a table.

R	A	G
3	1	20
6	2	12
9	3	8
12	4	4

answer

2	The pet store sold 5 puppies that were either spotted or brown in colour. The spotted ones were sold for $100 each, and the brown ones were sold for $120 each. The store collected $540. How many spotted ones and browns each the store sold?

This is a Chickens and Rabbits problem, but since the number of pets is very small and multiple pets were sold on each kind, so we can use a table to solve it.

3 of $100 + 2 of $100 each = $540

3	Joseph wanted to buy 6 fish of 3 kinds goldfish, guppies, and catfish. Show how Joseph could buy all the combinations of fish if he buys at least one fish of each kind.

It can be solved by using a table to have at least one fish of each kind. 7 combinations.

$6 = \square + \bigcirc + \triangle$ answer

goldfish	guppies	catfish
4	1	1
3	1	2
2	1	3
1	1	4
1	2	3
1	3	2
1	4	1

answer

Handshakes problem 握手問題

Introduction

There are many variations of handshakes problem, but the way to solve it is to use a list for small numbers, otherwise, use a sum formula to solve it such as $\frac{(a+l)n}{2}$, where a is the first term, l is the last term, and n is the number of terms.

Renee invited 4 of her friends to her birthday party. Each person in the party must shake hands with every other person once. What is the total number of handshakes?

$4 + 3 + 2 + 1 = 10$

How many rectangles are in the following figure?

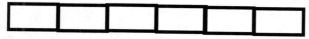

$6 + 5 + 4 + 3 + 2 + 1 = 21$

There are 6 distinct whole numbers $a < b < c < d < e < f$ and there are 15 pairs of numbers that are formed by choosing two different numbers. The sums of these 15 pairs of numbers are

12, 15, 17, 18, 20, 22, 23, 24, 26, 27, 28, 30, 31, 34, 39

The paired numbers produced from a list of numbers have appeared in many math contests in the past.

What is the sum of $c + d$?

5, 7, 10, 13, 17, 21 so c + d = 23

A pair of skates at Super Save is discounted 15% on the first day of next month if it is not sold by the end of the month. After 4-month, the price of skates is at what percent of the original price?

1	How many two-digit counting numbers exist such that the ones digit is larger than the tens digit?

12, 13, 14, 15, 16, 17, 18, 19
23, 24, 25, 26, 27, 28, 29
. . .
$8 + 7 + 6 + 5 + 4 + 3 + 2 + 1 = \textbf{36}$

2	A line segment that joins two points on a circle is called a chord of that circle. What is the greatest number of intersecting points on a circle with 4 points?

chord	points
1	2
3 ?	3 ?
6 ?	4 ?

1	When two the numbers 2, 9, 11, 17 are added, how many different sums are there?

2, 9 (11)   2, 11 (13)   2, 17 (19)   9, 11 (20)   9, 17 (26)   11, 17 (28)

6 different sums

2	When the following three numbers 9, 17, 22 are picked with no restriction on how many times each number can be chosen, how many least times of numbers can be picked to make a sum of 65?

2 of 17's, 22, 9
Try to get the largest number the highest times to get the least number of choices.

3	Thomas has 3 blue cards, 3 white cards, and 3 black cards in a box. If he chooses 3 cards at a time, what are the different combinations of cards he can pick? The order of 3 picked cards does not matter. Change each colour to a digit.

111   222
112   223
113   233
122   333
123
133
10 combinations

1	There are 6 people in a room. They all shake hands with each other. How many handshakes will there be? Use table. Connecting dots. List three methods to solve this problem. **15= (5+4+3+2+1)** **answer** $\frac{6\times5}{2} = 15$
2	Thomas has 1 blue card, 1 white card, 1 red card, and 1 black card in a box. If he chooses 1 card at a time, what are the different combinations of cards he can pick? No colour can be repeated. *Use the box method* $4 \times 3 \times 2 \times 1 = 24$ or list method
3	Thomas has 5 cards with dots 0, 1, 2, 3, and 4 marked on each card. If he chooses 2 cards at a time, what are the different combinations of cards he can pick? Each digit can be repeated. 00, 01, 02, 03, 04 11, 12, 13, 14 22, 23, 24 33, 34 44 5+4+3+2+1 = 15
4	Jennifer has $2.30 in 10 cents and 25 cents. She has more 25 cents than 10 cents. How many of each coin does she have? 8 of 25 cents and 3 of 10 cents.

Math Contest Preparation, Problem Solving Strategies, and Math IQ Puzzles for Grades 4 and 5
Ho Math Chess 何数棋谜 奥数,解题策略,及 IQ 思唯训练宝典

Frank Ho, Amanda Ho © 1995 - 2020   All rights reserved.

Student's name: _____   Assignment date: _____

English and math 英文数学

Some words used in the Kangaroo Math Contest appeared in grades were not understood by children such as distinct divisors, factors, a palindrome. Some math vocabularies are not used by children's daytime schools, so they do not understand them.

Some problems require students to understand English thoroughly; for example, the following English has got a lot of grade 3 students confused.

What time is it now if what is left of the day is half of the time that has passed it so far?

This problem can be considered as a multiple problem.

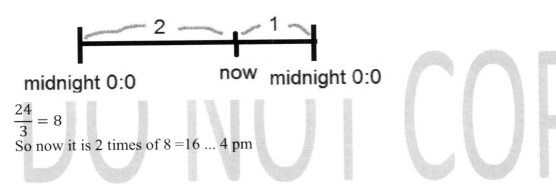

$\frac{24}{3} = 8$

So now it is 2 times of 8 =16 ... 4 pm

Language is important when solving math problems 文智弱不能解文字题

Thirty less 2, plus 5 = 30 - 2 + 5 = 33	Thirty less than 35, plus 6 = 35 - 30 + 6 = 11
The sum of 14 and 6, divided by 2 = $\frac{14+6}{2} = 10$	The sum of 14 and 6 divided by 2 = $14 + \frac{6}{2} = 17$
The number 7 is multiplied by itself, minus 5 = $7 \times 7 - 5 = 44$	The number 7 is multiplied by itself minus 5 = $7 \times (7 - 5) = 14$

Ho Math Chess　何数棋谜 奥数,解题策略,及 IQ 思唯训练宝典
Frank Ho, Amanda Ho © 1995 - 2020

Student's name: _____   Assignment date: _____

Wording can make problems complicated 咬文嚼字的文字题

The following problem demonstrates how a subtraction problem can create more complicated conditions (more information) and thus, students could get confused.

Adam has 42 apples, and Bob has 28 apples. How many apples does Adam have more than Bob? 42-28=14	Adam bought 3 apples for 51 cents, and Bob bought 2 apples for 34 cents. What is the price cost for one apple? No division is allowed. 51-34=17 cents	William bought a pencil and an eraser for 45 cents, later he bought a pencil and 2 erasers for 64 cents. How much was the cost of an eraser? 64-45 = 19 cents

Trial and Error method (Guess and check) vs. systematic method 试对错法及系统法

Veronica and Cathleen have 10 apples altogether, and Veronica has 2 more apples than Cathleen. How many apples does each one of them have originally?

Method 1 - Trial and Error for small numbers	Method 2 - a systematic method
$10 = 10 + 0$ $= 9 + 1$ $= 8 + 2$ $= 7 + 3$ $= 6 + 4$	$\dfrac{10 - 2}{2} = 4$ $4 + 2 = 6$ .... Veronica Cathleen has 4.

Student's name: _____ Assignment date: _____

Marking or writing method 标註及写中途答案

In China, grade 5 students are required to learn to solve word problems using algebraic equations, so in this case, the universal method such as Line Segment Diagram (or Bar Chart) is not necessarily needed. So, in contrast, student's abilities in different countries may reflect the difference in math curricula in different countries.

One popular way of solving algebra to solve word problems is the "Let statement". We have found one good way to solve word problems using algebra is to mark the known information right on the problem and then connect them with an equal sign. This method is very similar to mark information on the geometry figure and then figure out the answer using the known information.

Algebra	Geometry
Adam has twice as much as Bob. Cathy has $5 more than Bob. The The sum of their money is $53. How much does each person have? **2B**　　　　　　　　**B** \　　　　　　　　/ 　　Adam has twice as much as Bob. 　　Cathy has $5 more than Bob. The **B + 5** / 　　sum of their money is $53. How 　　/ 　　much does each person have? **2B + B + B + 5 = 53** Bob =12, Cathy = 17, Adam = 34	$\triangle$ABC has $\angle$A = 15^0, and the size of $\angle$B is twice the size of $\angle$C. Draw a triangle and mark known information on it as follows. $15 + 2C + C = 180$ $C = 55$ 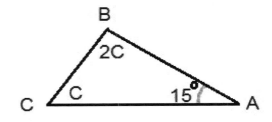

Patience and organizing abilities are required in math contest 耐力及組織力

To only concentrate on a student's math ability is not good enough to be an excellent math contestant. The personality traits such as patience and organizing etc. are equally important.

We have found many students who lack the patience even to complete the \t \table of the following problem to get the answer.

Jessica gave $2.85 in dimes and quarters to a store clerk. If she gave 4 more dimes than quarters to the clerk, how many dimes did she give?

Method 1 - Use algebra

$$10 (4 + Q) + 25 Q = 285$$
$$40 + 10Q + 25Q = 285$$
$$35Q = 245$$
$$Q = 7$$

Method 2 - Make a list or T Table

Number of dimes	Number of quarters
15	11, not possible
14	10, not possible
13	9, not possible
12	8, not possible
11, $1.10	7, $1.75
8, $0.80	4, $ 1.00, not possible
7, $0.70	3, $0.75, not possible

Ignoring unnecessary information 不必为沒用资料担心

Some students do not care if they have read the problems carefully or even totally understood the problems. The problem is they lose the ability to store problems in their data bank, so the capability of solving one problem to expand the soling ability to many problems may be lost.

We have seen some problems in the kangaroo Math Contest containing unnecessary information, so if students do not read carefully, then they could get very confused.

In an exercise survey, 150 reported that they have attempted to do exercises. Of those 150 reported, 16 reported that they actually had exercised at least once a week.

If 25% of the people have exercised at least once a week surveyed have done 3 times a week, how many people who have exercised 3 times a week?

$16 \times 0.25 = 4$

Similar Solution for Different Problems 異體同解

Problem 1	Problem 2
Isaac has $25. He gives all $25 to 5 of his friends equally. How much does each of his friends get? $5	Mr. Ho gives $30 to Isaac and Issac. If Isaac gets 4 times as much as Isaac, how much will Isaac get? Isaac: $24 Issac: $6

Student's name: _____ Assignment date: _____

Similar problems with different solutions using substitution 同題異解

All the following problems with a = sign can be turned into scale problems.

$$\bigcirc + \bigcirc = 12$$

$$\bigcirc + \triangle = 13$$

$$\triangle = ?$$

A + B = 23
A − B = 5

$$\bigcirc + \triangle = 23$$

$$\bigcirc = \triangle + 5$$

$$\bigcirc = ?$$

$$\triangle = ?$$

Transferring learned knowledge to solve other problems 举一反三

One problem facing students is once they learned how to solve one type of problem; some of them do not know how to transfer the learned knowledge to solve other problems. There are many math concepts which we learned in solving one type of problems can be transferred to solve other types of math problems, for example,

1. Times tables can be used to find the factors or common factors, GCF, LCM.
2. Multiplication can be used to find the answers for % problems.
3. Chickens and Rabbits problem can be used to find solutions for Travelling problems.
4 Work problems can be used to find answers to ravelling problems.
5. Sum and Difference and Sum and Multiplier can be used to find the answers for Age problems.
6. The methods of fraction, ratio and % can be transferred to each other.

Basic fraction to solve Age problems

The following demonstrates that we can use the basic property of fractions to solve age problems.

1. Equivalent fraction concept.
2. When a number is added or subtracted to numerator or denominator, then the difference of the numerator and dominator will not be changed. This property can be used to solve age problems since the difference between the ages of two people will not be changed.

Example 1

$\frac{11+x}{41+x} = \frac{3}{8}$, find out what is x?

This problem can be solved by using algebraic cross-multiplication to solve x. We like to demonstrate an idea that is to transfer the learned knowledge of a fraction reducing the concept to solve it.

The new fraction $\frac{3}{8}$ is a simplified fraction from $\frac{11+x}{41+x}$. so, the new difference is now 5 (8 − 3), but it was 41 -11 = 30, so it was reduced by a common factor of 6 (30 ÷ 5). To get back the original, resulting fraction, $3 \times 6 = 18, 18 - 11 = 7$ So x =7.

This above fraction problem can be easily changed to an age problem.

Jocelyn is 11 years old, and her mother is 41 years old. In how many years later, will the age ratio of Jocelyn to her mother be 3:8?

The age difference is constant. $41 - 11 = 30$

$\frac{30}{8-3} = 6$ years for each ratio unit.

$30 \div 5 = 6$ This is the common factor in reducing the number of $11 + x$ to 3.

$11 + x = 18$
$x = 7$ years later.

Practice

$\frac{53+x}{263+x} = \frac{2}{7}$, find out what is x?

Find the ratio difference.
$263-53=210, 7 - 2 = 5$

Find the ratio unit.
$210 \div 5 = 42$

Work backwards.
$42 \times 2 = 84, 42 \times 7 = 294, 84 - 53 = \mathbf{31}$

Example 2

$\frac{11+x}{37+x} = \frac{8}{21}$, find out what is x?

5

Example 3

$\frac{11+x}{36+x} = \frac{1}{2}$, find out what is x?

14

Example 4

Basic Problem	Enrichment problem	Enrichment problem
What number shall be added to the numerator and denominator of $\frac{7}{37}$ such that the result of a new fraction will be $\frac{7}{22}$? It does not matter what number is added to the numerator or denominator. The difference will still be $37 - 7 = 30$. Now the difference of new fraction is $22 - 7 = 15$, so we know the new difference was simplified by a common factor of 2 ($30 \div 15 = 2$) after a new number was added to top and bottom. The original new fraction must be $\frac{14}{44}$. $14 - 7 = 7$ so that 7 shall be added.	**Jim is 5 years old, and his father is 35. In how many years will his father be three times as old as Jim's age?** Method 1 –The age difference will not change, the same method as the left problem. The difference of fraction (It means the difference of age which will always be the same.) will always be $35 - 5 = 30$, but now it has changed from 30 to 2 (3-1), so we know the new fraction has been reduced by a common factor of 15 ($30 \div .2$) The original new fraction is $\frac{1 \times 15}{3 \times 15} = \frac{15}{45}$, $15 - 5 = 10$ years later. Method 2 – Use ratio The age difference is always 30, and when the unit difference is 2 (3 times – 1 time). Each unit is $30 \div 2 = 15$. $15 - 5 = 10$. Method 3 – Use algebra	Jim is 9 years old, and his father is 33. In how many years will his father be three times as old as Jim's age? Method 1 –The age difference will not change, the same method as the left problem. $\dfrac{9 + x}{33 + x} = \dfrac{1}{3}$ $33 - 9 = 24$ $\dfrac{24}{3 - 1} = 12$ $\dfrac{1}{3} = \dfrac{12}{36}$ $12 - 9 = 3$ Method 2 – Use ratio Method 3 Use algebra

Sum and Difference to solve the more complicated problem

Basic sum and difference model	Complicated problem
Adam and Bob had 212 apples together, and Adam had 80 more apples than Bob. Find out how many apples did each of them have? Bob = 66 apples Adam =146 apples	**A sequence consists of 2010 terms. Each term after the first is 1 larger than the previous term. The sum of the 2010 terms is 5307. What is the sum when every second term is added up, starting from the first term and ending with the second last term?** (Modified from 2010 Pascal math contest.) The problem is really asking what the sum of all odd numbers is when the sum of all numbers is 5307. The student must know how to get the difference, and this can be done by using a small sample to find out. The sum difference between even numbers and odd numbers is the $\frac{the\ number\ of\ terms}{2}$. (Use 1, 2, 3, 4, 5, 6 or 2, 3, 4, 5, 6, 7 to figure this out.) There are even-numbered terms of 2010. Started with the odd number 1, 2, 3, 4, 5, 6 the difference between (1,3,5) and (2, 4, 6) is $\frac{\#\ of\ terms}{2}$. Start with eve number 2, 3, 4, 5 6 (246), (2,3,5) (The difference is still $\frac{\#\ of\ terms}{2}$. It does not matter if the sequence starts with an even number or odd number; the even-numbered term is always one bigger than the odd-numbered terms. Therefore, the sum of the even-numbered terms is 1005 greater than the sum of odd-numbered terms. The sum is in 5307 — the difference between. So, we use the Sum and Difference to get the sum of odd numbers. $\frac{5307-1005}{2} = 2151$

Ho Math Chess 何数棋谜 奥数,解题策略,及 IQ 思唯训练宝典

Frank Ho, Amanda Ho © 1995 - 2020

Student's name: _____   Assignment date: _____

From a whole number to decimal, fraction, percent, and ratio 從正整数至分数及百分比

Whole number Grade 1 and above	Decimal Grade 3 and above	Fraction and % Grade 5 and above
60 people surveyed were women, and 20 of them were under 21. How many people surveyed were women and under the age of 21?	0.6 of the people surveyed were women, and 0.3 of them were under 21. What part of people surveyed were women and under 21?	$\frac{3}{5}$ of people surveyed were women, $\frac{3}{10}$ of the women were fewer than 21. What percent of people surveyed were women and under 21?

Whole numbers Jocelyn has triple as many white blocks as black blocks. The number of red blocks is four more than the number of white blocks. How many blocks of each colour are there?	White = 15 Black = 5 Red = 4 = 25 = 19
Adam ate $\frac{2}{5}$ of his apples, and he had 36 apples left. How many apples did he have in the beginning?	$36 \times \frac{5}{3} = 60$
Fraction Adam had $\frac{2}{3}$ more apples than Bob, but if Adam gave 150 apples to Bob, then they each had an equal number of apples. How many apples did each of them have in the beginning?	The difference is $150 \times 2 = 300$ $300 \times \frac{3}{1} = 900$
Fraction On Monday, Adam sold 10 more than half of all his apples. On Tuesday, he sold 20 more than half of the remaining apples, and there were 90 apples left. How many apples did he have at the start of Monday?	

Decimal Jocelyn bought an ice cream cone for \$2.50 and spent double that amount on lunch, and she then spent \$2.50 playing games. If she had \$4.95 left, how much did she have in the beginning?	$4.95 + 5 + 2.5 = 12.45$
Percent Bob ate 35% of his apples, and he had 260 apples left. How many apples did he have in the beginning?	$$260 \div 0.65 = 260 \times \frac{100}{65} = 260 \times \frac{100}{65}$$ $= 400$
Sum and Multiplier Adam's apples are 5 more than three times of Bob's apples. Together they had 169 apples. How many apples did each of them have in the beginning?	$169 - 5 = 164$ $\frac{164}{4} = 41$ ...... Bob Adam $= 41 \times 3 + 5 = 128$
Percent After 20% of the taxes, Steven bought his notebook for \$139. What was the original price?	$139 \div 1.2 = 115.83$
Ratio The ratio of seated to unseated seats in a classroom is 3 : 2. There were 24 unseated seats in the classroom, how many seats were seated in the classroom?	$S : U = 3 : 2$ $\quad = x : 24$ $x = 36$
Ratio There are 15 more girls than boys in Jim's class, and the ratio of the number of girls to the numbers of boys is 5 to 2. How many boys and how many girls are in Jim's class?	$\frac{15}{5-2} = 5$ Girls $= 5 \times 5 = 25$ Boys $= 5 \times 2 = 10$
Ratio Adrian won Anderson 40% more in all their chess matches. Adrian won 24 more games than Anderson. How many matches did they play?	They played $24 \div 0.4 = 60$ matches.

When there are no obvious clues on how to solve word problems

I remember when I was teaching my son Andrew chess, he was quite good at book opening lines, so other experienced adult players tried to take him out of book lines. The purpose of playing non-book lines is, of course, to bring the competition to a level playing field so Andrew cannot rely on his pet openings. In contrast, often, math contests will have a few problems which are not related to specific model problems or having any clear strategies. It means the contest problems presenter(s) purposely create some problems to see if students are able to solve them in a situation that they have never seen similar problems before or have had some experiences of working on them.

There are three types of data that bother elementary students a lot, and they are fractions, decimals, and percents. Fortunately, there is a powerful technique or strategy which can be used to solve most of these applications problems in fractions, decimals, or percentage. To understand this method, students need to learn a math term called **Fractional Number** and the strategy of working backwards. It also involves the concept of the meaning of 1 or 100%. This method is called the **Corresponding Method**. Once the students understand the idea of the Corresponding Method, then many problems such as the following three models of solving percent problems can be easily solved, and so are many other word problems involving three types of data.

Model 1: What is $33\frac{1}{3}$% of $\frac{99}{101}$?

$\frac{33}{101}$

Model 2: What % is 0.11111... of 909?

8181

Model 3: 102 is what % of $\frac{1}{7}$?

71400%

Corresponding Method

The corresponding is always to look for a quantity and then find its corresponding fractional number to match it. Often the quantity is divided by its corresponding fractional number to get the original number (In a fraction, this is the concept of 1. In %, it is the concept of 100%, and in algebra, it is the concept of x.). For example, 20% of what number is 100? In this case, we use 100 (the quantity) divided by its corresponding fractional number 20%, the answer is $100 \div 0.2 = 500$. The Corresponding Method is very powerful when using it in solving fractions backwards problems.

For example, Eric spent $\frac{1}{4}$ of his money and had \$999 left. How much did he have in the beginning? You can solve this problem by using multiple steps, but in math contest, the one statement is very quick to get answer $999 \div (1 - \frac{1}{4}) = 999 \times \frac{4}{3} = 1332$.

A line segment diagram can be used to illustrate the concept of the Corresponding Method.

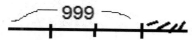

The Corresponding Method teaches *partial ÷ fractional number = whole*.

How to solve the above problem in algebra?

Let Eric's original money $= x$.

$$x - \frac{x}{4} = 999$$

$$x(1 - \frac{1}{4}) = 999$$

$$x = 999 \div (1 - \frac{1}{4})$$

$$= 1332$$

We can see, from the above, very clearly, the Corresponding Method is a short-cut method before using algebra, and yet it is even more powerful than using the algebraic method if the student can understand it by using the line segment to analyze.

Student's name: _____ Assignment date: _____

Fractional Number (Chinese call this 分率)

The concept of Fractional number is extensively used in Chinese math contest books.
A **fractional number** can be defined as a number that can be written in the form of $\frac{p}{q}$. The difference between a **fractional number** and a **rational number** is the denominator (q) of a fractional number can be zero but in this case the meaning of $\frac{p}{q}$ is not division but a ratio.

In elementary school math, when a notation of $\frac{p}{q}$ is written, it could mean a lot of different math concepts and the real meaning is only known until it is explained. For example, $\frac{p}{q}$ could be $\frac{3}{2}$, $\frac{3}{2}, \frac{3}{0}, \frac{0}{2}, \frac{3}{3}$. A fractional number could be division, or just a fraction, ratio, rate.

How to find a fractional number?

Use unit 1 or 100% as the standard value and then find the fractional number from the standard value.

%	fraction	ratio
The interest has gone up 10%. The new interest rate is _____. 110%	The stock price increased $\frac{1}{3}$ of its original price on day 1 and on day 2, it dropped 20% of day 1 price and the closing price at the end of day 2 was _____ (Leave an answer in a fraction.) $$\frac{4}{3} \times 0.8 = 1\frac{1}{15}$$	Every 3 girls there are 2 boys. If there are 5 children, then how many boys will be there? _____ 2 What is the fractional number of the boy? _____ $\frac{2}{5}$ What is the fractional number of the girl? _____ $\frac{3}{5}$
The interest has gone down 10%. The new interest rate is _____. 90%	The stock price dropped 10% and then dropped 10 % again. The new price is what % of the old price? $1 \times 0.9 \times 0.9 = 0.81 = 81\%$	
The tax rate is 25% of the purchase price. The new purchase price in % is _____. 125%		

Example

Grace spent her money as follows:

Day 1: $\frac{1}{3}$

Day 2: $\frac{1}{4}$ of the remaining of day 1.

Day 3: $\frac{1}{5}$ of the remaining of day 2, and she had $250 left.

How much did Grace have originally?

Arithmetic	Algebra
Draw a line segment diagram and use one statement to solve it. Use one statement. $= 250 \times \frac{5}{4} \times \frac{4}{3} \times \frac{3}{2}$ $= 625$ Using three steps: $250 \div \frac{4}{5} = 312.5$ $312.5 \div \frac{3}{4} = 416$ $416 \div \frac{4}{5} = 625$ In this case, the one statement is better than the multi-step method because the fractions can be reduced with no intermediate decimal results.	

The importance of a fractional number is to match it with a quantity.

Grace read 40 pages on the first day and 35 pages on the second day and the remaining pages left was $\frac{1}{4}$ of the whole book. How many pages had not been read? $75 \div \frac{3}{4} - 75 = 25$	Grace read 40 pages on the first day and 35 pages on the second day. The total number of pages read 25% of the entire book. How many pages had not been read? $75 \times 4 - 75 = 225$	Grace read 40 pages on the first day and 80 pages on the second day. The number of pages left unread was 75% less than the number of pages already read. How many pages had not been read? This is very similar to the Sum and Difference model problem. If the original number of pages is 100%, then the number of % left is 25%. It means 75% corresponds to 120 pages. $120 \div 0.75 = 160$

Problem

The number of concert tickets sold was 232 more than the unsold tickets. The unsold tickets are $\frac{4}{7}$ less than the number of sold tickets. How many tickets were there for sold and unsold altogether?

We can think about this problem as a Discount problem. $232 \div \frac{4}{7} = 406$, which is the number of sold tickets (like the original price in the Discount problem.)

Sold number of tickets = $406 \times \frac{3}{7} = 174$

Unsold number of tickets = $174 + 406 = 580$

Adam and Bob are to drive towards each other at the same time in 468 km. Adam's driving speed is 52 km/hour and is $\frac{1}{5}$ slower than Bob. How far had they each driven when they met?

Bob's speed = $52 \div \left(1 - \frac{1}{5}\right) = 65$

$\frac{468}{65 + 52} = 4$

$52 \times 4 = 208$ *Adam's distance*

$65 \times 4 = 260$ *Bob's distance*

Jenny spent 20% of her entire pay and $100 extra in the first week. The second week Jenny spent $250 more than the first week. She had $500 left. How much did she have originally?

$\frac{500 + 250 + 100 + 100}{0.6} = 3250$

The first week spent 0.2 of 1 whole (or unit 1) + $100

The second week spent 0.2 of 1 whole (or unit 1) + 100 + $250

Finally, there was $500 left.

All candy and box weighed 550 g. After $\frac{10}{17}$ of candy had been eaten, the box and the remaining candy weighed 250 g. How much does the candy and box each weighs originally?

The candy eaten was $\frac{10}{17}$ which corresponds to the amount of candy 300 (550-250)

The original amount of candy $= 300 \div \frac{10}{17} = 510$

The box weighs $= 550 - 510 = 40$

The first time, $\frac{2}{5}$ of a bucket was filled with water. After more water was poured into the bucket the second time, the bucket had filled up with water up to 13 l, and at this point, the bucket would be totally full if 12 l more water was poured. How much water was poured into the bucket the second time?

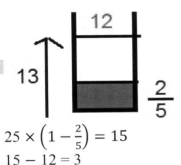

$25 \times \left(1 - \frac{2}{5}\right) = 15$

$15 - 12 = 3$

Student's name: _____   Assignment date: _____

A fraction is a bridge from arithmetic to algebra

Often when parents bring their middle grades children to me for an assessment, I like to test their fraction manipulation ability. There is one simple reason for this that is fraction is the most confusing notation in elementary school math, but it serves as an important bridge between arithmetic and algebra.

The following table gives a contrast on how important it is to understand fractions and be very skilful in fraction manipulation.

Arithmetic fraction	Algebra rational expression
$\dfrac{1}{2} + \dfrac{1}{3}$	$\dfrac{1}{2x} + \dfrac{1}{3x}$
$\dfrac{1}{2} + \dfrac{1}{3} + 1$	$\dfrac{1}{2x} + \dfrac{1}{3x} + x$
$\dfrac{1}{2} \times 6$	$\dfrac{1}{2} \times 6x$

Example

Arithmetic fraction	Algebra rational expression
Simplify $1 - \dfrac{1}{1 - \dfrac{1}{1 - \dfrac{1}{\frac{2-1}{2}}}}$	Simplify $1 - \dfrac{1}{1 - \dfrac{1}{1 - \dfrac{1}{\frac{x-1}{x}}}}$

Student's name: _____   Assignment date: _____

Fraction factoring

One area which is lacking in elementary math curriculum is factoring in which students are required to the concept to work on rational expressions and equations, so the training of working on fractional factoring is very important.

The Corresponding Method can be used to solve many fractions, ratios, and percents problems, but there are also other strategies that could be considered if no clues can be found.

1. Do not just look at the computation problems from left to right in a sequential manner.
    See Example 12.

2. Look for a pattern.
    Before you can see a pattern, you must patiently list all possible results and observe the pattern rule. The student must know how to calculate the sum of the arithmetic series to get sum (Gauss sum).
    See example 3.

3. Use a simpler case.
    Use a small sample size to figure the pattern formula. For example, you can use a smaller sample size to figure the probability problem for a large sample size. See example 10.

4. Look for answers indirectly.
    For example, to get congruent triangles first to get corresponding equal angles. See example 1.

5. Look at problems from different angles.
    For example, to convert ratios to fractions. See example 6.

6. Think out of the box.

See example 2 below.

To be able to solve some problems which have no model problems to follow, no apparent strategies to use, students can reach the highest level of ability to solve math contests problems. When working on these types of word problems, students must have possessed solid basic math contests concepts, know how to use different strategies under what conditions, know how to transfer a problem to another problem in such a way that student may be able to use a known method to him or her to solve it.

This technique of transferring a chess opening to some lines that Andrew is familiar with or comfortable with was often used by him, and sometimes his opponent was not aware of it.

Example 1

The following needs two moves to checkmate the black king, so the first move simply is to assist, not a direct attack. Show your moves by drawing lines.

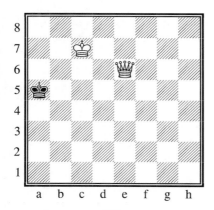

Example 2
Circle the following piece on the left column
which fits together with the piece given in the right column?

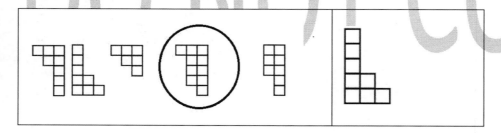

Example 3
Observe the following table and find the answer to the question?

1	1
3	4
5	9
7	16
9	25
11	36
99	?

The answer is 2500 and shows how you get it.

Student's name: _____   Assignment date: _____

Example 4

Cindy and Veena took turns, dividing a bag of apples. Veena took out odd number of apples every time which means she took out apples in the sequence of 1, 3, 5, 7, Cindy took out even number of apples every time which means she took out apples in the sequence of 2, 4, 6,8 …. When all apples had been divided, Veena had ten fewer apples then Cindy. How many apples did each girl have, and how many apples were in the bag originally when they started?

Method 1 – Use formula

$$\frac{2+2+(n-1)2}{2} \times n - \frac{1+1+(n-1)2}{2} \times n = 10$$

Method 2 – Use table

	1	2	3	4	5	6	7	8	9	10
Veena	1	4	9	16	25	36	49	64	81	100
Cindy	2	6	12	20	30	42	56	72	96	110

Example 5

Calculate

$$\frac{1+2+3+4+5+6+7+8+9+8+7+6+5+4+3+2+1}{999999999 \times 999999999}$$

$$\frac{1}{12345678987654321}$$

Example 6

Calculate
$$\frac{1}{2} + \frac{1}{4} + \frac{1}{8} + \frac{1}{16} + \frac{1}{32} + \frac{1}{64} + \frac{1}{128}$$

You can use LCD to solve it, or you can use 0 property to solve it. By adding one $\frac{1}{128}$ and then subtract $\frac{1}{128}$, then the answer will not change. 2 of $\frac{1}{128} = \frac{1}{64}$, 2 of $\frac{1}{64} = \frac{1}{32}$. Keeping adding by using the double additions, we can get 1.

The final answer $= 1 - \frac{1}{128} = \frac{127}{128}$.

$$\frac{127}{128}$$

Practice

Calculate
$$\frac{1}{2} + \frac{3}{4} + \frac{7}{8} + \frac{15}{16} + \frac{31}{32} + \frac{63}{64} + \frac{127}{128}$$

$$6\frac{1}{256}$$

Example 7

There are three distinct non-zero digits. All possible three-digit numbers are made of these 3 digits, and their sum is 1332. What is the largest 3-digit number out of all these numbers?

3 different non-zero digits can make 6 numbers. So, the average of 1332 is $1332 \div 6 = 222$. This means $\frac{2(100a+10b+c)}{6} = 222$, so $\frac{(100a+10b+c)}{3} = 222$, It means $a = b = c = 6$, so the three digits are 1, 2, and 3. The largest is 321.

Example 8

The sum of four reciprocals of 4 consecutive natural number is $\frac{19}{20}$. What is the total of all products of each natural number multiplied by every one of other numbers?

The 4 consecutive natural numbers give a lot of hints. W can get the 4 consecutive natural numbers from 20. But $\frac{19}{20}$ maybe a reduced fraction, so if we cannot get 4 consecutive numbers from 20, then we must try to get the 4 consecutive numbers from the multiple of 20 such as 40, 60 etc. We cannot get from 20 and 40. 60 but we can get from 60, $60 = = 2 \times 2 \times 3 \times 5$ which gives 4 numbers 2, 3, 4, and 5 or 3, 4, 5, and 6.

$$\frac{1}{2} + \frac{1}{3} + \frac{1}{4} + \frac{1}{5} = \frac{30+20+15+12}{60} = \frac{77}{60}$$

$$\frac{1}{3} + \frac{1}{4} + \frac{1}{5} + \frac{1}{6} = \frac{20+15+12+10}{60} = \frac{57}{60} = \frac{19}{20}$$

The sum of products $= (3 \times 4) + (3 \times 5) + (3 \times 6) + (4 \times 5) + (4 \times 6) + (5 \times 6) = 119$

Example 9

A sequence of natural numbers starting from 1 to n, what is its sum?

You may have to use the result of the above problem to get the answer to the following problem.

After one number was removed from a list of consecutive natural numbers starting from 1, the average of the remaining numbers is $35\frac{7}{17}$. What is the removed number?

By looking at the fraction, it appears 17 is the number of divisors, but it may not be since the fraction is reduced, so it must be a multiple of 17. The number of natural numbers after removing one of them must be 17, 34, 51, 68, …. (appears in a sequence of odd, even, odd even…)

1. A sum divided by $17a$ its remainder is $7a$, and its quotient is 35, what is the number? The number is $35 \times 17a + 7a = 602a$, Now the question becomes if 602 a sum of a list of natural numbers starting from 1? It is nice that we know the natural numbers starting from 1 so we can try to see if any sum, which will add up to a bit above 602. $\frac{1+l}{2} \times l > 602$, $l = 36$. Plug in, and we get sum 666. 666-602=58, which is not right for the removed number. So, it means we must try $a = 2$. There will be many trials to get the right answer. Is there any other method?

2. The odd and even sequence offers some clue here. Will the original number of terms be odd or even? How can we find it out? The sum of the original terms is $\frac{1+n}{2} \times n$ and its average is $\frac{1+n}{2}$ but if n is odd, then we get an average number, and if n is even, we get the average as a fraction which

n terms	sum	average	Difference in average
n terms	$\dfrac{1+n}{2} \times n$	$\dfrac{1+n}{2} = \dfrac{n}{2} + \dfrac{1}{2}$	
$(n-1)$ terms after removing the largest term	$\dfrac{1+n-1}{2} \times (n-1) = \dfrac{n(n-1)}{2}$	$\dfrac{n}{2}$	N term –(n-1) term $\dfrac{1}{2}$
$(n-1)$ terms after removing the smallest term which is 1	$\dfrac{2+n}{2} \times (n-1)$	$\dfrac{2+n}{2} = \dfrac{n}{2} + 1$	N term –(n-1) term $-\dfrac{1}{2}$

3. Now we know the original average of n terms after removing one term is $35\frac{7}{17} - \frac{1}{2} \le$ *original average* $\le 35\frac{7}{17} + \frac{1}{2}$ so the original average must be between 35 and 35.5.

4. $\frac{n}{2} + \frac{1}{2} = 35, n = 69,$ *The removed term is* $\frac{69 \times 70}{2} - 35\frac{7}{17} \times 68 = \mathbf{7}$

5. $\frac{n}{2} + \frac{1}{2} = 35, n = 70,$ *The removed term is not a whole nuber so no solution for* $n = 70.$

Example 10

How many numbers are there if two non-repeating digits are selected from 1, 2, 3, and 4? What is the sum of all these numbers?

There are 12 numbers if two non-repeating digits are selected from 1, 2, 3, and 4.
12 13 14 21 23 24 31 32 34 41 42 43
The tens place has 1, and there are 3 different numbers.
The tens place has 2, and there are 3 different numbers.
The tens place has 3, and there are 3 different numbers.
The tens place has 4, and there are 3 different numbers.

The above pattern repeats for the ones place too for digits 1, 2, 3, and 4
So, the total is $(1 + 2 + 3 + 4) \times 3 \times 10 +$ is $(1 + 2 + 3 + 4) \times 3 = 300+30=330$

Practice

How many numbers are there if 4 non-repeating digits are selected from 1, 2, 3, 4, 5, 6, 7, 8, and 9? What is the sum of all these numbers?

So, the total is $(1 + 2 + 3 + 4 + 5 + 6 + 7 + 8 + 9) \times 336 \times (1000 + 100 + 10 + 1)$
$=16798320$

Problem

Select 4-digit numbers from 1000 to 9999 such that the absolute value of the difference between the thousands place digit and the ones place of digit each number is 2. How many numbers are there?

The thousands place and ones place digit can be 20, 13, 24, 35, 46, 57, 68, 79
For 20, there are $1 \times 8 \times 7 \times 1 = 56$ numbers. For all others, there are $1 \times 8 \times 7 \times$
2 (*switch thousands and ones digit*) $\times$ 7 sets$=784$, $784 + 56 =$**840**

The area of each small square is 2cm² in the following figure, find the shaded area.

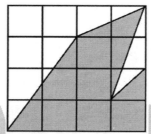 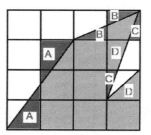

Move A to A, B to B, C to C, and D is equal to D. You will get 18 cm².

In an investing club, the total of ages of members ranging from 30 to 79 is 4476. No more than 3 members have the same age. At least how many members are 60 and older?

If we get the number of how many people less than 60, then we might be able to figure how many people are 60 and over.

The sum of 30 to 59 is $\frac{30+59}{2} \times 30 = 15 \times 89 = 1335$

No more than three people have the same age, and since the answer wants, "at least," so, we try to get at most for members who are less than 60. $1335 \times 3 = 4005$, 4476-4005=471.

471 is the age sum of members form 60 and over, and we want the least members, so it means we want older members to lower the number of members.

60	79	
	6	$79 \times 6 = 474$ which is over 471
	5	$79 \times 5 = 395$, 471-395=76 **There are 6 people who are o**
	4	$79 \times 4 = 316$, 471-316= 155=78+77
7		$60 \times 7 = 420$, 474-420= 54 which is less than 60.
8		$60 \times 8 = 480$ Which is over 471,
6		$60 \times 6 = 360$, $471 - 360 = 111$ which is over 79,

Student's name: _____   Assignment date: _____

The following table gives a breakdown of term marks of students. Find the number of students whose term marks are from 70 to 79.

The marks of each group of students	Total number of students (x)is $200 < x < 300$	The fraction of each group students out of total students
90 - 100	?	$\frac{1}{7}$
80 - 89	?	$\frac{1}{5}$
70 - 79	?	$\frac{1}{3}$
< 70	?	?

$1 - \frac{1}{7} - \frac{1}{5} - \frac{1}{3}) = \frac{34}{105}$

It means a number must be a common multiple of 7, 5, and 3, and 105 but larger than 200. It is 210.

$210) \times (1 - \frac{1}{7} - \frac{1}{5} - \frac{1}{3}) = \mathbf{68}$

A trapezoid has an area of 1400 m2. The height of it is 50 m, and its top base and the bottom base are all whole numbers with their total divisible by 8. Find out what the possible values of the top and bottom are?

7 = 1+6=2+5=3+4

What abilities shall a math contesting student possess?

- A very strong desire to do well and is a self-motivator
- Has excellent analytical ability with great patience.
- Has an excellent ability to recall a repertoire of previously learned knowledge and apply them to good use?
- Has excellent visualization and be keen ability to observe the pattern and find out pattern rules.
- Has excellent ability to create a table or list all possible outcomes.
- Know very well on how to find out computation tricks to do fast computing.
- Has excellent ability in using a smaller sample to figure out complicated problems.
- Knows very well on when to use formulas when needs arise.
- Has an excellent and reasonable strategy and a very clear direction on how to tackle problems and is be able to adjust when getting stuck.

Part C – Computations and other word problems 数的基本功及其他文字应用题

Ho Math Chess workbooks are created to reach or match the highest math standard in many countries, including some countries that consistently rank high on international math tests. This section is a collection of a variety of word problems to meet students' challenges. More problems can be found in the series of Ho Math Chess contests workbooks.

Standard and expanded form representations for decimals 标準式及展開式塊條形式

Standard form	Block representation?		Expanded form?
1.23	answer		$1 + 0.2 + 0.03$
123	answer		100+20+3
3	answer		3
0.3	answer		0.3

Decimal	fraction	%
0.01	$\frac{1}{100}$?	1% ?
?	$1\frac{1}{2}$	150% ?
0.1	? $\frac{1}{10}$	? 10%
$0.\overline{1}$	$\frac{1}{9}$ answer ?	$\frac{100}{9}\%$?

Speedy multiplication 心算

$2 \times 8 \times 25 \times 5 =$
10 x 200 = 2000

$150 \times 15 \times 84 \times 1505 \times 5 =$

= 2250 x 21 x 2 x 2 x 5 x 5
= 2250 x 21 x 10 x 10
= 225000 x 7 x 3
= 1575000 x 3
= 4725000

$50 \times 2 \times 100 \times 5 \times 20 =$
= 100 x 100 x 100
= 1,000,000

$18 \times 4 \times 2 \times 100 \times 25 =$

= 36 x 100 x 100
= 360000

$15 \times 35 \times 2 \times 4 =$

= 70 x 60
= 4200

Speedy division 心算

It is easier for the students to get a solution if the horizontal format is converted to the vertical format.

$100 \times 13 \div 25 \div 4 + 10 \times 3 \div 2 \div 5$

16

$35 \div 2 \div 5 \times 100$

350

$36 \div 25 \times 100 + 100 \div 3 \times 300$

10144

$2000 \div 2 \div 5 \div 8 \div 2$

20

$1000 \times 15 \div 8 \div 125$

15

$125 \times 3 \div 25 \times 100$

1500

$375 \times 13 \div 25 \times 6$

1170

$231 \times 10 \div 11 \times 2$

105

$45 \times 13 \div 9$

65

Student's name: _____ Assignment date: _____

Clever computation 巧算

$10 - 5.98 = 10 + 6 -$ _____ $=$ _____ .	$11.98, 4.02$
$10 - 7.865 = 9.999 - 7.865 +$ _____ $=$ _____	**0.001** $= 2.134 + 0.001 = $**2.135**
$10 - 5.499 = 9.999 - 5.499 +$ _____	$0.001 = 4.5 + 0.001 = 4.501$
$10 - 8.888 = 9.999 - 8.888 +$ _____	$0.001 = 1.111 + 0.001 = 1.112$
Write 2.79813 in expanded form. $2 + 0.7 + 0.09 + 0.008 + 0.0001 + 0.00003$	
Write 27.9813 in expanded form. $27 + 0.9 + 0.08 + 0.001 + 0.0003$	

Evaluate by rearranging so to make the calculation easier.

$6.47 + 1.51 + 0.19 - 1.37 - 1.43 - 5.47$

$6.47 - 1.37 + 1.51 + 0.29 - 1.43 - 5.47$

$= 5.30 + 1.70 - 6.90 = 7 - 6.9 = 0.1$

Evaluate by rearranging so to make calculation easier.

$64 \times 2.5 \times 0.125 \times 4 \times 8$

$64 \times 2.5 \times 4 \times 0.125 \times 8 = 64 \times 10 \times 1 = 640$

Evaluate by rearranging so to make calculation easier.

$-397 + 97 = -300$

$9723 - 397 + 97 = 9723 - 300 = 9423$

$0.875 + 0.125 = 1$

$3.98 - 0.875 - 0.125 = 3.98 - 1 = 2.98$

Calculate (Leave answers in simplified fraction)

$1 \div 4 \div 6 = \dfrac{1}{4 \times 6} = \dfrac{1}{24}$

$7.2 \div 4 \div 6 = \dfrac{7.2}{4 \times 6} = = \dfrac{72}{240} = \dfrac{3}{10}$

$125 = \dfrac{1000}{\Box} = \dfrac{1000}{8}$ (Replace box by a number.) 25

$32000 \div 125 = 32000 \times \dfrac{1000}{8} = 4,000,000$

Calculate.
$13789 \times 1111 = 13789 \times (1000 + 100 + 10 + 1)$
$= 13789000 + 1378900 + 137890 + 13789 = 15319579$

Calculate.
$8888 \times 9999.$
$= 8888 \times (10000 - 1)$
$= 88880000 - 8888 = 88871112$

Calculate.
$600 = \underline{\hspace{2cm}} - 1 \quad 601$
$89 = 90 - \underline{\hspace{1.5cm}} \quad 1$

$7 \times 699 + 7 \times 89$
$= 7 (699 + 89) = 7 \times 788 = 5516$

Computation in queen's 8 directions 计算皇后的 8 个方向

If 2 W + 4 B = 24 find the different values which satisfy the equation.

W	B

(2, 5) (4, 4) (6, 3) (8, 2)

Basics Computing	Thinking skills
$\dfrac{1}{2} + \dfrac{1}{3} = \dfrac{5}{6}$	Convert to the same measuring unit.
♘ + ♕ = -12	White knight and white queen assume to carry negative signs.
$3 + 2 = 1$	Light **2** is - 2. (We can use light coloured number for negative number.)
♕ + ♗ = 6	White bishop carries the minus sign.
$\dfrac{1}{2} + \dfrac{1}{3} = \dfrac{5}{6}$	
$\dfrac{1}{2} + \dfrac{1}{3} = \dfrac{1}{6}$	Light $\dfrac{1}{3}$ carries minus sign.
- (+3) = **-3**	
- dark **3** = **-3**	
- light **3** = **3**	

Student's name: _____ Assignment date: _____

List all points. A, B, C	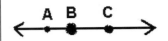
List all line segments. AB, AC, BC	
List all lines. AB, AC, BC	
List all rays. AB, BA, AC, CA, BC, CB	
Rank all points. None, all points have no sizes.	

Student's name: _____ Assignment date: _____

Basics Computing	Thinking skills
$x+\dfrac{1}{3}=2$, $\frac{5}{3}$	✛ Computing from left to right.
$3=x+\dfrac{1}{2}$, $\frac{5}{2}$	✛ Computing from right to left.
$\dfrac{3}{x}=\dfrac{0.5}{2}$, 12	⤢ Cross-multiplication.
$\dfrac{\dfrac{1}{1+\dfrac{1}{2}}}{\dfrac{3}{2}}$, $\frac{4}{9}$	⬌ Computing from top to down.
$\dfrac{1}{1+\dfrac{1}{1+\dfrac{1}{2}}}$, $\dfrac{3}{5}$	⬌ Computing from bottom to up.
$24\times\dfrac{1}{2}=12$	✕ Computing diagonally.
$48\times\dfrac{2}{3}=32$	✕ Computing diagonally.

$\dfrac{1}{\text{⤢}} + \dfrac{2}{\text{⬌}} = \dfrac{?}{15}$? shall be 11.	Express result in decimal. $0.2\% + 0.4 + \dfrac{1}{2} = 0.902$
1 m + 20 cm = _____ m = _____ cm = 1.2 m = 120 cm	Express result in fraction. $2\% + \dfrac{1}{100} + 5\%$ $\dfrac{2}{25}$
$0.2 \times 10^3 = 200$	$0.2 \div 10^3 = 0.0002$
$0.2 \times 0.001 = 0.0002$	$0.2 \div 0.001 = 200$
$0.2 \times 1\% = 0.002$	$0.2 \div 1\% = 20$
$0.2 \times 0.5\% = 0.001$	$0.2 \div 0.5\% = 40$
$4 \div 5 = 0.8$	$0.1 \div 0.5 = 0.2$
$4 \div 0.05 = 80$	$0.04 \div 0.05 = 0.8$
Express result in %. $1.1\% + \dfrac{2.02}{100} - \dfrac{1.81}{50} = -0.5\%$	$3 \times (91 + \dfrac{1}{2}) + 2 \times (89 + \dfrac{1}{2}) = 453.5$ ½ shall be 1/3 and the answer shall be 453.

Student's name: _____ Assignment date: _____

$4(21 + \dfrac{1}{4}) + 3(19 + \dfrac{1}{3}) = 143$

$\dfrac{3 \times 10 + 4 \times 10}{10} = \dfrac{10(\quad + \quad)}{10} = 7$ 4, 3

$2 \nwarrow\!\searrow + 3 \updownarrow\!\leftrightarrow = 21$

$4 + 2 = 30$

The pie mass (not including crust) is 75 g, and its crust is $\dfrac{1}{10}$ of the entire pie. What is the

mass of the pie? $\dfrac{x}{10} + 75 = x$, $x = 83\dfrac{1}{3}$

Odd and even numbers 奇偶数

Many students will answer that even numbers are 2, 4, 6, 8, ... etc., but what happens to 1212? Is it even or odd? So, to understand that if the last digit (the rightmost one) of a number is 0, 2, 4, 6, 8, then it is an even number is important. In contrast, if the last digit (the rightmost one) of a number is 1, 3, 5, 7, 9, then it is an odd number.

Circle the following numbers which are even.

2, 14, 13, 29, 24, 102, 0, 100, 231 437, 500, 502, 609, 111, 102, 134

There is a 2-digit number. If the one place digit must be even and the tens place digit must be odd, what could be the largest 2-digit number?

98

How many even numbers are there from 100 to 200 inclusive?

There are 200-100 + 1 = 101 numbers

$\frac{101+1}{2} = $ **52** (Use a small sample 2, 3, 4, 5, 6 to figure out this relationship.)

Is the sum of an even number + an even number odd or even?

even

Is the difference between two even numbers − an even number odd or even?

even

Is the sum of an even number + an odd number odd or even?

odd

Is the sum of an even number − an odd number odd or even?

odd

Is the sum of an odd number + an odd number odd or even?
even

Is the sum of an odd number − an odd number odd or even?
even

Is the produce of an even number × an odd number odd or even?
Even

Student's name: _____ Assignment date: _____

Circle the answer such that $\boxed{}$ is the smallest.

Odd number + odd number = Even or Odd
Even number + even number = Even or Odd

$\bigcirc \times \triangle = 35$

$\bigcirc + \triangle = 2 \times \boxed{}$　　7, 5, 6

$\bigcirc \times \triangle = 48$

$\bigcirc + \triangle = 2 \times \boxed{}$　　8, 6, 7

$\bigcirc \times \triangle = 21$

$\bigcirc + \triangle = 2 \times \boxed{}$　　7, 3, 5

$\bigcirc \times \triangle = 49$

$\bigcirc + \triangle = 2 \times \boxed{}$　　1, 49, 5

$\bigcirc \times \triangle = 27$

$\bigcirc + \triangle = 2 \times \boxed{}$　　3, 9, 6

$\bigcirc \times \triangle = 63$

$\bigcirc + \triangle = 2 \times \boxed{}$　　9, 7, 8

Divisibility rule of 7 的約数

Check to see if the difference of the last digit multiplied by 2 and subtracted from the rest of the number is divisible by 7 or not. Continue the above procedure until the result is either 0 or divisible by 7.

91	$9 - 2 \times 1 = 7$
203	$20 - 3 \times 2 = 14$
22344	Last digit multiply by 2, $4 \times 2 = 8$ Subtracted rest of digits, 2234 - 8 = 2226 Last digit multiply by 2, $6 \times 2 = 12$ Subtracted rest of digits, 222 - 12 = 210 The rest of the number is 2. Divisible by 7, $\frac{21}{7} = 3$
177	Last digit multiply by 2, $7 \times 2 = 14$ Subtracted rest of digits, $17 - 14 = 3$ 3 is not divisible by 7.

Exercise

Is 72429 divisible by 7?

Yes.

Is 25109 divisible by 7?

Yes.

Divisibility rule of 13 的約数

Check to see if the sum of the last digit multiplied by 4 and added to the rest of the number is divisible by 13 or not. Continue the above procedure until the result is either 0 or divisible by 13.

91	$9 + 4 \times 1 = 13$ … yes
949	$94 + 4 \times 9 = 130$ 130 is divisible by 13.
468	$46 + 4 \times 8 = 78$ 78 is divisible by 13.
1768	$176 + 4 \times 8 = 208$ $20 + 4 \times 8 = 52$ 52 is divisible by 13.

Exercise

Is 26897 divisible by 13?

Yes

Is 474852 divisible by 13?

No.

Frank Ho, Amanda Ho © 1995 - 2020　　　　　

Student's name: _____　Assignment date: _____

Estimate 估算

Estimate

$582 \div 18 =$
$= 600 + 20 = 620$

$2347 \div 39 =$
$= 2400 \div 30 = 80$

$3949 \div 10.101 =$
$= 3950 \div 10 = 395$

$275 \div 3.999 =$
$= 270 \div 4 = 75$

$257 \div 5.105 =$
$= 260 \div 5 = 52$

$361 \div 5.888 =$
$= 360 \div 6 = 60$

$299 + 199 + 99 + 999$
$= 300 + 20 + 100 + 1000 = 1600$

Evaluate 计算

Evaluate

$149 \div 10 = \quad 14.9$

$149 \div 100 = \quad 1.49$

$1.49 \div 1000 = \quad 0.0149$

$149 \times 10 = \quad 1490$

$1.49 \times 100 = 149$

$1.49 \times 0.01 = 0.0149$

$1.2 \times \underline{\quad\quad} = 12000$
10000

$12 \div \underline{\quad\quad} = 0.012 \quad\quad 1000$

$1.2 \div \underline{\quad\quad} = 0.0012 \quad\quad 1000$

$12 \times \underline{\quad\quad} = 12000 \quad\quad 1000$

$0.12 \times \underline{\quad\quad} = 12000$
1200000

$275 + 248 + 425 + 752 =$
$= 300 + 250 + 400 + 750$
$= 1700$

Ho Math Chess 何数棋谜 奥数,解题策略,及 IQ 思唯训练宝典

Student's name: _____   Assignment date: _____

只见棋谜不见题　劝君迷路不哭涕　数学象棋加谜题　健脑思维眞神奇

Multi-grade multi-level math 多年级多功能计算题---

You are a chess piece located at c3.

	☼	▢	▭	◯	△
Fraction	$\frac{1}{2}$	1	$\frac{1}{2}$	$\frac{4}{4}$	$\frac{3}{4}$
decimal	0.2	0.40	0.8	0.2	0.6
Whole	2	12	22	32	42
%	100%	200%	300%	400%	500%

Whole number

Decimal

Fraction of multiplication and division [Do not need to have the same measuring unit (denominator).]

Fraction of addition and subtraction [Must have the same measuring unit (denominator).]

Percent

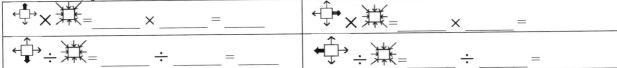

6, 44, 2, 4, ½, 3/2, ½, 2, 4   16, 21, 1, 3, ¼, 1, ¼, 3, 5

Scientific notations 科学符号

Write the following in scientific notation.

$600 = \qquad 6 \times 10^2$

$3000 = \qquad 3 \times 10^3$

$0.000123 = \qquad 1.23 \times 10^{-4}$

$12.3 \times 0.01 \times 100^2 = \qquad 1230 = 1.23 \times 10^3$

Calculation problems in China including factoring common numbers

Many calculation problems in China require advanced skills such as "factoring". This type of problem does not appear in North America.

$4.68 \times 1.1 - 0.468 + 4.68 \times 9 =$
$= 4.68 \times 1.1 - 4.68 \div 10 + 4.68 \times 9$
$= 4.68 (1.1 - 0.1 + 9)$
$= 4.68 (1 + 9)$
$= 46.8$

Multiples 倍数

A number can be multiplied by 1, 2, 3, …etc.. These products are also called multiples. A number has infinite multiples. The results in the times tables from 1×1 to 1×9 are multiples of 1.

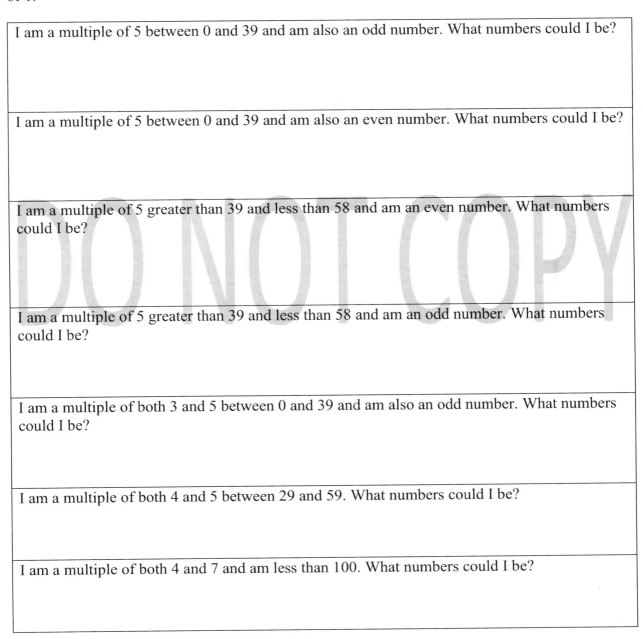

I am a multiple of 5 between 0 and 39 and am also an odd number. What numbers could I be?

I am a multiple of 5 between 0 and 39 and am also an even number. What numbers could I be?

I am a multiple of 5 greater than 39 and less than 58 and am an even number. What numbers could I be?

I am a multiple of 5 greater than 39 and less than 58 and am an odd number. What numbers could I be?

I am a multiple of both 3 and 5 between 0 and 39 and am also an odd number. What numbers could I be?

I am a multiple of both 4 and 5 between 29 and 59. What numbers could I be?

I am a multiple of both 4 and 7 and am less than 100. What numbers could I be?

as ... as 跟 ... 一樣

Kumar has $309. Pauline has twice as much as Kumar. How much does Pauline have?

$618

Kumar has $44. Pauline has half as much as Kumar. How much does Pauline have?

$22

Kumar has 212 marbles. Pauline has 3 less than half as many as Kumar. How many does Pauline have?

103

Kumar has $214. Pauline has $15 more than half as much as Kumar. How much does Pauline have?

$122

Kumar has $129. Pauline has 3 times as much as Kumar. How much does Pauline have?

$387

After Pauline gave $3 to Kumar, then Kumar had $217. Kumar had twice as much as Pauline had before getting $3. How much did Pauline have at the beginning?

$\frac{217-3}{2} = \$107$

Joanne told her mother. "If I had done twice as correct as I answered in the test, I would have 6 more points than I have now.". How many points did Joanne get in the test?

6

Brent rode 15 km to a park and on the way home, he rode three times as far to his uncle's home. How far did he ride to his uncle's house from the park?

45 km

Brent sold 219 raffle tickets. Pauline sold 9 times as many. How many tickets did Pauline sell?

1971 tickets

Pauline and her 4 friends like to share 705 candies equally. How many candies would each person get?

141 candies

Pauline memorizes 23 vocabularies per day. How many vocabularies will she memorize in 25 days?

575 vocabularies

Brent buys lunch meat at $0.99 per 100 g. How much will it cost him if he buys 1.2 kg?
1 kg = 1000 g
$11.88

Brent makes half a much as Pauline per hour. Pauline makes $75 per 5 hours. How much will Brent make in 5 hours?
1.2 kg = 1200 g
$187.50

Pauline finishes reading a book in 10 days. At half of the reading speed, how long will it take Pauline to finish reading the same book?

5 days

Brent runs 15 km per day. At the same rate, how many days would Brent have run if his total distance is 225 km?

15 days

Student's name: _____   Assignment date: _____

Prime 質数

N=1+2+3+4+5+6+…+10.   Find the largest prime factor of N.   The sum is 55, and the largest prime is 11.
N=1+2+3+4+5+6+…+98+99+100.   Find the largest prime factor of N.   The sum is 5050. The largest prime is 101.
Is 13411341 a composite number?   Yes, 1341 x 1001 = 13411341
The sum of 2 primes is 40, what is the largest product of these two primes?   23 x 17=391
The sum of 2 primes is 1995, what is the product of these two primes?   2x1993=3986
N is a prime and N+4, N+6, N+10 are all primes. Find the smallest N?   7
N is a prime and N+6, N+8, N+12, N+14 are all primes. Find the smallest N?   5
Find the sum of all different odd primes that divide 2009.   200 = 7 x 287, 187 = 7 x 41   7+41=**48**

Student's name: _____   Assignment date: _____

Prime numbers

Guide [rook] from a8 to h1 through squares occupied by prime numbers only.

	a	b	c	d	e	f	g	h
8	[rook]	8	3	4	6	18	20	32
7	5	2	4	37	10	8	15	4
6	9	3	7	6	17	18	16	6
5	8	4	2	6	10	23	8	12
4	12	8	11	13	5	15	4	31
3	16	12	16	15	17	18	10	8
2	8	15	37	8	19	29	6	4
1	4	6	16	12	10	31	2	29

Circle the prime number(s).

0, [rook] ,1, [bishop] ,
2, [queen] ,31, [pawn] ,13, [knight] ,97, [king] ,91

After how many terms is the sum $2 + 7 + 16 + 29 + \ldots$ a prime number?

2, 7, 16, 29, 46, 67
6th term
The difference between numbers are 5, 9, 13, 17, 21

The number 13 is a prime. If you reverse the digits, you also obtain a prime number, 31. What is the larger prime of the pair of primes that satisfies this condition and has a sum of 110?

73

Many prime numbers can be expressed as the sum of a prime and twice a square other than zero. For example, $41 = 23 + 2 \times 3^2$. What is the largest prime number less than 25 that cannot be expressed as the sum of a prime and twice a square?

$23 = 5 + 2 \times 3^2$
$19 = 17 + 2 \times 1^2$
17

How many ordered triples of primes (a, b, c) exist such that $a + b + c = 7$?

(2, 2, 3) (2, 3, 2) (3, 2, 2) **3**

How many ordered triples of primes (a, b, c) exist such that $a + b + c = 26$ and $a \leq b \leq c$?

(2, 7, 17) (2, 11, 13) (2, 5, 19)   total **3**

How many prime numbers are there to satisfy $\sqrt{300} < x < \sqrt{700}$ $(17 < x < 26)$?
2
19,23

Units digit 个位数

Find the units digit of the following sum: $2008^4 + 2009^2 + 1010^5$. $6 + 1 = 7$
Find the units digit of the following $2^{2009} + 3^{2009} + 7^{2009} + 8^{2009}$. $2+3+7+9=0$
Find the units digit of the following $419^{209} + 30^9 - 47^9 + 8^{2009}$. $9+0-9+8=8$
Find the units digit of the following $(2009^{2001} + 2010^{2009} + 2011^{2009}) \times 2009^{2009}$. $(9+0+1)9=0$
Find the units digit of the following $2^{20} \times 3^{39}$. $6 \times 7 = 2$
How many zeros at the end of the following product? $1 \times 2 \times 3 \times 4 \ldots \times 8 \times 9 \times 10$ $\left[\frac{10}{5}\right]=2$
How many zeros at the end of the following product? $1 \times 2 \times 3 \times 4 \ldots \times 18 \times 19 \times 20$ $\left[\frac{20}{5}\right]=4$
How many zeros at the end of the following product? $1 \times 2 \times 3 \times 4 \ldots \times 98 \times 99 \times 100$ $\left[\frac{100}{5}\right]= 20, \left[\frac{100}{25}\right]= 4, 20 + 4 = 24$

Counting digits 算数字

From 00 to 99, each digit 0, 1, 2, ….to 9 appears 20 times.

The reason is from 00 to 99. There are 200 digits (100 of 2-digit numbers), and each digit happens to appear the equal number of times, so each digit appears $\dfrac{200}{10} = 20$ times except 0 if leading 0 is not considered as a number. The digit 0 only appears 9 times if leading 0's are not counted. This is a very useful tip for counting digits problems.

Example 1

Count the number of total digits from the numbers 1 to 99.

From 1 to 9, there are 9 digits.
From 10 to 99, there are 2 digits $\times$ (99-10+1) = 180 digits.
From 100 to 199, there are 3 digits $\times$ $(199 - 100 + 1) = 300$ digits.

Example 2

If 492 digits are used to assign lockers to students starting from locker number 1, how many lockers could be assigned with 492 digits used in total?

lockers	Number of lockers	Number of digits	Cumulative digits
1 to 9	9	9	9
10 to 99	$90 = (\ 99 - 10 + 1)$	180	189
100 to ?	?	?	492

So $492 - 189 = 303$ digits, so the number of lockers needed is $\dfrac{303}{3} = 101$

The last locker number is $101 + 100 - 1 = 200$
So, there are 200 lockers.

Student's name: _____　Assignment date: _____

	Lockers are numbered with consecutive positive integers beginning with 1, and the digit 2 is used exactly 106 times. What is the number of the last locker? **250**
	How many digits does it take to number a book from 1 to 250 inclusive? **642** 1 − 9 (9) 10 − 99 (180) 100 − 199 (300) 200 − 250 (51 x 3 = 153) 9 + 180 + 300 + 153 = 642
	How many times does the digit 5 appear in digits from 1 to 1 million? **600,000** From 1 to 1 million there are 000000 − 999999, 6 million digits (6 x 1,000,000). 6 million divided by 10 so there are 600,000 of 5's.
	How many times does the digit 9 appear in digits from 1 to 199? **40**
	Niamey wrote down all numbers from 100 to 1000, one after the other. How many 5's did he write? **280** 9x20+100 (500 to 599)

To write all the integers from 0 to 9 on a piece of paper, how many times will the digit '7' be written?

1

To write all the integers from 10 to 99 on a piece of paper, how many times will the digit '7' be written?

19

To write all the integers from 100 to 999 on a piece of paper, how many times will the digit '7' be written?

280

To write all the integers from 1 to 2009 on a piece of paper, how many times will the digit '7' be written?

601
0000 to 1999 there are 20 of 100 so 20 x 20 =400
700 – 799 there are 100 of 7's
1700 – 1799, there are 100 of 7.s
2007 has one 7.
400 + 200 + 200 + 1 = 601

Coin problems 硬币问题

Mike has 9 coins. Each coin is worth less than $1.00. The coins represent four different denominations and include exactly one fifty-cent piece and three nickels. Find the largest amount he could have.

$1(0.5) + 4(0.25) + (1(0.1) + 3(0.05) =$ **$1.75**

Standard Canadian coins are: 1c, 5c, 10c, 25c, 1$ and 2$. Find the smallest sum of money that you can't pay using ten or fewer standard coins. Express your answer in cents.

1c	5c	10c	25c	1$	2$
4	1	1	3	1	1

4 of pennies, 1 of nickel, 1 of a dime, 3 of quarters, and 1 of 1$. This total amount of $1.94 with 10 coins cannot be replaced by fewer coins. One can get $1.94 for ten coins, but with 11 coins, one can get **$3.94,** which you cannot get with just 10 or fewer coins.

Standard Canadian coins are: 1c, 5c, 10c, 25c, 1$ and 2$. Find the smallest sum of money that you can't pay using nine or fewer standard coins. Express your answer in cents.

Find the smallest amount you can pay for 10 coins. 4(1), 1(5), 1(10), 3 (25), 1($1) **$1.94**

Standard Canadian coins are: 1c, 5c, 10c, 25c, 1$ and 2$. Find the smallest sum of money that you can't pay using seven or fewer standard coins. Express your answer in cents.

Find the smallest amount you can pay with 8 coins. 4 of 1 cent, 1 of 5 cents, 1 of 10 c, 2 of 25 c, total **69** cents

Number with remainder 餘数问题

 What is the smallest whole number greater than 2 that will have a remainder of 2 when divided by any member of the following set {3, 4, 5, 6, 8}?

LCM of 5, 6, and 8 is 120. 120 +2 = **122.**

What is the smallest whole number greater than 2 that will always short of 2 when divided by any member of the following set {6, 7, 8}?

LCM of 6, 7, and 8 is 168. 168 - 2 = **166.**

Find the remainder of 111…11 (2002 of 1s) divided by 13.

111111 is divisible by 13, so we can find out how many groups of 111111 there are. 2002 divided by 6, the remainder is 4. So, there are 4 of 1: 1111.   1111/13 = 85 ….6, **the remainder is 6.**

Find the remainder of 111…11 (2009 of 1s) divided by 7.

2

Crypt-arithmetic 数字谜

Replace each letter with a number. The different letter means a different number.

```
  MATH
x    9
------
  HTAM
```
1089 x 9 = 9801

Replace each letter with a number. The different letter means a different number.

```
  A B C
x     C
------
  D B C
```
125 x 5 = 625 or 175x5=875

Ho Math Chess   何数棋谜 奥数,解题策略,及 IQ 思唯训练宝典

Frank Ho, Amanda Ho © 1995 - 2020   All rights reserved.

Student's name: _____   Assignment date: _____

Replace each letter with a number. The different letter means a different number.

```
      A B C D E F G H
  x                 H
  _____
    A A A A A A A A A
```

12345679x9

Replace each letter with a number. The different letter means a different number.

```
    R E D A C T I O N S
  x                   C
  _____
  T T T T T T T S T S
```

Since the multiplicand contains all 10 digits (total is 45), it is divisible by 9 or 3. If REDACTIONS is a multiple of 9 or 3, then its product is also a multiple of 9. Hence the sum of the digits of the product $9T + 2S$ is divisible by 9 or 3; thus, S must equal 9 or 0 or 3.

If S = 9, then C must be 1, which is not correct. If S = 0, then C can be 1 to 9. If S is 3, then C must be 1, which is not reasonable. We conclude S must be 0.

8641975230 x 9 = 77777777070

Sum of arithmetic series $\frac{a+l}{2} \times n$ 算術级数和

N=1+2+3+4+5+6+…+9   Find the sum of N. 45
N=1+2+3+4+5+6+…+98+99+100.   Find the sum of N. 5050
N=2+4+6+…+50+52.   Find the sum of N. 702
N=4+6+8 + …+100+102.   Find the sum of N. 2650
N is a whole number that satisfies N^2=1+2+3+4+3+2+1. Calculate N^3. 64

Ho Math Chess 何数棋谜 奥数,解题策略,及 IQ 思唯训练宝典

Student's name: _____   Assignment date: _____

Counting principles 数数的原理

Using the pennies, nickels, dimes, and quarters, in how many ways can you have 30 cents in change?

Make a table and start with the highest value of the coin and gradually reduce the number of higher value coins by the lower values of coins.

Q	D	N	P
1		1	
1			5
	3		
	2	2	
	2	1	5
	2		10
	1	4	
	1	3	5
	1	2	10
	1	1	15
	1	0	20
		6	
		5	5
		4	10
		3	15
		2	20
		1	25
			30

18

How many poles will you need to make a straight 50-metre fence with 10 m apart?

6

A holiday fruit box contains a dozen each apple, oranges, and grapefruits. What is the least number of pieces of the fruit must you pick to guarantee that you have three of the same kind?

AOG
AOG
7

A bar of chocolate is packaged in a box that holds only one chocolate, a box that holds 5 chocolates, or a box that holds 25 chocolates. How many boxes are needed to fill an order for 116 chocolates if the fewest number of boxes is used and each box is filled?

$1 + 5 \times 3 + 25 \times 4 = 116$ **8 boxes**

A book contains 250 pages. How many times are the following digits used in numbering the pages?

Digit	Number of times used	Comments
0		00-99: **9**, 100 – 199:**20**, From 200 to 250: 200, 201, 202, 203, 204, 205, 206, 207, 208, 209, 210, 220, 230, 240, 250 **16** **Total 45**
1	155 ?	00 – 99 has 20, 100 – 199 has 120, 200 – 250 has 15 ?
2	106	00-99: **20**, 100 – 199:**20**, From 200 to 250: **66** **Total 106**

What is the 50th odd whole number?

99

What is the maximum number of possible diagonals in an octagon?

Shape	Number of diagonals
triangle	$\dfrac{3 \times 2}{2} - 3$
quadrilateral	$\dfrac{4 \times 3}{2} - 4$
pentagon	
hexagon	
heptagon	
octagon	**20** You can use the diagram method to draw diagonals from one point. $$\dfrac{8 \times 5}{2} = 20$$ 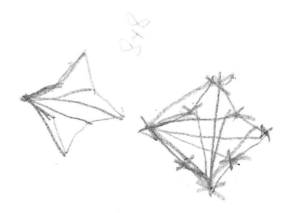 It is difficult to draw an octagon, so draw 8 points on a circle to help you.

In how many ways can change be made for a dollar bill using coins from a collection that contains four nickels, four dimes, four quarters, and two half-dollars?

5	10	25	50
0	0	0	2
0	0	2	1
3	1	1	1
1	2	1	1
3	4	0	1
2	3	0	1
0	0	4	0
1	2	3	0
2	1	3	0
2	4	2	0
4	3	2	0

A dartboard is designed to have two scoring areas, as shown. If an unlimited number of darts is allowed, what is the largest score that cannot be attained?

7x15-7-15 = **83 (LCM – 7 – 15)**
There are many scores that cannot be attained with a combination of 7 and 15. For example, 1 to 6, 16, 17, 18, 19, 20 etc. but the largest number cannot be attained 83. After 83, every number can be attained.

How many triangles are there in the figure shown?

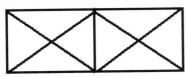

small triangles:8
middle triangles: 8
large triangles: 2
18

How many triangles are in each of the following figures?

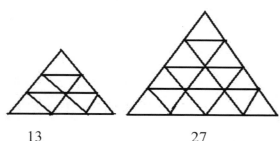

13   27   15

 =10

▽ = 3   13 + the above 2 = 15

Ten days from Thursday, it will be on Sunday. What day of the week will it be 1,000,000 days from Thursday?

Friday

How many three-digit numbers have the units digit larger than the tens digit?

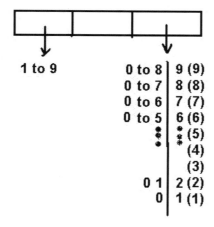

1 to 9		0 to 8	9 (9)	
		0 to 7	8 (8)	
		0 to 6	7 (7)	
		0 to 5	6 (6)	
			(5)	
			(4)	
			(3)	
		0 1	2 (2)	
		0	1 (1)	

$(1+2+3+\ldots+8+9) \times 9 = $ **405**

Student's name: _____   Assignment date: _____

Number of factors 几个因素

What is the smallest whole number with exactly three factors?

4

To find the number of factors of a number, use POP (Product Of Prime). Any integer (n) can be expressed as the product of one and only one set of primes (POP). So, n = $2^a 3^b 5^c$ …

Note that the integer n may contain only partial listed primes; the primes 2, 3, 5 listed here are only for explanation purposes.
The number of factors of n = (a + 1) (b + 1) (c + 1) … (by using the rule of multiplication for different ways). For example, 8= 2^3, it means that the number 8 has 4 factors (exponent 3 +1) of 1 (2^0), 2^1, 2^2, 2^3.

Complete the following table.

Least positive integers	Number of distinct positive integral factors
$2^2=4$	3
$2×3=6$	4
$2^4=16$	5
$2^2×3=12$	6
$2^6=64$	7
$2^3×3=24$	8
$2^2×3^2=36$	9
$2^4×3=48$	10
$2^{10}=1024$	11
$2^2×3×5=60$	12

What is the smallest positive whole number whose square is divisible by every whole number from 1 to 10?

420

What is the greatest odd factor for 7992?

999

How many factors in 4000 are perfect squares?

$4000 = 10^2 × 40 = 2^2 × 5^2 × 2^3 × 5 = 2^5 × 5^3 = (2^2)^2 × 2 × 5^2 × 5 = (2^2 × 5)^2 × 2 × 5$
So, the number of perfect square = (2+1) (1+1) = **6**

The perfect squares are $[(1+2+4)(1+5)]^2$ = $(1, 2, 4, 5, 10, 20)^2$ = **1, 4, 16, 25, 100, 400counting shapes**

Prime and factor 質数与因素

What is a prime number?
A number can only be a product of 1 and itself, or a number can only be divided by 1 and itself.

Give 5 examples.
2, 3, 5, 7, 11

What is a factor?
A number can be a product of two other numbers. These two other numbers are called factors.

Give 5 examples.
2 x 3 = 6, 3 x 4 = 12, 4 x 5 = 20, 5 x 6 = 30, 6 x 7 = 42.

What is a prime factor?
A number is both a prime and a factor.

Give one example.
$24 = 2^3 \times 3$, 2 and 3 are prime factors.

What are prime factors of 6?   2, 3

What are prime factors of 12×2?   2, 3

What are the prime factors of 0.24×200?   2, 3

If A and B are one-digit whole numbers, then find the answers to the following questions.
$45 = \underline{\hspace{1cm}} \times 3 = (A + B) \times 3$
15
There are multiple answers for A and B. Find them all by making a T table.

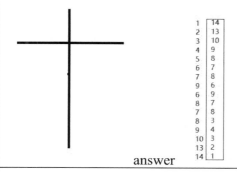

1	14
2	13
3	10
4	9
5	8
6	7
7	8
9	6
6	9
8	7
7	8
8	3
9	4
10	3
13	2
14	1

answer

If A and B are whole numbers, then find the answers A and B for the following questions.

$$51 = \underline{} - 17 = (A + B) \times 3 \div 3 - 17 \quad \text{-------} \rightarrow A + B = 68$$

$A - B = 12$

$A = 40, B = 28$

The number of students in Marcus's class is a two-digit number. For every boy, there are three girls in his class, what could be the number of students in his class?

Starts at 12, then add 4, all the way to 96.

12, 16, 20, 24, 28, 32, 36, 40, 44, 48, 52, 56, 60, 64, 68, 72, 76, 80, 84, 88, 92, 96

GCF and LCM

There are many ways which students could use to find GCF and LCM, but the List method or Factor Tree method is slower in finding answers when compared to the following methods.

Watch the videotape for more information. https://www.youtube.com/watch?v=kAVMTu1cg9A

numbers	**Find GCF and LCM using repeated division method** 连續短除法	Use multiple of the small number to find GCF 小数倍数法	Use difference of 2 large numbers to find GCF 差数法	Use multiple of the large number to find LCM 大数倍数法	Product of relative primes to find LCM 数的乘绩
1728, 2304 GCF = 576 LCM = 6912			See note 1 below.	3 times of 2304 = 6912	
3450. 4140 GCF = 690 LCM =20700					
12, 36 GCF = 12 LCM = 36					
28, 42 GCF = 14 LCM = 84					
7, 11 GCF = 1 LCM = 77					

Note 1

	2304	1728	
$2304 - 1728 = 576$	576	576	$1728 - 1152 = 576$

$$\text{GCF} = 576$$

$$\text{LCM} = \frac{2304 \times 1728}{576} = 6912$$

LCM, GCF, prime, multiple, factor word problems 最小公倍数, 最大公约数, 质数, 因数文字问题

The smallest prime number is _____. The smallest composite number is _____. 2, 4
Use 4 digits 0, 3, 5, 7 to make a 4-digit number such that it is a multiple of both 2 and 5. The largest multiple is _____, the smallest multiple is _____. 3570, 7530
A number is a multiple of 3 and 5. It also has a factor of 7 then such number with the smallest value is _____. 105
Is the following problem true or false?

Problems	T or F
If a and b are whole numbers and a ÷ b = 4 then the GCF of a and b is 4.	F
GCF of a number is = LCM of that number.	T
There are at least two factors for any natural number.	F
There are no common factors for 1 and any non-zero natural numbers.	F
LCM of two primes is their product.	T

a and b have GCF 6 and LCM 72. If a is 18, what is b? GCF × LCM = a × *b*, b = 24
Jordan used a fence with 25 posts every 5 m and with 2 posts at two ends. Now she wants to build the same length of the fence with posts every 6 m and with posts at two ends. How many do old posts in the middle of the fence not need to move? 3, the posts are 30 m, 60 m, and 90 m -- LCM of 5 and 6
Jordan painted a red spot from left to right every 6 m and painted a white spot from right to left every 5 m on a 100-m street. How many spots on the street where it was painted in both red and white colours? 30, 60, 90

Student's name: _____ Assignment date: _____

What is the minimum number of tiles needed to have a square-shaped patio laid with 45 cm by 30 cm tiles?

First, we calculate the length of the square using LCM.

The LCM of 30, 45, is 270 m.

The tiles needed for length is 270 ÷ 30 = 9.
The tiles needed for width 270 ÷ 45 = 6.
6 × 9 = 54 squares

Fill in the squares using non-zero digits. Also, place the decimal point correctly.

```
    3.□
  × .25
  ─────
   17□
  □00
  □75
```

5, 5, 7, 8

What is the probability of getting the sum of 7 of two numbers appearing on the top surfaces of a pair of standard dice?

$\frac{1}{6}$ is the answer.

How many problems can be missed of a 40 problems test and still make an 85%?

6

Find out the information on the following hexagonal prism.

Total faces (F) = _____   8
Total edges (E) = _____   18
Total vertices (V) = _____   12

V+ F – E = _____   2

Patterns to learn to analyze, sort, classify, conclude 规律分析, 排序, 分类, 総结

Downward pattern 下行规律

Complete the following pattern. Match the right-hand side column's pattern to the left-hand side column's pattern.

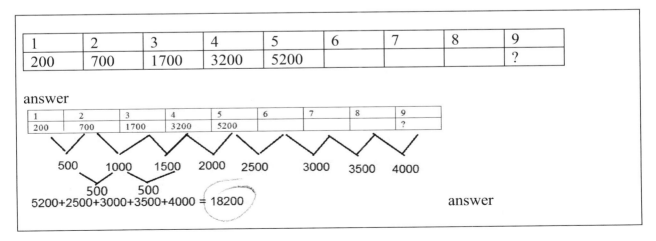

Double patterns 双规律

1	2	3	4	5	6	7	8	9
200	700	1700	3200	5200				?

answer

1	2	3	4	5	6	7	8	9
200	700	1700	3200	5200				?

500   1000   1500   2000   2500   3000   3500   4000

500   500

5200+2500+3000+3500+4000 = 18200   answer

A recursive pattern 递归规律 has a pattern that gives the next term value based on the present term.

For example, $t_n = t_{n-1} + 2$. 4, 6, 8, 10, …….

5, 7, 9, _____, _____   11, 13

15, 26, 48, _____, _____   81, 125

13, 41, 97, _____, _____   **13** +28=41, **41**+56=97, **97**+84=181, **181** + 112=293

Fibonacci sequence (Fee-Bo-Nah-Chi)

1, 3, 4, 7, 11, _____   18

Every number after the first two is the sum of the previous two numbers. Add the current and the previous numbers to get the next number.

1, 1, 2, 3, 5, 8, _____

Recursive pattern
Find the next 2 numbers 2, 6, 14, _____, _____.

Pattern rule is _____.

**Add 4, 8, 12, 16, … So, the answers are 26. 42
Or 30, 62 … Times 2 plus 2 to get the next one.**

Explicit pattern 顯性規律

An explicit pattern is a pattern using a general rule based on the first term. There is a common difference between each term. An arithmetic sequence is an explicit pattern.

Find the next term.

6, 20, 34, _____   48
2.5, 2.7, 2.9, _____, _____   3.1, 3.3
51, 49, 47, 45, _____   43
$1.99, $1.97, $1.95, $1.93, _____ $1.91

The pattern in words 文字規律

The sum of the digits of the number 4210 is 7. How many numbers between 100 and 1000 also have 7 as the sum of their digits?

106 (160, 601, 610), 115 (151, 511), 124 (142, 214, 241, 412, 421), 133 (313, 331) …….16
205 (250, 502, 520), 223 (232, 322, 223)   8
304 (340, 403, 430) ………………4

We know the number of sum 7 numbers is **28**.

Pattern with multi-answer 多答規律

Find the next 2 numbers 1, 3, _____, _____

5, 7 (Add 2 to get the next number.) or 9, 27 (Multiply 3 to get the next number.)

Pattern

$10 - 1 = 9$
$100 - 11 = 89$
$1000 - 111 = 889$

What does $100000 - 11111 =$ _____ **88889**

If the following pattern is continued, then how many 5 squares will be shaded in the 5th grid?

5

     answer

Find the next number.

$1, 4, 9, 16,$ _____ **25** $(+ 3, +5, +7, + 9)$

Replace ? by a number.

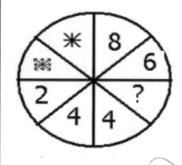

answer

13, the right side minus 4 is the left side.

Leo has 150 beads of a necklace with the following pattern. What figure is the 67th bead on the necklace? How many beads are black altogether?

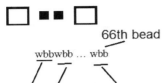

66th bead

wbbwbb ... wbb

1st set   2nd set   22nd set   The 67th bead on the necklace is white.

For every 3 beads, there are 2 black beads. $150 \times \frac{2}{3} = 100$ black beads.

What is the next shape? Draw it.

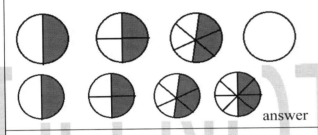

answer

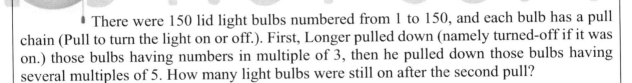

There were 150 lid light bulbs numbered from 1 to 150, and each bulb has a pull chain (Pull to turn the light on or off.). First, Longer pulled down (namely turned-off if it was on.) those bulbs having numbers in multiple of 3, then he pulled down those bulbs having several multiples of 5. How many light bulbs were still on after the second pull?

$\frac{150}{3} = 50$ .... Off including those with numbers in multiple of 15's.

$\frac{150}{5} = 30$ .... Off but those numbers in multiple of 15's were turned after on this pull.

$\frac{150}{15} = 10$ ....numbers in the multiple of 15's.

The number 50 includes numbers in multiple of 3 and 15, but the numbers of multiples of 15 were on after the second pull, so we need to take away 10 from 15. The number 30 includes numbers in multiple of 5 and 15, but the numbers of multiples of 15 were on after the second pull, so we need to take away 10 from 30

$150 - 40 - 20 = 90$

Find all possible answers to the following equation.

$$\bigcirc \times 4 + \square \times 2 = 32$$

◯	□
8	0
7	2
6	4
5	6
4	8
3	10
2	12
1	14
0	16

Mr. Ho's class was observing birds in the trees. On each tree, there were 3 cardinals and 2 mockingbirds in each tree. The class counted 35 birds altogether. How many birds did they see?

21 mockingbirds and 14 cardinals.

Patterns in tables 列表规律

1. A snail is at the bottom of a wall and is trying to climb up out of the wall. The snail climbs in the following distance pattern.

Number of days	1	2	3	4
Distance in cm	2	4	6	? 2 x 4 = 8

The gap (distance between days) = _____ cm. 2

The pattern rule is Distance = Number of days × gap = _____ 2d

2. A snail is at the location of 2 cm from the bottom of a wall and is trying to climb up out of the wall. The snail climbs in the following distance pattern.

Number of days	0	1	2	3	4
Distance in cm	2	4	6	8	? 10

The gap (distance between days) = _____ cm. 2

The pattern rule is Distance = Number of days × gap + _____ = _____ 2, 2d + 2

Student's name: _____ Assignment date: _____

3. A snail is above the ground of a wall and is trying to climb up out of the wall. The snail climbs in the following distance pattern.

Number of days	1	2	3	4
Distance in cm	4	7	10	? 13

The gap (distance between days) = _____ cm.   3

The pattern rule is Distance = Number of days × gap + _____ = _____

1, 3d + 3

4. A snail is at the bottom of a wall and is trying to climb up out of the wall. During the day, the snail climbs 4 cm, but at night, she drops 2 cm, and if this pattern continues, when will be the number of days the snail climbs out of the10-cm wall?

Use the following table to solve the above problem.

Number of days	1	2	3	4
Distance in cm	? 4	? 6	? 8	? 10

5. Jaden owes some money to Rain, and the amount is a multiple of 3 and 4 but at least as possible. How much does Jaden owe?

12

6. Jaden owes some money to Rain, and the amount is a multiple of 14 and 12 but at least as possible. How much does Jaden owe?

84

7. Issac has $19 on day 1, and he gets $3 from his mother every day. How much money does he have on day 5?

Number of days	1	2	3	4	5
Accumulated amount	19	? 22	? 25	? 28	? 31

It is easy to use the above pattern table to solve the problems of a few days, but how about the problem is changed to the following?

8. Issac has $19 on day 1, and he gets $3 from his mother every day. How much money does he have on the 365th day?

19 + 364 x 3 = 1111

9. Use the core pattern method to solve the following problem.

Today is Monday. What day will it be on the 209th days later?

Sunday, 209 divided by 7 with remainder 6

10. Explain how you could find the colour of the 142nd block in the following pattern block using the core pattern idea.

W	W	R	R	R	W	W	R	R	R	...

White

11. Us the pattern to solve the problem. Bennie is on a bicycle tour 520 km from his home, and he can cycle 25 km per day. If he starts riding from home on Tuesday morning, when will he reach his destination? On what day will he reach his destination?

21 days, Tuesday

12. Use a pattern to solve the problem. A recipe calls for 2 tablespoons of sugar, 4 tablespoons of orange juice, and 6 tablespoons of apple juice. If you had 18 tablespoons of apple juice, how many tablespoons of sugar and orange juice would you need?

6 tablespoons of sugar. 12 tablespoons of orange juice.

13. Use a pattern to solve the problem. A recipe calls for 3 tablespoons of sugar, 4 tablespoons   of orange juice, and 8 tablespoons of apple juice. If you had 15 tablespoons of sugar, how many tablespoons of apple juice and orange juice would you need?

20 table of spoons of orange juice, 40 tables of spoons of apple juice

14. On Monday, a magic plant is 3 cm high. By Tuesday, the plant has doubled its height to 4 cm. If this pattern of doubling its height from the day before continues. How high will the plant be on Saturday?

3 x 2 x 2 x 2 x 2 x 2 = 12 x 8 = 96

15. Look at the following pattern and find an answer to the question mark.

Number of days	0	1	2	3	4
Accumulated amount	2	8	13	17	? 20

Ho Math Chess 何数棋谜 奥数,解题策略,及 IQ 思唯训练宝典
Frank Ho, Amanda Ho © 1995 - 2020

Student's name: _____ Assignment date: _____

Below is a table that shows the relationship between x and y.

The pattern rule is $y = x + 2$

x	y
1	3
2	4
3	5
4	6
5	7

Below is a table that shows the relationship between x and y.

The pattern rule is $y =$ _____ $x + 3$

x	y
2	5
3	6
4	7
5	8
6	9

Below is a table that shows the relationship between x and y.

The pattern rule is $y =$ _____ $70 - x$

x	y
1	69
2	68
3	67
4	66
5	65

Below is a table that shows the relationship between x and y.

The pattern rule is $y =$ _____ $10x + 1$

x	y
1	11
2	21
3	31
4	41
5	51

Student's name: _____ Assignment date: _____

Pattern attributes (for higher grades)

Figure pattern has some attributes such as colours, sizes, shapes, directions, and fonts. For example, the following pattern has the attributes of sizes, shapes, and colours.

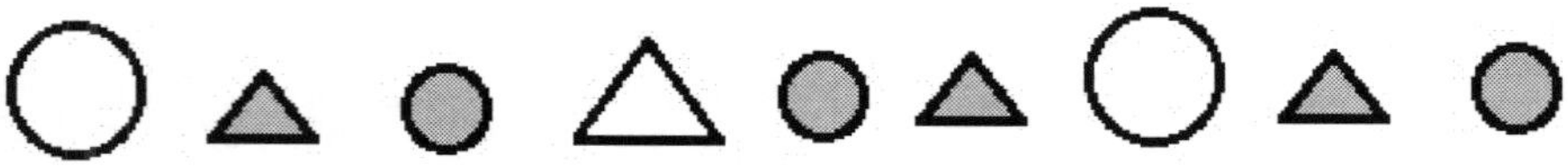

    A. The above pattern has 3 attributes size, colour, shape.

    B. How does the size change?
It changes in the order of circle, triangle, …

    C. How does the shape change?
It changes in the order of circle, triangle, ….

    D. What are the next three shapes in the pattern?

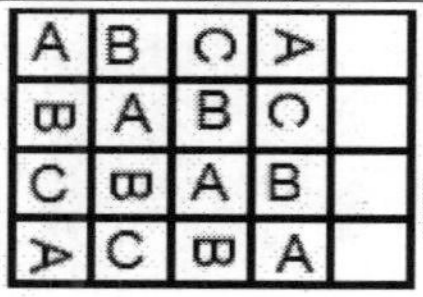

answer

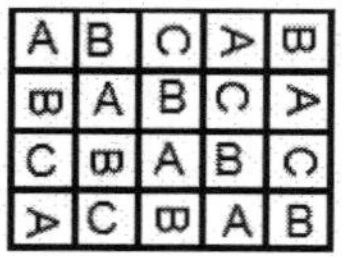

    A. What attributes do they change in the above pattern?
Letter and orientation

    B. What is the next column in the above pattern?

… answer

    A. What attributes do they change in the above pattern?
Shape and size
    B. What is the next column in the above pattern?

Pattern core and pattern rule (for higher grades) 规律的起点及规则

There are many kinds of patterns, such as all numbers pattern, a pattern with figures, a pattern with repeated core pattern or 2-dimensional pattern etc.

Pattern core

Example

What is the pattern core of the pattern ABCABCABCABCABC….?

The pattern core of the above pattern is ABC.

What is the 110th letter of the pattern ABCABCABCABCABC….?

Use the division method by dividing 110 by 3 and the remainder is 2, so the letter is B because the pattern core is ABC.

Predict the colour of the 112th block of the following pattern.

red	yellow	yellow	red	red	yellow	yellow	red	red	yellow	yellow	red

$\frac{112}{4}$ has remainder 0, so the colour is red because the pattern core is ryyr.

---

predict the 57th term of A1B2A1B2A1B2…
Each letter or number is considered as one term.

57 divided by 4 with the remainder of 1, so the 57th term is A.

What is the 20th term of the following pattern?

RYRRYYRRRYYYRRRRYYYY…

The RY appears in a pattern of 1, 4, 6, 8, 10 so the 20th term is R.

RYRRYYRRRYYYRRRRYYYY…

How to find the number pattern? 如何找数字規律?

How to find the next number?

Step 1

Finding the next number of a number pattern, we often use the difference or quotient (or called gap) between two adjacent numbers.

Step 2

To predict the next number, one should figure out the pattern rule.

1-dimensional pattern

3, 5, 7, 9, 11, _____

The gap is always 2 by using the larger – small number.
The pattern rule is as follows.
Start at 3, add 2 to get the next number.
The answer is 13.

2, 4, 8, 16, _____
The pattern rule is _____
Stat at 2, multiply 2 to get the next number.

Row 1	1	2	3	4	5
Row 2	3	4	5	6	?

The pattern rule is _____.
 row 2 = row 1 + 2

Continue the pattern in the following table.

1			
3	6		
?	?	20	
7	14	?	56

5, 10

28

Student's name: _____ Assignment date: _____

In and out Tables 進出表

In	1	3	5	7
Out	3	5	7	?

Pattern rule: Out = In + 2

In	1	3	5	7
Out	3	5	7	?

Pattern rule: Out = In + 2

In	1	3	5	7
Out	3	5	7	?

Pattern rule: Out = In + 2

In	1	3	5	7
Out				

Pattern rule: Out = In + 2

In	1	3	5	7
Out				

Pattern rule: Out = In × 2

In	4	6	7	8
Out				

Pattern rule: Out = In - 1

In	Out
2	
4	
5	
7	

Pattern rule: Out = In × 3

In	Out
12	
9	
6	
5	

Pattern rule: Out = In add 2

In	Out
19	
18	
17	
13	

Pattern rule: Out = In subtract 6

Student's name: _____   Assignment date: _____

Number patterns or letter pattern 数字与文字规律

1.	1	2	3	___	___	___	**4,5,6**
2.	2	4	6	___	___	___	**8,10,12**
3.	5	10	15	___	___	___	**20,25,30**
4.	10	100	1000	___	___	___	10000,100000,1000000
5.	325	335	345	___	___	___	**355,365,375**
6.	4236	5236	6236	___	___	___	**7236,8236,9236**
7.	270	280	290	___	___	___	**300,310,320,**
8.	1150	1200	1250	___	___	___	**1300,1350,1400**
9.	7385	7375	7365	___	___	___	**7355,7345,7335**
10.	4350	4250	4150	___	___	___	**4050,3950,3850**
11.	1007	1008	1009	___	___	___	**1010,1011,1012**
12.	4256	4506	4756	___	___	___	**5006,5256**
13.	21	32	43	___	___	___	**54,65,76**
14.	613	524	435	___	___	___	**346,257,168**
15.	987	876	765	___	___	___	**654,543,432**

Student's name: ____________________________ Assignment date: ____________________

English Letters pattern 英文字母規律

Continue the following patterns.

B, D, F. H, ____ J

ABAABA __ __ __ __ __ __ __ __ AABAAAAB

GH1GH2GH3 __ __ __ GH4

BAABBAAABBB___ ___ ___ ___ ___ ___ ___ ___ AAAABBBB

Looking for number patterns 数字规律

1.	3	_____	15	31	63	127	255	7
2.	10	20	40	80	160	_____		320
3.	2	4	16	_____	65536			256
4.	16	8	_____	_____	1			4, 2
5.	_____	12	36	108	324	972		4
6.	_____	_____	20	24	96	100	400	1, 5
7.	600	600	300	100	25	_____		5
8.	784529	78452	7452	452	_____			42, 2
9.	11	18	25	32	39	_____	53	46
10.	810	270	_____	30	10			90
11.	1	4	16	64	256	_____		1024
12.	$400	$200	$100	$50	_____			$25
13.	100	99	97	94	90	_____	_____	85, 79
14.	15	12	14	11	13	_____	_____	10, 12
15.	1	3	7	15	31	_____	_____	63, 127
16.	67	35	19	11	7	_____	_____	5, 4

Look for patterns.

```
                    1
                  2   2
                3   4   3
              4   7  __   4                    7
            5  11  __  11   5                  14
          6  __  25  __  16   6              16, 25
        7  22  41  __  41  __  7              50
```

```
                    1
                  2   4
                3   9   27
              4  16  __ 256                    64
            5  __  __ 625 3125               25, 125
```

```
                    1
                  2   4
                3   6   9
              4   8  __  16                    12
            5  __  15  __  __              10, 20, 25
          6  __  __  __  __  __          12, 18, 24, 30, 36
```

Figure pattern 图形规律

Fill in the missing terms to complete the pattern.

Student's name: _____ Assignment date: _____

Put ♖ in the following board in such a way that each row, each column has one and only one ♖. Can you find more than one way?

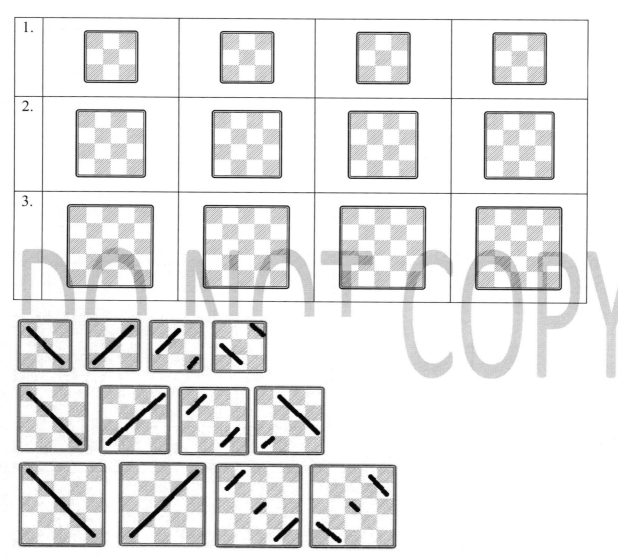

2-dimensional pattern 二维规律

Look for Pattern and Complete T-table.

1.

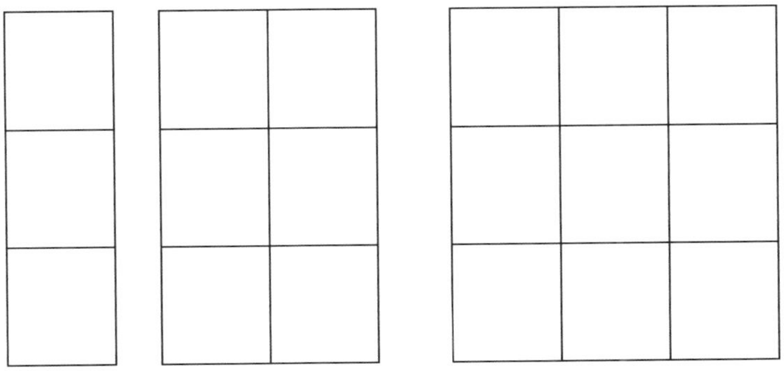

Number of columns	Number of squares
1	3
2	6
3	9
4	12
5	15
6	18

2.

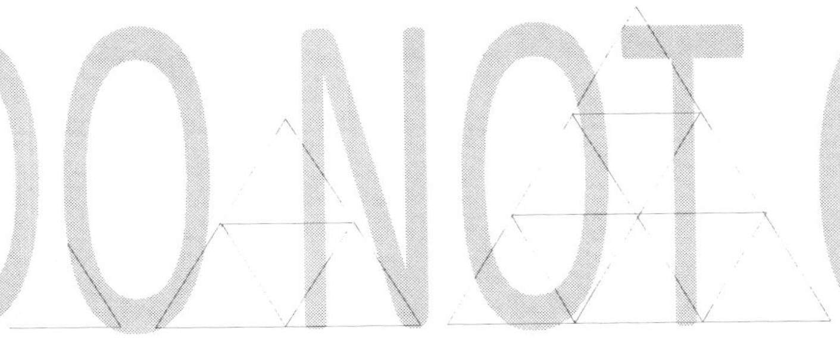

Number of rows	Number of triangles
1	1
2	4
3	9
4	16
5	25
6	36

3.

Number of rows	Number of squares
1	1
2	4
3	9
4	16
5	25
6	36

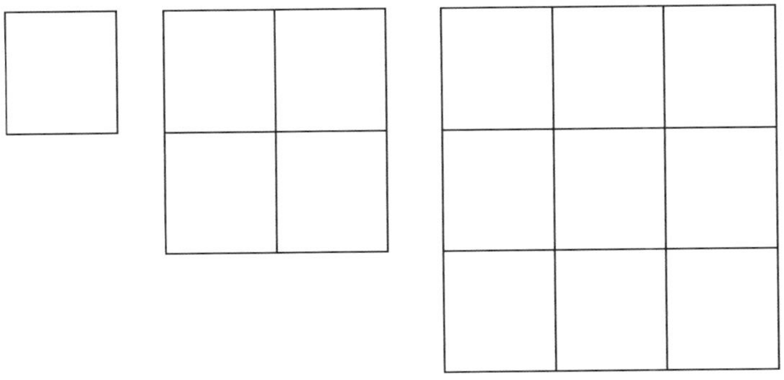

Look for Pattern and Complete T-table.

4.

```
* * *        * * * *        * * * * *
*            *              *
*            *              *
             *              *
                            **
```

Number of rows	Number of apples
3	5
4	7
5	9
6	11
7	13
8	15

5.

```
★ ★          ★ ★ ★          ★ ★ ★ ★
★ ★          ★   ★          ★       ★
             ★ ★ ★          ★       ★
                            ★ ★ ★ ★
```

Number of rows	Number of stars
2	4
3	8
4	12
5	16
6	20
7	24

6.

```
• • •        • • • •        • • • • •
  •              •                •
  •              •                •
                 •                •
                                  •
```

Number of rows	Number of dots
3	5
4	8
5	11
6	14
7	17
8	20

Look for Pattern and Complete T-table.

7.

7.

Number of rows	Number of apples
3	5
5	9
7	13
9	17
11	21
13	25

8.

Number of rows	Number of stars
3	6
5	12
7	18
9	24
11	30
13	36

9.

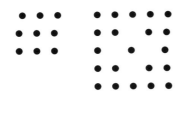 

Number of rows	Number of dots
3	9
5	21
7	33
9	45
11	57
13	69

Ho Math Chess   何数棋谜 奥数,解题策略,及 IQ 思唯训练宝典

Student's name: _____ Assignment date: _____

Pattern word problems 文字規律題

1	Alvin saves \$11 in February, and he saves \$5 after that every month. How much will he have saved by the end of August? $11 + 5 \times 6 = $ **\$41**
2	Adam saves \$17 in January and \$5 each month after that. Bob saves \$15 in January and \$7 each month after that. Who has saved more money by the end of November? Adam = $17 + 5 \times 101 = 67$ Bob = $15 + 7 \times 10 = 85$ …. Bob saved more.
3	Heather has biked 10 km from her home. After that, she cycled 7 km per hour. She biked 38 km altogether, how many more hours had she biked after the initial 10 km? $38 = 10 + 7 \times 4$ Heather would have biked 4 more hours. 38
4	Two cats, Kiko and Snow, share cat food one can for every 5 days. How many cans should Frank buy in December if there are no more cans left? Frank needs to buy 7 cans.
5	Kiko, the cat, likes to go out in the very early morning at about 5 a.m. She usually will come back every 45 minutes, then rests for 5 minutes and then go out again until noon, then she likes to take a nap. If Kiko goes out at 6:30 a.m. for 45 minutes and then comes back resting for 5 minutes if this pattern continues until 12 noon, how many times would she have gone out, and how many times would she have come back if Kiko stayed at home the last time before noon? From 6:30 a.m. to 12 noon, there are 6 and a half hours = 390 minutes. 45 minutes + 5 minutes = 50 minutes 390 divided by 50 = 7 times of going out after 5 minutes of resting with 40 minutes left, 7 times of going out and 8 times of coming back.

Student's name: _____   Assignment date: _____

The two cats Kiko and Snow, like to collect leaves. Yesterday Kiko collected 3 leaves, and Snow collected 1 leaf. If starting from today, Kiko collects 1 leaf every day, and Snow collects 2 leaves every day, then on what day will they collect the same number of leaves?

Snow: 1, 2, 2
Kiko: 3, 1, 1

The second day.

In Ethan's class, three out of every five students are male. There are 125 students in his class, how many of them are female

50

Up to today, Adam has read 7 pages of his book and will read one page thereafter. Bob has read 4 pages and will read 2 pages thereafter. How many days later will Adam and Bob read the same number of pages?

name	To begin	Week 1	2	3			
Adam	7	8	9	10			
Bob	4	6	8	10			

3 days

Kiko, the cat, goes out every 6 minutes and the cat Snow goes out every 8 minutes. If both go out at 6:30 a.m., when would be the next time they go out together?

Use LCM or pattern to solve it. 6:54 a.m.

Banno has 8 books and buys 1 new book every week. Benni has 4 books and buys 2 new books every week. After how many weeks will Banno and Benni have the same number of books?

	To begin	Week 1	2	3	4	5	6
Banno	8	9	10	11	12	13	14
Benni	4	6	8	10	12	14	16

Pattern in $ax + by$ model $ax + by$ 规律模式

| 1 | Renee is working to raise money for her gymnastics competition trip. She has two options:
Option A – She works 7 days, and each day, she makes $8.
Option B – She makes different money each day. |

Day 1	Day 2	Day 3	Day 4	Day 5	Day 6	Day 7
$1	$3	$5	$7	$9	?	?

To raise the most money, which option should Renee choose? Show all your work.

Option A: $8 x 7 = $56
Option B: 1+ 3 + 5 + 7 + 9 + 11 + 13 = $49

Option A is better.
    Blank line   blank line
    Blank line   blank line
    Blank line   blank line
    Blank line   blank line

| 2 | Renee wants to grow 50 seedlings in two kinds of trays. One tray can hold 4 seedlings, and the other tray can hold 6 seedlings. How many ways can she fill in the two trays if each tray must be in full? |

Each drop of two of the six-seedling tray would require the fill of 3 of four-seedling trays.

Number of 6 seedlings	Number of 4 seedlings
7	2
5	5
3	8
1	11

There are 4 ways to plant.

Fractions 分数

Can you describe five meanings of $\frac{p}{q}$, where p and q are whole numbers?

1. P $\div q$
2. p $\times \frac{1}{q}$
3. The ratio of p to q.
4. P out of q parts
5. The probability of $\frac{p}{q}$
6. The scale factor is $\frac{p}{q}$.
7. A fraction

Blank line   blank line
Blank line   blank line
Blank line   blank line
Blank line   blank line

Ho Math Chess   何数棋谜 奥数,解题策略,及 IQ 思唯训练宝典
Frank Ho, Amanda Ho © 1995 - 2020
Student's name: _____ Assignment date: _____

Fraction models 分数的模式

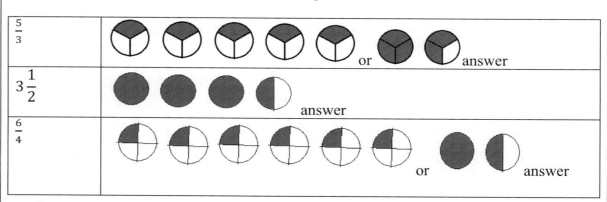

Write the fraction for the following fraction models. All pieces are selected.

Fraction model	fraction
	2 2/3
	1 3/5
	2
	1 2/5

The Smiths cut 2 pizzas into seventh each. They ate 12 pieces. What fraction of the pizzas did they not eat?
$\frac{1}{7}$ *answer*

Name the fraction of the shaded area. 見图写分数

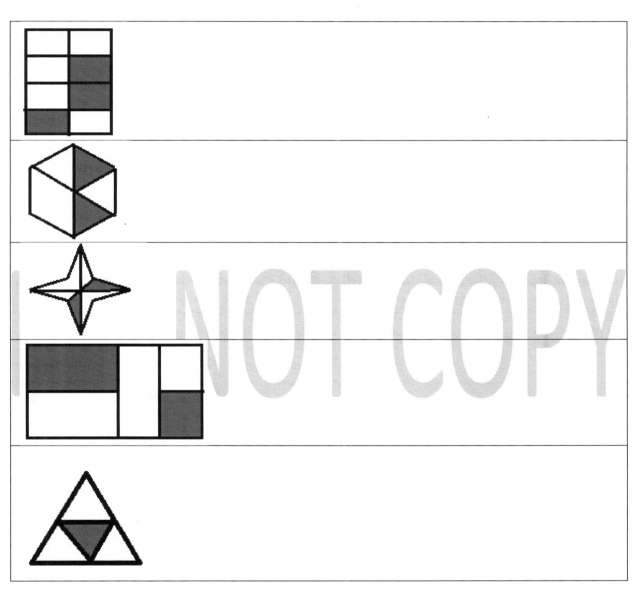

This figure represents $\frac{3}{5}$ of one whole, shows what the whole might look like. The answer may vary.   answer

Using a graph to represent fractions 以图代表分数

$\frac{1}{2}$ of a chocolate ⬜◼ + $\frac{1}{3}$ of the same chocolate ⬜⬜◼ = 5 of $\frac{1}{6}$ the same chocolate

Divide the above chocolates to show $\frac{3}{6}$ and $\frac{2}{6}$.

$\frac{2}{3}$ of chocolate ☐ + 1 of chocolate ☐ = ◼ ◼⬜ = $1\frac{2}{3}$

$\frac{1}{4}$ of chocolate ☐ + $\frac{1}{2}$ of chocolate ☐ = ▦ = $\frac{3}{4}$

$\frac{1}{3}$ of chocolate ☐ + $\frac{1}{2}$ of chocolate ☐ = ▦ = $\frac{2}{6} + \frac{3}{6} = \frac{5}{6}$

$\frac{1}{8}$ of chocolate ☐ + $\frac{1}{4}$ of chocolate ☐ = ▦ = $\frac{3}{8}$

$\frac{1}{2}$ of chocolate ☐ + $\frac{1}{8}$ of chocolate ☐ = ▦ = $\frac{5}{8}$

$\frac{1}{3}$ of chocolate ☐ + $\frac{1}{6}$ of chocolate ☐ = ▦ = $\frac{3}{6} = \frac{1}{2}$

Hidden treasures offered by a fraction 分数是个宝

Many math educators have published articles attempting to explain the reason why a fraction is so difficult for elementary students to master and its concept is so hard to understand when compared to other math concepts. Many also attempted to explain that the fraction must be taught from the concept, instead of a drill. This ration makes sense, but students continue to get confused. Why?

My thinking is the complication of the fraction symbol itself has been ignored by many math teachers. Many math books did not discuss the symbol $\frac{x}{y}$ hidden properties. When a symbol $\frac{p}{q}$ is written, it does not necessarily mean a fraction. A fraction is defined as $\frac{partial}{whole}$. A ratio (with the same measure unit for 2 or more numbers) is defined as $\frac{partial1}{partial2}(for\ 2\ numbers) = \frac{partial}{whole} = \frac{whole1}{whole2} = \frac{whole}{patial} = \frac{partial\ or\ whole}{0} = \frac{0}{whole\ or\ partial}$, when the number is 0, the computation is not meaningful. So. A fraction could be considered as a special case of ratio. A % could be considered as a special case of fraction when its dominator is 100.

For example, what does $\frac{1}{2}$ mean?
  (1) Is it 1 divided by 2?
  (2) Is it one half?
  (3) Is it one out of 2?
  (4) Is it $1 \times \frac{1}{2}$?
  (5) Is it 1 (partial) to 2 (partial) ratio?
  (6) Is it one of every two?
  (7) Is it reduced form of $\frac{2}{4}$?
  (8) Is it 50%
  (9) Is it 0.5?
  (10) Is it a fraction?
  (11) Is it 2's reciprocal?
  (12) Is it a unit fraction of 2?

Can many elementary students answer and explain the above answers clearly?
The reason that many students cannot answer clearly to the above questions is the reason why students are confused about fractions.

Many concepts learned in operating whole numbers do not necessarily apply to a fraction operation. The following demonstrates some examples.

Student's name: _____ Assignment date: _____

Fraction not only has a horizontal operation but also has a vertical operation. BEDMAS order of operation does not necessarily apply to a fraction.

$$\frac{13}{30} \times \frac{15}{26}$$

The above multiplication needs to be reduced in cross diagonals before multiplying.

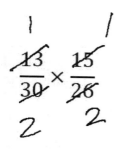

The ratio of partial 1 : partial 2 can be converted into a fraction for calculation purpose; this concept is not clearly talked about in most math textbooks.

Ratio = partial1 : partial2, whole = partial1 + partial2

The fraction of partial 1 = $\dfrac{partial1}{partial1+partial2}$

The ratio of boys to girls in Martin's class is 2 to 3. Martin has 25 students in his class, how many boys in his class?

We can convert the ratio to a fraction. It means that the fraction of boys is $\frac{2}{5}$. So, for the entire class, the number of boys $= 25 \times \frac{2}{5} = 10$.

The whole 1 (unit 1) concept in the fraction is given all the time naturally, and often, it acts as a variable in algebra. Different 1's exist at different stages of the remaining fraction word problems. The whole 1 often can be obtained by using a quantity divided by its corresponding fractional number, this concept never stressed in the math textbooks.

Johnny spent one-third of his money and had $24 left. How much did he have in the beginning?

$$24 \div \left(1 - \frac{2}{3}\right) = 72$$

When a fraction word problem is given, often, other information is also given without explicitly stated. At this point, the students must know them and use hidden information to solve the problems.

When a fraction $\frac{p}{q}$ is given.	Other "hidden" information comes with it.
A computer keyboard costs $100 which is $\frac{1}{10}$ of a computer.	**The whole of unit 1 is automatically offered.** The whole is 10 parts, and the $100 is for 1 part. So, the total is $100 \times 10 = $1000
A pair of wheels cost $\frac{2}{5}$ of a hand truck, the hand truck costs $100. How much is the pair of wheels? A pair of hand truck wheels costs $40 which is $\frac{2}{5}$ of the hand truck. How much is the hand truck?	**Of the hand, truck/ Multiplication and division operations are automatically offered.** Students must understand the following. $\frac{p}{q} = p \div q$ for division (In division, the q is the divisor) $\frac{p}{q} = p \times \frac{1}{q}$ for multiplication (In the fraction form $\frac{p}{q}$, q means $\frac{1}{q}$) $$\cancel{100}^{20} \times \frac{2}{\cancel{5}_{1}} = 40$$ **Use Quantity divided by its corresponding fractional number to get a whole (not necessary the original amount if it is a fraction remaining problem).** $40 \div \frac{2}{5} = $40 \times \frac{5}{2} = $100 **Use $\frac{quantity}{partial} \times whole = $40 \times \frac{5}{2} = $100**
After Jenny spent $\frac{2}{3}$ of her money, what fraction of her money was left?	**Fraction of part 1 + fraction of part 2 = 1** $1 - \frac{2}{3} = \frac{1}{3}$

Student's name: ______________________ Assignment date: ______________________

Why convert % or ratio to a fraction? Emily has \$125, and she spent 60%. How much did she have left?	It is easier to reduce the number such that it is easier for computation. $125 \times \frac{2}{5} = 50$ Calculate with decimal. $125 \times 0.4 = 60$
Calculate the following. $120 \times 0.75 = ?$	120×0.75 $= \overset{30}{\cancel{120}} \times \frac{3}{\underset{1}{\cancel{4}}}$ $= 90$
1. $16000 \div 125 = ?$	$16000 \div 125$ $= \frac{16000}{125}$ $= \frac{16 \times \overset{8}{\cancel{1000}}}{\underset{1}{\cancel{125}}}$ $= 128$

Matching a partial number to a partial fraction or a unit one (whole)

Harry is $\frac{2}{3}$ of Ethan's age. Ethan is 12 years old.	Harry is $\frac{2}{3}$ of Ethan's age. Ethan is 12 years old. 3 matches 12 (12 is divided into 3 equal parts.) 2 is Harry's parts. Harry is 8 years old.
Harry has $\frac{2}{3}$ more than his brother. His brother has \$36. How much does Harry have?	$1 + \frac{2}{3} = \frac{5}{3}$ (The unit 1 is Harry's brother's money.) $36 \times \frac{5}{3} = 60$ ..... Harry's money
There are 8 rabbits which are $\frac{2}{3}$ of the number of chickens. How many chickens are there?	Match 8 to $\frac{2}{3}$. There are 8 rabbits which are $\frac{2}{3}$...... Each part is 4. There are 8 rabbits which are $\frac{2}{3}$..... 3 parts are 12.
Eight people playing basketballs who are $\frac{4}{5}$ the number of people playing baseball. How many people play baseball?	Match the number to the fraction in "Eight people playing basketballs who are $\frac{4}{5}$ ....". 8 divided by 4 = 2 Eight people playing basketballs who are $\frac{4}{5}$ 2 x 5 = 10

Student's name: ______________________ Assignment date: ____________________

Karissa brought 6 books to school, and they are $\frac{3}{5}$ of her books at home. How many books does she have at home in total? Blank line blank line Blank line blank line Blank line blank line Blank line blank line Blank line blank line Blank line blank line Blank line blank line Blank line blank line	Each part has 6 divided 3 = 2 books. Karissa brought 6 books to school and they are $\frac{3}{5}$ of her books at home. Total books at home = 5 times 2 = 10.

Fraction multiplication model 分数乘法的模式

Decimal, fractions, % # 39

Ho Math Chess (何數棋谜　趣味數學)

Use the empty area of this page or back page as a work area to calculate the following problems.

Use array(s) to explain $1\frac{3}{4} \times 1\frac{1}{2}$. $2\frac{5}{8}$

(1) Use the array model to explain the distributive law calculation of $1\frac{3}{4} \times 1\frac{1}{2} = (1 + \frac{3}{4})(1 + \frac{1}{2})$.

The basic unit for one whole is $\frac{1}{8}$ (dimension is 4 by 2).

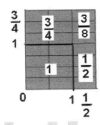

answer

(2) Use the array model to explain the improper fraction conversion way of calculating $1\frac{3}{4} \times 1\frac{1}{2}$.

answer

Use array(s) or area model to explain $\frac{4}{5} \times 1\frac{2}{3}$.

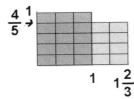

The answer is $\frac{4}{3}$.

Why we use the technique "multiply and invert" to do fractions division?

Because it is much easier to get answers by "multiply and invert".

Fraction division 分数的除法

Decimal, fractions, % # 52

Ho Math Chess (何數棋谜　趣味數學)

Use the empty area of this page or back page as a work area to calculate the following problems.

Samantha did the following problem, find out if anything wrong with her calculation and explain.

If there are 150 oranges to be shared by 40 people, then how many oranges will each person get?

Samantha calculated her answer as follows:

$\frac{150}{40} = \frac{15}{4}$ (equivalent fractions) $= 3\frac{3}{4}$ (change to mixed fraction, so the quotient is 3 and the remainder is 3.)

Each person gets 3 oranges, and there will be $\frac{3}{4}$ of an orange left.

The left-over oranges are 30 oranges, not $\frac{3}{4}$ of an orange.

"Onederful" and magic unit 1 神奇單位一

I saw a magician who could grab a few play cards in the air out of nowhere and later, he could even grab a deck of cards, and all these cards seem to come out of nowhere (www.youtube.com). The similar "trick" I can think of in arithmetic mathematics is to grab the "magic" number 1 in the air to solve some math problems.

If the elementary math is limited to natural numbers only, then it would be much easier math but less challenging, and the most difficult challenging area in arithmetic is a fraction. Percent can be considered as a special case of a fraction, and the ratio can be converted to a fraction in computation, so if students master the skills of fraction, then many similar types of problems in percent and ratio can also be solved.

The most difficult concept in the fraction is the concept of whole "1" (called unit 1 單位 1) since unit 1 has a concept that is different from the natural number of 1. The concept of unit 1 in a fraction represents a "whole," which may not be even countable such as the liquid inside a bottle. The fraction of unit 1 can be used to evaluate the value of the remaining number and to calculate the original value. All these concepts are very different from the whole numbers students learned before learning the fractions.

Is it the identity of one that helps the student solve the most challenging fraction probes? In multiplication, when you multiply a number by 1, and you have the same number, that's called the identity property of one. It is this identity property that helps students solve many fraction problems.

The numeral 1 in math is a magnificent number. It simplifies computational procedure when used properly, and yet it becomes redundant in some cases such as the power of 1 in exponential number or when a number multiplied by 1. So, while 1 is very useful, it also can cause problems if not handled carefully.

There are three major areas that use lots of unit 1 in their word problems: fraction word problems, Work problems, Travelling problems. We discuss many examples in these areas in this workbook.

Student's name: _____ Assignment date: _____

How useful is 1? Look at the following examples. 1 有多么有用? 見例题

1 can be used as a parameter. For example, in work problems, we can assume the work amount to be unit 1, and it acts like a variable of an unknown quantity. Students should not think that unit 1 is just a numerical one with a value of 1. **This unknown quantity 1 is used very often in solving arithmetic word problems**.

1 is used to turn a fraction upside down. For example, one half when written in fraction, the 1 turns 2, upside down, so it becomes $\frac{1}{2}$. In this case, 1 has the meaning of a reciprocal command. By knowing this, we then can do 1 over a fraction very quickly, for example, if $\frac{1}{\frac{1}{3}}$ then we know the answer is 3.

1 can also be used to convert a radian to a degree and vice versa (You learn this in grade 11 or 12 in Canada.).

1 can be used to convert any numbers to % by multiplying that number by 100%.
When working on fractions, it is easier to change a whole number to a fraction by dividing 1, such as $2 = \frac{2}{1}$.

We use 1 concept in fraction as "whole" or "entirety".

While the above list is not meant to be exhaustive, it does indicate the usefulness of 1.

How useless is 1? Look at the following.

$1x + 2$, the coefficient 1 in front of x is useless.

How about 2 x to the power of 2 $[(2x)^2]$? Often, a wrong answer is written as 2 times power 2 of x ($2 x^2$) and the correct answer of number 2 to the power of 2 is forgotten ($2^2 x^2$). It all is caused by the problem that 2 to the power 1 was not written originally to give us a reminder ($2 = 2^1$).

The common factor of 1 is between any numbers, so we do not consider 1 as a factor of a relative prime between 2 numbers.
For an exponential number a to the power x, the base a should not be 1.
1 is not a prime number, nor a composite number.

Student's name: _____   Assignment date: _____

Reciprocal and 1 倒数及 1

Fill in each ⬜ by a number. $\dfrac{\frac{1}{a}}{b} = \dfrac{b}{a}$

If $1 = a \times \dfrac{1}{\boxed{}}$ then $a = 1 \div \dfrac{1}{\boxed{}}$

a, a

$1 = 3 \times \dfrac{1}{\boxed{}}$ 3

$1 = \dfrac{1}{2} \times \boxed{}$ 2

If $1 = 2 - \boxed{}$ then what $\boxed{}$ is in $1 = 2 - (-\boxed{})$? $\boxed{} = -1$

$1 = \boxed{} - 3$ 4

$1 = 1 - \boxed{}$ 0

$1 = \boxed{} - 0$ 1

$1 = \boxed{} + 0$ 1

$0 \div 1 = \boxed{}$ 0

$1 = 0 \times \boxed{}$, $1 \div 0 = \boxed{}$ undefined, undefined (no answer)

$1 = \dfrac{2}{3} \times \boxed{} = \dfrac{\frac{2}{3}}{\boxed{}} = \dfrac{1}{2} \times \boxed{} = \dfrac{2}{3} \times \dfrac{1}{\boxed{}} = 1 \div \dfrac{2}{3} \times \boxed{}$ $\dfrac{3}{2}$, 3, 2, $\dfrac{2}{3}$, $\dfrac{2}{3}$

$1 = 0.1 \div \boxed{} = 0.1 \div \dfrac{1}{\boxed{}} = \boxed{} \div 0.1 = 10 \div \boxed{} = \dfrac{0.1 \times 100}{\boxed{}} = \dfrac{\boxed{}}{0.01 \times 100} = \dfrac{\frac{1}{0.01}}{\boxed{}}$

  0.1, 10, 0.1, 10, 10, 1, 100

$1 = 10 \div 0.1 \times \boxed{} = 1000\% \times \dfrac{1}{\boxed{}} = 100\% \times 0.1 \times \dfrac{1}{\boxed{}}$ 0.01, 1000%, 0.1

Find the value of $\dfrac{1}{1 + \dfrac{1}{1 + \frac{1}{2}}}$ $\dfrac{3}{5}$ answer

---

Ho Math Chess 何数棋谜 奥数,解题策略,及 IQ 思唯训练宝典
Frank Ho, Amanda Ho © 1995 - 2020   All rights reserved.

Student's name: _____   Assignment date: _____

Whole and partial one (fraction)

Calculation methods

The whole 1 can be graphically represented as a circle as an entirety such that whole 1 is also called a unit 1 and each unit one can be divided into equal parts. We can use a fraction to get back the original amount by using division and use the fraction to get the new value by using multiplication.

Fraction: Use the product ÷ its corresponding fraction to get the original amount.
Percent: Use the product ÷ its corresponding partial % (or % increase/decrease) to get the original or new amount.

Example – division method

Melody spent $\frac{5}{8}$ of her money and had $333 left. What was her original amount?

$333 \div \frac{3}{8} = 888$

Example - calculation method

Melody spent $\frac{2}{7}$ of her money and had $444 left. If she spent $\frac{1}{2}$ more of her total money, then how much did she have left now?

$444 \div \frac{2}{7} = 621.6$

$444 - 621.6 \times \frac{1}{2} = 133.20$

Using unit 1 as the whole 用單位一

Andria's money is three times as much as Bob's. Andria has $111, how much does Bob have?

37

After Andria spent $\frac{1}{3}$ of his money, he had $1372 left. How much did he have originally?

2058

Method 1 - Use 1 idea.	Method 2 - Use ratio idea	Method 3 - Use proportion	Method 4 - Use Line segment diagram
$1372 \div \frac{2}{3} = 2058$	Unspent: Spent = 2:1 So, the total money has 3 units. $1372 \div 2 \times 3 = 2058$;	$\frac{1}{x} = \frac{\frac{2}{3}}{1372}$ $x = 2058$	

After Andria spent 20% of his money, he had $1372 left. How much did he have originally?

1710

Jason finished reading a book in 3 days. On day 2, Jason read 2 times as many pages as day 1. On day 3, he read 2 times as many pages as day 2. What is the fraction of the entire book Jason read on day 2?

When water is freezing, it increases its volume by $\frac{1}{10}$. By what part of its volume will ice decrease when the ice melts and turns back into the water.

Let the water volume be 1.
Ice $= 1 + \frac{1}{10} = \frac{11}{10}$
$\frac{11}{10} \times x = 1$
$x = 1 \div \frac{11}{10} = \frac{10}{11}$

Magic unit 1 and assuming a number 神奇單位一及假设数

On a line segment $\overline{ABCDE}$, D is the midpoint of AE. The length of BD is $\frac{4}{5}$ the length of AB and BC = CD. What percent of AE is AC?

This problem has no quantity, how to solve it?

Andria's money is three times as much as Bob's. Adrian has $111, how much does |Bob have?

Adam can finish a painting in 25 days. If Adam and Bob work together, then they can finish the same job in 20 days. How many days will it take if Bob paints alone?

Fraction has two operations: Multiplication and Division 自帶乘除的分数

Diagram	English explanation by multiplication	English explanation by division	English explanation by the ratio
	Take one of one half.	Divide one into two equal pieces, and one part is taken,	One half to two halves = 1:2

It is important that students understand a fractional number can be interpreted in multiple ways unless it has been specified defined in advance. For example

$\frac{3}{5}$ divided by 3 is a lot easier to think the problem is $\frac{3}{5}$ multiplied by $\frac{1}{3}$.

English words	Written in multiplication	Written in division
2 of one half	$2 \times \frac{1}{2}$	$\frac{2}{2}$
2 of one-third	$2 \times \frac{1}{3}$	$\frac{2}{3}$
2 of one-fourth	$2 \times \frac{1}{4}$	$\frac{1}{2}$
2 of one-fifth	$2 \times \frac{1}{5}$	$\frac{2}{5}$
2 of one-eighth	$2 \times \frac{1}{8}$	$\frac{1}{4}$

Students are confused about fractions from 1 + 1 to 100%. 学生被 1+1 到 100%搞混了

What is 1 + 1? _____   answer   2

Show 1 + 1 is not 2 by one example (The answer is not "window".)

_____.

1 dog + 1 cat

Can you change 1 + 1 to a fraction problem? _____

Yes. $\frac{1}{1} + \frac{1}{1} = \frac{2}{1} = 2$

Show by the diagram on why $\frac{1}{2} + \frac{1}{4} \neq \frac{2}{6} \left(\frac{1+1}{2+4} \right)$?

 $= \frac{3}{4}$

The fractions with different values of numerators imply that they have different measuring units, do you agree? Explain your answer by reasons.

_____

Yes. $\frac{3}{2}$ means 3 of $\frac{1}{2}$ unit. $\frac{3}{4}$ means 3 of $\frac{1}{4}$ unit. $\frac{3}{2} + \frac{3}{4}$ means we are adding 3 of $\frac{1}{2}$ unit to 3 of $\frac{1}{4}$ unit. $\frac{1}{2}$ unit is different from $\frac{1}{4}$ unit.

Both of the following models showing $\frac{1}{4}$, how are their meanings different? Give one

example of each model.

Model A	One example of expressing the left Model A.
	Jocelyn cuts a squared pizza into 4 equal parts, and she takes one part of it. The part she takes is $\frac{1}{4}$ if expressed in a fraction.

Model B	One example of expressing the left Model B.
	Jocelyn has 4 squared pizzas with equal size. She takes one of them and the part she takes is $\frac{1}{4}$ if expressed in a fraction.

$\dfrac{p}{q}$ is not always $\dfrac{part}{whole}$. For example, a rate could be expressed as $\dfrac{1}{\#\ of\ hours}$, 1 is not a part, but a whole.

You can show the meaning of fractions by using a line segment. Show $\dfrac{1}{2}+\dfrac{1}{2}=1$ by a line segment as follows.

Assume you have shown the above line segment correctly and now mark the endpoints of the line segment as A and B at each end and mark its midpoint as C. Now, let's use the same line segment to create a work problem.

The distance (value, amount) from A to B is 1. Assume the above value from A to B is the amount of paintwork needed to complete, and it takes 2 hours for you to finish, then what is the value (work time) from A to C or C to B? One hour. This vale of either A to C or C to B will be your work rate per hour. Now try the following problem.

It takes Cecelia 3 hours to finish painting her room and 5 hours for her sister to finish if both work together then how long does it take for them to finish together?

$$answer\ \ 1 \div \left(\frac{1}{5}+\frac{1}{3}\right) = \frac{15}{8} = 1\frac{7}{8}\ hours$$

From 1 + 1 to 100% 1+1 到 100%

Convert the following division to a mixed fraction $\frac{p}{q} = \frac{dividend}{divisor} = \frac{7}{2}$. $3\frac{1}{2}$

$$2 \overline{\smash{)}\,7} \quad \begin{array}{r} 3 \\ \hline 7 \\ 6 \\ \hline 1 \end{array}$$

Is $\frac{2}{3}$ a multiplication problem or a division problem?

Why it is a division problem? _____ $2 \div 3$

Why it is a multiplication problem? _____ $2 \times \frac{1}{3}$

If you think fraction is a "division" problem, then do $2 \div 3 \times 6$. $\frac{2}{3} \times 6 = 4$

If you think fraction is a "multiplication" problem, then do $2 \times \frac{1}{3} \times 6$. 4

Does "order of operation" apply to fraction operation? If not, then what is normally done first in fraction operation? _____

No. the division is done first to convert to multiplication. For example, $\frac{1}{2} \times \frac{1}{3} \div \frac{3}{2} = \frac{1}{2} \times \frac{1}{3} \times \frac{2}{3} = \frac{1}{9}$.

How is fraction operation different from "normal" whole number or decimal operation?

Fraction has the chance of reducing.

The fraction operation not only has left to right operation, but it also has _____ operation.

Top and down or diagonal operation. Look at $6 \times \frac{15}{2}$, shall the "multiplication be done first, or shall the "division" be done first? The numbers can be reduced to be done first.

Why do we not have to convert the fraction multiplication to have the same denominators?

Even convert all the denominators to the same LCD, we still need to reduce the product, so there is no point to convert.

How is a fraction different from the "division" problem?

For example, what does $\frac{3}{2}$ mean in division or fraction (part and whole)? Explain by examples.

$\frac{3}{2}$ in the division means to 3 is equally shared by 2.

$\frac{3}{2}$ in a fraction means to 3 of $\frac{1}{2}$.

Student's name: _____ Assignment date: _____

Fractions comparison 分数的比较

Decimal, fractions, % # 39

Ho Math Chess (何數棋谜　趣味數學)

Use the empty area of this page or back page as a work area to calculate the following problems.

Which fraction $\frac{3}{4}$ or $\frac{2}{3}$ is larger? How much is the difference? Use rectangular arrays as an area model to explain your reasoning.

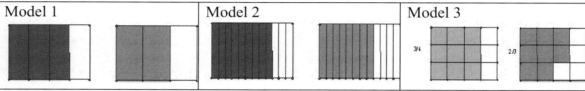

| Model 1 | Model 2 | Model 3 |

Model 2 and 3 are much clearer than model 1.

Use arrays to multiply fractions $\frac{2}{3} \times \frac{3}{4}$.

$. = \frac{2}{3} \times \frac{3}{4} = \frac{6}{12}$ answer

Fraction computations 分数计算

What does $\frac{2}{3}$ mean? Can you come up with at least 3 answers?

$2 \div 3$

$2 \times \frac{1}{3}$

2 to 3

2 out of 3

Insert 3 fractions between $\frac{1}{5}$ and $\frac{1}{6}$?

Convert to LCD $\frac{6}{30}$ and $\frac{5}{30}$, cannot insert whole number fractions.

Convert to LCD $\frac{30}{150}$ and $\frac{25}{150}$, insert 3 fractions $\frac{26}{150}, \frac{27}{150}, \frac{28}{150}$.

Insert 3 fractions between $\frac{6}{13}$ and $\frac{7}{13}$?

$\frac{24}{52}, \frac{28}{52}$

$\frac{25}{52}, \frac{26}{52}, \frac{27}{52}$

Without using common denominators, find 3 fractions between $\frac{7}{8}$ and $\frac{7}{9}$.

$\frac{7}{8} = 0.875$

$\frac{7}{9} = 0.778$

Insert 0.80 ($\frac{20}{25}$), 0.82 ($\frac{21}{25}$), 0.84 ($\frac{22}{25}$)

Use LCN (**L**owest **C**ommon **N**umerator) to compare $\dfrac{5}{7}$ and $\dfrac{8}{11}$.

$\dfrac{5}{7} = \dfrac{40}{56}$

$\dfrac{8}{11} = \dfrac{40}{55}$

$\dfrac{5}{7} < \dfrac{8}{11}$

Does the following shaded area show 1 of $\dfrac{3}{8}$ pie, 3 of $\dfrac{1}{8}$ pie, or $1\dfrac{1}{2}$ of $\dfrac{1}{4}$ pie?

The shaded area can be 1 of $\dfrac{3}{8}$ pie, 3 of $\dfrac{1}{8}$ pie, or $1\dfrac{1}{2}$ of $\dfrac{1}{4}$ pie, but the real meaning is only meaningful if the graph truly represents the real meaning.

Fractions

Fill in the blank $\dfrac{1}{1.2} = \dfrac{\square}{9.6} = \dfrac{10}{\square}$		8, 12
Fill in the blank $\dfrac{1}{1.2\%} = \dfrac{\square}{1.2} = \dfrac{10}{\square}$		100, 0.12
Fill in the blank $\dfrac{5}{tenth} = \dfrac{\square}{100\%} = \dfrac{\square}{0.75}$		50, 3.75
Fill in the blank below $\dfrac{20}{120} = \dfrac{\square}{90} = \dfrac{\square}{112.5}$		15, 18.75
Fill in the blank $\dfrac{0.2}{0.25} = \dfrac{\square}{25\%} = \dfrac{\square}{\frac{1}{4}}$		0.2, 20
Fill in the blank $\dfrac{\frac{2}{5}}{1} = \dfrac{\square}{12.5}$	5	

Use the figure on the right, the probability of getting 1 is _____ $\frac{1}{2}$ answer

Use the figure below, the ratio of 1 to 3 is _____.   2 : 1
Use the figure below, the ratio of 2 to 3 is _____.   1 : 1

How difficult is it for students to solve fraction problems? 为何分数很难?

I did an experiment as follows. I presented a whole number problem and a fraction problem to students.

Whole number problem	Fraction problem	
Adam and Bob shared 200 apples. Adam had three quarters fewer apples than Bob. Find out how many apples did each one of them have in the beginning. A : B = 1 : 4 A = $200 \times \frac{1}{5} = 40$ B = 200 - 40 = 160	Adam and Bob divided 200 apples. Adam had $\frac{3}{5}$ fewer apples than Bob's apples **out of 200 apples**. Find out how many apples did each one of them have in the beginning.	
	Arithmetic method	Algebraic method
	Let the total apples be 1. $B - A = \frac{3}{5}$ $B + A = 1$ $B = 200 \times \frac{1}{5} = 40$ Adam $= 1 - \frac{1}{5} = \frac{4}{5}$ Adam $= 200 \times \frac{4}{5} = 160$	Let Bob's apples of fraction $= x$ $(x - \frac{3}{5})200 + 200x = 200$ Bob $= x = \frac{4}{5}, 200 \times \frac{4}{5} = 160$ Adam $= 200 - 160 = 40$
	Adam and Bob divided 210 apples. Adam had $\frac{3}{5}$ fewer apples than Bob's apples. Find out how many apples did each one of them have in the beginning.	
	Arithmetic method	Algebraic method
	Let Bob's apples be 1. Adam $= \frac{2}{5}$ Bob's apples $= \frac{210}{1 + \frac{2}{5}} = 150$ Adam $= 210 - 150 = 60$	$x + \frac{2}{5}x = 200$ $x = 150 = $ Bob Adam $= 200 - 150 = 60$

The first difficulty students will face is the concept of remaining and the concept of using the remaining quantity and its corresponding remaining fraction to get a whole. This concept does not exist in whole-number computations.

The second difficulty students will face is some math contest books will talk about Sum/Difference, Sum/Multiplier etc. types of problems in whole numbers, but these types of problems seldom given in the fractions sections.

Clearly, even with the same problem presented above, by just changing the numbers from whole numbers to fractions, the difficulty level increases dramatically, and most students encountered difficulties. So, the skills of solving the whole number problems are not totally helpful to the fraction type of word problems, and students require a very different training of fraction skills to solve fraction word problems in the areas of working on the remaining fractions or using the remaining fraction and its corresponding quantity to get back the original whole value.

Fractions calculations

If you forget how to calculate fractions, then you will have difficulty in doing problems in this section. It is surprising that many students simply forgot how to do addition, subtraction, multiplication and division of fractions. A very simple-minded rule is to convert all fractions to improper fractions and then carry out fraction calculations for all four operations. The drawback of this method is you might encounter large numerators; see the following examples for details.

To convert all fractions to improper fractions first,

$$13\frac{2}{3} + 12\frac{2}{5} = \frac{41}{3} + \frac{62}{5} = \frac{41\times5+62\times3}{15} = \frac{391}{15} = 26\frac{1}{15}$$

If you do not convert fractions to improper fractions, then you do the following way

$$13\frac{2}{3} + 12\frac{2}{5} = 13\frac{10}{15} + 12\frac{6}{15} = 25\frac{16}{15} = 26\frac{1}{15}$$

Tangram and fraction 七巧板与分数

	a	b		c
3	$1\frac{1}{9}$	$3\frac{1}{2}$		$2\frac{1}{3}$
2	$2\frac{1}{8}$			$3\frac{3}{4}$
1	$1\frac{1}{7}$	$3\frac{1}{6}$		$1\frac{1}{5}$

The **tangram** invented by the ancient Chinese hundreds of years ago. (七巧板; literally "seven boards of skill") is a dissection puzzle consisting of seven flat shapes (2 large right triangles, 1 medium right triangle, 2 small right triangles, 1 square, and 1 parallelogram) which are put together to form shapes. The objective of the puzzle is to form a specific shape (given only in outline or silhouette) using all seven pieces, which may not overlap. You are at b2 and the area of the entire square is 1.

$$\underline{\quad} + \underline{\quad} = 3\frac{1}{2} + \frac{1}{16} = \underline{\quad} + \underline{\quad} = \underline{\quad}$$

$$\underline{\quad} - (1 + \underline{\quad}) \underline{\quad} =$$

$$\underline{\quad} \times (1\frac{1}{3} + \underline{\quad}) \underline{\quad} =$$

$$\underline{\quad} \div (2\frac{2}{3} + \underline{\quad}) \underline{\quad} =$$

$$\underline{\quad} + \underline{\quad} = \underline{\quad}$$

$$\underline{\quad} - (1\frac{2}{5} + \underline{\quad}) \underline{\quad} =$$

$$\underline{\quad} + \underline{\quad} = \underline{\quad}$$

$$\underline{\quad} \underline{\quad} = \underline{\quad}$$

$$\underline{\quad} + \underline{\quad} = \underline{\quad}$$

$$\underline{\quad} - \underline{\quad} = \underline{\quad}$$

$$\underline{\quad} + \underline{\quad} + \underline{\quad} = \underline{\quad}$$

$$\underline{\quad} \underline{\quad} \underline{\quad} = \underline{\quad}$$

$\frac{1}{16}$ $\frac{1}{8}$ $\frac{1}{8}$ $\frac{1}{4}$

$3\frac{9}{16}, 2\frac{7}{12}, 3\frac{7}{8}, 1\frac{21}{80}, 2\frac{1}{4}, 1\frac{61}{144}, 2\frac{7}{16}, \frac{4}{5}, 2\frac{1}{10}, 1\frac{11}{80}, 2, \frac{115}{144}$

Fraction multiplication 分数乘法

No reducing beforehand.	
$2 \times \frac{1}{3} = \frac{2}{3}$ answer	$21 \times \frac{3}{74} = \frac{63}{74}$ answer
$12 \times \frac{1}{13} = \frac{12}{13}$ answer	$5 \times \frac{1}{32} = \frac{5}{32}$ answer

Reducing beforehand.	
$2 \times \frac{1}{6} = \frac{1}{3}$ answer	$24 \times \frac{3}{74} = \frac{36}{37}$ answer
$24 \times \frac{1}{3} = 8$ answer	$25 \times \frac{1}{30} = \frac{5}{6}$ answer

Reducing beforehand.	
$\frac{2}{10} \times \frac{4}{6} = \frac{2}{15}$ answer	$\frac{4}{13} \times \frac{13}{6} = \frac{2}{3}$ answer
$\frac{2}{3} \times \frac{21}{9} = 1\frac{5}{9}$ answer	$\frac{2}{24} \times \frac{8}{2} = \frac{1}{3}$ answer

Reducing beforehand.	
$2\frac{2}{10} \times \frac{4}{6} = \frac{22}{15}$ answer	$\frac{4}{13} \times 3\frac{13}{6} = \frac{62}{39}$ answer
$2\frac{2}{3} \times \frac{21}{9} = \frac{56}{9}$ answer	$2\frac{2}{24} \times \frac{8}{2} = \frac{25}{3}$ answer

Reducing beforehand.	
$2\frac{2}{10} \times \frac{4}{6} \times \frac{12}{8} = \frac{11}{5}$ answer	$\frac{4}{12} \times \frac{8}{6} \times \frac{36}{12} = \frac{4}{3}$ answer
$1\frac{2}{3} \times 2\frac{2}{5} \times 2\frac{20}{18} = \frac{96}{9}$ answer	$1\frac{2}{13} \times \frac{26}{15} \times 1\frac{17}{15} = \frac{64}{15}$ answer

Student's name: _____   Assignment date: _____

Converting order of operation into fractions 将横式運算转换或分数

$42 \times 8 \div 7 =$	$43 \div 6 \times 48 =$
48	364
Blank line blank line	
Blank line blank line	
Blank line blank line	
Blank line blank line	
$88 \div 45 \times 90 =$	$28 \times 18 \div 14 =$
176	36
Blank line blank line	
Blank line blank line	
Blank line blank line	
Blank line blank line	
$14 \times 18 \div 7 =$	$25 \div 6 \times 72 =$
36	300
Blank line blank line	
Blank line blank line	
Blank line blank line	
Blank line blank line	
$20 \div 45 \times 90 \div 5 =$	$35 \div 45 \times 85 \div 5 =$
8	$\frac{85}{9}$
Blank line blank line	
Blank line blank line	
Blank line blank line	
$100 \div 45 \times 90 \div 20 =$	$100 \div 45 \times 90 \div 20 \div 36 \times 720 =$
10	200
Blank line blank line	
Blank line blank line	
Blank line blank line	

Ho Math Chess 何数棋谜 奥数,解题策略,及 IQ 思唯训练宝典

Student's name: _____   Assignment date: _____

Faction, %, ratio, equation conversion 5 大運算的转换 分数, %, 比, 方程式, 英文题

Fraction	%	Ratio	Equation	English statement
$\dfrac{A}{B} = \dfrac{}{}$ $\dfrac{2}{3}$	A= _____ % of B $66\frac{2}{3}$	A : B = ___ : ___ $\overline{2:3}$	___ A = ___ B $3A = 2B$	The ratio of Adam's oranges to Bob's orange is 2 to 3.
$\dfrac{A}{B} = \dfrac{}{}$ $\dfrac{5}{6}$	A= _____ % of B $83\frac{1}{3}$	A : B = ___ : ___ $\overline{}$ 5:6	___ A = ___ B $6A=5B$	Veena paid $120 (A) for a pair of shoes. Originally, she thought that she would have to pay 20% more than she paid, what was the original price that she thought (B)? $144
$\dfrac{A}{B} = \dfrac{}{}$ $\dfrac{3}{1}$	A= _____ % of B 300	A : B = ___ : ___ 3:1	___ A = ___ B $1A=3B$	Adam (A) had three times of apples as Bob (B)
$\dfrac{A}{B} = \dfrac{}{}$ $\dfrac{3}{4}$	B= _____ % of A $133\frac{1}{3}$	A : B = ___ : ___ $\overline{}$ 3:4	___ A = ___ B $4A=3B$	Adam (A) has $\frac{3}{4}$ of Bob's (B) apples.
$\dfrac{A}{B} = \dfrac{}{}$ $\dfrac{3}{2}$	A= _____ % of B 150	A : B = ___ : ___ $\overline{}$ 3:2	___ A = ___ B $2A=3B$	Adam (A) took $\frac{1}{3}$ of apples and Bob (B) took $\frac{1}{3}$ of the remaining.
$\dfrac{A}{B} = \dfrac{}{}$ $\dfrac{8}{9}$	A= _____ % of B $88\frac{8}{9}$	A : B = ___ : ___ $\overline{}$ A : B = 8 : 9	___ A = ___ B $9A=8B$	Nine times of Adam's apples (A) are eight times of Bob's apples.

Example 1

Gina took one-half of apples out of the basket, and there were 1999 apples left, how many apples were there in the beginning?

Method 1 – work backwards

If 1999 was what left after Gina took one half, then 1999 times 2 must be the total.

$1999 \times 2 = 3998$

Method 2 – Division method using 1 as the whole

If Gina took one-half of all apples, then there was one half left, so the quantity of 1999 apples corresponds to the 1 part out of 2, The partial number is 1998, and the whole is 2, so the total is $1999 \times 2 = 3998$.

We can also use the method of Quantity divided by its corresponding fraction to get the whole $1998 \div \frac{1}{2} = 1999 \times 2 = 3998$

The above method uses the same idea of having original numbers to be 1 whole. Fractions have the implicit meaning of using the denominators as "wholes". Percents have the implicit meaning of having 100% as the whole or having 100 as the denominator and be treated as the whole of being 100. The ratio can be treated as simplified fractions, so they can be converted to fractions. Since both percent and ratio can be transferred to fractions, the most important learning is still to learn how to do fraction word problems and then we can use the skills in solving fraction problems to solve ratio and % problems. In high schools, fractions problems are called rational problems.

Example 2

Adam had three times of apples as Bob and Adam gave 4932 apples to Bob, then Bob had three times as many apples as Adam. How many apples did each one of them have in the beginning?

This is a difference and ratios/multiples problem. The ratio changes after the amount are changed.

Method 1 – algebraic method

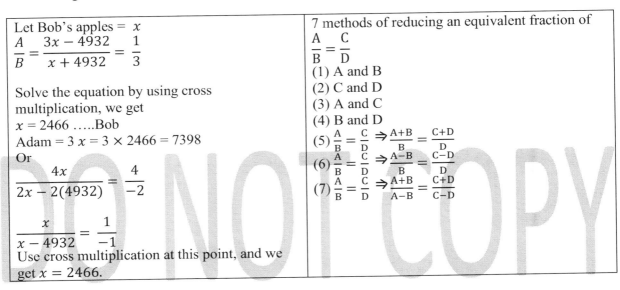

Method 2– arithmetic ratio method

We can use the ratio method to solve the problem.
A:B= 3:1(3:1 is a reduced form)
(A−4932) : (B+4932) = 1:3
Compare the above two rations, we know that Adam has reduced apples by 4932 and his ratio dropped from 3 to 1 so that each ratio unit corresponds to the amount of $\frac{4932}{3-1} = 2466$.
Adam = 3 × 2466 = 7398
Bob = 2466

By comparing the algebraic method and the arithmetic method, we know that the arithmetic method follows the exact steps of the algebraic method and uses the algebraic concept to solve the problems. The algebraic method is easier once the equation is set up. The arithmetic is ironically using the same concept of the algebraic method, but if the students do not understand algebra, then we teach students to use the concept that is to have the difference divided by the difference of ratios to get back the original amount. Many times, the reason why the arithmetic method works can be "easily" explained by using algebra.

The concept of using the difference amount by is corresponding ratios difference can be explained by the line segment diagram as follows. My experience of teaching students shows that, sometimes, the line diagram may not be "easy" for students to draw to show the correct scale. If the scale is drawn totally out of proportion, then it will not be helpful for students to solve the problems.

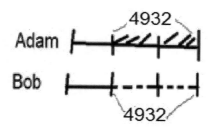

Method 3– arithmetic fraction method

We can just use one statement to get back the original amount.

$4932 \div \left(\frac{3}{4} - \frac{1}{4}\right) = 4932 \times 2 = 9864$, this is to say this is the amount of 2 parts out of 4 parts (total).

Adam $= 9864 \times \frac{3}{4} = 7398$

Bob $= 9864 \times \frac{1}{4} = 2466$

Example 3

Cecilia can finish a science project in 7 days, and Joyce can finish it in 3 days. If they work together with their individual speeds, then how long will it take for them to finish the science project?

Assume the work amount for the science project is 1.

Cecilia's work rate will be $1 \div 7 = \frac{\square}{\square}$ and Joyce's work rate will be $1 \div 3 = \frac{\square}{\square}$.

The days take together to finish will be $1 \div \left(\frac{1}{7} + \frac{1}{3}\right) = 2\frac{1}{10}$. **days.**

How do some students do so fast on $1 \div (\frac{1}{a} + \frac{1}{b}) = ?$ The trick is 1 is here to serve the purpose of flipping the fraction. So, the answer is $\frac{ab}{a+b} \cdot (\frac{Multiply\ 2\ numbers}{Add\ 2\ numbers})$

Example 4

Travelling problem

Trucks A and B are travelling in a circular motion, and it takes truck A 50 minutes to finish and truck B 30 minutes to finish. After truck A travels a 25-minute circle, truck B starts to catch up. How long does it take for truck B to catch up to truck A?

Use 1 as the length of the circle. 25 minutes means $\frac{1}{2}$ circle.

$$\frac{\frac{1}{2}}{\frac{1}{30} - \frac{1}{50}} = 37.5 \text{ minutes}$$

Example 5

Reciprocal

1 is used as a variable. 1 is to turn fraction upside down - $\frac{1}{\frac{a}{b}} = \frac{b}{a}$.

Calculate

$$\frac{1}{1 + \frac{1}{2 + \frac{1}{2}}}$$

$$\frac{5}{7}$$

Example 6

1 is used as a media to do the "trick" to convert numbers to percents.

1 is 100%.

What % is 2? _____ 200

Example 7

By using 1 as a whole in fraction, it is easier to solve some problems than the algebraic method

Sometimes, it is easier to use a line segment to solve fraction problems than an algebraic way.

After Frank spent 20 % of his pay on a computer. He spent $\frac{2}{5}$ of the remaining on a DVD. He had $72 left. How much money did he have at first?

To solve it using algebra by forwarding method, the equation is

$$x - 0.2x - \frac{2}{5}(x\text{-}0.2) = 72$$
$$x = 150$$

Most elementary students cannot solve the above equation, but they can use the line segment to solve the above problem.

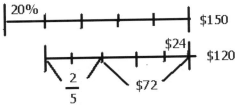

By providing a set of tools to elementary students, elementary students can solve some difficult problems, which sometimes they see these word problems again when they are in secondary schools.

Use one statement only to solve fraction remaining word problems by the backward method.

Many fraction word problems involving remaining can be "easily" solved by using only one statement instead of multi-step when using the algebraic method.

$$72 \div \frac{3}{5} \div \frac{4}{5}$$
$$= 72 \times \frac{5}{3} \times \frac{5}{4}$$
$$= 150$$

Example 8

No quantity is mentioned in the problem.

Benjamin has $\frac{3}{5}$ of Jocelyn's money and Andrew has as twice as much as Benjamin's money. How much does Andrew have Jocelyn's money in terms of a fraction?

If Jocelyn has money of 1, then Andrew has $\frac{6}{5} = 1\frac{1}{5}$ of Jocelyn's money.

\

Problem

If A = 50 and B= 120, how many % is A less than B? How many % is B more than A?

Less:

$\frac{120-50}{120} = 58\frac{1}{3}$ %   Blank line   blank line

More   Blank line   blank line

$\frac{120-50}{50} = 1.4 = 140\%$ Blank line   blank line

All 61 students in Cindy's class attended a math contest, and the students who did not get awards were 12 more than $\frac{2}{5}$ of those who got awards. How many students in Cindy's class got awards?

Arithmetic method   Blank line   blank line

Use 1 as the number of those who got awards, and it is equivalent to x in algebra, then this problem becomes the sum dividing by its corresponding total of fractions.

$\frac{61-12}{\frac{2}{5}+1} = 35$ Blank line   blank line

         Blank line   blank line
         Blank line   blank line

Algebraic method

Let the number of students who got awards = x.

$x + 12 + \frac{2}{5}x = 61$ Blank line   blank line

         Blank line   blank line

$x = 35$ Blank line   blank line

The ratio of A :B : C = 1 : 2: 4 and if C − B = 18 what is the value of A + B + C?

$\frac{18}{4-2} = 9$ Blank line   blank line

A + B + C =$9 \times 1 + 2 \times 9 + 4 \times 9 = 63$ Blank line   blank line

         Blank line   blank line

A tin of oil is $\frac{3}{5}$ full. 3.4 l of oil is required to fill it completely. If one full tin of oil costs $51, how much does $\frac{3}{4}$ l of oil cost?

$3 \times 4 \div \frac{2}{5} = 8.5$ Blank line   blank line

$\frac{51}{8.5} \times \frac{3}{4} = \$4.5$ Blank line   blank line

Student's name: _____   Assignment date: _____

Mixed fraction word problems 分数混合文字题

Using the pie chart is a method to learn fractions concept, but in actual computation, the Line Segment Method is more useful.

Calculate the shaded areas. Show the answer by a diagram.

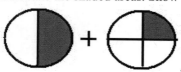

answer $\frac{3}{4}$

Calculate $\frac{1}{2} + \frac{1}{4}$.   answer $\frac{3}{4}$

Calculate $\frac{1}{2} + \frac{1}{3}$.   answer $\frac{5}{6}$

Calculate the shaded areas.

answer $\frac{3}{4} +$

Calculate $\frac{1}{2}$ of one apple and $\frac{2}{3}$ of one apple. All apples are the same size. _____

answer $\frac{7}{6}$ apple

Calculate $\frac{1}{2}$ of one apple and $\frac{2}{3}$ of one pineapple. _____ $\frac{1}{2}$ of one apple and $\frac{2}{3}$ of one pineapple

Calculate $\frac{1}{2}$ of one small apple and $\frac{2}{3}$ of one large apple. _____ $\frac{1}{2}$ of one small apple and $\frac{2}{3}$ of one large apple

Sam ate $\frac{1}{2}$ of a small apple and $\frac{3}{4}$ of a large apple. Amanda ate 3 times as much as Sam ate in the total amount. How much did Amanda eat?

$\frac{3}{2}$ of one small apple and $\frac{9}{4}$ of one large apple

Sam's mother cut one pizza into pieces of size $\frac{1}{8}$. How many $\frac{1}{8}$ pieces of $\frac{1}{2}$ size and how many $\frac{1}{8}$ pieces of size $\frac{1}{4}$ are there?

4, 2

Student's name: _____   Assignment date: _____

Bob's garden is 20 ft × 10 ft rectangle. Bob plants tomatoes in half of his garden. $\frac{1}{4}$ of the remainder are radishes. $\frac{1}{2}$ of what is left containing cucumbers. The last area is planted in peppers. What fractional part of the garden is planted in peppers?

Blank line   blank line
Blank line   blank line
Blank line   blank line
Blank line   blank line

3/16

Forty less than one-third of a number is equal to thirty more than one-quarter of its number. What is the number?

Number dividing by its corresponding fractional number.

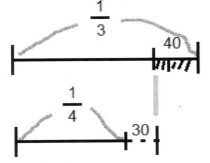

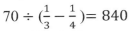

$70 \div (\frac{1}{3} - \frac{1}{4}) = 840$

Blank line   blank line
Blank line   blank line
Blank line   blank line
Blank line   blank line

Student's name: _____ Assignment date: _____

A merchant carrying rice passes through three stations. At the first station, he sells one-quarter of his rice. At the second station, he sells one-fifth of what remains and at the last station, one-sixth of what remains. He ends up with 9.5 kg of rice. How much rice (in kg) did he start with?

1. $\dfrac{1}{4}$

2. $\dfrac{3}{4} \times \dfrac{1}{5}$

3. $\dfrac{9.5}{\left(1 - \dfrac{1}{4} - \dfrac{3}{4} \times \dfrac{1}{5}\right) \times \dfrac{1}{6}}$

19 kg

Blank line	blank line
Blank line	blank line
Blank line	blank line
Blank line	blank line

The airplane was full when it left Vancouver. At the first stop (Kelowna), half of the people got off the plane, and 8 got on. At the next stop (Prince George), half of the people who were on board got off, 11 got on, and the plane was full again. How many people were on the plane when it left Vancouver?

Line Segment Diagram	**Algebraic method**
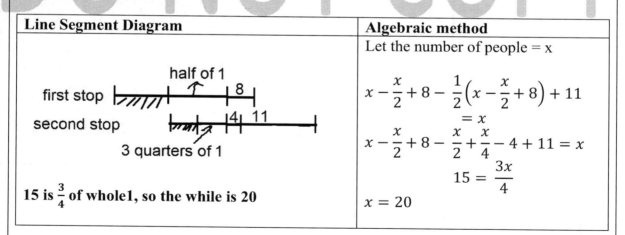 15 is $\frac{3}{4}$ of whole1, so the while is 20	Let the number of people = x $$x - \frac{x}{2} + 8 - \frac{1}{2}\left(x - \frac{x}{2} + 8\right) + 11 = x$$ $$x - \frac{x}{2} + 8 - \frac{x}{2} + \frac{x}{4} - 4 + 11 = x$$ $$15 = \frac{3x}{4}$$ $$x = 20$$

20 people

| Blank line | blank line |

Student's name: _____   Assignment date: _____

Evaluate $4 \times \left(\dfrac{1}{2} + \dfrac{1}{4} \right) + 56 \times \left(\dfrac{1}{7} + \dfrac{1}{8} \right) = 2 + 1 + 8 + 7 = \mathbf{18}$

Rank the following fractions from the least to the largest.

	2 fractions	2 or more fractions	Comments
Same bottom	$\dfrac{1}{2}, \dfrac{3}{2}$ >	$\dfrac{1}{2}, \dfrac{3}{2}, \dfrac{0.5}{2}$ 3/2 > ½ > 0.5/2	
Same top	$\dfrac{4}{3}, \dfrac{4}{5}$, >	$\dfrac{4}{3}, \dfrac{4}{5}, \dfrac{0.4}{0.6}$ 4/3 > 4/5 > 0.4/0.6	
Top and bottom all different	$\dfrac{3}{7}, \dfrac{5}{9}$ <	$\dfrac{2}{3}, \dfrac{3}{4}, \dfrac{6}{7}, \dfrac{1}{2}$ 6/7 > ¾ > 2/3 > 1/2	The top times 100 to get 2-digit results.
Top and bottom all different		$\dfrac{16}{23}, \dfrac{10}{21}, \dfrac{11}{18}, \dfrac{8}{17}, \dfrac{1}{2}$ 16/23 > 11/18 > ½ >> 8/17	

What must the stock price be increased in % to its original price if the price dropped to $\dfrac{1}{2}$ of its original price? 100 divided by 100 = 200%.

After a $\dfrac{1}{4}$ discount, Austin paid $115. What was the original price?

115 x 4 divided by 3 = **153.33**

Evaluate

$$9 \times \frac{1}{18} + 8 \times \frac{1}{16} + 7 \times \frac{1}{14} + 6 \times \frac{1}{12}$$

2

| Blank line | blank line |
| Blank line | blank line |

If $A + B + C + D = 10$
$0.2A + 0.2B + 0.2\,C + 0.2\,D = ?$

2

| Blank line | blank line |
| Blank line | blank line |

Evaluate

$$\frac{0.2}{0.04} + \frac{0.3}{0.06} + \frac{0.35}{0.07} + \frac{0.4}{0.08} + \frac{5}{0.1} + \frac{5}{0.01}$$

Blank line	blank line
Blank line	blank line
Blank line	blank line

570

Find $\dfrac{x}{y}$ if $\dfrac{x+2y}{x-y} = \dfrac{1}{2}$

-5

In how many ways can a debt of $69 be paid exactly using only $5 bills and $2 bills? 7 ways

$2	$5
2	13
7	11
17	7
27	3

$2	$5
22	5
27	3
32	1

Find angle x and angle y.

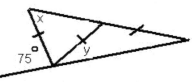 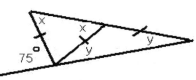

$x + y = 105$, $x = 2y$, so $3y = 75$, $y = 25$, $x=50$

Evaluate

$$\frac{1}{1\times3}+\frac{1}{3\times5}+\frac{1}{5\times7}+...+\frac{1}{n(n+2)}, n \text{ is odd whole number.}$$

$$\frac{1}{2}\left(\frac{1}{1}-\frac{1}{3}\right)+\frac{1}{2}\left(\frac{1}{3}-\frac{1}{5}\right)+...+\frac{1}{2}\left(\frac{1}{n}-\frac{1}{n+2}\right)=$$

Blank line   blank line   —
Blank line   blank line

$$\frac{n+1}{2(n+2)}$$

Evaluate

$$\frac{n(n+1)(n+2)}{n}+\frac{n(n+1)(n+2)}{n+1}+\frac{n(n+1)(n+2)}{n+2}=74$$

N= 4

Blank line   blank line

Three containers hold 19, 13, and 7 ml juice separately. The 19 ml container is full, but the 13 ml and the 7 ml containers are empty. How to get 10 ml by using these 3 containers without dumping any juice or adding any more juice but by only pouring juice to each other to 10 ml in one container?

	19 ml	13 ml	7 ml
	0	13	7
Step 1	7	13	0
Step 2	19	1	0
Step 3	12	1	7
Step 4	12	8	0
Step 5	5	8	7
Step 6	5	13	2
Step 7	18	0	2
Step 8	18	2	0
Step 9	11	2	7
Step 10	11	9	0
Step 11	4	9	7
Step 12	4	13	3
Step 13	17	0	3
Step 14	17	3	0
Step 15	10	3	7

Student's name: _____ Assignment date: _____

Convert $\frac{1}{8}$ to be a sum of 2-unit fractions (a fraction with numerator as 1). (Hint: Convert $\frac{1}{8}$ to its equivalent fractions and make sure that each term in the numerator is the factor of its denominator.). For example, $\frac{1}{8} = \frac{3}{24} = \frac{1+2}{24} = \frac{1}{24} + \frac{1}{12}$. Come up with 4 more answers

$$\frac{1}{8} = \frac{6}{48} = \frac{2+4}{48} = \frac{1}{24} + \frac{1}{12} \qquad \frac{1}{8} = \frac{2}{16} = \frac{1+1}{16} = \frac{1}{16} + \frac{1}{16}$$

$\frac{4}{5}$ = the sum of unit fractions. $\frac{16}{20} = \frac{1}{20} + \frac{5}{20} + \frac{10}{20}$

$\frac{3}{4} = \frac{1}{?} + \frac{1}{?} + \frac{1}{4} + \frac{1}{2}$

$\frac{2}{5}$ = the sum of unit fractions $\frac{1}{4} + \frac{1}{10} + \frac{1}{20}$

Convert the following to the difference of 2-unit fractions.   answer $\frac{1}{18} + \frac{1}{9}, \frac{1}{12} + \frac{1}{24}, \frac{1}{15} + \frac{1}{30}$

$\frac{1}{6} =$

$\frac{1}{8} =$

$\frac{1}{10} =$

Two trains start at the same time. After two trains past each other, they arrive at their destinations for one hour and four hours, respectively. How much faster is one train running than the other?

One train was running twice as fast as the other.

A ————————— B — C
  4 hours   1 hour

s = slow speed, f = fast speed. The time took to meet is the same regardless of their speeds, so this concept is used for the equation to solve.

Time $= \frac{4s}{f} = \frac{f}{s}$, $4s^2 = f^2$, $2s = f$

Fraction maze 分数谜题

- Move only vertically down or horizontally to a square where its value is less than the fraction of the square you are currently in.
- Stop when you cannot move anymore.
- Start at the square where its value is fenced by a rectangle to reach a circled square finally.

$\frac{41}{6}$	$\frac{42}{7}$	$\frac{27}{5}$	$\frac{40}{8}$	$\frac{5}{2}$
$\frac{21}{7}$	$\frac{22}{6}$	$\frac{21}{4}$	$\frac{20}{5}$	$\frac{4}{3}$
$\frac{11}{3}$	$\frac{22}{7}$	$\frac{20}{3}$	$\frac{3}{5}$	$\frac{5}{4}$
$\frac{22}{6}$	$\frac{20}{8}$	$\frac{5}{2}$	$\frac{2}{6}$	$\frac{8}{2}$
$\frac{1}{4}$	$\frac{1}{5}$	$\frac{3}{2}$	$\frac{5}{2}$	$\frac{7}{2}$

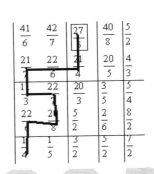

Samantha has a basket of apples. If she had half as many more as she now has, and two apples and a half, she would have 100. How many apples did she have?

$$x + \frac{1}{2}x + 2.5 = 100$$

$x = 65$

Julian has some pennies, nickels, dimes, and quarters. The total value of each different number of coins is the same (total value of pennies = total value of nickels = total value of dimes = total value of quarters). If the value of all these coins is $8, how many quarters are there?

800 / 4 = 200, 200 /25 = 8 quarters

Express the answer to the following in common fraction ($\frac{p}{q}$).

$$\left(1 - \frac{1}{2}\right)\left(1 - \frac{1}{3}\right)\left(1 - \frac{1}{4}\right)...\left(1 - \frac{1}{50}\right)$$

Do subtraction and then cancellation of the denominator of the current fraction with the numerator of the next fraction. $\frac{1}{50}$

Student's name: _____　Assignment date: _____

All decimals 小数

Decimal computations for advanced students 挑战生小数计标

The whole number divided by the whole number	Decimal divided by whole	Whole divided by decimal	Decimal divided by decimal	Operated by the power of 10
$1 \div 3$	$12.12 \div 3$	$300 \div 0.3 = \frac{300}{0.3} =$	$3.9 \div 0.3$	$3.9 \div 10$
$1 \div 5$	$10.05 \div 5$	$1515 \div 0.03$	$15.15 \div 0.03$	$15.15 \div 10000$
$1 \div 7$	$21.021 \div 7$	$1414 \div 0.7$	$14.14 \div 0.3$	$14.14 \div 0.1$
$21 \div 5$	$0.002525 \div 5$	$25251414 \div 0.5$	$252514.14 \div 0.5$	$252514.14 \div 0.001$
$31 \div 4$	$2829.028 \div 4$	$2829028 \div 0.04$	$28.29028 \div 0.04$	28.29028×0.01
$205 \div 25$	$0.502625 \div 5$	$502625 \div 0.05$	$5026.25 \div 0.05$	5026.25×10000
$125 \div 8$	$125.125 \div 25$	$125125 \div 2.5$	$1251.25 \div 2.5$	$1251.25 \div 10$
$18 \div 15$	$30.015 \div 15$	$30015 \div 1.5$	$300.15 \div 1.5$	$30015 \div 100$

Student's name: _____   Assignment date: _____

Evaluate

$10.82 + 0.28 + 0.73 + 0.57 + 0.37 + 0.91 + 0.43 + 0.62 + 0.62 + 0.91 + 0.43 + 0.69 + 0.77$

$= 10.82 + 0.28 + 0.73 + 0.37 + 0.57 + 0.43 + 0.28 + 0.62 + 0.91 + 0.69 + 0.43 + 0.77 = 16.9$

| Blank line | blank line |
| Blank line | blank line |

Evaluate $0.9 + 0.99 + 0.999 + 0.99999$ 3.88899

| Blank line | blank line |
| Blank line | blank line |

Evaluate $100 \times (0.21 + 0.47) + 100(0.37 + 0.29)$ 134

| Blank line | blank line |
| Blank line | blank line |

Evaluate $9 \times (0.1 + 0.11 + 0.111 + 0.1111)$

3.88899

0.2 is ____ % of 5?   4

What is 0.2 of 200 _____.   40

0.6 is what times 3 _____.   0.2

11− 0.0019 =   1.0981

Convert each of the following to a decimal.

$\frac{3}{5} = 0.6$	$\frac{0.3}{5} = 0.06$	$\frac{3}{0.5} = 6$	$\frac{0.3}{0.5} = 0.6$	$\frac{0.3}{0.05} = 60$
$\frac{6}{5} = 1.2$	$\frac{0.6}{0.5} = 1.2$	$\frac{6}{0.5} = 12$	$\frac{0.6}{0.05} = 120$	$\frac{0.6}{5} = 1.2$

How many pieces of ribbon does Austin need to cut from a length of 0.24 m and each cut piece is 0.0008 m?

30

Without calculating 0.4 × 0.9, how do you know the result is less than 0.4 or 0.9? Explain.

Since 0.4 times 1, the answer will still be 0.4, so by comparison, if 0.4 times something less than one (one time), then its answer will be less than 0.4. For the same reason, we can explain its answer will also be less than 0.9 if its answer is less than 0.4.

Use only two 8s to get an answer 10. **8/.8=10**	
Blank line	blank line
Blank line	blank line

Use only one 2 and one 3 to get an answer 8. 2^3	
Blank line	blank line
Blank line	blank line

Use 2, 4, 9, 6, 7, 3 only once to find two numbers whose sum is 112. 69+43 or 49+63	
Blank line	blank line
Blank line	blank line

Use 2, 4, 9, 6, 7, 3 only once to find two 3-digit numbers whose difference is 263. 732-469	
Blank line	blank line
Blank line	blank line

Rectangle B will be four times the area of rectangle A (as shown below). What are the dimensions of rectangle B?

7m

A 6m

1 by 168, 2 by 84, 4 by 42, 6 by 28, 7 by 24, 8 by 21, 12 by 14

Tammy had 10 more hockey cards than Tina, but she gave all her cards to Tina and then Tina ended up with 992 cards. How many cards did Tammy start with?

501 A variation of Sum and Difference problem. $\frac{992-10}{2} = \frac{982}{2} = 491$ …. Tina

$491 + 10 = 501$ ……. Tammy

A 1L can of paint covers 8m². Tammy needs to paint 8 rectangle-shaped posters for her science project that measure 60 cm by 100 cm in total area. Will 1L be enough to paint? Show your work.

1L is enough since 60 cm=60/100 m and 100 cm = 1 m Total area is 0.6 m².

(1) Place a decimal point in number 475 to make a new number between 4 and 5. _____   4.75
(2) Switch 2 digits in the result of (1) such that a new number is greater than the resulting number in (1). 7.45
(3) Switch 2 digits in the result of (1) such that a new number is less than the resulting number in (1). 4.57

(1) Place a decimal point in number 908 to make a new number 9 and 10. _____   9.08
(2) Switch 2 digits in the result of (1) such that a new number is greater than the resulting number in (1). 9.80
(3) Switch 2 digits in the result of (1) such that a new number is less than the resulting number in (1).   0.98

(1) Place a decimal point in number 768 to make a new number between 7 and 6. _____   7.68
(2) Switch 2 digits in the result of (1) such that a new number is greater than the resulting number in (1).   7.86
(3) Switch 2 digits in the result of (1) such that a new number is less than the resulting number in (1).   6.78

(1) Place a decimal point in number 102 to make a new number between 1 and 2. _____   1.02
(2) Switch 2 digits in the result of (1) such that a new number is greater than the resulting number in (1).   10.2
(3) Switch 2 digits in the result of (1) such that a new number is less than the resulting number in (1).   0.12

Student's name: _____　Assignment date: _____

Fill in each [　　　　　] by a number.

$0.001 = [\quad\quad\quad] \times 10$　　　**0.0001**

$2.014 = 100 \times [\quad\quad\quad]$　　　**0.02014**

$3000.03 = 10 \times [\quad\quad\quad]$　　　**300.003**

$45 = 10 \times [\quad\quad\quad]$　　　**4.5**

$7500 = 7.5 \times [\quad\quad\quad]$　　　**1000**

$6.231 = 6231 \times [\quad\quad\quad]$　　　**0.001** $\dfrac{1}{1000}$

Fill in each box by a number.

$0.00001 = 10 \times \boxed{}$ 0.000001

$0.0001 = 1 \div \boxed{}$ 10000

$0.1 = 10 \div \boxed{}$ 100

$0.000001 = 1000 \div \boxed{}$ 1000000000

$0.1 = 100 \times \boxed{}$ 0.001

$20.576 = 2.0576 \times \boxed{}$ 10

$0.0020576 = 2.0576 \times \boxed{}$ 0.001

$100 \times 10 \times 0.01 = 10 \times \boxed{}$ 1

$0.01 \times 100 \times 0.1 \times 10000 = 0.01 \times \boxed{}$ 100000

$0.0000034 = \boxed{}\%$ 0.00034

$10000.03 = \boxed{}\%$ 100.0003

$2345.0001\% = \boxed{}$ 23.450001

$0.00001234\% = \boxed{}$ 0.0000001234

Student's name: _____   Assignment date: _____

Percent 百分比

Computation of percent 百分比计算

Often, we translate percent to either divided by 100 or multiplied by $\frac{1}{100}$ in the computation of %.

Original amount × percent = partial amount

In lower grades, most problems are to find the partial amount when a percent is given. A direct method using multiplication could be used to solve it.

Example 1

A dress is selling for $20. If Sophie buys it at a 20% discount, how much will she save, and how much will she have to pay?

$20 \times 0.2 = 4$ …… The Amount Sophie will save.
$20 - 4 = 16$ …….. The amount Sophie will have to pay.

Use one statement

Students should also understand that without getting the amount of discount, use the concept of the whole in a fraction, how much does Sophie have to pay could also be solved by using only one statement.

$20 \times 0.8 = 16$ … Sophie only pays 80%.

Example 2

Twelve students of Alvin's borrowed books for the library, which is 75% of the entire class. How many students in Alvin's class did not borrow any books?

Method 1

Convert the percent to a fraction and then convert fractions to groups.

$75\% = \frac{3}{4}$ which could mean Alvin's class is divided into 4 groups and 3 groups of them borrowed books and the number of students in that 3 groups is 12. To find how many students in each group, we just use $\frac{12}{3}=4$. We know there is only one group of students who did not borrow any books, so the answer is **4**.

Method 2

Use the Line Segment Method by drawing line segments.

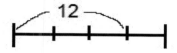

Method 3

A quantity divided by its corresponding value (to work backwards to get the original amount.)

This method is difficult for lower grades students to understand, so we suggest using this method for higher grades students.

$12 \div 0.75 = 12 \times \frac{4}{3} = 16$ …. The number of students for the entire class

$16 - 12 = 4$

Review of Percent 百分比複習

Information		Problem	Answer
(square divided into 4 parts, bottom-left shaded)		Find the % of the shaded area. Find % of the not shaded area.	
Annie		Find the letter of n's percentage in the name as spelt on the left.	
25% 50%		Which one is the larger percentage?	
(3×2 grid of shaded squares)		Find the percent of shaded squares.	
Annie's class has 10 boys and 15 girls.		Find the percent of boys in Annie's class.	

Ho Math Chess 何数棋谜 奥数,解题策略,及 IQ 思唯训练宝典
Frank Ho, Amanda Ho © 1995 - 2020   All rights reserved.

Student's name: _____   Assignment date: _____

From the whole number to fraction, decimal, percent or ratio

The percent, decimal, or fraction has hidden information that the student must know to solve word problems. The original amount of decimal, decimal, or fraction is 1.

		Meaning and concept	Example
Fractional number *Which is represented by $\frac{p}{q}$. p and q are integers, but q can not be zero unless it is a ratio. In the case of q = 0 for ratio, no computation can be done.*	fraction	• A fraction is a part out of a whole. A fraction is a ratio of part to whole. • Whenever you multiply or divide a fraction, it involves 2 operations: multiplication and division. • The original amount is 1. This concept applies to also percent. • The remaining fraction can be found by using 1= a fraction. This concept applies to percent. • No fraction divisions because all fractions are converted to fraction multiplications. • A fraction could have many meanings if used in different places. For example, when the bottom is 100, it could be called a percent. When doing division, it could be converted to a decimal number. When two numbers are compared, it is called a Ratio.	$9 \times \frac{2}{3}$, 9 is divided by 3 and then multiplied by 2. $8 \div \frac{2}{3}$, 8 is divided by the top number and then multiplied by the bottom number. The meaning of division of a fraction gives the original total of parts "3".
	decimal	See above.	$\frac{2}{3} = 3\overline{)2}$
	percent	See above.	$\frac{7}{100} = 7\%$
	ratio	See above. A horizontal form of ratio problem such as a : b = 2 : 3 often is converted to a fraction to do computations.	The number of girls to the number of boys is $\frac{2}{3} = 2$ to 3.

Example

Alina bought a pair of shoes for $80 with a 20% discount. What was the original price.?

Use Ratio

original	Sale price
?	$80
100% = 1	80%

After 20% discount, it means Alina paid her price at 100% − 20 % = 80%.
$80 at 80%, it means $10 at 10%. So, at 100%, the original price will be $100. The student can also use the cross-multiplication to solve the above ratio problem whenever there is a single fraction on each side of the equation.

Use Equation

Original × discounted percent = discounted price

So, to get back the original price, use discounted price ÷ discounted percent = original price

The same concept could be used for price increase, tax, commission by changing the above-discounted percent. Once the student understands the above concept, then they can use a short-cut method as follows:

Quantity ÷ its corresponding fractional number (fraction, %, or decimal) = original amount

Many students could not understand the concept when the original quantity could be found by using a division when using the above equation (Original × discounted percent = discounted price) to explain. A simple way to explain would be to use the whole number times table, and most students could link the idea of times table to **Quantity ÷ its corresponding fractional number (fraction, %, or decimal) = original amount.**

If 2 × 3 = 6, then how to get back 2 when 3 and 6 are given?
We know factor 1 × factor 2 = product
So, the unknown factor can be found by using **product ÷ a known factor** which is equivalent to **Quantity ÷ its corresponding fractional number (fraction, %, or decimal) = original amount.**

Frank Ho, Amanda Ho © 1995 - 2020   All rights reserved.

Student's name: _____   Assignment date: _____

Work and finish all the top row problems first before working on the bottom row problems.

Whole number	fraction	decimal	percent	ratio
Jennifer had 17 questions correct in her 25-question test. Oscar had 19 questions in his 20-question test. How many questions did they get correctly altogether?	Together how many questions did they get correctly in fraction out of two tests? *This problem illustrates the fraction is part out of the whole.* $$\frac{17+19}{25+20} = \frac{36}{45} = \frac{4}{5}$$	Together how many questions did they get correctly in decimal out of two tests? *This problem illustrates the concept of converting a fraction to a decimal.* $$\frac{4}{5} = 0.8$$	What percent did Jennifer get correctly? *Use the equivalent fraction to convert the bottom number to 100.* $$\frac{17}{25} = \frac{68}{100} = 68\%$$ What percent did Oscar get correctly? $$\frac{19}{20} = \frac{95}{100} = 95\%$$	What is the ratio of Jennifer's correct questions to Oscar's correct questions? 17: 19
The above is a very simple one-step addition model which is the following: $J + O = ?$ *A more complicated multi-step model could be created by adding another equation, such as the following:* $J + O = a$ $J = O + b$, *"O + b"* *can be changed to a multiplier relationship.* *These complicated multi-step word problems will fall into Sum and Addition, Sum and Difference, Addition and Multiplier model problems etc.*	What is the fraction of incorrect questions that Jennifer got? Use the concept of 1 − fraction = remaining fraction $1 - A = \bar{A}$ $1 - \frac{17}{25} = \frac{8}{25}$	What is the % of incorrect questions that Oscar got? Method 1 – use %. $100\% - 95\% = 5\%$ Method 2 – use fractions. $$\frac{1}{20} = \frac{5}{100} = 5\%$$	If Jennifer's correct percent is increased by 20%, how many correct questions will she get? $68\% + 20\% = 88\%$ $25 \times 0.88 = 22$ If Oscar's correct percent is decreased by 20%, how many correct questions will he get? $75\% \times 20 - \frac{3}{4} \times 20 = 15$	What is the number of correct questions Jennifer and Oscar each gets if the ratio of Jennifer's to Oscar's correct questions is 9 to 10? *Use the idea of an equivalent ratio.* $J : O = 9 : 10$ $= 18 : 20$ Jennifer gets 18 correct questions and Oscar gets 20 questions.

Student's name: _____   Assignment date: _____

Finding equal to, more than, less than of the originals 找 =, >, < 的原数

Emily has 20% of Mable's money. Mable has $15. How much money does Emily have?

$15 \times 0.2 = 3$

Emily has 20% more money than Mable. Mable has $15. How much money does Emily have?

$15 \times 1.2 = 18$

Emily has 20% less money than Mable. Mable has $15. How much money does Emily have?

$15 \times 0.8 = 12$

Emily has as much as $\frac{2}{5}$ of Mable's money. Mable has $15. How much money does Emily have?

$15 \times \frac{2}{5} = 6$

Emily has $\frac{2}{5}$ more money than Mable. Mable has $15. How much money does Emily have?

$15 \times 1.4 \ (1\frac{2}{5} = \frac{7}{5}) = 21$

Emily has $\frac{2}{5}$ less than Mable. Mable has $15. How much money does Emily have?

$15 \times 0.6 = 9$

Without calculating, use a shortcut to get the answer of 5% of 1200.

10% of 1200 is 120. 5% is half of 120 = 60.
60

Without calculating, use a shortcut to get the answer of $\frac{3}{4}$% of 884.

$\frac{1}{4}$% of 884 is 221%, so $\frac{3}{4}$%.of 884 is 3% times 221 = 663%
663%

Without calculating, use a shortcut to get the answer of $\frac{2}{3}$% of 399.

Find one-third of 399 first, then times the answer by 3.

266%

Student's name: _____ Assignment date: _____

Computation of decimal, %, or fractions 小数, %, 分数 计算

Do not use a calculator to calculate. Only use a pencil to write answers.

$\$100 \times 0.5 = \$50 \times$ _____	1
$\$120 \times 20\% = \$$ _____ $\times 10\%$	240
$\$170 \times 0.5\% = \$$ _____ $\times 50\%$	17
$\$30 \times 100\% = \$$ _____ $\times 60\%$	48
$\$120 \times \frac{1}{2}\% = \$240 \times$ _____	$\frac{1}{4}\%$
$\$170 \times \frac{3}{4} = \$340 \times$ _____	$\frac{3}{8}$ answer
$\$140 \times 50\% = \$$ _____ $\times 25\%$	240

Before and after problems with conditions 開价与賣价

Ryan bought a pair of pants. Answer the following questions.

Paid price	Condition 1 Discounted price	Condition 2 Clearance price	Calculation space	What was the regular price?
$75	Bought at 10% off the clearance price.	The clear price was $20 off the regular price.		? $$\frac{75 + 20}{0.9} = 105.56$$
$60	Bought at 25% off the clearance price.	The clearance price was $15 off the regular price.		? $$\frac{60 + 15}{0.75} = 100$$
$150 bought at the clearance price	Bought at 10% off the regular price. This is a discounted price.	The clearance price was $10 off the discount price.		$$\frac{150 + 10}{0.9} = 177.78$$?
Bought at $120	What was the percent of decreased price (discount)?	none	$\frac{10}{130} \times 100\% =$ 7.69% answer	$130
Bought $150	What was the price of the increased price?	none	$\frac{150-135}{135} \times 100\% =$ 11.5% answer	$135

Student's name: _____ Assignment date: _____

Jasmine has $50 in her pocket. She spends 0.25 of her money. How much does she have left?

$37.50

Jimmy and Bruce play on the same soccer team. Each game is 1.5 hours. Jimmy plays $\frac{1}{3}$ of a game. Bruce plays $\frac{5}{6}$ of a game. How many more minutes does one person play than the other?

45 minutes

An individual carton of 1 L milk costs $4.96. It will cost $4.50 each when buying 2 cartons together at the same time. What percent is saved if buying 2 cartons together than buying 2 cartons individually?

1.78

Find the missing number.

$$57$$
$$\times 4?$$
$$\overline{3?2}$$
$$\underline{2????}$$
$$????$$

$57 \times 46 = 2622$

The area of a rectangular room is 63 m². The longest side is 9 m long. What is the perimeter of the room?

32 m

Student's name: _____ Assignment date: _____

Counting cubes 算立体数

Find out the information in the following table using the 3 by 3 by 3 cube as an example.

Cube dimensions	$2 \times 2 \times 2$	$3 \times 3 \times 3$	$4 \times 4 \times 4$	$5 \times 5 \times 5$	$n \times n \times n$
3 sides painted	8	8	8	8	8
2 sides painted	0	12	24	36	(side) $(n - 2) \times 12$
1 side painted	0	6	24	54	(area) $(n - 2)^2 \times 6$
0 side painted	0	1	8	27	(volume) $(n - 2)^3$
Total number of cubes	8	27	64	125	n^3

A cube measuring 4 units on each side is painted only on the outside. It is cut into 1-unit cubes. How many cubes have paint on 3 sides? 2 sides?

Statistics 统计

The term Central Tendency refers to the "middle" value or typical value of a data set, and it is measured by mean, median, or mode.

Mean and average 平均数

A mean means average. The mean is valid only for interval data or ratio data.

An interval variable is a measurement where the difference between the two values is meaningful. The difference between a temperature of 100 degrees and 90 degrees is the same difference as between 90 degrees and 80 degrees. A weight of 4 grams is twice the weight of 2 grams because the weight is a ratio variable. A temperature of 100 degrees C is not twice as hot as 50 degrees C because temperature C is not a ratio variable.

$$\text{An average} = \frac{sum\ of\ a\ list\ of\ numbers}{the\ number\ of\ numbers\ in\ the\ list}$$

A sum = average × the number of items
Often an average is converted to a sum to solve the problem.

The average speed problem must use the following speed and distance formulas.

$$\text{Speed} = \frac{distance}{time}$$

Distance = speed × time

$$\text{Time} = \frac{distance}{speed}$$

Median 中位数

Take the middle value of sorted data in ascending order or descending order.
Median is used when there are a few extreme values that could influence the mean such as house prices or salary etc. The best measure of the median is ordinal data. An ordinal variable is one where the order matters but not the difference between values. For example, movie ratings from 1 to 5

Mode 众数

The most frequently occurred data value in the data set, such as a popular song. Best measure data for mode is nominal (categorical). For example, sex is coded as 1 for female and 2 for a male.

Student's name: _____ Assignment date: _____

Statistics and equation 以方程式解统计题

> The average height of a group of boys is 1.65 cm. When two more boys each of height 1.70 cm joined the group, the average height became 1.66 cm. How many boys were in the group at the end?
>
> Let x be the number of boys at first
> $1.65x + 1.7 \times 2 = 1.66(x + 2)$
> X=8
> There were 10 boys at the end.
> | Blank line | blank line |
> | Blank line | blank line |

Average of averages 平均数的平均

Example

The average of 11 girls' math scores is 78, and the average of the 13 boys' math scores is 75. What is the average of the class?

The average of two averages $= \dfrac{average1 \times the\ number1\ of\ items + average2 \times the\ number2\ of\ items}{the\ number1\ of\ itmes + the\ number2\ of\ items}$

$= \dfrac{78 \times 11 + 75 \times 13}{11 + 13}$

$= \dfrac{858 + 975}{24}$

$= 76.38$

Problem

> The average score of 23 students in a math class is 78. The average of 15 female students is 81. What is the average score of the remaining boys?
>
> $\dfrac{78 \times 23 - 15 \times 81}{23 - 15}$
> | Blank line | blank line |
>
> $= \dfrac{1794 - 1215}{8}$
> | Blank line | blank line |
>
> $= \dfrac{579}{8}$
> | Blank line | blank line |
>
> $= 72.38$
> | Blank line | blank line |

Average of two average speeds

Oscar drove from his home to the park at 60 km per hour and came back home from the park to his home at a speed of 50 km per hour. It took 2 hours to comp0lete the round trip. What was the average speed of his round trip?

Wrong solution

$\frac{60+50}{2} = 55$ km per hour

Correct solution

Average speed $= \frac{distance1 + distance2}{time1 + time2}$ Blank line   blank line

Method 1   Blank line   blank line

Let the distance be d.   Blank line   blank line

$\frac{d}{60} + \frac{d}{50} = 2$ Blank line   blank line

$\frac{d(5+6)}{300} = 2$ Blank line   blank line

$d = \frac{2 \times 300}{5+6}$ Blank line   blank line

$d = 55\frac{5}{11}$ Blank line   blank line

The average speed $= \frac{2 \times 55\frac{5}{11}}{2} = 55\frac{5}{11}$ Blank line   blank line

          Blank line   blank line

Method 2   Blank line   blank line
Let the distance be 1.   Blank line   blank line

$\frac{1}{60} + \frac{1}{50} = 2$ Blank line   blank line

$\frac{1 \times 50 + 1 \times 60}{300} = \frac{1 \times (5+6)}{300} = 2$ Blank line   blank line
The "1" acts like a variable, so the 1 should be thought of as an unknown quantity with value 1.
$1 \times (5+6) = 2 \times 300$
1 of distance $= \frac{2 \times 300}{5+6} = 55\frac{5}{11}$.   Blank line   blank line

$d = 55\frac{5}{11}$ Blank line   blank line

The average speed $= \frac{2 \times 55\frac{5}{11}}{2} = 55\frac{5}{11}$ Blank line   blank line
          Blank line   blank line

Student's name: _____ Assignment date: _____

Average of averages

Average of two averages $\neq \dfrac{average\ 1 + average\ 2}{2}$

Average of two averages $= \dfrac{average\ 1 \times n1 + average\ 2 \times n2}{n1 + n22}$, n1 and n2 are the numbers of numbers added to get the sum.

Example Average of two average speeds

> Adam drove his car uphill at 30 km per hour, and then he drove downhill at 40 km per hour. The road length is 35 km. What was his two-way average speed?
>
>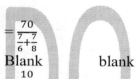
> $\dfrac{35 \times 2}{\frac{35}{30} + \frac{35}{40}}$
> Blank   blank
>
>
> $= \dfrac{70}{\frac{7}{6} + \frac{7}{8}}$
> Blank   blank
> $= \dfrac{10}{\frac{1}{6} + \frac{1}{8}}$
> Blank   blank
>
> $= \dfrac{10}{\frac{7}{24}}$
> Blank   blank
>
> $= 10 \times \dfrac{24}{7}$
> Blank   blank
>
> $= 34.29$ km per hour
> Blank   blank
> Blank   blank
> Blank   blank

Ho Math Chess 何数棋谜 奥数,解题策略,及 IQ 思唯训练宝典

Frank Ho, Amanda Ho © 1995 - 2020

Student's name: _____ Assignment date: _____

Problem

A class of 30 students took a math test. 11 students had an average (arithmetic mean) score of 81. The other students had an average score of 65. What is the average score for the whole class?

The average of averages $= \dfrac{11 \times 81 + 19 \times 65}{30}$
$$= \dfrac{891 + 1235}{30}$$
$$= \dfrac{2126}{30}$$
$$= 70.81$$

Alan's average of his 5 math tests is 78, and he got 85 for his 6th test. What is his overall average?

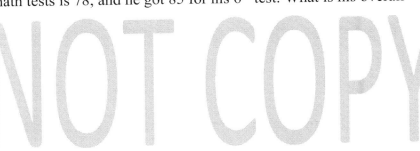

$\dfrac{78 \times 5 + 85}{6}$
$$= \dfrac{390 + 85}{6}$$
$$= \dfrac{475}{6}$$
$$= \mathbf{79.17}$$

Karissa's average of her five tests is 86, and the average of her six tests is 88. What is the score on her 6th test?

$6 \times 88 - 5 \times 86 = 528 - 430 = \mathbf{98}$

Weighted average

A weighted average of two averages $= \dfrac{rate\ 1 \times n1 + rate2 \times n2}{n1 + n2}$

Rachel's car uses 5.3 litres of gas per 100 km in the city, and 4.3 litres of gas per 100 km on the highway. Rachel drove 60 km in the city and 40 km on the highway., What was her average consumption of gas (in litres per 100 km) Give the answer correct to one decimal place.

$$\dfrac{\dfrac{5.3}{100} \times 60 + \dfrac{4.3}{100} \times 40}{60 + 40} \times 100 = 4.9 \text{ litres} / 100 \text{ km}$$

Blank   blank
Blank   blank

if Five darts are thrown at the following dartboard, and no darts hit a line, what is the average score of a dart?

The scoring record is as follows.

Dart numbers	Dartboard score got thrown at.
2	2
2	5
1	7

Average $= \dfrac{2 \times 2 + 2 \times 5 + 1 \times 7}{5}$

$= \dfrac{21}{5}$

$= \mathbf{4.2}$

A car left Kamloops at 9:00 AM and arrived at Vancouver, 340 km away from Kamloops, at 1:15 PM the same day. What was the average speed of the car in km per hour?

80 km /hour

Blank   blank
Blank   blank

On a certain test, seven students scored 70, seven scored 75, seven scored 80, nine scored 85, and ten scored 90. What was the average of all these students?

81, 340 divided by 4.25 = 80

Blank   blank

David wrote eight math tests, all graded out of 100. he calculated his average after six tests and found that his seventh test raised his 6th tests average by 2 marks, and his eighth test raised his 7th tests to be average by 2 marks. How many more marks did he get on the eighth test than on the seventh test?

18 marks

Use a small sample to find out the answer.
Assume 50   52   54 are 3 test averages.
Total are 300 364 422
The difference is 422 – 364 = 18.

Blank   blank
Blank   blank   Blank   blank

The average age of Alan, Betty and Cathy is 36. Alan is 8 years older than Betty. The average of Alan and Cathy is 40. How old is Alan?

Alan = Betty + 8 Blank   blank
36 x 3 = 108   Blank   blank
40 x 2 = 80   Blank   blank
108-80=28 ... Betty   Blank   blank
Alan = 28 + 8 = **36**   Blank   blank
Blank   blank

There are 180 campers at Ho Math Chess Summer Camp, and each camper can choose 2 out of 6 activities. How many campers, on average, can choose each activity?

$$\frac{180 \times 2}{6} = 60$$

Blank   blank

There were 5 children in the Ho Math Chess class, and the average weight of each child is 42 kg. When a sixth child joined the class, the average weight of each child increased to 43 kg. What was the weight of the sixth child?

Blank   blank

Method 1

Blank   blank

Use the total to figure out.

Method 2

Blank   blank

Use the average to figure out.

Blank   blank

If the sixth child also weighs 42 kg, then the average will still be 42 kg, but it is 43 kg, so it means every one increased 1 kg and all the increases must be added on to the sixth child so 42 + 6 = 48.

Blank   blank

Adam wants to buy a bike but is $123.23 short and Bob wants to buy the same bike but is $427.25 short. If they put their money together, then they will just have enough to buy the bike together. How much is the cost of the bike?

Blank   blank
Blank   blank

The key thing is their combined money = the bike money.

It is very similar to the supplementary angles problem; their supplementary angles add to 180^0.

So, the bike cost will be $123.23 + $427.25 = $550.48.

Blank   blank

Each of the two boxes contains 180 candies. On the first day, Andy ate some candies from the first box. On the second day, Andy ate as many candies from the second box as it was left in the first box. How many candies did he eat during the two days?

$x + 180 - x = \mathbf{180}$

You can use the Line Segment Diagram to give a visual effect.

Blank   blank
Blank   blank

The mean, the median, and the mode of the six numbers below are all equal. What number does A represent?

A   1.8   1.5   1.6   1.9   2.2

Blank   blank

The total of 5 numbers = 9 so we now know $\frac{9+x}{6}$ = one of those 6 numbers., $x = 1.8$

Blank   blank

Which statistics of mean, mode, median shall be used for the following data? State your reason.

99, 98, 97, 94, 93, 92, 91, 89, 5, 4, 3

Median 92
There is no mode, and you cannot use the skewed average

51, 51, 53, 79, 88, 87, 86, 85, 88, 89, 88, 90

Mode 88

88, 89, 87, 88, 85, 88, 99, 98

The median is 88, and the mean is 90.25

98, 88, 87, 85, 84, 75, 74

The median is 85.

Jocelyn took 5 math tests and had an average of 85. In order to get an average of 89 for all 10 tests. What average shall she get for the remaining tests?

92

The mode is 88, and the average is 90.43. Find the 2 missing numbers.

88, 89, 90, _____, _____, 91, 92

The smallest is 70. The range is 16, and the median is 85. The mode is 81. Find the missing data.

70, 81, 85, 81, 86

Student's name: _____ Assignment date: _____

There are 6 whole numbers. The median is 36, and there is no mode. The largest number is 47, and the range is 17. Two of the numbers are 34 and 39. What is the mean?

34.6

30, 32, 34, 38, 39, 47

There are 5 numbers. The smallest is 11, but it is not a mode. The range is 23. One of the numbers is 23. If the mean is 19.2, find the mode.

11, 14, 14, 23, 34

There are 6 whole numbers. One-fifth of its total is 17. Two-thirds of media is 12. The difference between mode and the media is 2. One of the numbers is 4. Find these 6 numbers.

4, 5, 16, 20, 20, 20

Student's name: _____   Assignment date: _____

Angela's average score for her 5 subjects is 90. If 10 more points add one of her subject scores, what is her new average?

Method 1, $\frac{5 \times 90 + 10}{5} = \frac{460}{5} = 92$

Method 2, $90 + \frac{10}{5} = 92$

What is the average of $\frac{2}{3}$, $\frac{1}{5}$, 0.7?

$\frac{4}{9}$ answer

The average of two numbers is 8. If one of the numbers is –6, what is the other number?

22

Triangular number

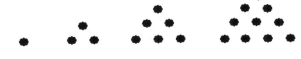

If the above pattern continues, what is the total number of dots of the 100th figure? 5050

Calculate $4000 - 5 - 10 - 15 - \ldots - 95 - 100$

$4000 - \frac{5 + 100}{2} \times 20 = 2950$

Pan balance weighing problem 天平称重

A double-**pan balance** is a **scale** that has 2 pans that are balanced against each other. The scale functions like a seesaw, with each of the 2 pan**s** attached to a beam over a centred pivot point.

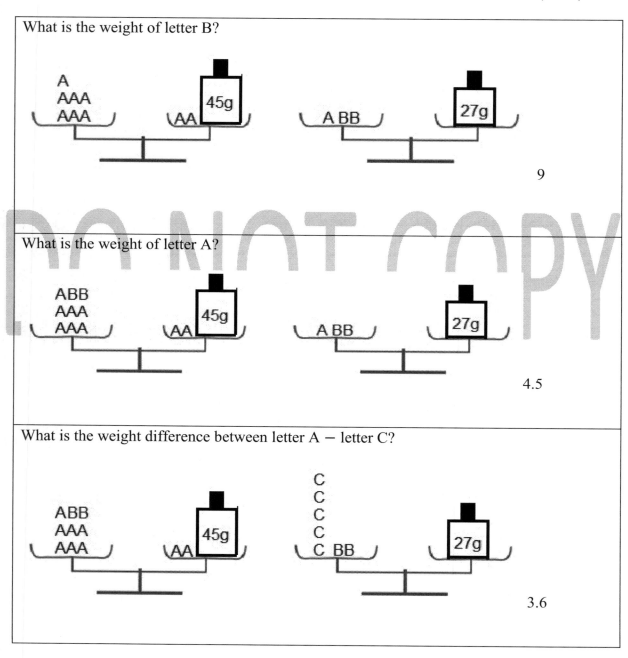

What is the weight of letter B?

9

What is the weight of letter A?

4.5

What is the weight difference between letter A − letter C?

3.6

Clock problem 时鐘問題

Here are 4 clocks on the wall. Only one of them is correct. One is 30 minutes ahead, another is 30 minutes late, and the other is stopped. What is the correct time?

6:10

Here are 4 clocks on the wall. Only one of them is correct. One is 30 minutes ahead, another is 30 minutes late, and the other is stopped. What is the correct time?

1:45

Here are 4 clocks on the wall. Only one of them is correct. One is 30 minutes ahead, another is 30 minutes late, and the other is stopped. What is the correct time?

9:40

What time is the following clock to the nearest 5 minutes? 1:20 a.m. or 1:20 p.m.

Logic Problem 罗辑問題

Sam, Bob, Victor, and David have these numbers 17, 18, 23, 36 on their basketball uniforms. Use the following strategies to find each boy's number.
- Bob has consecutive numbers, and Bob has an even number.
- David's number is not a multiple of 4.

Sam 17, Bob 18, Victor 36, David 23

Adam has more books than Bob. Bob has fewer books than Charlie. David has more books than Adam but does not have the largest number of books. Who has the largest number of books?

Charlie

Adam, Bob and Charlie went shopping, and each bought a pair of pants. Each pair of pants is made either of cotton or polyester material. Adam's pants are not made of cotton. Bob's pants are made of a material different from Adam's, and Charlie bought a pair of pants which was made of a material different from Bob's pants. Find out what material made each of their pants?

Adam – Polyester, Bob – Cotton, Charlie – Polyester

Sylvia made a 4-digit number from 4 digits: 1, 2, 3, and 4. The 1 was between 2 consecutive numbers. The 2 had no numbers to its left. What did the number Sylvia make?

2134

An odd number has 4 digits, and no digits are repeated. The hundreds place digit is three times the value of the ones place digit. The sum of all digits of the number is 27. What is the number?

7983

What number am I?

I am a three-digit number and less than 360. I am divisible by 24 and 18. My tens digit is the same as the ones digit.

288

Six classmates: Adam, Bob, Cathy, David, Ethan, and Frank are in a line-up for a school assembly. Adam is ahead of Frank and Bob is the first one in the line. Frank is between Cathy and David, and Ethan is the last in the line. David is before Ethan.

Who is the fourth in line? Frank There are 2 answers BACFDE or BCAFDE.

liar or truth-teller?

Simon, John and Tom had a track and field meet. When they were asked about the result,
"I was the first." Simon said.
"I was the second." John said.
"I was not the first." Tom said.
One of them told a lie. Who is the first, the second and the third, and who told a lie?

Simon, John and Tom had a chess tournament. When they were asked about the result, they answered as follows:

"I'm not the first," Simon said.
"I'm the third," John said.
"I'm the first," Tom said.
One of them told a lie. Who is the first, the second and the third?

Simon lied	John lied	Tom lied
S - 2, 3	S – 1	S – 1
J- 2	J – 1, 3. > 1	J - 2
T – 2, 3	T – 2, 3 > 2	T – 1

John told a lie and Simon was first, John was third, and Tom was second.

Simon lied	John lied	Tom lied
S -1	S – 2, 3 > 2	S – 2, 3 > 2
J- 3	J - 3	J - 3
T - 1	T - 1	T – 2, 3 > not possible

John told a lie, and Tom is the first. John is the second, and Simon is the third.

Logic Problems – liar or truth-teller?

You arrive at a fork in the road; only one way leads to the truth-tellers village, the other way leads to the liar's village. A guard who comes from one of the villages stands at the fork. You may ask the guard one question with only "yes" or "no" as an answer to try to find the way to the truth-tellers village, what question would you ask?

You point at one way and ask, **"Does this way lead to your village?"**

If the guard answers "no," then you go to the other way where you did not point at. If the guard answers "yes," then you go to the way where you pointed at. Reason? The following is not correct? Since if you know which way is the truth teller's way, then why even bother to ask?

If you pointed to the truth-tellers way and if the guard is that way, then the answer "yes" would be truthful. If the guard is a liar, then he/she would also answer "yes" to lie.
When you point to the liar's way and if the guard is a truth-teller, then the answer would be "no," but the liar would also answer "no" to lie.

So, the conclusion is the "yes" answer would lead to the truth-tellers way where you pointed at and "no" would lead to the truth-tellers way when you pointed to the liar's way.

Logic Problems – liar or truth-teller?

You arrive at a fork in the road; only one way leads to the truth-tellers village, the other way leads to the liar's village. Two guards who each come from one of the villages stand at the fork. You may ask one of the guard's one question with only "yes" or "no" as an answer to try to find the way to the truth-tellers village, what question would you ask?

The fact that there are 2 guards is red herring – you only need to ask any one of them the same question as to the previous question. How about asking, "Are you a guard?"

Logic Problems – liar or truth-teller?

There are 2 brothers, one always tells the truth, and the other always lies. What question would you ask with only "yes" or "no" as an answer to either one of them to figure out which one he is?

There are a man and a woman, and one is a liar, and the other is honest. The woman says, "None of us is a liar." Who is honest?

Ask one of them, "If I were to ask your brother whether you always tell the truth, what would he say?"

If the answer is "no," then he is a truth-teller, the "yes" answer tells he is a liar. Just ask, "Are you two brothers?". The liar would answer "no" when, in fact, they are.

If the brother had been asked is a truth-teller, then he would answer "no" since he knows his brother always lies.

If the brother had been asked is a liar, then he would answer "yes" since he knows his brother is honest and he would lie.

The woman is a liar since there is no such thing as "none of us is a liar" if indeed one of them is a liar.

Logic Problems – liar or truth-teller?

There are three persons, and they are either a truth-teller or a liar. When asked what type of person each is, the following happened.

Person A answered but was not heard.
Person B says, "Person A said he was a liar."
Person C says to Person B, "You are lying."
Is person C a liar or truth-teller by analyzing the above statements?

Kerry and Dennis, one is a liar, and another is a truth-teller.
Kerry said, "At least one of us is a liar."
Who is the liar? Who is honest?

Person C is a truth-teller. If person A were a truth-teller, he would have said," I am a truth-teller" He would have said," I am a truth-teller" if he were a liar. So, no one would ever say, "I am a liar." Therefore, Person B lied, and Person C spoke the truth.

Student's name: _____ Assignment date: _____

Consecutive numbers 连續数

Find the least number of consecutive positive integers that add up to 10. 1, 2, 3, 4
Find the least number of consecutive positive integers that add up to 100. 18, 19, 20, 21, 22
Find the least number of consecutive positive integers that add up to 1000. 198, 199, 200, 201, 202
Find the next number of the following pattern. 16 11 16 _____ 1, 6, 11, 16, **21**
Find a group of five consecutive numbers with a sum of 240. 46, 47, 48, 49, 50 Hint: the average of consecutive numbers must also be the median.
What three consecutive numbers have the same total and product? 1, 2, 3 or –1, -2, -3
What three consecutive odd numbers total of 273? 89, 91, 93
What five consecutive odd numbers total 75? The middle one is 75/5=15 11, 13, 15, 17, 19
What five consecutive even numbers total 320? The middle one is 320/5=64 60, 62, 64, 66, 68

Pages and Sheets 頁数与張数

The following table illustrates the relationships between pages and sheets.

	The page number on the left side	The page number on the right side	How many missing sheets between pages
A book has missing pages between pages	1	4	
	24	45	
	3	56	

0.7 of the people surveyed were men, 0.7 of these men were over 21. What part of the people surveyed were men who were 21 or over?

Black bears have all black paws, and white bears have all white paws. There are some black bears and some white bears, and all the number of black paws and the number of white paws is 52. The number of black bears is 3 more than white bears. How many are white bears and how many black bears there?

$52 \div 4 = 13$

$B + W = 13$
$B - W = 3$
$B = 13, W = 5$

Isabella travelled on a Saturday morning and arrived at the destination on a Saturday evening. She travelled a total of 100 km. Each day she travelled one km less than the previous day. Find out how many kilometres all in whole numbers she travelled each day?

(Hint: where is the average of the sum of consecutive numbers?)

Isabella travelled on a Saturday morning and arrived at the destination on a Saturday evening. She travelled a total of 116 km. Each day she travelled one km less than the previous day. Find out how many kilometres all in whole numbers she travelled each day?

(Hint: where is the average of the sum of consecutive numbers?)

This problem is included here because we found some students seem to only care about getting the answer instead of really understanding it, so the above way of getting the answer is not deposited in the brains. When the same problem presents to them again, they still do not know how to do it.

23, 22, 21, 20, 19, 18, 17, 16

Julia was talking to her friend and said, "If I get twice as many cookies as I got from my sister, then I would get 20 more cookies to eat than I have now." How many cookies did Julia get from her sister?

Student's name: _____ Assignment date: _____

When 36 is added to a number, the result is the same as when the number is multiplied by two and half of the original number. What is the original number?

The 36 increase corresponds to the ratio increase of $1\frac{1}{2}$.

$36 \div 1\frac{1}{2} = 24$

Find the fraction.	Find quantity.
Fernando spent $\frac{2}{5}$ of his money. How much did he have left in a fraction?	Work forward Fernando spent $\frac{2}{5}$ of $1235. How much did he have left? $741
Fernando had $\frac{3}{7}$ of his money left. How much did he have spent in a fraction?	Work backwards Fernando spent $\frac{2}{5}$ of his money, and he had $1275 left. How much did he have originally? $2125

Vera divides the number by 8 and gets 0.25 as her answer. Leon multiplies the same number by 8, what answer should he get?

Two fractions in lowest terms add together is $\frac{31}{35}$. The denominators of two fractions are consecutive odd numbers. What are these two fractions?

$\frac{3}{5} + \frac{2}{7}$

If 20 is dived by a number n and n is a 2-digit number less than 20 but more than 10, then the remainder cannot be over _____.

Justin has 7 more pogs than Jocelyn. After he gave 10 pogs to Jocelyn, how many pogs will Jocelyn have more than Justin?

This problem is much easier just to act out using self-created numbers. This method is even easier than using the Line Segment Diagram method.

Justin	Jocelyn
17	10
7	20

The answer is 13

When 21 is divided by the whole number x, the remainder is 5. How many different values are there for x?

$21 - 5 = 16$

x could be the factors of $16 = 1, 16, 2, 8, 4$

What is the remainder when 10^{24} is divided by 1997?

# of ending 0's as dividend	4	8	12	24
Remainder when divided by 1997	$3^1 = 3$	$3^2 = 9$	$3^3 = 27$	$(3^3)^2 = \mathbf{729}$

$$\bigcirc - \square = 10$$

$$\square - \triangle = 24$$

$$\bigcirc - \triangle = ?$$

Venn diagram 思维图 Inclusive and exclusive 容斥原理

Introduction

This Inclusive and then exclusive method is different from the subtraction method in that the inclusive part may include the overlapping part, which is not the same as the subtraction method. A diagram explains the difference is as follows:

Subtraction method – The shaded area

The number of objects in the shaded ring is the difference between the number of objects of the outer circle – the objects of the inner circle.

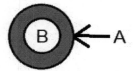

A is the outer circle, B is the inner circle.

Venn diagram method - Inclusive and exclusive method (set theory)

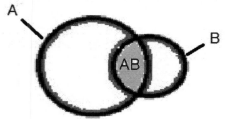

The number of objects in the following A and B and both AB is as follows:

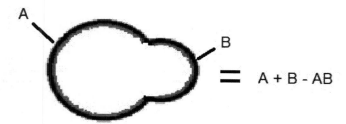

$$= A + B - AB$$

Fill in each ? by a number. Each circle has a sum of 19.

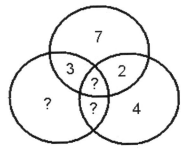

3, 7, 6

Fill in each ? by a number. Each circle has a sum of 19.

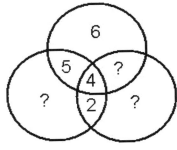

8, 4, 9

Fill in each ? by a number. Each circle has a sum of 19.

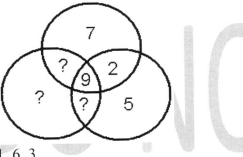

1, 6, 3

Fill in each ? by a number. Each circle has a sum of 19.

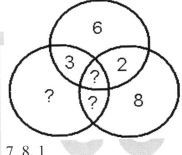

7, 8, 1

Fill in each ? by a number. Each circle has a sum of 19.

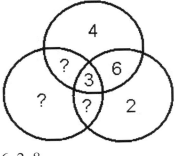

6, 2, 8

Fill in each ? by a number. Each circle has a sum of 19.

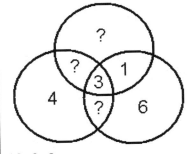

12, 3, 9

Place the multiples of 3 in the following table and the multiples of 2 in the following table in the Venn diagram.

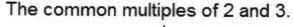

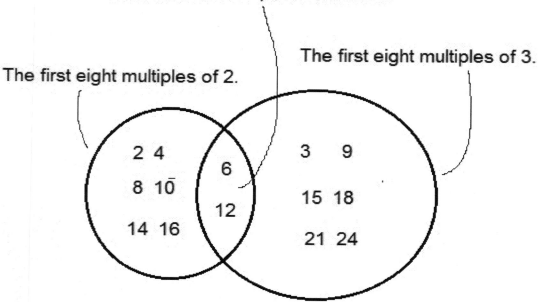

Place the first eight multiples of 6 in the following table and the first eight multiples of 9 in the following table in the Venn diagram.

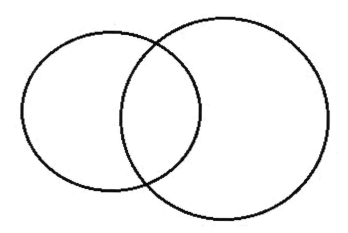

Venn diagram

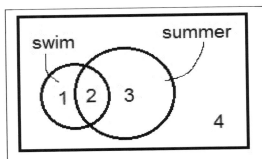

Use the above Venn diagram to answer the following questions.

A. In which part of the Venn diagram would you put on a summer swimming suit.

B. In which part of the Venn diagram would you put on your beachwear?

C. In which part of the Venn diagram would you swim outdoor?

Take a look at the following figures and then answer each question using All, Some, No, or Not.

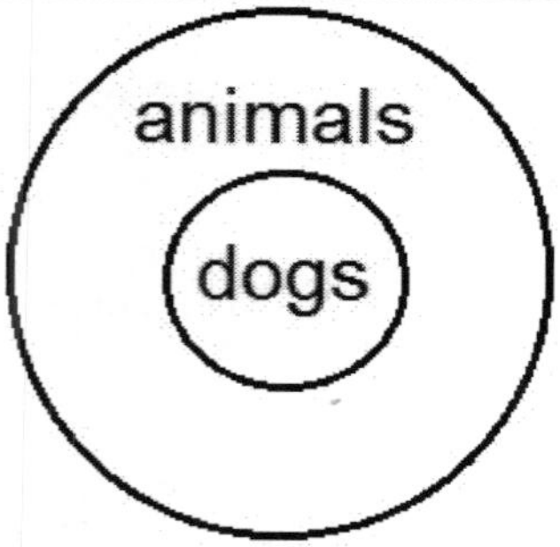

_____ dogs are animal. All

_____ animals are dogs. Some

_____ all animals are dogs. Not

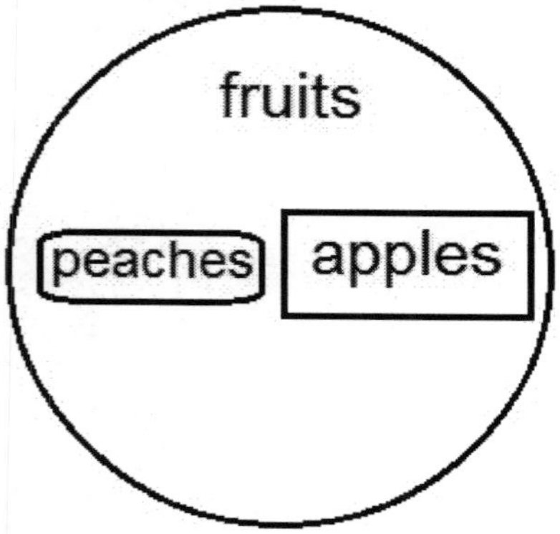

_____ peaches are fruits. All

_____ apples are fruits. All

_____ all fruits are apples. Not

Peaches and apples are _____ fruits. all

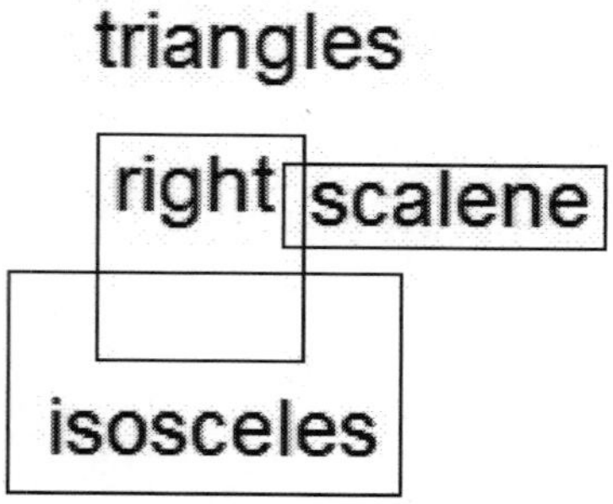

_____ right triangles are triangles. All
_____ scalene triangles are triangles. All
_____ isosceles triangles are triangles. All
_____ _____ triangles are scalene right triangles. Some
_____ triangles are isosceles right triangles. Some
_____ all triangles are isosceles triangles. Not
There are _____ scalene, isosceles triangles. some

Sort the following numbers according to the right attributes.

900, 176, 531, 384, 413, 679, 325, 424

Separate circles have the following attributes: Even and odd numbers

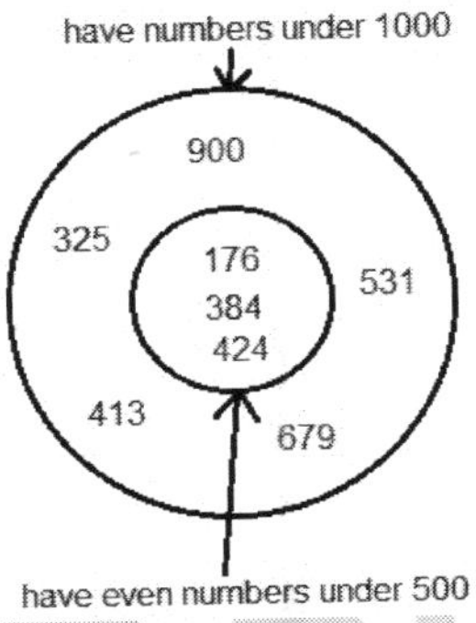

answer

900   176
424   384

531   413
679   325

Answer

Overlapping circles have a common attribute that is it has numbers over 300 and are even. The left side circle has numbers over 300, and the right-side circle has even numbers.

answer

531   900
679   384   176
413   424
325

answer

One circle inside the other one.

The inner-circle has even numbers under 500.

answer

have numbers under 1000

900
325   176   531
384
424
413   679

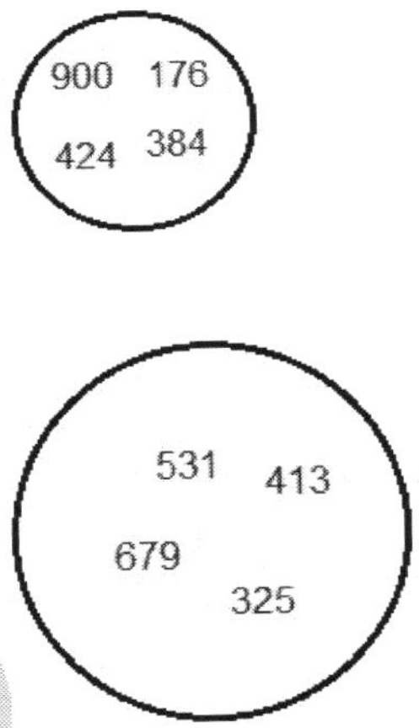

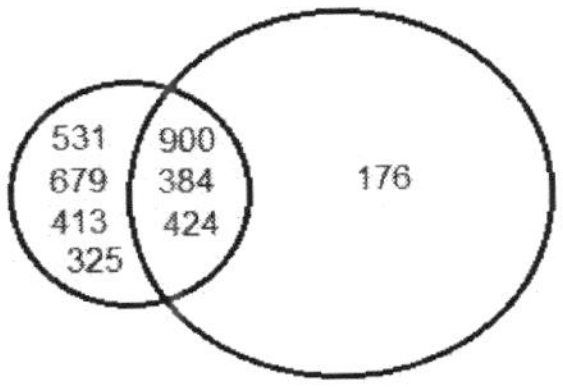

have even numbers under 500

answer

Twenty-three teenagers went hiking in Alaska. Eleven of them saw a deer; seven of them saw a polar bear and five of them saw both a deer and a polar bear. How many of them saw neither? How many of them only saw a polar bear? How many of them only saw only a deer? 10, 6, 2

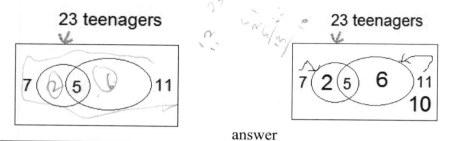

answer

In a small-town of 1000 families, 800 of them own a computer, a cell phone, or both. If 600 of the families own computers and 700 of their own cell phones, how many families own both a computer and a cell phone? How many families own only a computer and a cell phone but not both?

500 families own both computers and cell phones. 300 families own either a computer or cell.

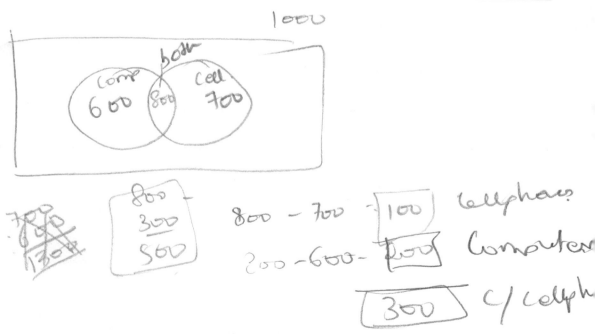

Carroll diagram vs. Venn diagram 從橫表与思唯图

Use the Carroll diagram and Venn diagram separately to solve the following problem.

Find out what are the common factors of 12 and 15.

Venn diagram	Carroll diagram		

Venn diagram

factors of 12

factors of 15

5
15

1
3

2
4
6
12

Carroll diagram

	12	15
Common factors of both 12 and 15	1, 3	1, 3
Non-common factors of 12 and 15	2, 4, 6, 12	5, 15

Which method is better for you to find the answer and why?

Venn diagram only gives you two separated information, but the Carroll diagram gives you 4 separated information.

Use the following Carroll diagram to sort out the following numbers.

16, 15, 23, 25, 21, 30, 43, 45, 18, 60

	Even	Odd
Multiples of 5		
Not multiples of 5		

	Even	Odd
Multiples of 5	30, 60	15, 25, 45
Not multiples of 5	16, 18,	21, 23, 43

Counting paths 计算通路

The path counting problems appeared in Kangaroo Math Contest in grade 3 before and without advanced knowledge. It is very easier for students to get inaccurate counts.

There are two ways of counting the paths: addition method and multiplication method, but which method to use depends on the directions of the path. Normally there are conditions restricting the paths: No direction of going back to the start direction is allowed, the shortest possible route must be sought, the same route can only go through once etc. The addition method is used when the intersection of the path does not allow any opposite direction; when the opposite direction is allowed, then the multiplication method is used.

1. Addition method

Example 1

How many ways are there when travelling from point A to point B in the directions of up and right (this is considered as north-east one direction for this type of example.)?

Method 1 - Counting on the Dots

Use Pascal's triangle property, and we find the paths of any intersection by adding the values of two previous points (counting on the dots).

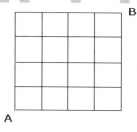

There are 70 ways of reaching B from A. Note that the values are symmetric, so one should check to ensure that all numbers are in symmetry. Note that if this question allows going down, then it will become a multiplication question. Compare this question to the same diagram in the Multiplication Method for the difference of direction.

Method 2 - Permutation

Going from A to B, there are only 4 vertical ways | | | | and 4 horizontal _ _ _ _ altogether for every route (since this shape is a square so we can find it out the vertical bars and horizontal lines easily from the board of the square). So, the number of ways of going from A to B is equivalent
to the question of finding out how many different ways that 4 vertical lines and 4 horizontal lines can be arranged? The answer is $\frac{8!}{4! \times 4!} = \frac{8 \times 7 \times 6 \times 5 \times 4!}{4! \times 4 \times 3 \times 2} = 70$. The reason for dividing by 4! and 4! is because of the repetitions of 4 same vertical ways and the 4 same horizontal ways. This permutation method only applies if the shape is in a rectangular shape.

Example 2

Count the paths from A to B.

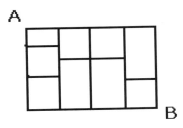

Use the Counting on the Dots method as follows:

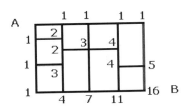

There 16 routes from A to B. When the direction changes, this same diagram could change to a multiplication problem. See the Multiplication Method for details.

Example 3

Count the paths when walking from A to B in directions of right, up, and northeast?

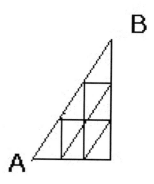

Since we cannot walk down and left, so the addition method should be used.

There are 22 ways.

Example 4

Find out how many routes going from A to B without going left or down.

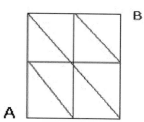

"Counting on the Dots" is used to count the number of paths.

2. Multiplication method

It is important to realize that we now talk about the possibility of going in the opposite way (going up and down), which suggests the multiplication method to solve this kind of problem.

Example 1

How many ways are there when travelling from point A to point B in the directions of up, down, and right?

This problem has the same routes as the above case 1; the only difference is this problem allows the opposite directions of going up and down.

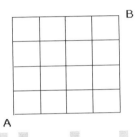

The possible routes are $5 \times 5 \times 5 \times 5$ (5 horizontal lines with 4 columns = 5^4) = 625.

Note 1:   Let's look at a simple example of 2 by 2 for going right and up only (addition method) and what happens when allowing going up, right, and down (multiplication method).

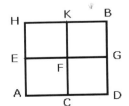

When allowing going up and right, there are 6 routes. In addition to the 6 routes, there are 3 more routes for allowing going up, down and right. These 3 new routes are: AHKFGB, AHKCDB, AEFCDB.

What happens when allowing going up, down, right, and left (this means allowing going back)?

Normally the path questions do not allow going back (left), the main reason is it adds too many complications for hand calculations, and the method of the addition will not work since Pascal's triangle only allows one direction travelling. Even with the permutation method, the conditions are complicated. See the following examples:

For the above 2 by 2 chessboard with the travelling route - AEFCDGFKB: $\dfrac{8!}{4!4!}$

For the above 2 by 2 chessboard with the travelling route - ACFEHKB: $\dfrac{6!}{4!2!}$

3. For the above 2 by 2 chessboard with the travelling route - ADGEHB: $\dfrac{8!}{6!2!}$

Note 2: A 3 by 2 chessboard multi-direction paths example ⊞ is very similar to the following questions:

Michelle has 4 different colours of shirts and 4 pairs of different colours of pants. How many different outfits can she have?

$4 \times 4 = 16$

From A to B, there are 4 possible routes. From B to C, there are also 4 possible routes. How many different trips can be taken from A to C and back without taking the same route from A to C?

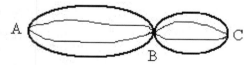

From A to C, there are 4×4 routes, but when going back from C to B, there will be one route taken when going from B to C and also there will be one route chosen from A to B, so the routes going from C to A will be 3×3, the total routes will be $4 \times 4 \times 3 \times 3 = 144$. Note that point B is the checkpoint.

Notice that there is one converging point B. The converging point signals the point for multiplication.

Student's name: _____   Assignment date: _____

3.   The above 3 by 2 multi-direction paths diagram ⊞ in the above point 2 can be modified as follows with the same answers (4 × 4) travelling from A to B.

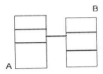

Example 2

We are counting paths from A to B.

Since it can go up and down, so the multiplication method must be used.
4 × 3 × 3 × 3 = 108

Example 3

Count the paths when walking from A to B in directions of right, up, down, and north-east?

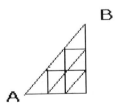

Since we can walk up and down, the multiplication method should be used.

There are 2 × 4 × 6 = 48 ways.

Student's name: _____ Assignment date: _____

3. A mixed-method of addition and multiplication

Example 1

Counting only the paths following the lines and going downward and to the right, how many paths from A to B?

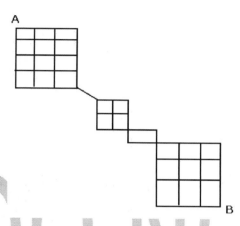

Either "Counting on the Dots" method or the permutation method can be used to find out the possible routes for each of 3 squares then multiply the results of squares to get the final answer.

$$\frac{7!}{3!4!} \times \,_{1 \times} \frac{4!}{2!2!} \times 2 \times \frac{6!}{3!3!} = 8400$$

Example 2

Count the number of routes from A to B.

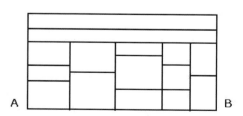

There are two parts to be computed, the top rectangle has 2 ways (2 horizontal lines), and the bottom rectangle uses the multiplication method.

Part 2: $4 \times 3 \times 4 \times 4 \times 3 = 576$.
The total number of ways $= 2 + 576 = 578$.

Example 3

Count the number of ways from A to D of the following diagram.

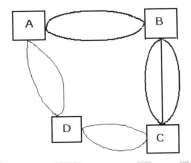

Path $A \rightarrow B \rightarrow C \rightarrow D$: $2 \times 3 \times 2 = 12$
Path $A \rightarrow D$: 2

Add the above 2 paths: $12 + 2 = 14$

Example 4

Use the following diagram and answer the questions.

Count the routes from A to B and must go through C.

A to C: $\dfrac{4!}{2!2!} = 6$

C to B: $\dfrac{4!}{2!2!} = 6$

The routes $= 6 \times 6 = 36$

2. Count the routes do not go through C.

$$\frac{8!}{4!4!} = 70$$
$$70 - 36 = 34$$

3. Must go through C and D.

A to C: 6
C to D: 2
D to B: 2

A to C to D to B: $6 \times 2 \times 2 = 24$

Must go through C or D.

A to C to B: 36 (see above)
A to D to B: $\frac{6!}{3!3!} \times 2 = 20 \times 2 = 40$
A to C to D to B: 24 (see above)

The routes must go through C or D: $40 + 36 - 24 = 52$.

3-Dimensional figure

Example 1

How many are the shortest ways there from A to B?

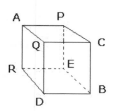

To go from A to B, it must travel through 3 vertices: P, Q, R and each vertex has 2 ways of travelling, so the answer is $3 \times 2 = 6$ or $\frac{(1+1+1)!}{1!1!1!} = 6$. The 6 ways are APCB, APEB, AQCB, AQDB, AREB, and ARDB.

Student's name: _____   Assignment date: _____

Example 2

How many are the shortest ways there from A to B?

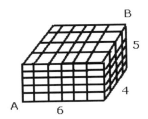

There are 6 bars for length and 4 bars for width and 5 bars for height. Altogether there are 15 bars, which is the shortest distance to reach B from A. The 15 bars can be considered as an arrangement problem with repetitions.

$$\frac{(6+5+4)!}{6!\,5!\,4!}=630630$$

Problem

How many paths are there from A to B? _____ **6**

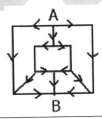

How many different routes are there from A to B in the following diagram?

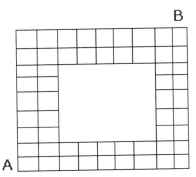

Find the number of different routes from A to B.

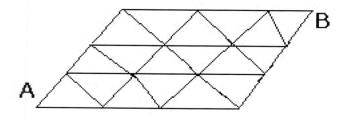

2756, 168

How many routes can a person choose from A to B going up only?

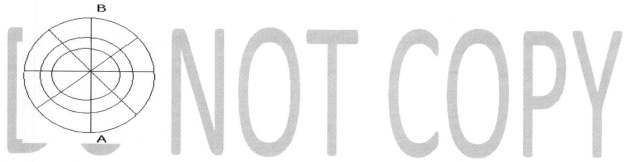

A, P, Q, R, S, T, B are 7 cities. Hubert starts at A and wishes to reach city B, but he likes to visit every other city only once before arriving at city B. How many different routes can he choose there?

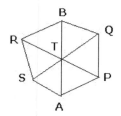

77

In the above question, if (a). Q is his destination; how many routes are there? (b). P is his destination; how many routes are there?

2

Find the number of routes from A to B.

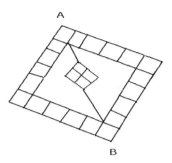

5, 98

How many routes are there from A to B when travelling downward or sideways?

444

How many routes are there from A to B if only the directions of moving horizontally and downward are allowed?

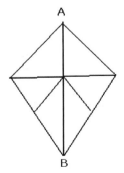

10

How many routes are there from A to B if only the directions of right, up and down are allowed?

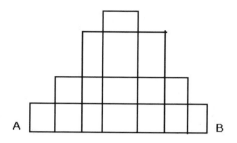

2880

Isaac drives from point A to point B. How many ways that he can drive with the minimum distance to reach point B?

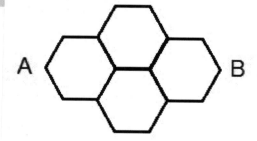

6

Student's name: _____ Assignment date: _____

Ratio problems 比

A lot of ratio problems can be solved by using ratio method, and often by using fractions. The following example demonstrates 5 solving methods.

In Sarah's class, there are 3 girls for every 4 boys, and there are 56 students in total. How many boys and girls are there in her class separately?

Method 1 Ratio	Method 2 List	Method 3 Algebra Assume there are x groups of pattern of a 3 to 4 ratio.	Method 4 Fraction	Method 5 Pattern figure
G B total 3 4 7 24 32 56 24 + 32 = 56	G B total 3 4 7 6 8 14 9 12 21 12 16 28 15 20 35 18 24 42 21 28 49 24 32 56	$3x + 4x = 56$ $x = 8$	$56 \times \frac{3}{7}$ $= 24$ $56 \times \frac{4}{7}$ $= 32$	OOO △△△ OOO △△△ ... $56 \div 7 = 8$ set of new and used cars $8 \times 3 = 24$ $8 \times 4 = 32$

Andy can ride 8 km in the same time as Bob can ride 6 km. They want to ride 12 km and finish together. How much of a head start should Bob start?

Andy: Bob = 8 : 6 = 4 : 3 = 12 : 9

So, Bob needs a head start of 3 km.

Student's name: _____ Assignment date: _____

The difference between the two numbers is 24. The ratio of the large number to the small number is 6 to 4. What are these two numbers?

The difference of 24 is the difference between tow ratio units $6 - 4 = 2$.
Each unit value is $\frac{24}{6-4} = 12$

The large number is $12 \times 6 = 72$. The small number is $12 \times 4 = 48$.

The sum of two natural numbers is 84. If the first number is multiplied by 8 and the second number by 6, then those two products are equal. What are these two natural numbers?

Arithmetic method - use ratio	Algebraic method
Let S = small number and L = large number $8S = 6L$ $S : L = 6 : 8 = 3 : 4$ (We need to reduce since $6 + 8 = 14$ and 84 is not a multiple of 14.) Ratio unit amount $= \frac{84}{3+4} = 12$ $S = 3 \times 12 = 36$ $L = 4 \times 12 = 48$	$8S = 6L$ $S + L = 84$ When participating in math contests, it appe that there is an advantage for young student learn how to solve the systems of equations instead of waiting until high school.

Student's name: _____   Assignment date: _____

Ratio and measurement 比及测量

The ratio of 3 angles of a triangle is 3:4:5, what are the sizes of 3 angles?

$$\frac{180}{3+4+5} \times 3 = 45, \qquad \frac{180}{3+4+5} \times 4 = 60, \qquad \frac{180}{3+4+5} \times 5 = 75$$

The ratio of the boys: girls in Samantha's class is 2:5, and there are 20 girls, what is the total number of students in her class?

$$\frac{20}{5} \times 7 = 28$$

The ratio of the boy : girl in Samantha's class is 3:2. Twenty-one girls (30% of all girls) showed up one day in the library, and the rest went on a field trip. What is her class size?

$21 \div 0.3 \div 2 \times 3 + 70 = 175$

Can a triangle with more than one obtuse angle? Explain
_____.

No, because with 2 obtuse angles in a triangle, a triangle could have 2 angles over 90 degrees. The sum of total angles in the triangle will be over 180 degrees.

At the popcorn factory, for every kilogram of popcorn that is popped, 110 grams do not pop. The factory pops 6 kilograms every day. What is the total weight, in kilograms, of the not popped corn in the mouth of June?

Hint: 1 kilogram = 1000 gram.

19.8 kg

For a digital clock, the time is shown by 4 digits such a 12:34. From 00:00 to 23:59, what is the largest sum of 4-digit time when adding all four digits?

The largest hour is 19 and the largest minute is 59 so the time is 12:59, so the sum = 1+ 9 + 5 + 9 = 24.

How many times do the hour hand, the minute hand, and the second hand circulate the clock entirely altogether in a 24-hour period?

In 24 hours, the hour hand circulates 2 times.
The minute hand circulates $\frac{24\times60}{60} = 24$ times. You can think if the hour hand circulates one tick, then the minute hand circulates 12 ticks. So, if the hour hand circulates 2 times, then the minute hand circulates 24 times.

The second hand circulates $\frac{24\times60\times60}{60} = 1440$.

You can think if the hour hand circulates one tick, then the second hand circulates 720 times. $2 \times 720 = 1440$.

Hour hand	Minute hand	Second hand
5 ticks	60 ticks	3600 ticks
1	12	720

The sum of circulation = 2 + 24 + 1440 = 1466.

Now it is at 3 o'clock. If the clock moves 1 minute more, then the angle formed by the hour hand and the minute hand is an acute angle or obtuse angle?

Acute angle because the minute hand moves faster than the hour hand.

Rational equation and ratio

A ratio is a comparison of two quantities measured in the same units.

In a school, the ratio of the number of students who wear glasses to the number of students who do not wear glasses is 10. 9. $\frac{2}{3}$ of the boys and $\frac{2}{5}$ of the girls wearing glasses. What is the ratio of the number of boys to the number of girls?

This problem has 2 unknowns but only with one equation, but luckily, the answer is to ask ratio, so we do not need to find out the specific number of boys or girls other than their equation.

An average Canadian grade-9 student may have difficulty to solve this rational equation.

$$(\frac{2}{3}B + \frac{2}{5}G) : (\frac{1}{3}B + \frac{3}{5}G) = 10 : 9$$

B : G = 9 : 10

Rate 單位数

A ratio is a comparison of two quantities measured in different units.

A $1 US can be exchanged for $1.06 Canadian. How much Canadian dollars can the US $300 exchange to Canadian?

Student's name: _____   Assignment date: _____

Probability 机率

Probability calculation using the diagram

	What is the probability of choosing  ▮? 100%
	What is the probability of choosing  ⬤⬤? 100%
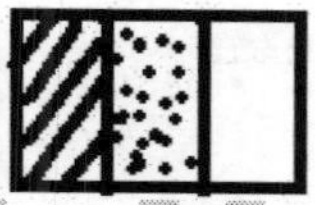	What is the probability of choosing  ▨? 1/3
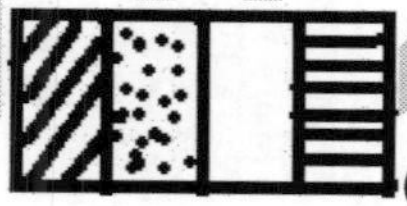 (123)(124)(134)(234)	What is the probability of choosing 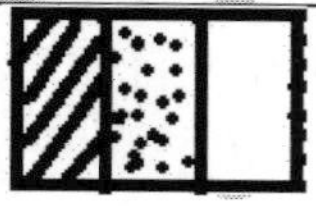 ? 1/4
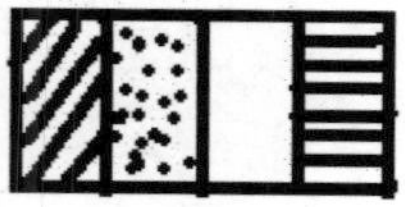	What is the probability of choosing  ▨? 1/4

Student's name: _____ Assignment date: _____

Pick one of the following letters without looking.
SUNNY TOMMY

P(aY) = 1/5
P(an O) = 1/9
P(a vowel) = 5/27
P(not a T) = 25/27

What are the outcomes of rolling a 6-faced die? _____
    Blank   blank
What is P(0)? _____   0   Blank   blank
What is P(1)? _____   1/6
    Blank   blank
What is P(2 or 3)? _____   1/3

Spin the spinner and answer the following problems.

P(white) = _____   1/4   Blank   blank
P(black) = _____   ½   Blank   blank
P(red or white) = _____   ½   Blank   blank
P(red and white) = _____   0   Blank   blank

Pick a marble from the bag.

P(black) = _____   3/5   Blank   blank
P(white) = _____   2/5   Blank   blank
P(black or white) = _____   1   Blank   blank
P(red) = _____   0

Draw a spinner that would give the following probabilities $P(red) = \frac{1}{4}$, $P(blue) = \frac{1}{8}$, $P(green) = \frac{1}{4}$, $P(black) = \frac{3}{8}$.

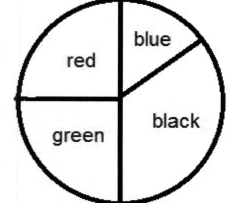

Probability calculation using diagram and decimals using %

	What is the probability of choosing ▉? 100%
● ● ●	What is the probability of choosing ● ●? 100%
	What is the probability of choosing ? 1/3
(123)(124)(134)(234)	What is the probability of choosing ? 1/4
	What is the probability of choosing ? 1/4

Tony's toy box had 3 red, 2 green, and 4 white pencils. Tony gave away 1 white, 1 green and 2 red pencils. What is the probability of getting a red pencil? Use ratio, fraction, and % to represent probability. What is the probability of not getting a red pencil?

$\frac{1}{5}$, 1:5, 20%

Each of the above letters represents the first letter of the column **Red**, **Blue**, and **Green**. Draw a tree diagram to list the probability of the following:

(1) The probability of getting red the first time. $\frac{1}{2}$

(2) The probability of getting green after getting a red. $\frac{1}{8}$

(3) The probability of getting the same colour in a row 3 times. Red: $\frac{1}{8}$, green and blue each $\frac{1}{64}$

(4) The probability of getting the first time green, the second time red, and the third time blue.

$\frac{1}{32}$

Problem

Two 6-sided dice are rolled, calculate the following probability.

P(Pair of odd numbers) (1,1) (3,3) (5,5) (1,3) (1,5) (3,5) (3,1) (5,1) $\frac{9}{36} = \frac{1}{4}$	

P(Sm of 1)
0

P(Sum between 2 and 8 (inclusive))

(11) …. 1
(21) …… 2
(22) (31) ……..3
(14) (23) …….4
(15) (24) (33) ……..5
(16) (25) 34) ………..6
(35) (26) …………..4
The total is $1 = 2 + 3 + 4 + 5 + 6 + 4 = 25$

$$\frac{25}{36}$$

P(Sum of 6, 7, or 8)

Use the result of the above problem, and we get the following.
$$\frac{15}{36} = \frac{5}{12}$$

P(Pair of even numbers)
$$\frac{1}{4}$$

P(Both numbers are > 3)
(44) …. 1
(45) …..2
(46) ….2
(55) ….1(56) …..2
(66) …..1
The total is $1 = 2 + 2 + 1 + 2 + 1 = 9$
$$\frac{9}{36} = \frac{1}{4}$$

P(both are the same numbers)

(11) (22) (33) (44) (55) (66)

$\frac{6}{36} = \frac{1}{6}$

Throw a die twice, what is the probability of the sum of points > 8?

(36) (45) (46) (55) (56)
The condition of the above total = 2 + 2 + 2 + 1 + 2 = 10

$\frac{10}{36} = \frac{5}{18}$

Three dice are thrown at random, what is the probability that the sum of numbers appearing on the top faces of 3 dice is 10?

136 6
145 6
226 3
235 6
244 3
334 3

$\frac{27}{216} = \frac{1}{8}$

Three cubes, each with faces numbered 1, 2, 3, 4, 5, and 6, are tossed. Each cube lands with a number on the top. What is the probability the sum of the top numbers is 15?

555 1
456 6
366 3

$$\frac{10}{216} = \frac{5}{108}$$

If a die is tossed 3 times, what is the probability that the product of the top 3 numbers > 100?
366 3
466 3
555..............1
566 3
666 1
556 3
456 6

$$\frac{20}{216} = \frac{5}{54}$$

Family members 家庭人数

Many family members' problems appeared in the kangaroo Math Contests.

William's dad and mom have 3 girls. Each girl has 2 brothers. How many members are there in William's family?

7

There are 3 girls in a family, and each of them has 2 boys. How many children are there in this family?

5

Sarah said to Annabelle, "I have 2 brothers in my family, and each of my brothers has 2 sisters." How many children are there in Sarah's family?

4

Part D – Geometry 几何

Vertex and faces 点与面

How to find the common vertex shared by three faces? (How to find 3 faces cube from a net?)

For a cube, each vertex is shared by three faces.

Problem 1

Which other 2 vertices meet with vertex 1 when the following net is folded?

Step 1
Draw a diagonal across 2 squares from vertex 1 to a point.

Step 2
From that point, draw 2 diagonals to reach 2 more vertices. These 2 vertices are 2 and 3 as follows.

Step 3
Vertices 1, 2, and 3 will share a common vertex when folded.

Problem 1

The following faces could share a common vertex:	The following faces could not share a common vertex
5, 3, 4 5, 3, 2 1, 2, 6 2, 6, 3 1, 2, 5 1, 4, 6	234 123 536 265 246

Student's name: _____ Assignment date: _____

Cube and nets 方块及折叠面

Many nets and cubes problems appear in the past Kangaroo Math Contests. So, practising more of these problems will make children be familiar with this type of problem. One of the very important exercises is for students to judge if the nets can be folded into a cube without using a physical cube.

Circle the following nets, if any, which can be folded into cubes. 折叠平面成方块

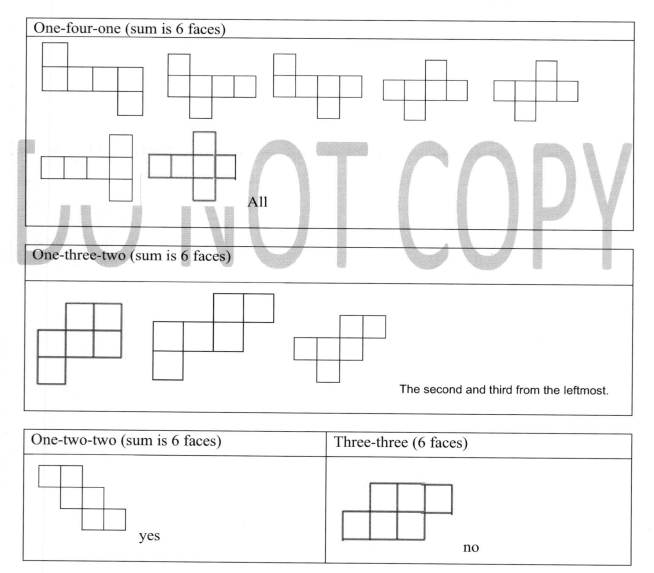

One-four-one (sum is 6 faces)

All

One-three-two (sum is 6 faces)

The second and third from the leftmost.

One-two-two (sum is 6 faces)

yes

Three-three (6 faces)

no

Circle the following nets, if any, which can be folded into cubes.

The second from the leftmost.

Transformation 旋转

Translation can be flip, rotate, or translate.
Describe how the figure moved from position 1 to position 2 using one transformation. Answers may vary.

Figure	Describe how the figure was transformed.
	Flip down or reflection
	Rotate CCW or CW
	Flip diagonally or translate right and down. Translation (right, down)

Student's name: _____　Assignment date: _____

Describe how the figure moved from position 1 to position 2 using two transformations.
Answers may vary.

Figure	Describe how the figure was transformed.
	Flip-up Move left
	Move right Flip down
	Move right Flip down Or Move left, flip-up

Angles, parallel, perpendicular 角, 平行, 垂直

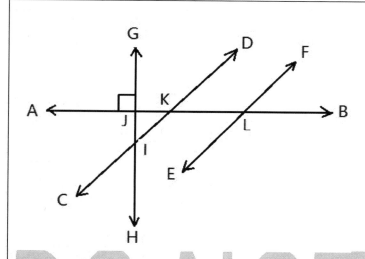

(A) Identify line segments online AB.   JK, KL, JL

(B) Identify rays online AB.   KA, KB, LA, LB, JA, JB

(C) What are the points of the above diagram? K, M, J, L

(D) Identify parallel lines.   CD //EF

    Identify perpendicular lines.   AB ⊥ GA

(E) Match left to right.

∠GJB	Reflex angle	∠CKB
∠AJB	Right angle	∠GJB
∠K turns 360°	Straight angle	∠AJB
∠CKB	The angle of resolution	∠K

Student's name: _____   Assignment date: _____

Making triangles 造三角形成

Make maximum triangles using the number of lines as indicated below such that no triangles overlap, and no triangles share sides.

Number of lines	Triangles	Number of triangles
4	Answer	2
5	?	3 ?
6	answer ?	4 ?
7	answer ?	5 ?

Make some triangles using the restrictions below.

Number of lines	Number of triangles	No triangles sharing sides
4	2	
5	2	answer ?
5	3	answer ?
5	4	answer ?
5	5	answer ?

Student's name: _____ Assignment date: _____

Make some triangles using the restrictions below.

Number of lines	No triangles sharing sides	Number of triangles
6	 answer	4
6	 answer	6
7	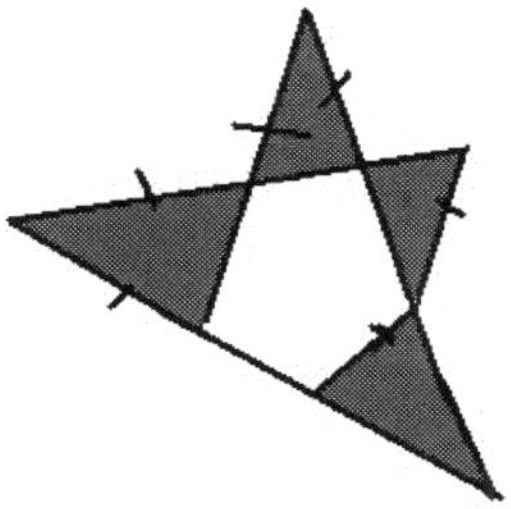 answer	4
8	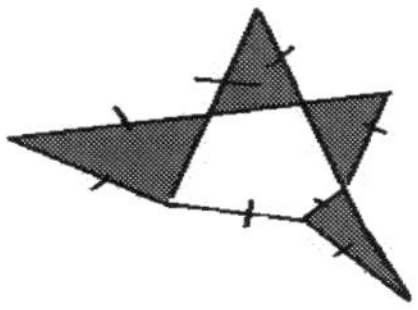 answer	4

Decimal, fractions, % # 34

Ho Math Chess (何數棋谜　趣味數學)

Use the empty area of this page or back page as a work area to calculate the following problems.

Drawing of different shapes 由点画图

Drawing of triangles 畫三角形

How many isosceles triangles (等腰三角形) you can draw in the following dotted diagram?

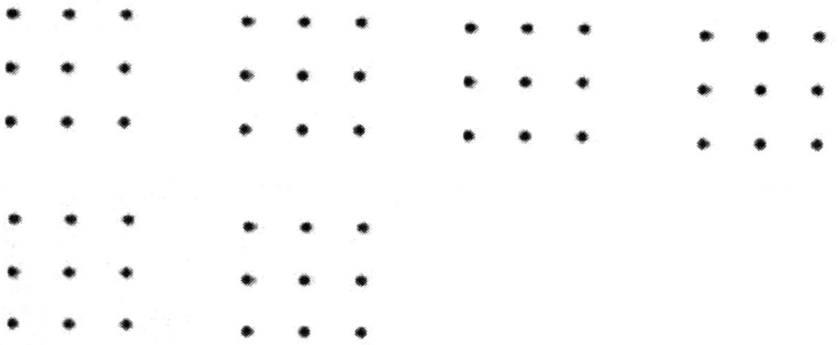

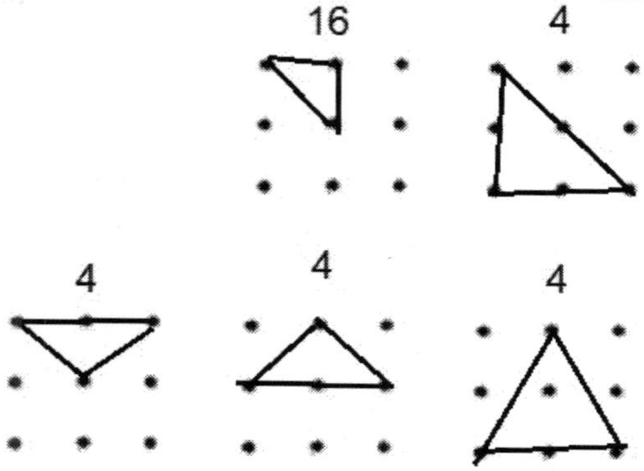

There are 32 isosceles triangles.

Student's name: _____ Assignment date: _____

Drawing of different sized squares 畫不等面積正方形

1. How many different sized squares you can draw from the following 2 by 2 dot paper. Square(s) must be drawn by connecting dots.   1

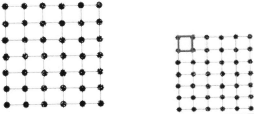

2. How many different sized squares you can draw from the following 3 by 3 dot paper. Square(s) must be drawn by connecting dots.   6

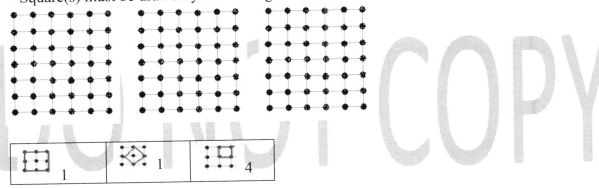

3. How many different sized squares you can draw from the following 4 by 4 dot paper. Square(s) must be drawn by connecting dots.   20

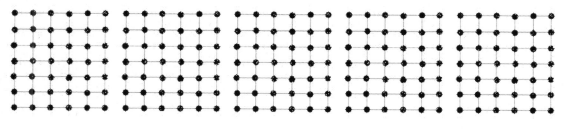

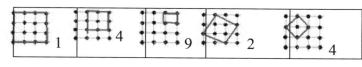

4. How many different sized squares you can draw from the following 5 by 5 dot paper. Square(s) must be drawn by connecting dots.   50

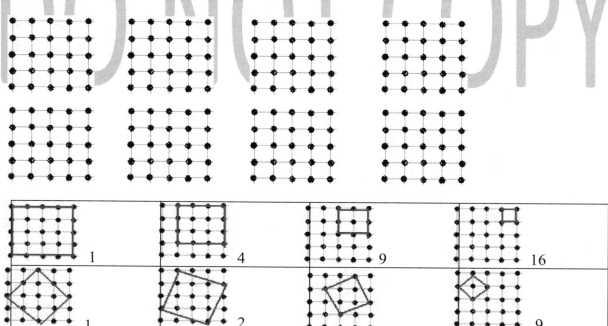

5. How many different sized squares you can draw from the following 6 by 6 dot paper. Square(s) must be drawn by connecting dots.   105

Answers for the previous page .

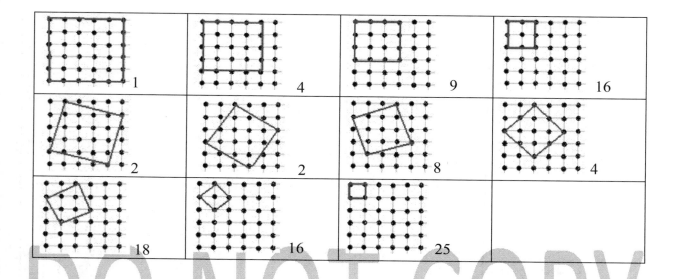

Student's name: _____ Assignment date: _____

Connect all dots in one stroke by drawing 6 straight lines. (more than 4 answers?)

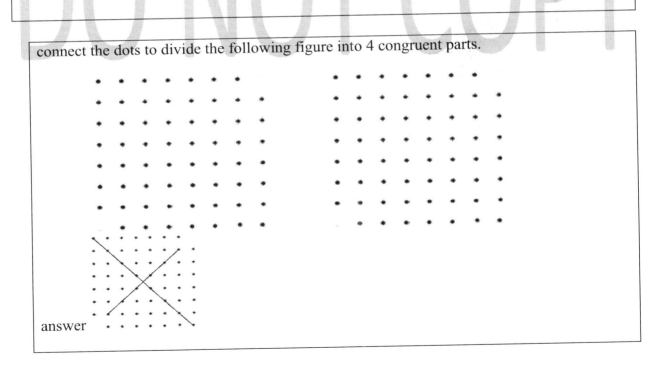

connect the dots to divide the following figure into 4 congruent parts.

answer

Circle dots 圈点
Decimal, fractions, % # 38

Ho **Math Chess** (何數棋谜　趣味數學)

Draw one curved line without lifting your pencil in such a way that each and only one dot is placed in one circled area. Draw it in a beautiful pattern. Do not use any tangent points such as

∞ , but crossed lines are allowed.

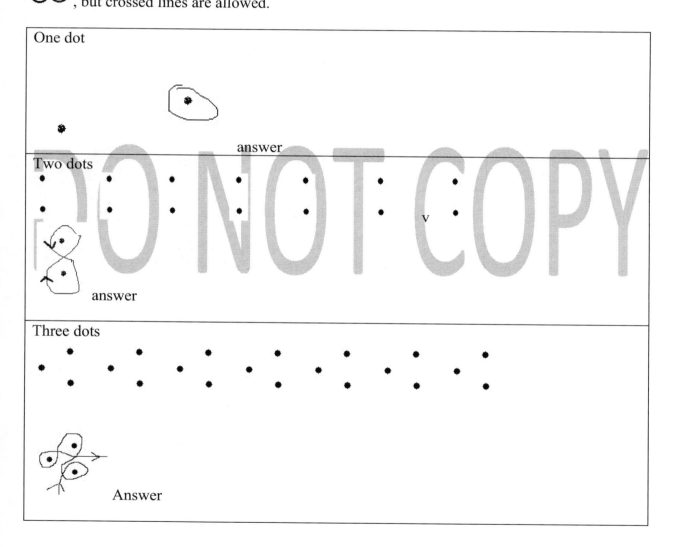

Four dots

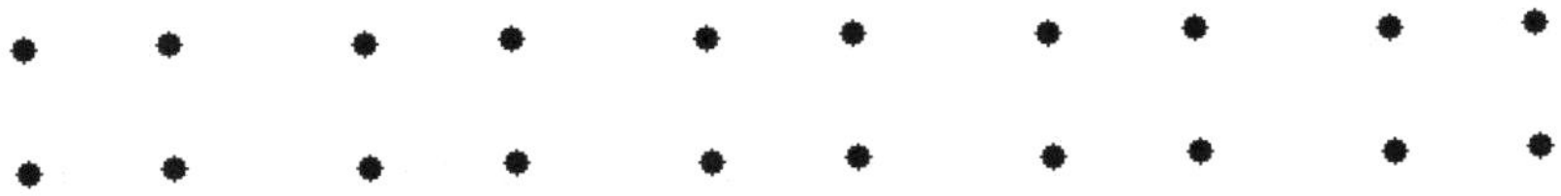

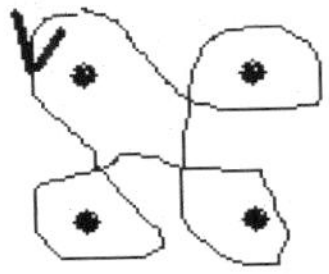

answer

Five dots

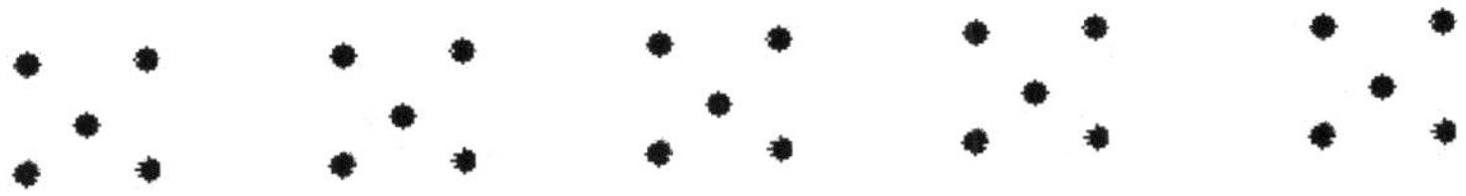

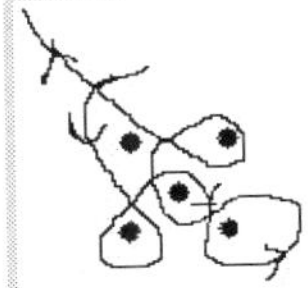

answer

Student's name: ______________________ Assignment date: ________________

Six dots

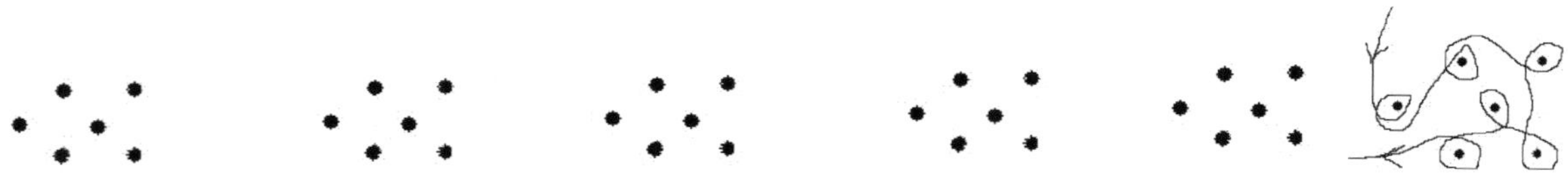

answer

Seven dots

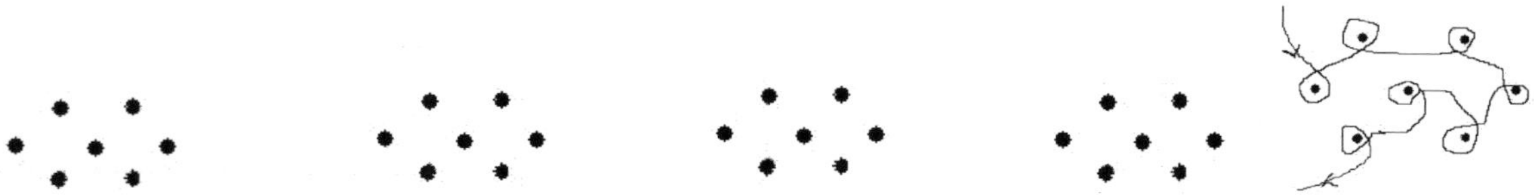

answer

Eight dots

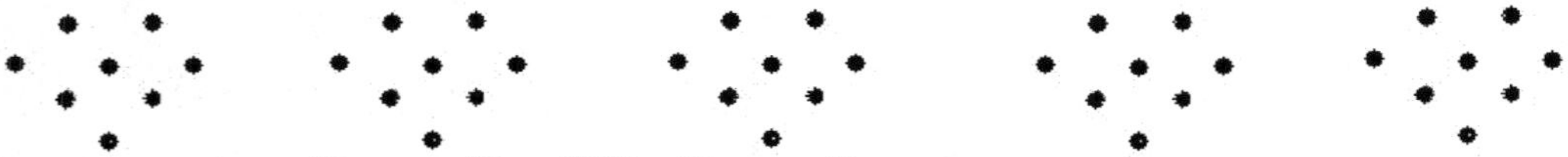

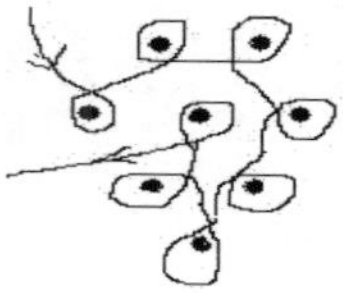

answer

Nine dots

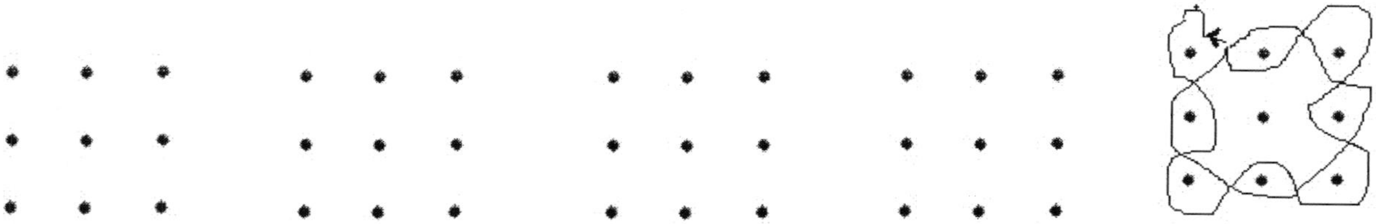

answer

Student's name: _____ Assignment date: _____

Ten dots

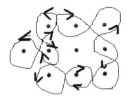

answer

Shape visualization 形状的視覺
Decimal, fractions, % # 46

Ho Math Chess (何數棋谜　趣味數學)

Use the empty area of this page or back page as a work area to calculate the following problems.

Ten identical squares are piled up as shown on the right-hand side. Place a number from 1 to 10 inside each square from the bottom square (number 1) to the very top one (number 10).

For example,

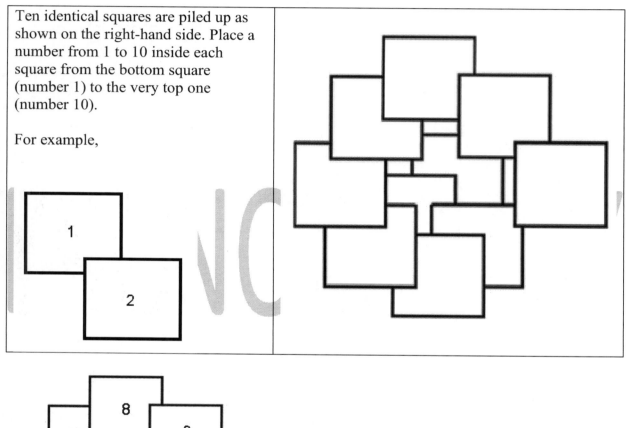

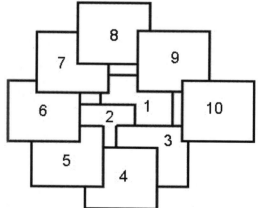

answer

Student's name: _____   Assignment date: _____

Position the numbers 1 to 8 in the following grid is such a way that no two consecutive numbers are touching along a side or from corner to corner. There is more than one answer.

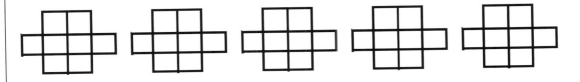

35 7182 46	63 2851 47	36 7182 54	81 6253 47	46 7182 35	57 3142 68			

Counting squares 数方块

What is the total number of squares with the same or different sizes, which can be chosen in the following diagram?

  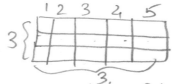 

1 by 1 has 21 or 5 x5 – 4 = 21 ⟹ total 21

2 by 2 has 12 or 4 x 4 – 4 = 16

3 by 3 has 5 or 3 x 3 – 4 = 5

Total is **38**

How many different squares altogether in the following figure?

1x1 = 21, 2 x 2 = 12, 3 x 3 = 5, 21+12+5=**38**

Geometry using algebra 以代数解几何

The figure below is made up of 2 parallelograms. Find∠x.

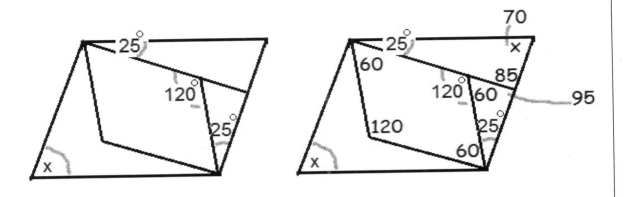

Algebra
Some word problems can be easily solved by using algebra, and many of these types of problems appear in Singapore as low as grade 5.

Tom's monthly salary is twice of Jerry's. If each of them spends $1200 monthly, then Tom's monthly savings is 5 times Jerry's. How much does Tom earn monthly?

2J-1200 = 5(J-1200)
J= 1600
Tom = 3200

There are three colours of LED lights in a store: red, blue and green. All three lights flash together when you walk in the store. The red light flashes every 12 minutes, the blue light flashes every 8 minutes, and the blue light flashes every 6 minutes. Including the flashes, you see when you first walk into the store, how many times will you see at least 2 LED lights to flash together if you are in the store for the next 60 minutes?

1st, 12 m, 24 m, 36 m, 48 m, 60m

Student's name: _____　Assignment date: _____

Basic methods for solving 2–D geometry contest problems and examples

Methods	Examples	Solution
Use helpline	The following rectangle is partitioned into 4 areas with known areas as 20cm², 25cm², and 30cm². Find the shaded area.	Method 1 Divide the entire rectangle into 5 equal areas, ∴ the shaded area = $\frac{25}{2} \times 3 = 37.5$ cm². Method 2 Use butterfly theorem variation, we know $25 \times 30 = 20 \times x$ $x = 37.5$ Method 3 Use the GCF. The shaded area $= 1.5 \times 25 = 37.5$ Method 4 – Ratio Shaded: 30 = 25 : 20 = 5:4 Shaded $= \frac{30}{4} \times 5 = 37.5$

Problem (all drawings are not to exact scale.)

The following squares are made from a right triangle. Find the shaded area of each square.

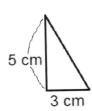  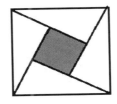

$8 \times 8 - \frac{5 \times 3}{2} \times 4 = 64 - 30 = 34$ cm^2 ….. left square

$34 - 30 = 4$ cm^2 … right square

Find the difference between the area of A part of the rectangle and the C part of the square.

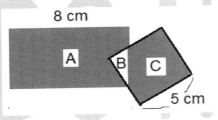

$A + B - (B+C) = A - C = 64 - 25 = 39$ cm^2

The radius of the following circle is 8m, and the circle touches only 4 points of a square. Find the shaded area.

$256 - 64\pi$

Diagram A and B have the same size as the square. Which square has a large shaded area?

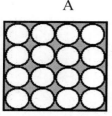

A

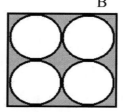

B

Both A and B are $16 - 4\pi$ assuming the side length of the square is 16.

Calculate the following area of triangle ABC.

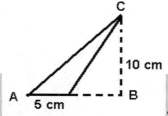

10 cm

A   5 cm   B

50 cm²

Student's name: _____ Assignment date: _____

Calculate the area of quadrilateral ABCD.
$25 + 20 = $ **45**

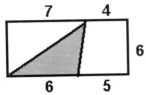

What is the area of the shaded triangle? **18 units²**   6x6/2=18

Find the area of the enclosed region. **72 units²**.
$100 - 36 + 8 = 72$

The side length of the square ABCD is 4 cm. All semicircles centred at the midpoint of the sides of square ABCD. Find the area to the nearest tenth of a square centimetre of the shaded portion. **6.9 cm²**

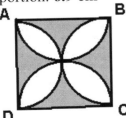

2 circle − square = 4 leaves.   Square − 4 leaves = **6.9 cm²**

How many triangles are there in the following figure?

answer

There are 10 triangles if all small triangles are numbered.

1+2:8, 1+2+3:4,

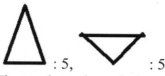   : 5,   : 5

The total number of triangles is $10 + 8 + 4 + 5 + 5 = 32$

Write the area in the fraction for the shaded area within a square ABCD.

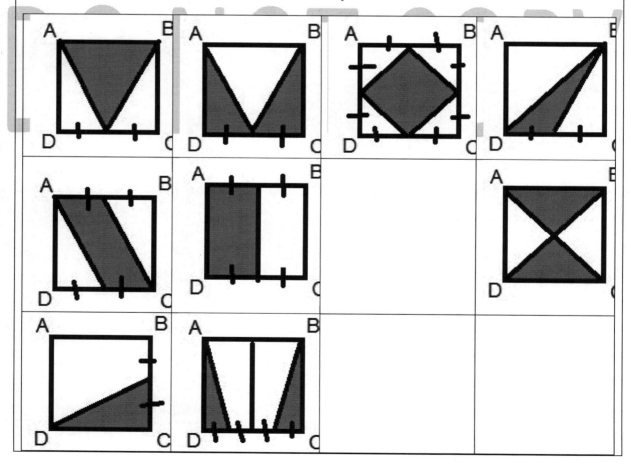

Student's name: _____ Assignment date: _____

Perimeter and area 周長及面積

A rectangular swimming pool measures 22 m by 16 m. A path 2 m wide is paved around the swimming pool. What is the area of the path?

$24 \times 18 - 22 \times 16 = 80 \text{ m}^2$

Find the shaded area.

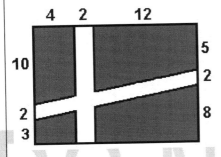

Method 1
$4 \times (10+3) + 12 \times (8+5) = 52 + 156 = 208$
Method 2

$(10+12+13) \times (4+12+12) - 2(4+12+12) - 2(10+2+3) + 2 \times 2$
$= 15 \times 18 - 2 \times 18 - 2 \times 15 + 2 \times 2$
$= 208$
Method 3
$15 \times 18 - 2 \times 15 - 2 \times 4 - 2 \times 12 = 208$

The area ratio of the three parts is 3: 7:7. What is the size of the fourth area (x + y)?
This problem involves the concept of a ratio, and the ratio of 2 triangles is the ratio of bases if their height is =. It also requires Systems of Equations to get x
and y.

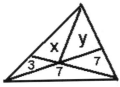

  x : (y+7) = 3:7 (The triangles of x : (y+7) share the same bases with 3 area and 7 area)
y:(x+3) = 7:7 (Because they share the same bases) with the same height
x=7.5, y=10.5 The total area = 7.5 + 10.5 = **18**

Student's name: _____ Assignment date: _____

A rectangle has volume 12 cm^3, what is the least surface area? What is the most surface area?

If 2x2x3=12, the least area = (4+6+6)x2=32, If 1x1x12=12, area = (1+12+12)x2=50, If 1x3x4=12, area = (3+4+12)x2=38
The most surface area = for the dimension 1 by 1 by 12. 2(1+12+12) = 50

Least 32 cm^3, most 50 cm^3

One side of Andy's rectangular garden measures 5.3 m. The perimeter of his garden is 19.8 m. Draw a sketch of Andy's garden. Label the side lengths.

$\frac{19.8}{2} = 9.9$

9.9-5.3=**4.6 … width**
5.3 unit … length

The length of a rectangle is increased by 1 unit. Its width is decreased by 1 unit. What happens to the area and the perimeter? Use an example to explain.
A square is also a rectangle, so we use 1 by 1. Its perimeter is 4. Its area is 1.
Increased the width and the length each by 1, the perimeter = (2+2) x 2 =8, its area = 2 x 2 =4
The new perimeter increased by 4 units; the new area increased by 3 units.

The length of a rectangle is increased by 2 units. Its width is decreased by 3 units. What happens to the area and the perimeter? Use an example to explain.

A square is also a rectangle, so we use 4 by 4. Its perimeter is 16. Its area is 16.
Increased the length by 2 and decreased the width by 3, the perimeter – (1+6) x 2 = 14, its area = 1 x 6 = 6
The new perimeter is decreased by 2, and the new area is decreased by 10 units.

The area of a rectangular room is 600 m^2, and the perimeter is 100 m. What are the dimensions of the room?
30 m by 20 m

What are the square metres of a rug which measured with the area as 650 cm^2?
1 m=100 cm, 1 m^2=10000 cm^2, 650 ÷ 10000 = 0.65 m^2

Student's name: _____ Assignment date: _____

Area and perimeter problem 周長及面積

Find the perimeter of the following figure.

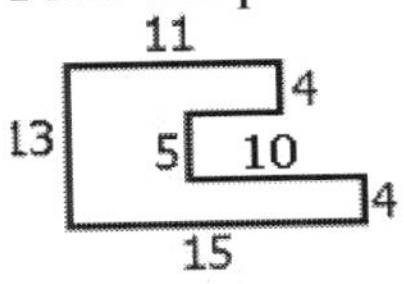

$13+13+11+15+10+[11-(15-10)]=$ **68**

Shapes	Perimeter	Area
rectangle	36cm	What is the least possible area?
rectangle	What is the greatest possible perimeter?	40cm^2

Which figure in the following table will have a perimeter of 36 units and an area of 81 square units.

Figure number	Perimeter	Area
1	4	1
2	8	4
3	12	9
4	16	16
9th figure	36	81

The mirror in Tammy's bedroom is 25 cm by 25 cm, so its area is 625 cm². Tammy would like a new mirror twice the area or the old mirror with one of the new dimensions to be 50 cm in order to fit on the wall. What is the missing dimension going to be?

125 cm

Tammy and Tina want to build a rectangular board with an area of 0.35 m². The width of the board must be 50 cm. What will the length be?

1 m² = 10000 cm² (1 m = 100 cm)
70 cm

A parallelogram has a base of 10 cm and a height of 5 cm. If its area is doubled, what base and height could be for the new parallelogram?

20 cm

A rectangle has a size of 6 m by 7 m. If its new area is 4 times bigger than the old area, what length and width could be the new rectangle?

1 m by 168 m
2 by 84
4 by 42
6 by 28
8 by 21
12 by 14

A 1L can of paint covers 8 m². Haruto and his sister need to paint 9 rectangle-shaped poster boards each measures 60 cm by 100 cm. Will 1L be enough to paint all 9 boards?

Yes because of $60\sqrt[4]{100} \times 9 = 54000$
$\frac{54000}{10000} = 5.4$ m²

Raymond's squared room is 144 m², with a rectangular closet build at one corner. Without counting the area of the closet, the remaining area is 120 m². What is the reasonable dimension of the closet?

144 − 120 = 24 m
The reasonable answers could be 3 m by 8 m, 4 by 6, 2 by 12

Student's name: _____   Assignment date: _____

Mixed geometry problems (All scales may not be exact.) 混合几何题

Calculate the perimeter and area of the following circle (leave answer in π).

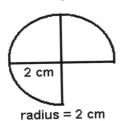

radius = 2 cm

Area $= \frac{3}{4} \times \pi r^2 = = \frac{3}{4} \times 4\pi = 3\pi$

Circumference $= = \frac{3}{4} \times 2\pi r + 4 = \frac{3}{4} \times 4\pi + 4 = 3\pi + 4$

AD // BC, Triangle ABC is a right triangle. Find the perimeter of ABCD and the area of triangle ACD.

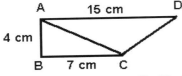

36 cm and 30 cm²

ABCD is a rectangle. AB=2×BC. The triangle ABE is equilateral. The point M is the midpoint of the side BE. Find the angle ∠ CMB (in degrees).

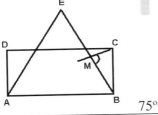

75°

In the picture, ABCDE is a regular pentagon, and ABFG is a square. Find the angle ∠ FBC (in degrees).

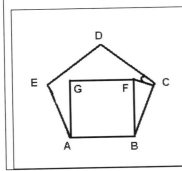

$\angle FBC = \angle ABC - 90^0$

$= \frac{(5-2)180}{5} - 90^0$

$= 108^0 - 90^0$

$= 18^0$

Student's name: _____ Assignment date: _____

Part E – School math mixed English word problems 学校数学混合文字题

Sum, Multiplier, Difference 和倍差問題

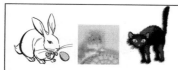

There are rabbits, gerbils, and cats in a pet store.

cats	rabbits	gerbils
3	6	4
1	2	10

- There are 13 animals in total.
- There are twice as many rabbits as cats.

How many of each animal could there be?

There are at least 2 animals each because the sentence uses a plural noun. Restrict cats first, then the number of rabbits must be divisible by 2. **The answer is 3 cats, 6 rabbits, 4 gerbils.**

The pet store sold 25 pets, including rabbits, cats, gerbils. It sold three times as many rabbits as gerbils. The gerbils sold were the same number as cats sold. How many of each animal was sold?

Method 1: Use a table
Gerbils sold = cats sold = 5
Rabbits sold = 15
Method 2: Use equation g + 3g + g = 45, g = 15

If you pick two digits from 1 to 5 to make a 2-digit number and no digit can be repeated, how many different numbers can you make?

5 x 4 = 20

If you choose two kinds of fruits from the following 4 fruits (strawberry, apple, banana, and orange) to make a fruit plate, then how many kinds of fruit plates can you have?

Code each fruit as 1, 2, 3, 4, and then you can list them all.
Or think this as a handshake problem, so the answer is 3 + 2 + 1 = **6**

Student's name: _____   Assignment date: _____

Mixed Combination problems 混合組合題

1	

Finish the following problems before working on word problems.

1 quarter = _____ cents = $\frac{\$1}{4}$ = \$0.25   25

2 quarters = _____ cents = $\frac{\$1}{2}$ = \$_____   50, 0.50

3 quarters = _____ cents = \$_____   75, 0.75

4 quarters = _____ cents = \$_____   100, 1

Oscar has the following number of coins.

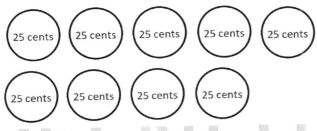

Question 1.

What is the total value of Oscar's coins? \$2.25

Question 2.

Jennifer has the same amount of money as Oscar with fewer than 9 coins. Find all the possible combinations of using the following coins that Jennifer could have of at least two of \$1 coins.

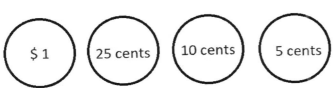

Make a table to solve this problem. Maximize the number of \$1 first and gradually reduce it.

\$1	25 cents	10 cents	5 cents
2	1	0	0
2	0	2	1
2	0	1	3
2	0	0	5

1 | Question 3.

Emma has the same amount of money as Oscar has with more than 9 coins. Find all the possible combinations of the following coins that Emma could have at least one of $1 and exact three of 25 cents.

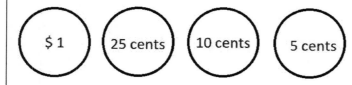

$1	25 cents	10 cents	5 cents
1	3	2	5
1	3	1	7
1	3	0	9

2 Jennifer, Emma, and Isabella went shopping. They bought some brushes, toy dogs, and a few ice cream cones.

$7.00 each $2.00 each $??? each

Question 1.

Jennifer bought 2 brushes and 3 ice cream cones. How much did it cost her altogether? $20

Emma bought 3 brushes and 2 ice cream cones. How much did it cost her altogether? $25

Who spent more money and by how much? Emma spent $5 more.

Question 2.

Isabell spent a total of $28. What combination of brushes and ice cream cones could she have bought?

$7	$2
4	0
2	7
0	14

Question 3.

What could be the price of a toy dog if Isabella bought 3 brushes and 2 toy dogs? Did she spend $27 altogether?

$3 for each toy dog. ($\frac{27-21}{2} = 3$)

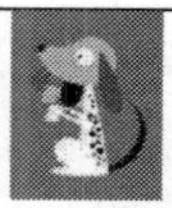

Kelly walks her dog 6 days each week for about 45 minutes each walk. What are the total hours and minutes taken each week for her dog-walk?

4 hours 30 minutes

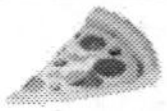

Each pizza is cut into 7 equal pieces. Each child will eat about 2 pieces of pizza. How many pizzas are needed for a class of 37 children?

11 pizzas

Kelly wants to have $35 changed in one-dollar or two-dollar bills or both bills. Find out all different combinations of bills to make $35 change. 17 ways

Kelly wants to have a 35 ¢ changed in 5 ¢, 10 ¢, or 25 ¢. Find out all possible ways that she can make 35 ¢ change. 4 ways

25¢	1	0	0	0
10¢	1	2	3	0
5¢	0	3	1	7

Student's name: _____ Assignment date: _____

Mixed Combination problem 混合組合題

Balls are thrown at the target. What are the possible scores that you could get if you throw two balls?

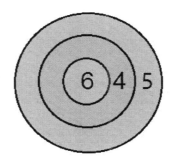

12 (6+6), 11 (6+5), 10 (6+4), 10 (5+5), 9 (5+4), 8 (4+4)

What are the different possible scores that you could get if you throw three balls?

12	13	14	15	15	16	17	18
444	544	554	555	654	655	566	666

7

What are the different possible scores that you could get if you throw five balls at target scores of 7 and 4 only?

20, 23, 26, 26, 33, 35

Student's name: _____ Assignment date: _____

Mixed Combination problem 混合組合題

Andy chooses 3 colours from a box of crayons, which only has 6 colours, red, blue, yellow, green, black, and white. How many ways can Andy choose crayons from the box?

15

Andy participates in 3 running events in a track meet, which has 50-m, 75-m, 100-m, and 200-m dashes. How many different choices does Andy have?

4 choices
Abv
Abd
Acd
bcd

There are 32 identical square desks. A large rectangular table is created to use these squares. How many possible ways can a rectangular table be put together by these square tables?

3 possible ways:
1 by 32; 2 by 16; 4 by 8

Terry counted there were 21 bicycles and tricycles in the park. He got a total of 53 when he counted the wheels. How many bicycles and tricycles were there?

10 tricycles and 11 bicycle

Student's name: _____ Assignment date: _____

Six people played in a chess tournament. Each played the other person twice. How many games were played in all?

If the problem is changed to play only once, then how many games were played?
5 + 4 + 3 + 2 + 1 = 15

$15 \times 2 = 30$ games

Show Andy what all possible 3-digit numbers you can make from the 4 digits 0, 5, 7, and 8 are. No digit can be repeated.

18 numbers = 3 x 3 x 2 x 1

How many different sums can you choose two digits from 3, 5, 7, and 9? No digit can be repeated.

5, the sums are 5, 6, 7, 8, 9

How many triangles are in the following diagram?

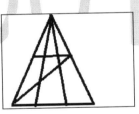

Answer The numbers are written on the sides of triangles.

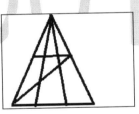	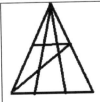 Left Slanted 3	Right bottom Slanted 3	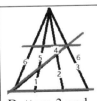 Bottom 3 and planted and horizontal intersection 3	Horizontal top 3

24 triangles
Blank line   blank line

Student's name: _____ Assignment date: _____

One car is needed to give a ride for every 4 students to Fun Fair. How many cars are needed for 37 students?

10 cars

Blank line   blank line
Blank line   blank line

Michael is about to cross a bridge, and we know the following information:

- The bridge is 8 m long.
- Michael's one-foot step is about 45 cm.

Blank line   blank line

About how many steps are needed for Michael to cross the bridge?

Blank line   blank line

18 steps

Blank line   blank line

There are 5 cedar trees for every 2 oak trees at the Nature Park. How many cedar trees are there if there are 12 oak trees?

Blank line   blank line

30 cedar trees

Blank line   blank line
Blank line   blank line
Blank line   blank line

It takes 12 seconds for the elevator from the first floor to the fourth floor, how many seconds does it take for the elevator to go from the first floor to the eighth floor?

$$\frac{12}{3 \text{ gaps}} \times 7 = 28 \text{ seconds}$$

Blank line   blank line

At the Pre-Loved Skates shop, the price of a pair of skates is reduced by half each day. If on the first day, a pair of skates cost $8, then how much will it cost on the fourth day?

$1

Blank line   blank line
Blank line   blank line
Blank line   blank line
Blank line   blank line

Student's name: _____ Assignment date: _____

There are three whole numbers ranked from the smallest to the largest and the difference between each number is 3. The total of three numbers is 24. What are these three numbers?

$$x + x + 3 + x + 6 = 24$$

Blank line   blank line
Blank line   blank line
5, 8, 11
Blank line   blank line

A basket of apples is divided into many piles. If each pile has 8 apples, then there is a short of one apple, and if each pile has 7 apples, then there are 8 apples left. Find how many apples are there and how many piles are there?

Blank line   blank line

Method 1

Find the number of apples which satisfies the condition 1 with 8 apples in each pile. The result is short of one apple.

The number of apples could meet the above condition 1 are 7, 15, 23, 31, 39, 47, 55, 63, 71, ...

Blank line   blank line

Find the number of apples which satisfy condition 2 with 7 apples in each pile. The result is 8 piles left.

The number of apples could meet the above condition are 15, 22, 29, 36, 43, 50, 57, 64, 71, ...

Blank line   blank line

The number of apples 71, which meets both conditions.   Blank line   blank line
Blank line   blank line

Method 2

Blank line   blank line

Let the number of piles $= x$

$8x - 1 = 7x + 8$ Blank line   blank line

$x = $ **9 piles**, $9 \times 8 - 1 =$ **71 apples.**

Blank line   blank line

Eric has 105 marbles, and Alex has 21 marbles. How many marbles does Eric have to give to Alex such that each of them has an equal number of marbles?

Blank line   blank line
Blank line   blank line
42
Blank line   blank line

Isaac wants to build a rectangular pen for his cat. He has 24 m of fencing. He wants the sides to be whole numbers. What are all the different rectangular areas he could possibly get?

11, 20, 27, 32, 35, 36 m^2
1 by 11 =11, 2 by 10 = 20, 3 by 9 =27, 4 by 8= 32, 5 by 7= 35, 6 by 6= 36,
Blank line   blank line

Isaac wants to build a rectangular pen for his cat. He has 12 m of fencing. He wants the sides to be whole numbers. What are all the different rectangular areas he could possibly get?

5, 8, 9 m^2
1 by 5, 2 by 4, 3 by 3
Blank line   blank line
Blank line   blank line

The pattern rule is to start the first number with 9 and adds 3 to the previous number. If the pattern continues, what is the fifth number? What is the total up and including the fifth number?

21, 75
Blank line   blank line
Blank line   blank line
Blank line   blank line

If 4.2 m roll of paper is cut into 3 equal pieces and each piece is 1.2 m long. How will much paper in cm be left in the roll?

4.2 – 3 x 1.2 =0.6 m = 60 cm   Blank line   blank line
Blank line   blank line
Blank line   blank line

Write 2222 in English words. _____. **Two thousand two hundred twenty-two**
Blank line   blank line
Blank line   blank line

Write 22.22 in English words. _____. **Twenty-two and twenty-two hundredth**

Student's name: _____ Assignment date: _____

James is 4 years older than his cousin Louise. In three years, Louise will be 16. How old is James now?

17

Blank line	blank line
Blank line	blank line
Blank line	blank line
Blank line	blank line

Each box carries 8 cans. You have 67 cans. How many boxes do you need to carry all these cans?

9 boxes

Blank line	blank line
Blank line	blank line
Blank line	blank line
Blank line	blank line

What is the positive difference between 14.8 and 3.19?

11.61

Blank line	blank line
Blank line	blank line
Blank line	blank line
Blank line	blank line
Blank line	blank line

What is the sum of 4 tenths and 21 hundredths?

0.61

Blank line	blank line
Blank line	blank line
Blank line	blank line

There are 32 children in Shelby's class. For every 3 girls, there is a boy. How many boys are in Shelby's class?

       Blank line   blank line

8   Blank line   blank line
       Blank line   blank line

---

   heron   duck   goose

There are 42 birds in the Nature Park. For every heron, there are 3 ducks. For every heron, there are three geese. How many of each bird are in the Nature Park?

6 herons   Blank line   blank line
18 ducks   Blank line   blank line
18 geese   Blank line   blank line
    Blank line   · blank line

A box of a dozen bags of biscuits along with a box altogether weigh 5000 g. Seven bags, along with a box, were sold, and they all weigh 3550 g. How much does each bag weigh, and how much does the box weigh?

Method 1

5000-3550=1450, 1450/5=**290 g weight of each bag**.   Blank line   blank line
3550 – 290 x 7 = **1520g weight of box**   Blank line   blank line

Method 2
12B + X = 5000   Blank line   blank line
7B + X =3550   Blank line   blank line

Alex's house is 1.5 km from school and Eric's house is 2 km from the school. How far is the distance from Alex's house to Eric's house?
Assume Alex's house, Eric's house and school are all on a straight line. Show two answers by drawing two diagrams.

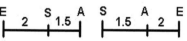

Show two answers by drawing two diagrams.   **0.5 and 3.5 km**

On the first day, Justin read half his book and 20 more pages. The second day he read half of what was left and 5 more pages, there were 40 pages left. How many pages were there in the book in the beginning?

       Blank line   blank line
45x2+20 =110, 110 x 2=**220**   Blank line   blank line

Is $\frac{4}{5}$ closer to 0 or 1? Draw a number line to show.

1

Is 150 closer to 100 or 200? Draw a number line to show.

the same

Is 1.51 closer to 1 or 2? Draw a number line to show.

2

Find the area of the following shaded rectangle when ABCD is a square.

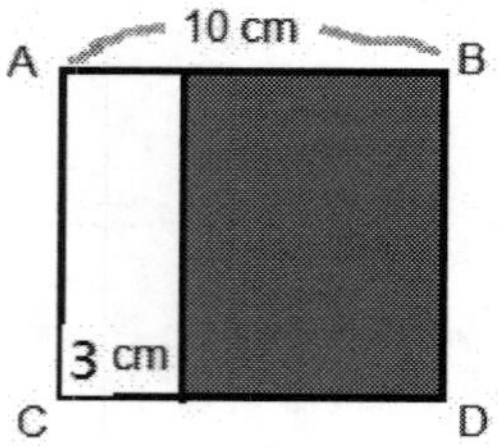

70 cm²

Use all the digits 9, 7, 0, 8, and 5 to form the greatest 5-digit even number.

98750

Pattern

Find the answers for the missing numbers by using a pattern rule.

A	B
3	180
7	420
9	540
13	? **780**

What is the pattern rule of getting B from A? _____ **B=A × 60**

What should be the next number for the following number sequence?

1, 8, 27, 64, _____ **125**

$\frac{5}{8}$ of guests at the party are boys and $\frac{1}{4}$ of the guests are girls, and the rest guests are adults. What fraction of the guests are adults?

1/8

Fernando used the following diagrams and figured out the answer was $\frac{3}{6}$, was he correct?

_____ **No, should be** $\frac{3}{8}$

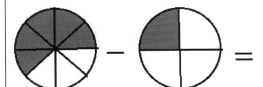 =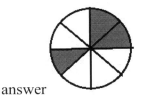

answer

What are 4 tens, 17 tenths and 8 thousandths in decimal numbers?

$40 + 0.17 + 0.008 = 40.178$

The measurements of a water tank are 35 cm long, 15 cm wide, and 25 cm high. Ten litres (L) of water are poured into this empty tank. How much is more water needed to fill the tank to its brim in L³? (1 L = 1000 cm³)

$\frac{35 \times 15 \times 25}{1000} - 10 = 13.125\,L - 10\,L = 3.125\,L$

Student's name: _____ Assignment date: _____

Fernando paid a total of $75 for a pair of earrings, a dress and a bracelet. The bracelet costs $6.60 more than the earrings. The dress cost triple as much as the bracelet. Find the cost of the dress.

$48.96

Use algebra to solve it. $X + x + 6.6 + 3x + 19,8 = 75$

The number of girls at the party was $\frac{4}{10}$ the number of boys. There were 24 more boys than girls at the party. How many boys were at the party? How many girls were at the party?

40 boys, 16 girls

$24 \div \frac{6}{10} = 40$ boys

$\frac{4}{10} \times 40 = $ **16 girls**

Aaron gets paid $3 per car wash and an additional $3 per hour. He worked three hours last week doing 15 car washes. How much did he earn?

$54 = $3 x 15 + $3 x 3

Rank the following number from lowest to greatest.

1.3, $\frac{1}{2}$, 1.032, $\frac{4}{10}$

$0.32, \frac{4}{10}, \frac{1}{2}, 1.032, 1.3$ **answer**

Write 3 dimes (each dime = 10 cents) and 2 nickels (each nickel = 5 cents) in decimal with a dollar sign. _____ **$0.40**

Write 3 dimes and 2 nickels in whole number _____ **40¢**

There are 6 soldiers in $\frac{1}{5}$ of a set of plastic army commandos. How many plastic army commando soldiers are there in a complete set?

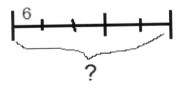

30

There are 8 soldiers in $\frac{2}{5}$ of a set of plastic army commandos. How many plastic army commando soldiers are there in a complete set?

20

Fernando studied at 8:30 a.m. and finished at 3:15 p.m. with a one-hour lunch break. Melissa studied at 12:35 and finished at 20:55 with a one-hour dinner break. Who studied longer and by how much time?

$$(15:15 - 8:30) - (20:55 - 12:35) = 6:45 - 8:20 = 1:35$$
Melissa by 1 hour and 35 minutes

A rectangular pool deck has a width of 4 m and a length of 6 m. It costs $4 to buy a meter fence. How much does it cost to install a fence around the pool deck?

$100

A rectangular pool deck has a width of 5 m and a length of 7 m. It costs $5 to buy a 120 cm of the fence. How much does it cost to install a fence around the pool deck?

$100

Is $\frac{1}{4}$ closer to 0 or 0.5? Draw a number line to show.

the same

Student's name: _____ Assignment date: _____

What is the next shape?　　hexagon

 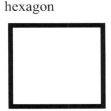 

?　answer

Blank line　　blank line
Blank line　　blank line
Blank line　　blank line

I am a 3-digit number. My tens digit is 3 times of my ones digit, and the sum of my digits is 12. What number am I?

831 or 732

Blank line　　blank line
Blank line　　blank line
Blank line　　blank line
Blank line　　blank line

Compare the following numbers using >, =, or <.

1. $\dfrac{0.1}{2}$　$\dfrac{0.01}{0.2}$　=

Blank line　　blank line
Blank line　　blank line

2. $\dfrac{0.001}{0.2}$　$\dfrac{0.01}{0.002}$　<

Blank line　　blank line
Blank line　　blank line

Blank line　　blank line

1 week = _____ days ✓

Blank line　　blank line

7

1 day = _____ week　$\dfrac{1}{7}$

Student's name: _____   Assignment date: _____

Jordan has 13 more than as many as four times of Jocelyn's apples. Jordan has 81 apples. How many apples does Jocelyn have?

Line Segment Method		Assumption Pattern method		Pre-algebra using symbol

		Jocelyn	Jordan	
		10	40+13 =53	
		11	57	
		15	73	
		16	77	
		17	81	

Line Segment Method: Jocelyn, Jordan, 13, 81

$$\frac{81 - 13}{4} = 17$$

Pre-algebra using symbol: $4 \times \square + 13 = 81$

17

The Spring fair director planned the daily sale of 3.5 tons of hot dogs, but the actual daily sale on average was 1 ton more than planned. The stock lasted for 7 days. How many days did the fair director originally plan to finish selling the hot dogs?

$$9 = \frac{4.5 \times 7}{3.5}$$

Compute $2.09 - 1.909 =?$

1.091

$2.64 - 1.909 =$

0.731

Two and one tenths + one hundred and three hundred two thousandths

102.402

Student's name: _____   Assignment date: _____

Add the face values of the underlined digits.

$5623\underline{6} + \underline{1}876453 + 623\underline{5}21 + 478\underline{20} + 45\underline{3} = ?$

1002029

Make a 3-digit number such that

- The hundreds place digit is 4 times of the ones place digit.
- The number is greater than 600.
- The number is divisible by 9.

882

Use the digits 1, 2, 3, 4, 5, 6, 7, and 8 once each to make the following sum greatest. What is the sum?

$$\square\square\square\square$$
$$+\ \square\square\square\square$$
$$\overline{\square\square\square\square\square}$$

8641+7532=16173

Use the digits 1, 2, 3, 4, 5, 6, 7, and 8 once each to make the following difference greatest. What is the difference?

$$\square\square\square\square$$
$$-\ \square\square\square\square$$
$$\overline{\square\square\square\square\square}$$

8765 - 1234 = 7531

Student's name: _____   Assignment date: _____

What is the missing number in the box if A is a number?

$$\square \times A \times \frac{2}{3} = A \times \frac{4}{7} \quad \frac{6}{7}\text{answer}$$

What is the reading indicated on the following weighing scale?

Answer: _____kg _____g 3, 750

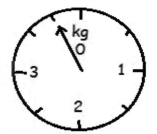

Find the missing numbers in the empty brackets.

$$\frac{(\ \ )}{18} = \frac{4}{[\ \ ]} = \frac{5}{15}$$

6, 12

Blank line   blank line
Blank line   blank line
Blank line   blank line
Blank line   blank line

Equation

When compared to North America elementary math, it is surprising to see many problems in Singapore, or China requires algebraic equations solving techniques which are very advanced for elementary students in North America.

Adam, Bob, and Cathy had 400 stamps altogether. After Bob had given 50 stamps to Adam, Bob had twice as many stamps as Cathy and Adam had 28 more stamps than Cathy. How many stamps did Cathy have?

Cathy = 108

Blank line   blank line
Blank line   blank line
Blank line   blank line
Blank line   blank line
Blank line   blank line
Blank line   blank line
Blank line   blank line

The False Creek, ice cream shop, has chocolate macadamia nut ice cream, honey nut ice cream, and blueberry ice cream. They also have wheat and rice cones. How many different double-dip ice cream cone combinations can they make from these selections?

12

Blank line	blank line
Blank line	blank line
Blank line	blank line
Blank line	blank line
Blank line	blank line

The gear pointed by an arrow is turned in a clockwise direction, in which direction will the right-most gear turn?

Clockwise

Blank line	blank line
Blank line	blank line
Blank line	blank line
Blank line	blank line
Blank line	blank line

Student's name: _____ Assignment date: _____

How many 2-digit numbers have a remainder of 4 when they divided by 5?

$$\frac{95}{5} - 1 = 18$$

Blank line   blank line
Blank line   blank line
Blank line   blank line
Blank line   blank line
Blank line   blank line

Find numbers to replace A, B, and C.

$$16 - 5A + 3B - 5C = 0$$

Blank line   blank line
Blank line   blank line
Blank line   blank line
Blank line   blank line

On Monday, September 1, after 10 hours and 35 minutes of darkness, the sun rose at 6:15 a.m. At what time was the sunset on Sunday, August 31st?

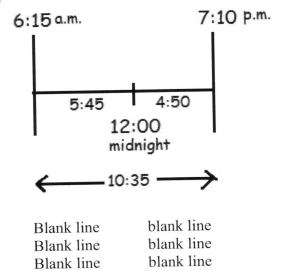

Blank line   blank line
Blank line   blank line
Blank line   blank line
Blank line   blank line

On the first Market Fair day, Tammy sold $\frac{1}{5}$ of her earrings. On the second day, she sold $\frac{1}{2}$ of the remainder. If she sold 17 more earrings on the second day than the first day, how many earrings did she sell for the two days altogether?

17~ (corresponds to) $\frac{2}{5} - \frac{1}{5} = \frac{1}{5}$ ($\frac{4}{5} \times \frac{1}{2} = \frac{2}{5}$ *the second day*)

17 ~ (corresponds to) $\frac{1}{5}$

$17 \times 5 = 85 \ldots \ldots$ original

$85 \times 2 + 17 = 187$

Blank line	blank line
Blank line	blank line
Blank line	blank line
Blank line	blank line
Blank line	blank line
Blank line	blank line

A circle-based water tank with a height of 6 m was $\frac{1}{4}$ full. When another 120 cm^3 of water was poured into the tank, it became $\frac{1}{2}$ full. Find the capacity of the water tank in litre. (1000 cm^3 is 1 L)

6B ~ (corresponds to) $\frac{1}{4}$

120+6B ~ $\frac{1}{2}$

120 ~ (corresponds to) $= \frac{1}{2} - \frac{1}{4} = \frac{1}{4}$

$\frac{120 \times 4 = 420 m^3}{1000} = 0.48$ L

Blank line	blank line
Blank line	blank line
Blank line	blank line
Blank line	blank line
Blank line	blank line
Blank line	blank line

Bob has 149 more stamps than Adam. Cathy has 229 more stamps than Bob. Altogether they have 767 stamps. How many stamps does each one of them have?
Hint: Use the Line Segment Diagram to solve.

9119 people were in the sports stadium last night. 3557 of them were women, and there were 879 fewer women than men. The rest were children. How many children were in the sports stadium last night?

1126

Vera wants to give two cans of fruit juice to each of her thirteen friends invited to her birthday party. How many of 6-pack of juice cans must she buy?

5 of 6-pack

Edna places 56 oranges into 4 baskets equally. How many oranges are there in 3 baskets altogether?

$54 \div 4 \times 3 = 48$

What number is just as far from 7 as it is from 21?

$\frac{7+21}{2} = 14$

If $11 + \boxed{} = 17 - \boxed{}$ then what is the value of $\boxed{}$?　3

Annabelle has a number. When 26 is added to her number, the result is the same as when her number is multiplied by 2. What is Annabelle's number?

26

　　Blank line　　　　blank line

Use the Line Segment Diagram.

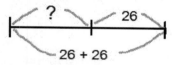

When 32 is added to a number, the result is the same as when the number is multiplied by 3. What is the original number?

It can be thought of as a ratio problem, so the ratio unit increase is 2.

$$\frac{32}{3-1} = 16$$

　　Blank line　　　　blank line

When 48 is added to a number, the result is the same as when the number is multiplied by 4. What is the original nu0mber?

16 ($48 \div 3 = 16$)

　　Blank line　　　　blank line
　　Blank line　　　　blank line

Sixty cents are made of an equal number of 10 ¢ and 5 ¢ coins. How many numbers of 10 ¢ and 5 ¢ are there?

Think 15 cents and as a new coin because of equal 10 cents and 5 cents. Figure out how many are needed.　4

Fernando has $3 in his pocket and $216 in his bank. He wants to share half of his bank money with Frank. How much money in total does Fernando have after sharing?

Multiplication method	Division method
$3 + 216 \times \dfrac{1}{2}$	$3 + 216 \div \dfrac{1}{2}$

For consecutive numbers, the difference between two even numbers or the two odd numbers is _____. 2

    Blank line   blank line
    Blank line   blank line

Find three consecutive whole numbers whose sum is 96.

    Blank line   blank line
    Blank line   blank line

31, 32, 33

Find three consecutive even whole numbers whose sum is 132.

    Blank line   blank line
    Blank line   blank line
    Blank line   blank line

43, 44, 45

Choose 3 digits from 1, 2, 3, 4, 5, 6, 7, 8, and 9 and calculate their sums. How many choices are there?

When a number divided by 3, then the remainder could be 0, 1, or 2. If these 3 digits added together, then the sum is divisible by 3.
The above 9 digits can be divided into 3 different categories when divided by 3.

    Blank line   blank line
  1. The remainder is 0: 3, 6, 9   Blank line   blank line
  2. The remainder is 1: 1, 4, 7   Blank line   blank line
  3. The remainder is 2: 2, 5, 8   Blank line   blank line

    Blank line   blank line

If we pick one digit from each of the above group, then the sum will be a multiple of 3. The choices are $3 \times 3 \times 3 = 27$. There are 3 more groups: $3 + 6 + 9 = 18$, $1 + 4 + 7 = 12$, $2 + 5 + 8 = 15$.
The total choices are $27 + 3 = \textbf{30}$.

    Blank line   blank line
    Blank line   blank line

Find two numbers such that one of them is 91 more than the other and their sum is 201.

$$\frac{201 - 91 = 110}{2} = 55 \; smaller$$

$55 + 91 = 146$ ...... larger

Blank line   blank line
Blank line   blank line
Blank line   blank line

Find a number when multiplied by 5 is the same as it is increased by 120.

$$\frac{120}{4} = 30$$

Blank line   blank line

Find two consecutive numbers when their sum is 183.

The sum of 183 and the difference is 1.

$\frac{183 - 1}{2} = 91$ .... smaller

$91 + 1 = 92$ .... larger

Blank line   blank line

Peter's father is three times as old as Peter if their sum of ages is 68. How old is Peter?

$\frac{68}{4} = 17$ .... Peter

Blank line   blank line

If 7 is subtracted from four times a number, the result is 68. What is the number?

Think reversely, the result of "four times a number" is $x \times 4 = 72$

$\frac{72}{4} = 18$ .... $darker$

Blank line   blank line
Blank line   blank line

Three erasers and one pencil cost $12. Three erasers cost as much as the cost of one pencil. How much is the cost of each pencil? How much is the cost of each eraser?
P = $6, E=$2

Blank line   blank line

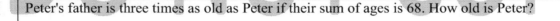

1. How many least colours do I need to paint each of the following squares, so any squares that touch each other are coloured differently?

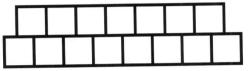

3

2. If today is Monday and if I started to read my book 14 days ago, then on which day did I first read my book?

Monday

3. $37 - 25 =$ _____ $=$ _____ $- 9 =$ _____ $+ 7 = 31 -$ _____ $= 1 \times$ _____ $=$ _____ $\div 1 =$ _____ $\times 6 = 3$
$\times$ _____ $= \frac{[\ ]}{4} \times 24$

12, 21, 5, 19, 12, 12, 2, 4, 2

4. How many triangles are there in the following square?

8+4+4 = 16

5. $1 + 1 + 1 + ... + 1 =$ _____
add one hundred times

100

6. How many pairs of parallel sides are there in the following figure?

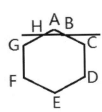

5, AB//FE, BC//FE, AH//DE, HG//DE, GF//CD

7. $12 + 12 = 2$ of _____ $=$ _____   12, 24

8. What is one half plus $\frac{1}{2}$? _____ 1

9. Show one quarter by shading the following squares.

3.75/15

10. Simplify the following division or fraction.

$\frac{2\ hours}{60\ minutes}$ 2
Blank line   blank line

11. Simplify the following division or fraction.
Blank line   blank line
$\frac{20\ seconds}{1\ hour\ 30\ seconds}$ 2/363
Blank line   blank line

12. 9 ones + 90 tens = _____ 99
Blank line   blank line

13. 9 tenths + 9 hundredths = _____ 0.99
Blank line   blank line

14. one half of one half = _____ of one-eighth 2
Blank line   blank line

15. 5 hundred + _____ = 100 of _____ + 12 12, 5

16. If Issac turned seven years old today, then 24 months ago, Issac was _____ years old. 5
Blank line   blank line

17. (9 + 9) + (1 + 1) = _____ + _____ = 2 × ____ 10, 10, 10

18. If $1 \div a = \frac{1}{a}$ then $1 \div 3 =$ _____ and $1 \div \frac{1}{3} =$ _____ 1/3, 3

19. $\frac{3}{1} \times$ _____ = 1 $\frac{1}{3}$
Blank line   blank line

20. In a rodeo, there are 3 horses for every 4 bulls. There are 280 hooves altogether. How many horses are in this rodeo? 30, convert the ratio to a fraction, then calculate.
Blank line   blank line

21. How many knight moves does it take to move from square 1 to square 9? 4
Blank line   blank line

Student's name: _____   Assignment date: _____

1.

English words	Math notation in a fraction	Math notation in decimal
One half	$\frac{1}{2}$	0.5
One quarter	$\frac{1}{4}$	0.25
Three quarters	$\frac{3}{4}$	0.25
Two thirds	$\frac{2}{3}$	$0.\overline{6}$
One eighth	$\frac{1}{8}$	0.125

What is one half plus $\frac{1}{4}$? _____ $\frac{3}{4}$

Blank line   blank line

2. An operation # is defined by A # B = 20 − (A+B) − (A−B).

Blank line   blank line

What is the value of (2 # 1)? _____ 16

Blank line   blank line

What is the value of (4 # 3)? _____ 12

What is the value of (4 # 3) # (2 # 1)? _____ -4

3. If one dozen erasers are $12, then what is the cost of 6 erasers? _____ 6

Blank line   blank line

4. If one dozen erasers are $12, then what is the cost of 5 erasers? _____ 5

Blank line   blank line

5. 18 − 9 = 20 − _____ + 10 − 1   20   Blank line   blank line

6. 8 × 60 = 8 × 10 × _____   6   Blank line   blank line

7. 8 × 125 = 8 × 5 ×5 × _____   5   Blank line   blank line

8. 6 × 3 ×5 = 30 × 3 × _____   1   Blank line   blank line

9. 4 ×18 = 18 ÷ ___ × 4 × 2   2   Blank line   blank line

10. 8 × 2 × 5 = 40 × _____   2   Blank line   blank line

11. 30 × _____ = 3 $\frac{1}{10}$ Blank line   blank line

Blank line   blank line

22, 6, 5, 1, 2, 2, 1/10

12. $16 \times 20 = 10 \times$ _____ $= 40 \times$ _____   8

13. $12 \times$ _____ $= 11 \times 24 =$ _____ $\times 33$ 8

14. Find the next term.

A, E, F, _____   H

15. What is the next figure?

answer

Part F – Ho Math Chess puzzles for the creative minds 何数棋谜培养金点子頭腦

Unequal Sudoku 不等数独

Every row and column must have only one number starting from 1 to the number of squares of each side (Sudoku), but all numbers must obey the inequality sign.

Example	Problem
231, 123, 312	2314, 3241, 4132, 1423

Fencing 盖围墙, 頭尾相连但不交义,不重複的循环围墙

Connect lines around each dot in such a way that each number indicates how many lines, connected by 4 dots only, surround it. The connected lines must form a single loop (like one rubber band) without lines crossed to each other.

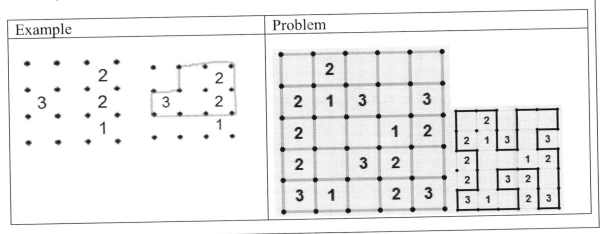

Amandaho Moving Dots Puzzle ™ 移点子

You are a rook at c3.

Move some dots in c4, c2, or d3 squares into c3 square such that the sum of dots + dots in each of rook's moves at c3 will be equal to the number shown on its destination square. See the following example.

Example

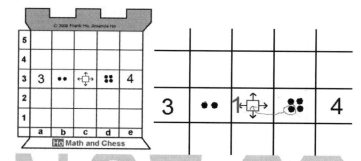

Problem

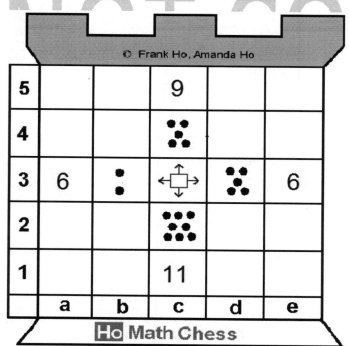

Move up 2, move down 1, move right 1, move left 1. 5 in the middle.

3-D Sudoku Buildings 看高楼数独

The number outside the large square shows the number of buildings that can be seen from that row or column when looking into the square from that direction. For example, the number "2" means you can see two buildings from that row or column. Each small square box must have the levels of the building. The final results must follow Sudoku law.

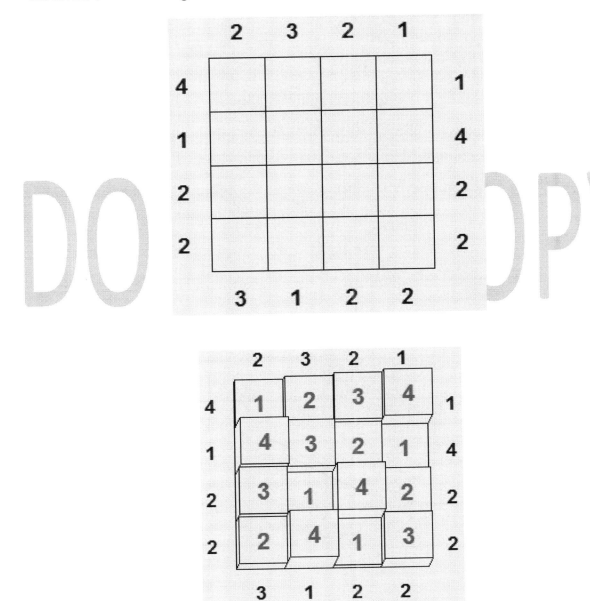

Fencing 盖围墙, 頭尾相连但不交义,不重複的循环围墙

Connect some dots around each number in the small square box in such a way that each number must be equal to the number within each small box. The connected lines must form a single loop (like one rubber band) without lines crossed to each other.

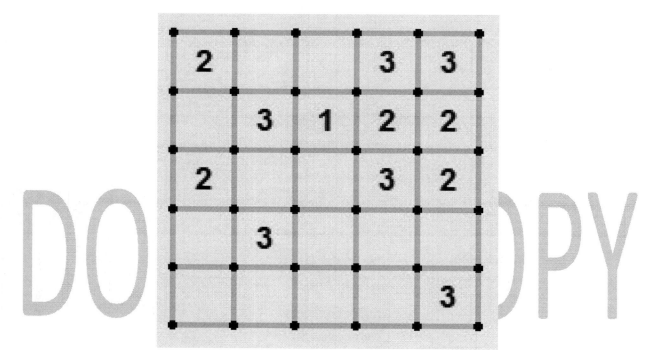

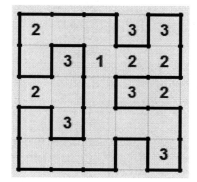

Student's name: _____   Assignment date: _____

Fencing 盖围墙, 頭尾相连但不交义,不重複的循环围墙

Connect some dots around each number in the small square box in such a way that each number must be equal to the number within each small box. The connected lines must form a single loop (like one rubber band) without lines crossed to each other.

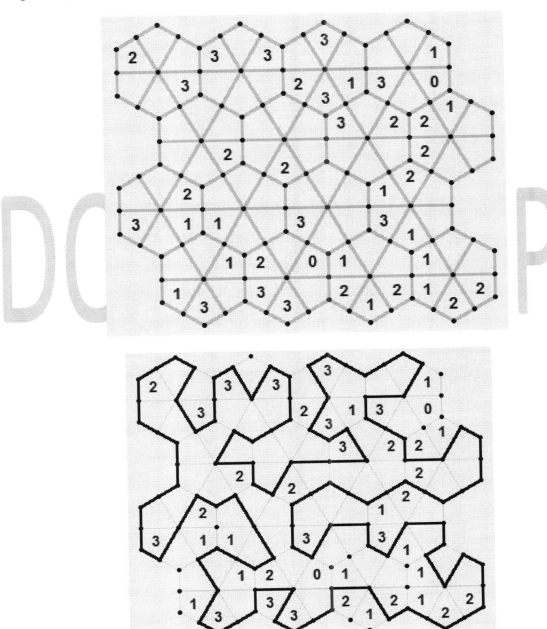

Frankho ChessDoku 何数棋谜算独

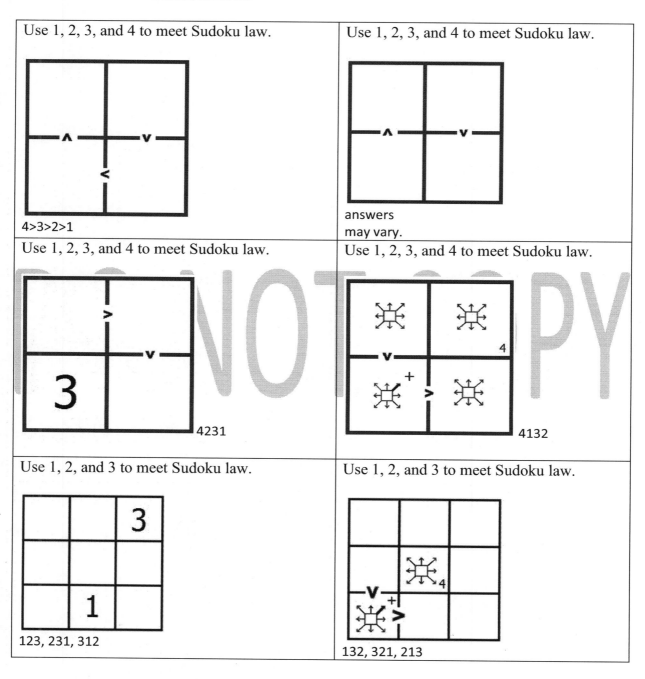

Use 1, 2, 3, and 4 to meet Sudoku law. 4>3>2>1	Use 1, 2, 3, and 4 to meet Sudoku law. answers may vary.
Use 1, 2, 3, and 4 to meet Sudoku law. 4231	Use 1, 2, 3, and 4 to meet Sudoku law. 4132
Use 1, 2, and 3 to meet Sudoku law. 123, 231, 312	Use 1, 2, and 3 to meet Sudoku law. 132, 321, 213

Unequal Sudoku 不等数独

Every row and column must have only one number starting from 1 to the number of squares of each side (Sudoku), but all numbers must obey the inequality sign.

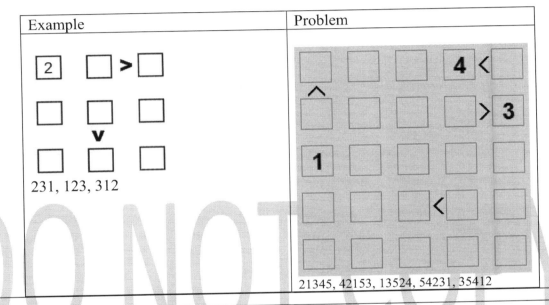

Example

231, 123, 312

Problem

21345, 42153, 13524, 54231, 35412

Fencing 盖围墙, 頭尾相连但不交义,不重複的循环围墙

Connect some dots around each number in the small square box in such a way that each number must be equal to the number within each small box. The connected lines must form a single loop (like one rubber band) without lines crossed to each other.

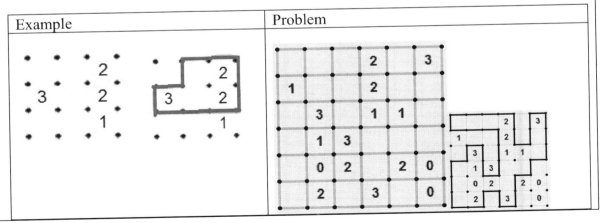

Example

Problem

Amandaho Moving Dots Puzzle ™ 移点子

You are a rook at c3.

Move some dots in c4, c2, or d3 squares into c3 square such that the sum of dots + dots in each of rook's moves at c3 will be equal to the number shown on its destination square. See the following example.

Example

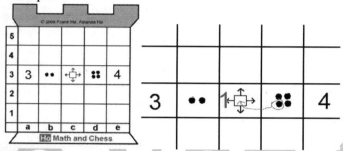

Problem

Move up 2, move down 1, move left 1. 4 in the middle.

Unequal Sudoku 不等数独

Every row and column must have only one number starting from 1 to the number of squares of each side (Sudoku), but all numbers must obey the inequality sign.

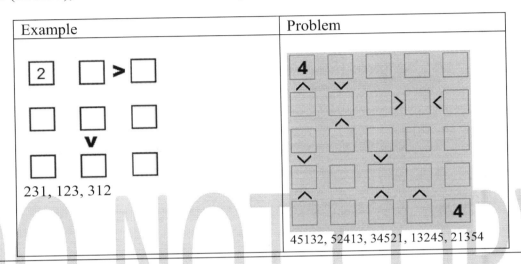

45132, 52413, 34521, 13245, 21354

Fencing 盖围墙, 頭尾相连但不交义,不重複的循环围墙

Connect some dots around each number in the small square box in such a way that each number must be equal to the number within each small box. The connected lines must form a single loop (like one rubber band) without lines crossed to each other.

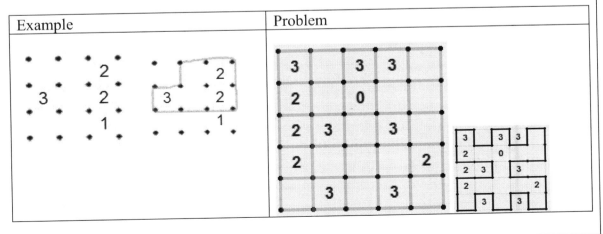

3-D Sudoku Buildings 看高楼数独

The number outside the large square shows the number of buildings that can be seen from that row or column when looking into the square from that direction. For example, the number "2" means you can see two buildings from that row or column. Each small square box must have the levels of the building. The final results must follow Sudoku law.

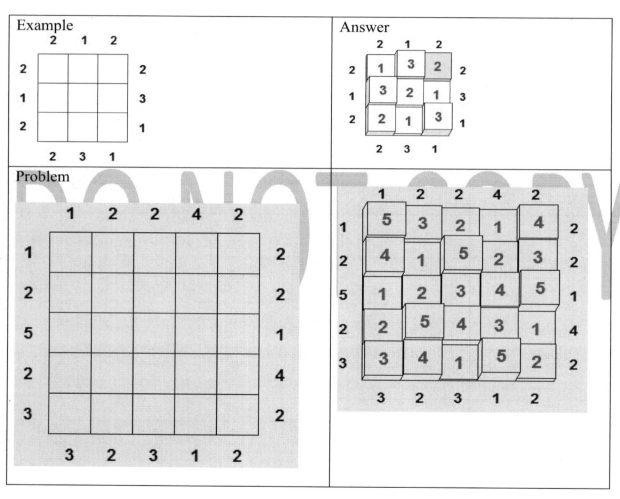

Sudoku 9 by 9 数独

Each row contains only one digit from 1 to 9.
Each column contains only one digit from 1 to 9.
Each box contains only one digit from 1 to 9.

					4		1	
	1					3	5	9
		5			6			
	7	2		6	8			
			7		1			
			3	5		8	7	
			9			7		
1	9	6					8	
	3		6					

CalcuDoku 算独

Each row contains only one digit from 1 to the size of the grid.
Each column contains only one digit from 1 to the size of the grid.
The digits in each block must satisfy the arithmetic operation given in the block.

Frankho ChessDoku 何数棋谜算独

Frankho ChessDoku™ is solved by using one or more operators of addition, subtraction, multiplication or division after following chess moves and logic.

Rule All the digits 1 to 3 must appear exactly once in every row and column. The number appears in the bottom right-hand corner is the result calculated according to the arithmetic operator(s) and chess move(s) as indicated by the darker arrow(s).

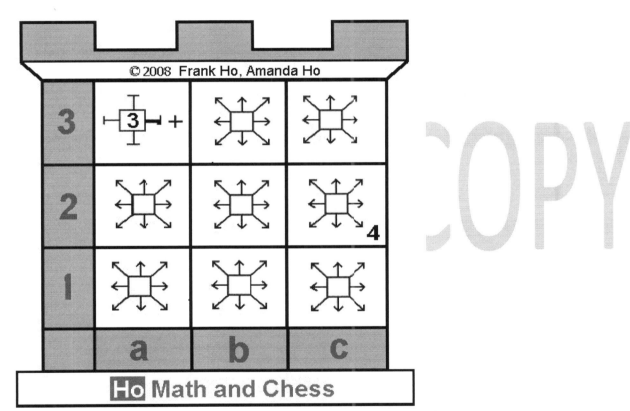

312, 231, 123

Unequal Sudoku（不等数独）

Every row and column must have only one number starting from 1 to the number of squares of each side (Sudoku), but all numbers must obey the inequality sign.

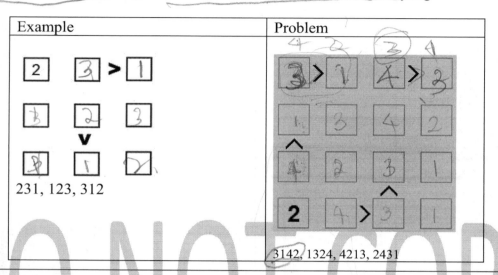

231, 123, 312

3142, 1324, 4213, 2431

Fencing 盖围墙, 頭尾相连但不交义,不重複的循环围墙

Connect some dots around each number in the small square box in such a way that each number must be equal to the number within each small box. The connected lines must form a single loop (like one rubber band) without lines crossed to each other.

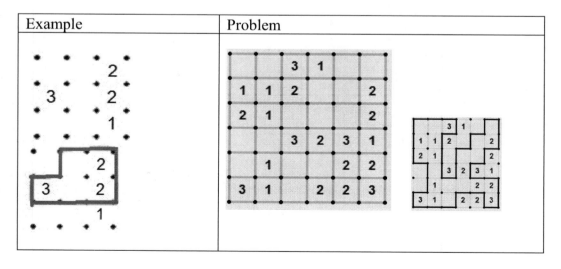

Student's name: _____　Assignment date: _____

Amandaho Moving Dots Puzzle ™ 移点子

You are a rook at c3.

Move some dots in c4, c2, or d3 squares into c3 square such that the sum of dots + dots in each of rook's moves at c3 will be equal to the number shown on its destination square. See the following example.

Example

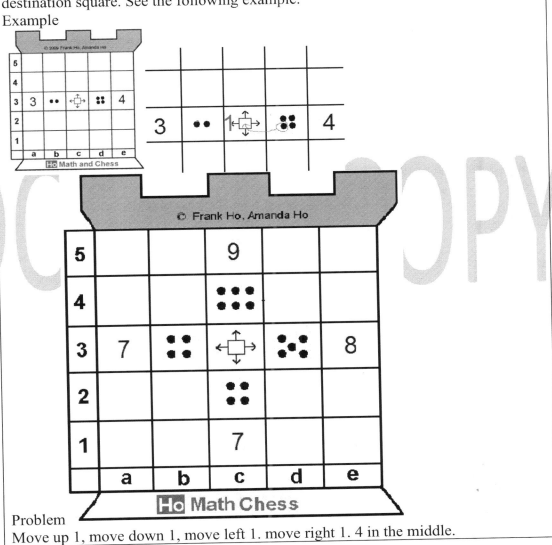

Problem

Move up 1, move down 1, move left 1. move right 1. 4 in the middle.

Student's name: _____   Assignment date: _____

3-D Sudoku Buildings 看高楼数独

The number outside the large square shows the number of buildings that can be seen from that row or column when looking into the square from that direction. For example, the number "2" means you can see two buildings from that row or column. Each small square box must have the levels of the building. The final results must follow Sudoku law.

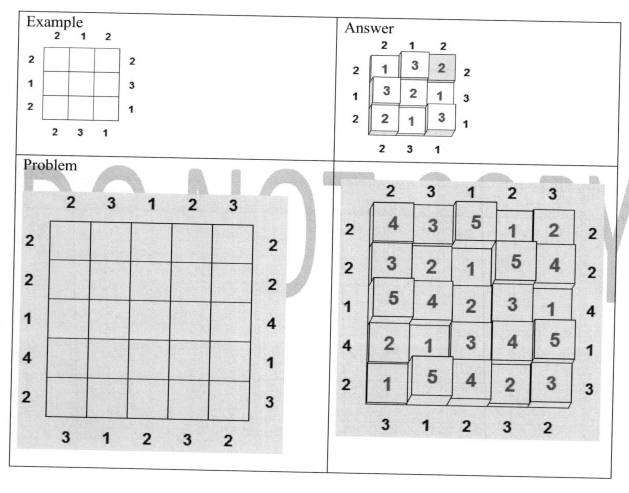

Student's name: _____   Assignment date: _____

Sudoku 数独

Each row contains only one digit from 1 to 9.
Each column contains only one digit from 1 to 9.
Each box contains only one digit from 1 to 9.

8								9
1	2			8			6	
					2		3	
			1		7			8
4	1						2	5
9			2		8			
	5		7					
	9			6			1	3
3								7

8	3	6	5	1	4	2	7	9
1	2	7	9	8	3	5	6	4
5	4	9	6	7	2	8	3	1
2	6	5	1	4	7	3	9	8
4	1	8	3	9	6	7	2	5
9	7	3	2	5	8	1	4	6
6	5	4	7	3	1	9	8	2
7	9	2	8	6	5	4	1	3
3	8	1	4	2	9	6	5	7

CalcuDoku

Each row contains only one digit from 1 to the size of the \grid.
Each column contains only one digit from 1 to the size of the grid.
The digits in each block must satisfy the arithmetic operation given in the block.

Example

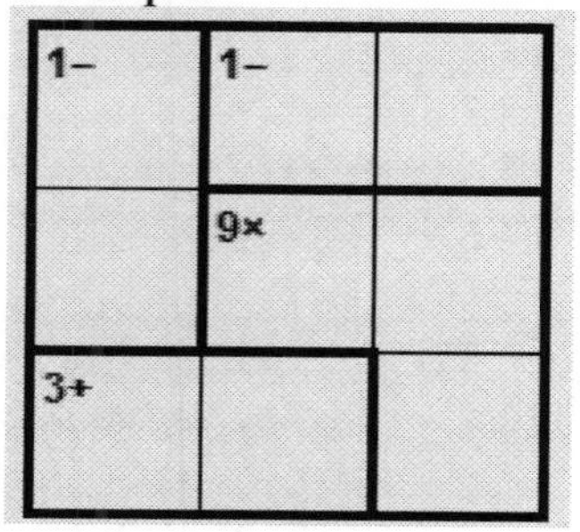

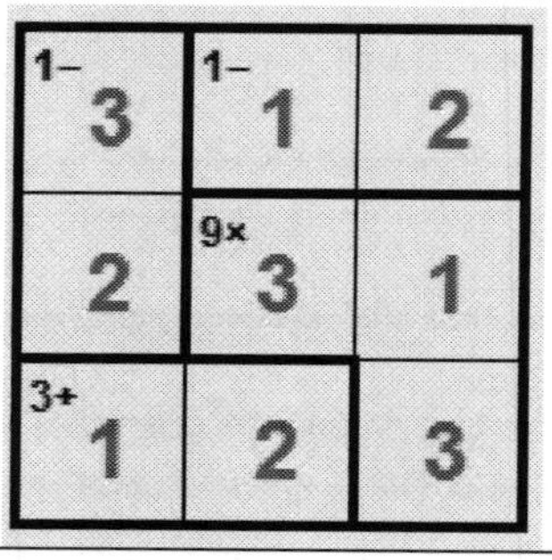

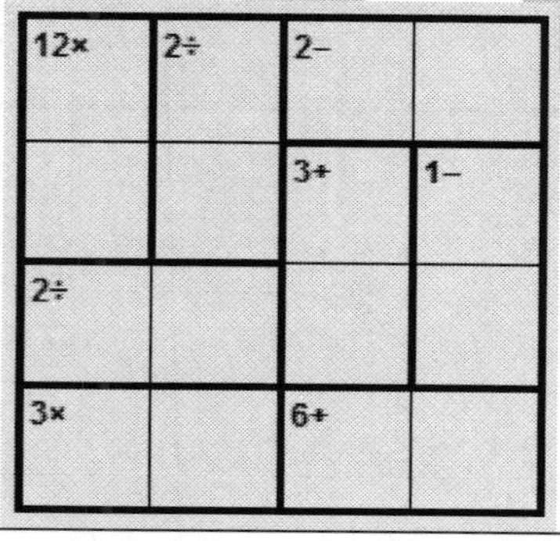

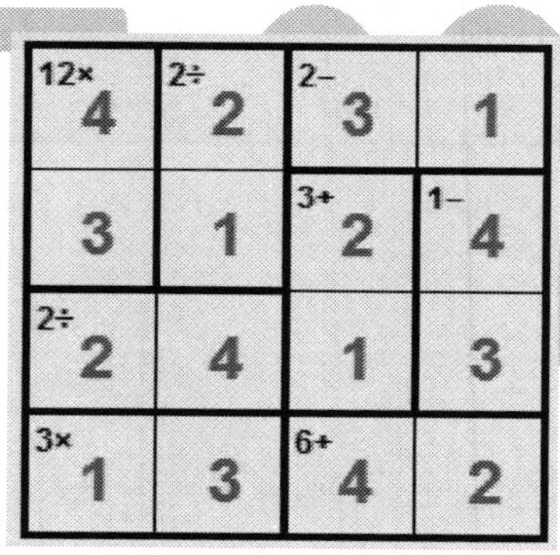

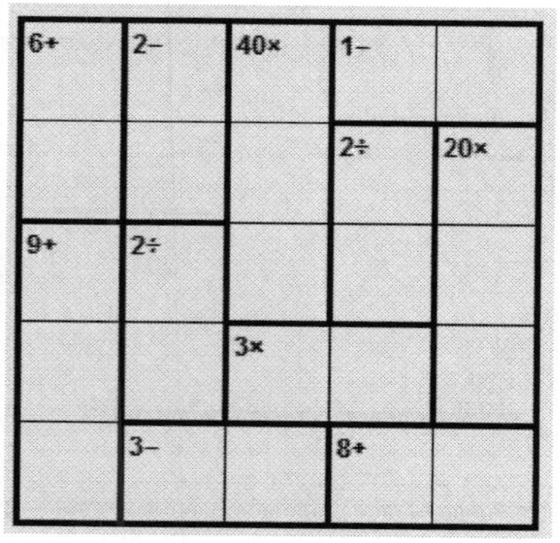

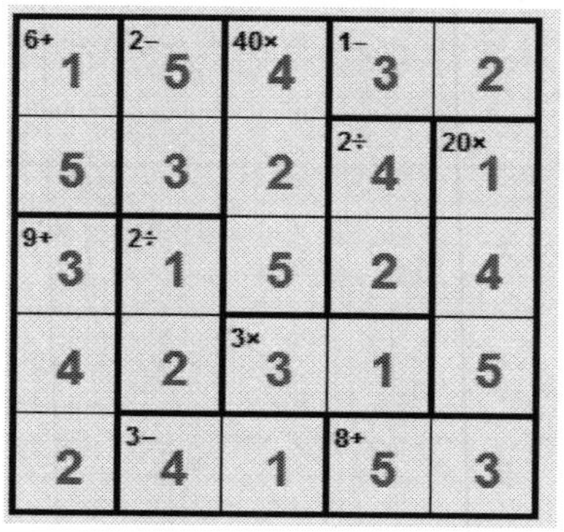

Student's name: _____ Assignment date: _____

Frankho ChessDoku 何数棋谜算独

Frankho ChessDoku™ is solved by using one or more operators of addition, subtraction, multiplication, or division after following chess moves and logic.

Rule All the digits 1 to 3 must appear exactly once in every row and column. The number appears in the bottom right-hand corner is the end result calculated according to the arithmetic operator(s) and chess move(s) as indicated by the darker arrow(s).

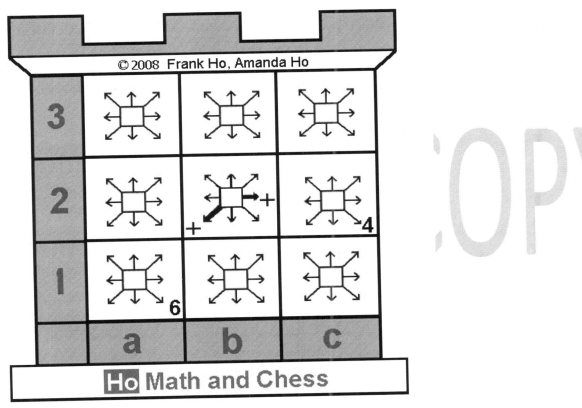

123, 231, 312

Unequal Sudoku 不等数独

Every row and column must have only one number starting from 1 to the number of squares of each side (Sudoku), but all numbers must obey the inequality sign.

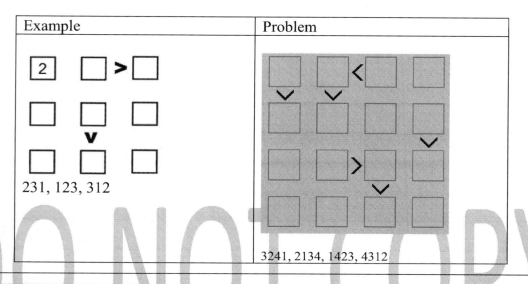

Example	Problem

231, 123, 312

3241, 2134, 1423, 4312

Fencing 盖围墙, 頭尾相连但不交叉,不重複的循环围墙

Connect some dots around each number in the small square box in such a way that each number must be equal to the number within each small box. The connected lines must form a single loop (like one rubber band) without lines crossed to each other.

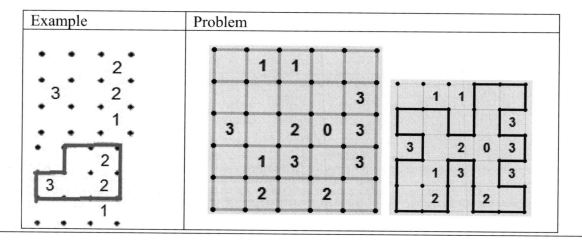

Example	Problem

Amandaho Moving Dots Puzzle ™ 移点子

You are a rook at c3.

Move some dots in c4, c2, or d3 squares into c3 square such that the sum of dots + dots in each of rook's moves at c3 will be equal to the number shown on its destination square. See the following example.

Example

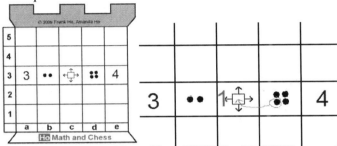

Problem

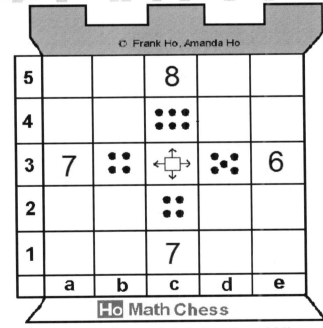

move down 1 and move left 2. 3 in the middle.

3-D Sudoku Buildings 看高楼数独

The number outside the large square shows the number of buildings that can be seen from that row or column when looking into the square from that direction. For example, the number "2" means you can see two buildings from that row or column. Each small square box must have the levels of the building. The final results must follow Sudoku law.

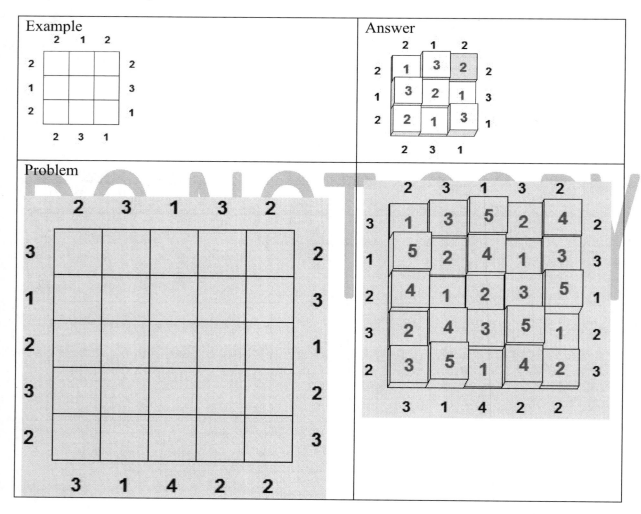

Sudoku 数独

Each row contains only one digit from 1 to 9.
Each column contains only one digit from 1 to 9.
Each box contains only one digit from 1 to 9.

CalcuDoku

Each row contains only one digit from 1 to the size of the grid.
Each column contains only one digit from 1 to the size of the grid.
The digits in each block must satisfy the arithmetic operation given in the block.

Student's name: _____ Assignment date: _____

CalcuDoku

Each row contains only one digit from 1 to the size of the grid.
Each column contains only one digit from 1 to the size of the grid.
The digits in each block must satisfy the arithmetic operation given in the block.

Sudoku

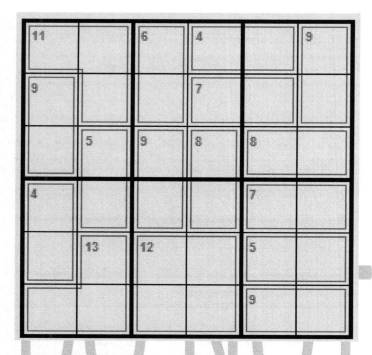

Fencing 盖围墙, 頭尾相连但不交义,不重複的循环围墙

Connect some dots around each number in the small square box in such a way that each number must be equal to the number within each small box. The connected lines must form a single loop (like one rubber band) without lines crossed to each other.

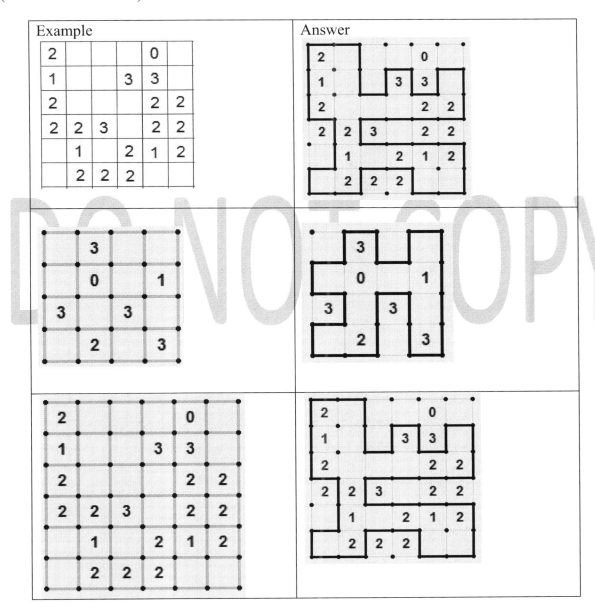

Ho Math Chess paper folding puzzle # **32** 何数棋谜折纸

5	1	6	5
5	1	6	5
3	4	2	8
3	4	2	8

Print the following sheets in double-sided format and then cut along with the 3 vertical bold lines as shown above.

The numbers on the front of the first sheet are 5165, 5265, 3428, 3428. The numbers on the back of the first sheet are 1376, 1376, 4782, 4782.

Fold each sheet (into 2 by 2) to four 1's to four 8's

Sheet 1 front

5	1	6	5
5	1	6	5
3	4	2	8
3	4	2	8

Sheet 1 back

1	3	7	6
1	3	7	6
4	7	8	2
4	7	8	2

Student's name: _____   Assignment date: _____

Sheet 2 front

8	7	1	8
8	7	1	8
2	1	7	6
2	1	7	6

Sheet 2 back

3	3	5	5
3	4	5	3
4	2	6	4
4	2	6	5

Sheet 3 front

1	1	3	5
2	2	3	4
3	3	2	2
1	1	4	5

Student's name: _____ Assignment date: _____

Sheet 3 back

6	7	8	6
6	7	8	6
7	8	5	4
7	8	5	4

Sheet 4 front

5	7	6	5
5	7	6	5
8	6	7	7
1	6	8	1

Sheet 4 back

2	2	8	8
4	4	1	1
3	3	4	4
2	2	3	3

Student's name: _____ Assignment date: _____

Sheet 5 front

2	2	3	3
1	2	1	1
4	4	4	4
2	1	3	3

Student's name: _____ Assignment date: _____

Sheet 5 back

6	7	8	6
5	7	8	5
5	8	7	5
6	8	7	6

Student's name: _____   Assignment date: _____

Sheet 6 front

1	2	2	3
4	3	3	3
2	1	4	2
5	4	4	6

Student's name: _____ Assignment date: _____

Sheet 6 back

7	5	5	6
8	8	6	6
1	7	7	8
1	5	7	8

Student's name: _____   Assignment date: _____

Decimal, fractions, % # 33 小数, 分数, 百分比

Ho Math Chess (何數棋谜　趣味數學)

Use the empty area of this page or back page as a work area to calculate the following problems.

---

1. Compute $1 \div 3 \times 6 \div 2 \times \dfrac{1}{2}$ 1/2

   Compute $6+3 \div 3 \div 14 \times 28$ 8

   23% of what is $\dfrac{4}{7}$?   0.13

   23.5% of what is 40% of $1\dfrac{2}{3}$? 67/300

---

2. Lily has some marbles (between 2 and 100, not inclusive), which is divisible by 8. She wants to use all marbles to form a square array. What could be the possible side lengths?

8, 4

---

3. Write the following word statement in standard form.

Four hundred twenty thousand thirteen.   420013

---

4. List all prime numbers between 13 and 43 inclusive.
13, 17, 19, 23, 29, 31, 37, 41

---

5. List all the composite numbers between 37 and 48 inclusive.
38, 39, 40, 42, 44, 45, 46, 48

---

6. A plant can produce 7 strawberries. There are 28 strawberries in a basket. How many plants will it take to produce 21 baskets of strawberries?
84 plants

---

7. Find the average of the numbers on the number line that is twice as far from 1 as from 7.
9   x-1 = 2 (x-7), x-1=2(7-x) The average = (13+15)/2=9

---

8. Find the average of the numbers on the number line that is twice as far from 5 as from 17.
21

---

9. A math lab seating 50 pupils have 3 times as many single desks as double desks. If all the seats are taken, find the number of double desks. 10

Student's name: _____ Assignment date: _____

Decimal, fractions, % # 35

Ho Math Chess (何數棋谜　趣味數學)

Use the empty area of this page or back page as a work area to calculate the following problems.
Compute the following expressions such that all numbers inside the parenthesis are all integers

and as small as possible, for example, $(2 + \frac{1}{2}) = \frac{1}{2}(4 + 1)$.

10.	Compute $(2 + \frac{1}{3})$. $\frac{1}{3}(6 + 1)$
11.	Compute $(3 + \frac{1}{4})$. $\frac{1}{4}(12 + 1)$
12.	Compute $(\frac{1}{3} \times 2 + \frac{3}{4})$. $\frac{1}{12}(8 + 9)$
13.	Compute $(3 + 0.1)$. $\frac{1}{10}(30 + 1)$
14.	Compute $(3 + 0.2)$. $\frac{1}{10}(30 + 2)$
15.	Compute $(0.1 + 0.2)$. $\frac{1}{10}(1 + 2)$
16.	Compute $(4 - 0.25)$. $\frac{1}{4}(16 - 1)$
17.	Compute $(20\% + 100.01)$. $\frac{1}{100}(20 + 10001)$
18.	Compute $(\frac{1}{2} + 0.75)$. $\frac{1}{4}(6 + 3)$
19.	Compute $(\frac{1}{2} + 0.25)$. $\frac{1}{4}(2 + 1)$
20.	Compute $(\frac{1}{2} + 0.2)$. $\frac{1}{10}(5 + 2)$
21.	Compute $(1\frac{2}{3} - 1.50)$. $\frac{1}{6}(10 - 9)$

Frank Ho, Amanda Ho © 1995 - 2020   All rights reserved.

Student's name: _____   Assignment date: _____

Decimal, fractions, % # 36

Ho Math Chess (何數棋謎　趣味數學)

Use the empty area of this page or back page as a work area to calculate the following problems.

22. 150, 50	Compute $(12\% \times 150 + 12\% \times 50). = 12\%($ _____ $+$ _____ $) =$
23. 5	Compute $(5\% \times 75 + 5\% \times 25) =$
24. 9	$0.2 \times 1 + 0.2 \times 2 + 0.2 \times 3 + 0.2 \times 4 + 0.2 \times 5 + 0.2 \times 6 + 0.2 \times 7 + 0.2 \times 8 + 0.2 \times 9$
25. 13.5	$0.3 \times 1 + 0.3 \times 2 + 0.3 \times 3 + 0.3 \times 4 + 0.3 \times 5 + 0.3 \times 6 + 0.3 \times 7 + 0.3 \times 8 + 0.3 \times 9$
26.	What % of $3\frac{1}{2} = 0.15$ of 1500?　$\frac{45000}{7}\%$
27. $\frac{31}{400}$	15.50% of 200 = what fraction of 400?
28. 8.5	$\frac{1}{2} \times 1 + \frac{1}{2} \times 2 + \frac{1}{3} \times 3 + \frac{1}{4} \times 4 + \frac{1}{5} \times 5 + \frac{1}{6} \times 6 + \frac{1}{7} \times 7 + \frac{1}{8} \times 8 + \frac{1}{9} \times 9$
29. $\frac{3}{16}$	$\frac{1}{2} \div \frac{2}{1} \div \frac{1}{3} \div \frac{4}{1}$
30. 3	$\left(\frac{1}{2} \div \frac{2}{1}\right) \div \left(\frac{1}{3} \div \frac{4}{1}\right)$

Student's name: _____   Assignment date: _____

Decimal, fractions, % # 37

Ho Math Chess (何數棋谜　趣味數學)

Use the empty area of this page or back page as a work area to calculate the following problems.

There are 3 people in a meeting: Mr. Yellow, Mr. Green and Mr. Blue. They are wearing yellow, green and blue ties. Mr. Yellow says: "Did you notice that the colours of our ties are different from our names?" The person who is wearing the green tie says, "Yes, you are right!" Do you know who is wearing what colour tie?

Mr. Blue- green
Mr. Yellow – blue
Mr. Green-yellow

$\frac{1}{5}$ of $\frac{3}{4}$ of what is equal to one half of a pizza?

$3\frac{1}{3}$

$0.002 \times 10^5 = 20\%$ of what?

100

If $6 + 3 = 3 (2+1)$ then

What is $24 + 18$? $6(4+3)$

What is $36 + 24$? $12(3+2)$

$1\frac{1}{2}\%$ of $150 = (0.04 + 0.02)$ divided by what fraction?

$$\frac{2}{75}$$

Decimal, fractions, % # 40

Ho Math Chess (何數棋谜　趣味數學)

Use the empty area of this page or back page as a work area to calculate the following problems.

1. List all integers between $-2\frac{2}{5}$ and $7\frac{1}{2}$.

-2, -1, 0, 1, 2, 3, 4, 5, 6, 7

2. Are $-\frac{6}{12}, \frac{1}{-2}$ equivalent?

Yes

3. Compare $-1\frac{31}{10}$ to $-\frac{21}{5}$ which one is larger?

$-1\frac{31}{10} > -\frac{21}{5}$

4. A cat and a dog are running a 52- feet race. The animals must run 26 feet and then retrace the same path to complete the race.

The dog leaps 3 feet per jump, and the cat leaps 2 feet per jump, so by the time the dog makes 2 leaps, the cat completes 3 leaps.

Who is the winner?

cat

5. Three customers went for a haircut and shave. In that saloon, two barbers operate at the same time and at the same speed. They take a quarter of an hour for the haircut and five minutes for the shave.

How quickly can they finish the haircut and shave for these customers?

30 minutes

Ho Math Chess 何数棋谜 奥数,解题策略,及 IQ 思唯训练宝典

Frank Ho, Amanda Ho © 1995 - 2020   All rights reserved.

Student's name: _____   Assignment date: _____

Decimal, fractions, % # 42

Ho Math Chess (何數棋谜　趣味數學)

Use the empty area of this page or back page as a work area to calculate the following problems.

---

1. one quarter of $2\frac{2}{5}$ + [(1+20%) of $7\frac{1}{2}$]. Express answer in a simplified fraction. $11\frac{2}{5}$

---

2. Express answer in simplified fraction

$\frac{13}{4} - \left(\frac{7}{4} - \square\right) = 1\frac{1}{2}$ 0

$\frac{13}{4} - \left(\frac{7}{4} + \square\right) = 1\frac{1}{2}$, what is $\square$?   0

$\frac{13}{4} - \frac{3+\square}{4} = 2$, what is $\square$?   2

$\frac{13}{4} - \frac{3-\square}{4} = 2$ what is $\square$?   2

3.

1 times _____ % = 2   200

10% times _____ = 2.   20

0.01% times _____ = 2.   20000

$\frac{0.01}{0.01\%}$ times _____ = 2   0.02

---

4. $\dfrac{\frac{2\%}{1}}{\frac{0.02}{2^2}}$,   8

---

5. $\square \times \left(2 \div 0.02 \times 10^2 + 3\% \div \frac{3}{2}\right) \times 3 - 100 = 200$, what is $\square$? $\frac{5000}{500001}$

Decimal, fractions, % # 44

Ho Math Chess (何數棋谜　趣味數學)

Use the empty area of this page or back page as a work area to calculate the following problems.

You are at c3.

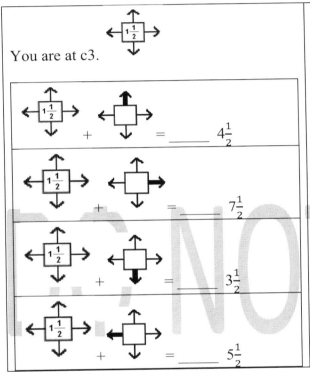

Amandaho Moving Dots Puzzle ™

You are at c3. Move some dots in b3, c2, c4, or d3 squares into a c3 square so that the sum of remaining dots + dots in each of rook's moves at c3 will be equal to the number shown on its destination squares.

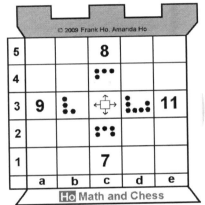

Move 1 down, move 3 up, move 1 left.

---

1. $5000 + 50 \times 10^2 + 25 \div 0.01 + 100 \times 0.002 + 100 \times 0.001$

12500.3

---

2. $\dfrac{23}{56} = \dfrac{A}{7} + \dfrac{B}{8}$, find out all possible values of A and B. A and B are whole numbers.

A2, B=1

---

3. Daniel's garden has flowers with only 5 and 6 petals. There are 44 flowers with 243 petals. How many flowers with 5 petals and how many flowers with 6 petals in Daniel's garden?

21 flowers with 5petals, 23 flowers with 6 petals

Decimal, fractions, % # 45

Ho Math Chess (何數棋谜 趣味數學)

Use the empty area of this page or back page as a work area to calculate the following problems.

You are at c3.

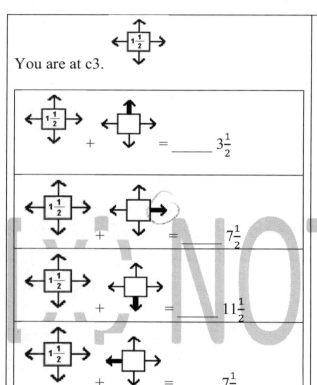

$$3\tfrac{1}{2}$$

$$7\tfrac{1}{2}$$

$$11\tfrac{1}{2}$$

$$7\tfrac{1}{2}$$

Amandaho Mov**ing** Dots Puzzle ™

You are at c3. Move some dots in b3, c2, c4, or d3 squares into a c3 square so that the sum of remaining dots + dots in each of rook's moves at c3 will be equal to the number shown on its destination squares.

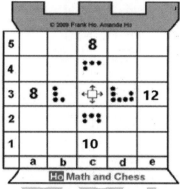

Move 2 down, move 2 right, move 1 left. Move 1 up.

1. Estimate 25% of 17 + 50% of 122= _____   4+61=65

   Estimate $\dfrac{3}{4.8}$ = _____ % $\dfrac{30}{50} = \dfrac{3}{5} = 60\%$

2. Estimate 10% of 19.89 = _____ % = _____ (standard form)   200, 2

3. What is 100% of 100% = _____ % = _____ (standard form)   100, 1
   What is 10% of 100 = _____ % = _____ (standard form)   10, 10
   What is 5% of 0.5% = _____ % = _____ (standard form)   1.025, 0.00025

Ho Math Chess   何数棋谜 奥数,解题策略,及 IQ 思唯训练宝典
Frank Ho, Amanda Ho © 1995 - 2020   All rights reserved.

Student's name: _____   Assignment date: _____

Decimal, fractions, % # 47

Ho Math Chess (何數棋谜　趣味數學)

Use the empty area of this page or back page as a work area to calculate the following problems.

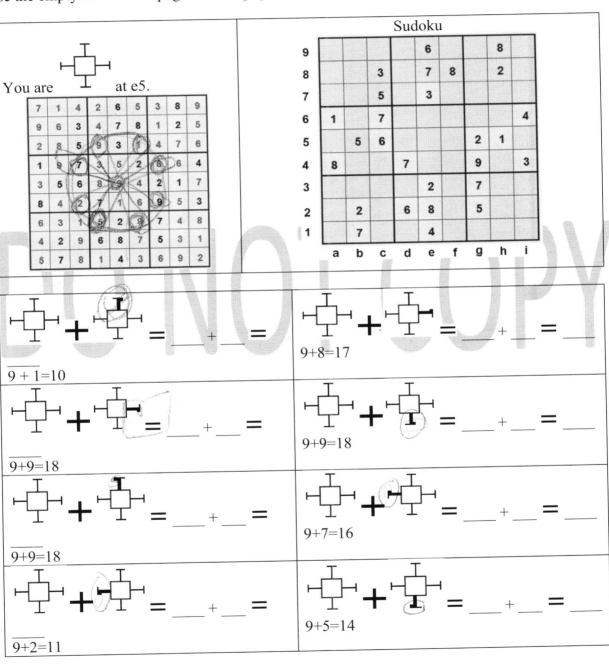

Decimal, fractions, % # 48

Ho Math Chess (何數棋谜 趣味數學)

Use the empty area of this page or back page as a work area to calculate the following problems.

1. Evaluate $\dfrac{1+\dfrac{1+\dfrac{1}{1}}{1+\dfrac{2}{1}}}{1+\dfrac{1}{1}}$ 5/6

2. 20% of 100 = what % of 100 − 80   100%

3. 45% of 120% = $\dfrac{1}{5}$ of _____ 10%   27

4. What is $\dfrac{1}{2}+\dfrac{1}{3}$?   5/6

   What is $1\dfrac{1}{2}+2\dfrac{1}{3}$?   3 5/6

5. $0.02 \times \dfrac{1}{5}$ of 20% of ___ = three quarters of 12 hundredth.   112.5 (225/2)

6. 20 % × 20% = 0.0001 × $\dfrac{\square}{\square}$ 400/1

7. 0.1 ÷ 0.0000001 = ?   1,000,000

8. $0.000001 \div \dfrac{2}{0.005}$ 0.0,000,000,025

Student's name: _____ Assignment date: _____

Decimal, fractions, % # 49

Ho Math Chess (何數棋謎　趣味數學)

Use the empty area of this page or back page as a work area to calculate the following problems.

1. Evaluate $\dfrac{0.2}{0.3} + \dfrac{0.3}{0.4}$ (leave answer in rational form $\dfrac{p}{q}$.)   17/12

2. Evaluate $\dfrac{20\%}{0.03} + \dfrac{0.4\%}{0.05}$ (leave answer in rational form $\dfrac{p}{q}$.)   506/75

3. Is 120% greater than 1? _____ , convert it to decimal _____ yes, 1.2
   Is 5% less than 1? _____ If 5% is the yearly interest rate, then what will be the total % you will get after one year including principal and interest?   Yes, 105%
   Is 85% less than 1? If the difference is a discount, then what % is the discount?
   _____ Yes, 15%

4. What is x?, $if\ 3 = \dfrac{1}{\frac{1}{x}}$.   3

5. $0.05(0.05 \div 0.02) = 4\left(2\dfrac{1}{2} - 1\dfrac{3}{4}\right) + 25\%\ of\ 1.2$ (leave answer in rational form $\dfrac{p}{q}$.)

   1/8

6. $\dfrac{1}{3}\% \times \left(3\dfrac{1}{2} \times 2\dfrac{1}{2} \div 3\dfrac{1}{4}\right) \div \dfrac{1}{25\%} \div \dfrac{1}{\frac{1}{25}}$ (leave answer in rational form $\dfrac{p}{q}$.)   35/624

Student's name: _____   Assignment date: _____

7. $\dfrac{200}{300} \times \dfrac{600}{200} \times \dfrac{400}{1000} \times \dfrac{2000}{8000}$ (leave answer in rational form $\dfrac{p}{q}$.)   1/8

8. $\dfrac{2}{4} \times \dfrac{5}{3} \times \dfrac{6}{10} \times \dfrac{24}{12} \times \dfrac{35}{70} \times \dfrac{28}{13} \times \dfrac{26}{14}$ (leave an answer in rational form $\dfrac{p}{q}$.)   2

Student's name: _____ Assignment date: _____

Decimal, fractions, % # 50

Ho Math Chess (何數棋谜　趣味數學)

Use the empty area of this page or back page as a work area to calculate the following problems.

1. Evaluate $\dfrac{1}{\frac{1}{2}} \times \dfrac{1}{\frac{1}{4}} \div \dfrac{1}{\frac{1}{16}} + \left(\dfrac{1}{\frac{1}{2}} \times \dfrac{1}{\frac{1}{4}} \right)$ (leave answer in rational form $\dfrac{p}{q}$.) 17/2

2. Evaluate $\dfrac{3(\frac{1}{4} - \frac{1}{2}) - 4(\frac{2}{5} - \frac{5}{2})}{3(0.04 - 0.2) - 4(0.2 - 0.5)}$ (leave answer in rational form $\dfrac{p}{q}$.) 85/8

3. Compare the followings.

a. $\dfrac{-1}{2}, \dfrac{3}{-4}$　　>

b. $\dfrac{-3}{2}, \dfrac{-4}{3}$　　<

4. Evaluate $\dfrac{3}{1}(3 - \dfrac{2}{1}) + \dfrac{4}{1}(1 - \dfrac{5}{1}) + \dfrac{2}{1}$ (leave the answer in rational form $\dfrac{p}{q}$.)

-11

5. No one in the chorus is younger than 10 years old. 19 kids are 10 or younger, 10 kids are older than 10, and 8 are older than 11. What is the largest possible number of kids in the chorus?

29

6. If $6 - x > 1$, then $x - 1 = $ _____, x is an integer. < or = 3

Decimal, fractions, % # 51

Ho Math Chess (何數棋谜　趣味數學)

Use the empty area of this page or back page as a work area to calculate the following problems.

Find the sum of $1 + 2 + 3 + 4 + 5 + 6 + 7 + 8 + 9 + 10$ without adding numbers from 1 to 10. Explain how you find it.

Method 1:

Draw from 1 to 10 then turn it upside down, we get $10 \times 11 = 110$, $110 / 2 =$ **55**

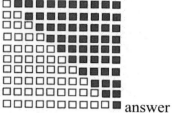 answer

Method 2: Find the media which must be also the average $(6+5)/2 = 5.5$, $5.5 \times 10 = 55$

2. Evaluate the result of 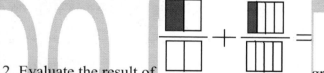 graphically.

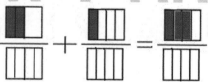

3. About 9% of Canadians watched the Vancouver 2010 Winter Olympic game opening ceremony live on TV. Canada's population is about 33 million. Kathy estimated the number of Canadians who watched the opening ceremony on TV live as 33 million ÷ 10. Does her estimate make sense? Explain your reason. **Yes**, 9% is 0.1 so × 0.9 is equivalent to × 10%. 0.1 = 10%. 33 million ÷ 10 = 33 million × $\frac{1}{10}$ = 33 million × 0.1

4. Three points of a 6 × 6 square array are connected. What is the largest possible triangle area that can be created? (5x5)/2=**12.5**

5. Cindy had 94 marbles, and Jenny had 13 marbles. Cindy gave some of her marbles to Jenny so that Cindy ended with twice as many as marbles as Jenny. How many marbles did Cindy give to Jenny? **26**

6. The area of a circle whose circumference is 36π is $c\pi$. What is the value of c?

$2\pi r = 36\pi$, $\gamma = 18$, c = 18 x 18 = **324**

Integer, expression, equation 整数, 代数式, 方程式

Integer, Expression, equation # 1

Ho Math Chess (何數棋谜　趣味數學)

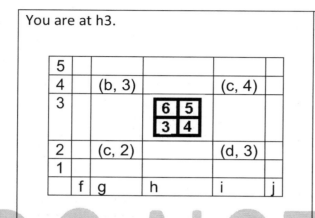

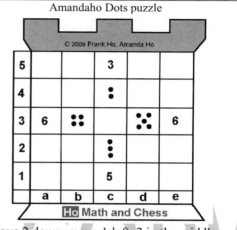

Move 2 down, move 1 left. 2 in the middle.

Amandaho Adjacent Numbers Difference Puzzle ™

Step 1. Solve the Amandaho Dots puzzle first.
Step 2 Solve the left top mini-chessboard puzzle.
Step 3. Find the difference (large number – smaller number) of the two adjacent corner numbers starting from the largest square until all four corner numbers are the same. Start from the left upper corner and fill in a number in each circle clockwise using the

following expressions.

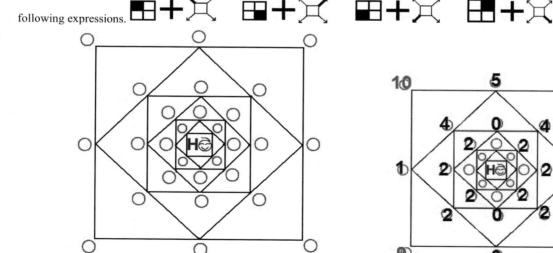

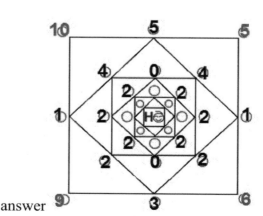

answer

6+4, 4+1, 3+3, 5+4

Integer, Expression # 2

Ho Math Chess (何數棋谜　趣味數學)

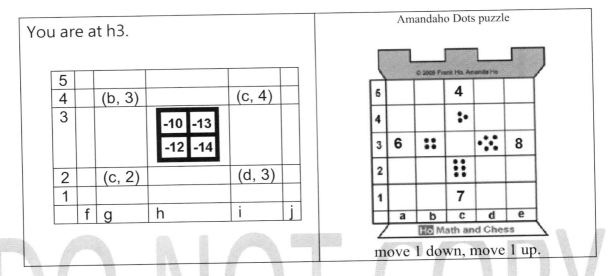

Amandaho Adjacent Numbers Difference Puzzle ™

Step 1. Solve the Amandaho Dots puzzle first.
Step 2 Solve the left top mini-chessboard puzzle.
Step 3. Find the difference (large number – smaller number) of the two adjacent corner numbers starting from the largest square until all four corner numbers are the same. Start from the left upper corner and fill in a number in each circle clockwise using the following expressions.

- 10 +4, - 14 +2, -12 +5, -13 +6

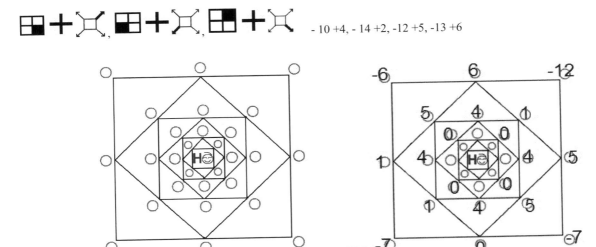

answer

Math IQ fitness advanced level 高难度题 - 训练批判力, 理解力, 抽象分析力, 觀察力

Math IQ fitness advanced level 1

One thing I noticed when teaching young students math is some of them are very weak in reasoning abstract or do not feel comfortable to sort out symbols or draw some relationships out of some seemly unrelated symbols. Because of this reason, they have a hard time understanding the meaning of functions or coming up with a mathematical formula for word problems. One way to improve their critical thinking ability is to give them more perception type of problems in improving their visual ability and make them feel comfortable to work with abstract symbols. This section includes math and chess integrated problems, computation problems using clever ideas, word problems to increase their comprehension ability and finally, the IQ puzzle type problems.

The purpose of this section not only improves children's math ability; it also increases their brainpower.

With such diversified problems all integrated into one place, young learners are more apt to embrace and engage in them than traditional repetitive worksheets.

Student's name: _____ Assignment date: _____

Math IQ Fitness Advanced level 1

Use distributive law $a(b + c) = ab + ac$ to find out which expression is larger. Show your work.

$2345 \times 5432 < 2346 \times 5431$
$2345 \times 5432 = 2345 \times (5431 + 1) = 2345 \times 5431 + 2345$
$2346 \times 5431 = (2345 + 1) \times 5431 = 2345 \times 5431 + 5431$

Use the number line concept to rank the following fractions from the least to the largest.
$\frac{12}{13}, \frac{44}{45}, \frac{29}{30}, \frac{1}{2}, \frac{2}{3}$ When the difference between denominator and numerator is only 1, the larger the denominator, the closer its value of the fraction is close to 1.

$\frac{44}{45} > \frac{29}{30} > \frac{12}{13} > \frac{2}{3} > \frac{1}{2}$

Naomy baked some pies for her party. She cut each pie into 6 pieces. After the party, she had some left between $2\frac{1}{2}$ to 3 pies with no partial pieces left. What could be the amounts of her leftover? (Answer in mixed number.)

$2\frac{1}{2} + \frac{1}{6} = 2\frac{4}{6} = 2\frac{2}{3}, \ 2\frac{4}{6} + \frac{1}{6} = 2\frac{5}{6}$

Which of the following products are not possible when a 2-digit number multiplied by a 3-digit natural number? Circle them.

100,000 0   11101(prime) 56,000,000 98910
(99 x 999= 98901) 99999

100,000	0	2400	1000	11101	56,000,000	98,910	99999

Evaluate the following using fractions but without using the same LCD method or converting to decimals.

$$\frac{1}{2} + \frac{1}{6} + \frac{1}{12} + \frac{1}{20}$$

$$(1 - \frac{1}{2}) + (\frac{1}{2} - \frac{1}{3}) + (\frac{1}{3} - \frac{1}{4}) + (\frac{1}{4} - \frac{1}{5}) = \frac{4}{5}$$

Evaluate the following.

$$8 \times 1 \times 4 \times 2 \times 100 \times 25 \times 50 \times 125$$

$$8 \times 125 \times 4 \times 25 \times 2 \times 50 \times 100 = 1000 \times 100 \times 100 \times 100 = 1,000,000,000$$

If $8 \; ♗ \; 3 = 24$, then what is $8 \; ♖ \; 3 =$? $8 + 3 = 11$

Harris saves pennies. He has 10 cents in his jar at the start. Harris starts on April 1st and saves 5¢ each day. (1) Write an equation to solve by which day Harris had saved a total of 57¢? (2) By which day Harris saved a total of $2.05?

$Y = 10 + 5x \leq 57$, **x ≤ 10 (April 10th)**
$205 = 10 + 5x$, x = **39 (May 9th)**

Evaluate 1,700,000,000 ÷ 125

Hint: (1700000000 × ?) ÷ (125 × 8) =

8,   13600000

Owen has 3 spades of playing cards: the ace, 2, and 3. Owen must choose two of these cards, how many possible combinations are there?

3

Harry drives 60 km/h. What distance does it cover in 5 minutes?

60 x 5/60 = **5**km

Arnold and his brother have 25 baseball cards altogether. He has one more than 2 times the number of cards his brother has. How many cards does Arnold's brother have?

method 1: 25 − 1 = 24, 24 / 3 = **8**
method 2: x + 2x + 1 = 25, x = **8**

Which of the following is the product of its digits?

24, 16, 18, 36, 30, 45, 78, area of ☐ , area of ▭ , area of △ , x^2, x^3

24, 16, 18, 36, 30, 45, 78, area of ☐, area of ▭, area of △ , x^3

Ho Math Chess 何数棋谜 奥数,解题策略,及 IQ 思唯训练宝典
Frank Ho, Amanda Ho © 1995 - 2020   All rights reserved.

Student's name: _____   Assignment date: _____

Find the value of $\Box$.

$$\Box \div 15, \times 4, + 3, - 15 = 20$$

$20 + 15 - 3 \div 4 \times 15 = 120$

If $1 + 3 + 5 + \ldots + 47 + 49 = 625$ then

$2 + 4 + 6 + \ldots + 48 + 50 =?$ **650**

From 1 to 50, there are 50 numbers and 25 of them are even and 25 of them are odd. So, if $1 + 3 + 5 + \ldots + 47 + 49 = 625$ then it means $2 + 4 + 6 + \ldots + 48 + 50 = 625 + 25 = 650$

The rectangular garden's perimeter is 28 m and its width measures 5 m, what is the side length?

28/2=14, 14 − 5 = **9 m**

The length of a rectangle is increased by 1 unit, and its width is decreased by 1 unit, what happens to its area and perimeter? Use an example to explain.

Area increases by 2 and the perimeter does not change.

3
[ ]2   4
       [   ]1

Old: Area = 6, perimeter = 10   New: Area = 4, perimeter = 10

Austin built a rectangular prism with 36 cm³. What might be the dimensions of the prism (all in natural numbers)?

Any 3 numbers multiplied together is 36.

Use the digits 4, 6, 7 and 9 to make the greatest quotient with no remainder. 976/4 = **244**

$$\Box \overline{)\ \Box\ \Box\ \Box}$$

What is the remainder of $\dfrac{24k-3}{12}$? K is a natural number.

$\dfrac{24k-12+9}{12} = \dfrac{12(2k-12)+9}{12}$ The remainder is 9.

Two-digit number AB − BA = 18 and AB + BA = 44. What is AB?

31− 13 = 18, 31 + 13 = 44

Give the equation of the rook's path that contains the squares of b1, b2, b3, b4, b5, b6, b7, b8.

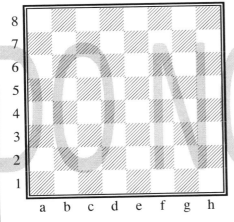

x = b

Write a number for the rightmost next figure.

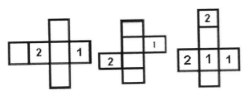

answer

Evaluate $\dfrac{\frac{1}{2}}{1}+\dfrac{1}{2}+\dfrac{\frac{1}{3}}{1}+\dfrac{2}{3}+\dfrac{\frac{1}{4}}{1}+\dfrac{3}{4}=?$ **3**

Two muffins are 45 ¢, and one muffin is 25 ¢. Christie has \$1.25 and would like to buy as many muffins as she can, how many can she buy?

Christie did the following way.

$\dfrac{125(125\,cents)}{45(45\,cents)}=\dfrac{25}{9}$, $9\overline{)25}$ with the remainder, 7 cents left, so she can buy 4 muffins (Quotient 2 × 2 muffins).

Is her answer correct? State the reason _____

25 divided by 9 gets the remainder 7 which does not represent the real money left. The money left should be 9 x 5 = 35 so she can have **5** muffins.

Student's name: _____　　Assignment date: _____

Evaluate $\dfrac{1}{\frac{1}{2}} + \dfrac{\frac{1}{2}}{1} + \dfrac{1}{\frac{1}{3}} + \dfrac{\frac{1}{3}}{1} + \dfrac{\frac{1}{4}}{1} + \dfrac{1}{\frac{1}{4}} = ?$　$2 + \frac{1}{2} + 3 + 1/3 + \frac{1}{4} + 4 =$ **10 1/12**

What is the total when each even number minus its neighbouring odd number from?
1 to 1000?

$(1000 - 999) + (998 - 997) + (996 - 995) + \ldots + (3 - 2) + (2 - 1) = ?$ **500**

Complete the following pattern to find out the total of sum of all digits from 1 to 99, i.e. $1 + 2 + 3 + \ldots + 9 + 1 + 0 + 1 + 1 + 1 + 2 + \ldots + 9 + 1 + 9 + 2 + 9 + 3 + \ldots + 9 + 9$.

The total of $0 + 1 + 2 + 3 + \ldots 1 + 0 + 1 + 1 + 1 + 2 + \ldots + 9 + 1 + 9 + 2 + 9 + 3 + \ldots + 9 + 9 = $ _____
$45 + 45 \, (10 + 20 + \ldots + 90) = 45 + (10 + 90)9/2 = 45 + 450 = $ **495**

Find the area of the following triangle.

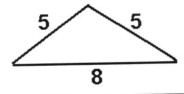 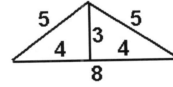

$3 \times 8 / 2 =$ **12**

Replace each ? with a number.

1. 9 2 3 4 7 1 ? 6　(9+2+3=14, 3+4+7=14, 7+1+6=14)
2. 9 1 3 8 2 5 ? 6　(9+1+3=13, 3+8+2=13, 2+5+6=13)

Evaluate $\left(\dfrac{1}{2} - \dfrac{3}{4}\right) \div \left(1\dfrac{3}{5} - 2\dfrac{3}{4}\right) - 0.02 \div 0.5$

$\dfrac{102}{575}$

Evaluate $\left(2(3-4) + 3(0.05 - 0.10) \times (0.01 - 0.8)\right) \div 0.01$

169.85

3	$\dfrac{2}{3}$	$\dfrac{1}{2}$	$\dfrac{1}{5}$
2	$\dfrac{3}{4}$	$\dfrac{1}{6}$	
1	$\dfrac{4}{5}$	$\dfrac{1}{4}$	$\dfrac{1}{7}$
	a	b	c

You are at c2 = ☐.

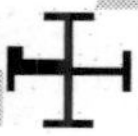

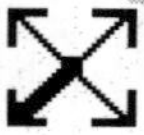

$\boxplus - \boxtimes = \underline{\hspace{3cm}} \dfrac{5}{12}$

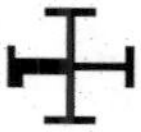

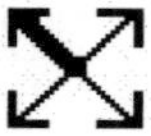

$\boxplus \times \boxtimes = \underline{\hspace{3cm}} \dfrac{2}{5}$

Ho Math Chess 何数棋谜 奥数,解题策略,及 IQ 思唯训练宝典
Frank Ho, Amanda Ho © 1995 - 2020

Student's name: _____ Assignment date: _____

Fill in each box by a number from 1 to 9. Each number can only be used once.

$$\frac{\Box}{\Box\Box} + \frac{\Box}{\Box\Box} + \frac{\Box}{\Box\Box} - 1 = 0 \quad 9/12 + 5/34 + 7/68 - 1 = 0$$

Observe the pattern and replace each ? by a number.

6, ?, 13, 12, 24, 25, ?, 5, 31, ?, 7, 29 Each 2 neighbouring numbers add up to a perfect square number. $6 + 3 = 9, 3 + 13 = 16, 25 + 11 = 36, 11 + 5 = 16, 31 + 18 = 49, 18 + 7 = 25.$ **3, 11, 18**

Evaluate $(w-a)(w-b)(w-c)...(w-x)(w-y)(w-z)$.
The answer is 0 since there is a term w-w=0

Which one of the following numbers does not belong in the following sequence?

1, 3, 7, 15, **32**, 63
15 x 2 + 1

2 is to $-\frac{1}{2}$ as -2 is to _____

½

Fill in blank boxes with digits 5, 6, 7, 8, 9.

$\square \times \square = \square + \square\square$ 8 x 9 = 7 + 65

Fill in blank boxes with digits 2, 3, 4, 5, 6.

$\square + \square = \square . \square \times \square$ 3 + 6 = 4.5 x 2

How many trailing zeros in the product of $500 \times 2 \times 5 \times 40 \times 5$?

Convert to product of primes. $500 \times 2 \times 5 \times 40 \times 5 = 5^6 \times 2^6 = 10^6$, **6 zeros**

How many trailing zeros are there in 75!? $\dfrac{75}{5} + \dfrac{75}{25} = 15 + 3 = $ **18**

How many trailing zeros in the product of $4^4 \times 25^5$? $= 2^8 \times 5^{10} = 10^8 \times 5^2$, **8 zeros**

How many trailing zeros are there in 20!? $\dfrac{20}{5} = 4$, **4** zeros

Circle the odd one below.

The third one, since all others have symmetry lines.

Student's name: _____　Assignment date: _____

Fill in blank boxes with digits 3, 4, 5, 6, 7.

$$\square^{\square} = \square\square + \square$$

$3^4 = 75 + 6 \text{ or } = 76 + 5$

The smallest composite number is _____. **4**

The sum of the largest 1-digit composite number and the largest 2-digit composite number is _____. **9 + 99 = 108**

Find the odd one in the following figures.

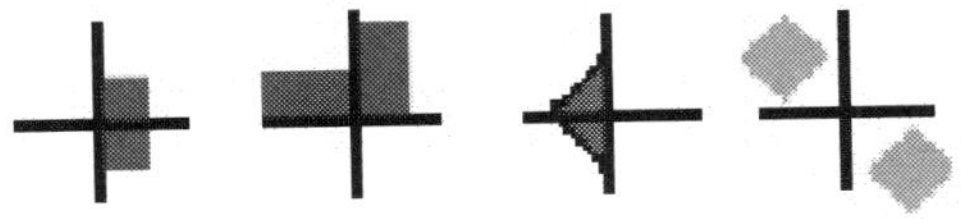

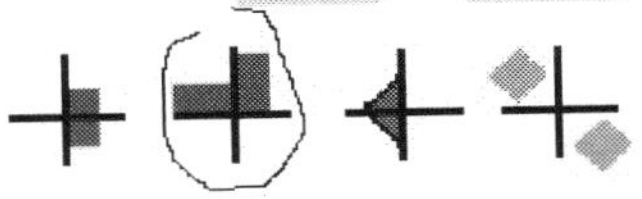

not a symmetry.

Student's name: ______________________ Assignment date: ______________________

Calculate. $-2^2 \times (-2)^3 \times (-2)^2 \times (-2^3)$ $=$ **-1024**
Calculate x. $2_{-x} = 1$ **0**
Calculate. $1\times\frac{1}{1}+2\times\frac{1}{2}+3\times\frac{1}{3}+\frac{1}{4}\times4+5+\frac{1}{5}\times5$ **10**
Calculate and leave the answer in fraction form. $\frac{\frac{1}{2}}{\frac{1}{3}}+\frac{\frac{1}{2}}{\frac{1}{\frac{1}{2}}}=\frac{7}{4}$
Calculate. (9% + 0.21 + 0.7 + 64% +0.36) ÷ 1% 200
Calculate. $7000 \times \left(\frac{1}{1000}+\frac{1}{100}+\frac{1}{10}\right)$ **777**

Evaluate

$$2 \times \dfrac{1}{\dfrac{1}{1}} + 2 \times \dfrac{1}{\dfrac{1}{3}} + 2 \times \dfrac{1}{\dfrac{1}{5}} + ... + 2 \times \dfrac{1}{\dfrac{1}{97}} + 2 \times \dfrac{1}{\dfrac{1}{99}}$$ (Hint: $1 + 3 = ?$, $1 + 3 + 5 = ?$, $1 + 3 + 5 + 7 = ?$)

$2 + 3 + 5 + 7 + ... + 97 + 99 = 1 + 1 + 3 + 5 + ... + 97 + 99 = 1 + 50^2 = 1 + 2500 =$ **2501**

Evaluate $\dfrac{0.02}{\dfrac{1}{2}} + \dfrac{0.045}{0.\overline{1}} + \dfrac{\dfrac{2}{3}}{0.\overline{6}}$ $\dfrac{0.02}{0.5} + \dfrac{0.045}{\dfrac{1}{9}} + \dfrac{\dfrac{2}{3}}{\dfrac{6}{9}} = 0.04 + 0.405 + 1 = 1.445$ $\left(1\dfrac{89}{200}\right)$

Evaluate

If 2♛$+ 3$♞$= X + $♛$+ $♞, what is X (in numeric value)?

15

Find the shortest distance when going around the circular movement from the lowest edge A to the highest edge at B (Leave the answer in exact form.). The circumference is 10π, AB =

$$\sqrt{25\pi^2 + 100} = 5\sqrt{4 + \pi^2}$$

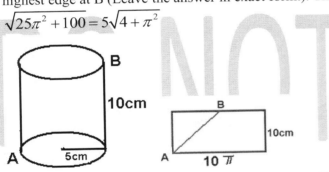

Find the shortest distance from A to B on the surface area and through inside the cube (Leave answer in exact form.). (1) Surface: $AC^2 = \sqrt{100 + 100} = 200$, $AB = \sqrt{100 + 200} = \sqrt{300} = 10\sqrt{3}$

(2) Inside: $AB^2 = 10^2 + 20^2 = 100 + 400$, $AB = \sqrt{500} = 10\sqrt{5}$

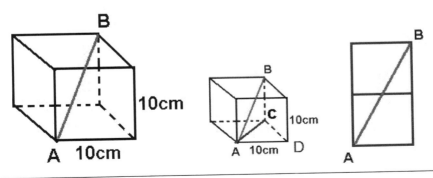

Student's name: _____ Assignment date: _____

Math IQ fitness advanced level 2

$$(\square + \bigcirc) \times 2 = 126, \quad 48 + 15; \ 52+11$$

$$\square - \bigcirc = \underline{\hspace{3cm}} \quad 48\text{-}15\text{=}33; \ 52\text{-}11\text{=}41$$

If n is an odd integer and $2 \le n \le 80$, how many integers is $\dfrac{(n-1)n(n+1)}{8}$ equal to multiples of 8?

The odd number will give multiples of 8, and there are **39** (from 2 to 80) odd numbers.

If n is an even integer and $2 \le n \le 80$, how many integers is $\dfrac{(n-1)n(n+1)}{8}$ equal to multiples of 8?

The even number will give multiples of 8, and there are **10** even numbers.

Two similar rectangles are the same shape. Circle true or false. false

Two rectangles are always similar. Circle true or false. false

Two squares are always similar. Circle true or false. true

Rank the following fractions.

$\dfrac{7}{8}, \dfrac{66}{77}, \dfrac{555}{666}, \dfrac{4444}{5555}, \dfrac{33333}{44444}$ 　　 $\dfrac{7}{8} > \dfrac{6}{7} > \dfrac{5}{6} > \dfrac{4}{5} > \dfrac{3}{4}$

If $a : b = 9 : 4$ and $b : c = 5 : 3$ then $(a - b) : (b - c)$ is equal to _____.

25:8

25 to 8. $a : b : c = 45 : 20 : 12$　a-b=45-20=25　b-c=20-12=8

If $\dfrac{x-3y}{y} = 12$ then $\dfrac{x}{y}$ is equal to _____. **15**

Student's name: _____ Assignment date: _____

$$\sqrt{\sqrt{81 \times 81 \times 81 \times 81}} = 3 \times 3 \times 3 \times 3 = 81$$

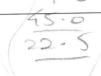

Find the next number is in the following pattern.

20, 30, 45, 67.5 _____ 67.5

67.5 x 1.5 = 101.25

Convert the following fractions to the sum of 2-unit fractions.

$\dfrac{2}{5} =$	$\dfrac{2}{5} = \dfrac{6}{15} = \dfrac{1+5}{15} = \dfrac{1}{15} + \dfrac{1}{3}$
$\dfrac{2}{7} =$	$\dfrac{2}{7} = \dfrac{8}{28} = \dfrac{1+7}{28} = \dfrac{1}{28} + \dfrac{1}{4}$
$\dfrac{2}{11} =$	$\dfrac{2}{11} = \dfrac{12}{66} = \dfrac{1+11}{66} = \dfrac{1}{66} + \dfrac{1}{6}$
$\dfrac{3}{4} =$	$\dfrac{3}{4} = \dfrac{1+2}{4} = \dfrac{1}{4} + \dfrac{1}{2}$
$\dfrac{3}{5} =$	$\dfrac{3}{5} = \dfrac{6}{10} = \dfrac{1+5}{10} = \dfrac{1}{10} + \dfrac{1}{2}$

$$\square + \bigcirc = 21$$

$$\square - \bigcirc = 11, \ \square = 16, \ \bigcirc = 5$$

$$2\square + \bigcirc = 28$$

$$\square + 2\bigcirc = 36, \ \square = 10, \ \bigcirc = 8$$

What time will be 52 minutes past 11:20 A.M.?

11:20 + 0:52= 12:12 P.M.

| Blank line | blank line |
| Blank line | blank line |

Julian has 5 coins, and only one of them is a penny. What is the least amount of money Julian can have?

1¢ + 5 ¢+ 5¢ + 5¢+5¢ = 21¢

| Blank line | blank line |
| Blank line | blank line |

5	87	86	89	86	85
4	86	87	83	81	82
3	89	87	100	84	83
2	81	87	85	84	89
1	83	84	86	89	82
	a	b	c	d	e

You are at c2 = $\square$.

$\square$ = ╪ (____) +____ 100 = 82 + 18

$\square$ = ╪ (____) +____ 100 = 89 + 11

$\square$ = ⤬ (____) +____ 100 = 84 + 16

Draw a rectangle with perimeter 36 cm and the least possible area.

cm by 17 cm

Student's name: _____   Assignment date: _____

Every number is a factor of _____. **Zero**

Blank line   blank line

_____ is a factor of every number. **One (1)**

Blank line   blank line

_____ is the only number that is neither positive nor negative. **0**

Blank line   blank line

At a party, everyone shook hands with everybody else. There were 66 handshakes. How many people were at the party?

$+ 2 + 3 + 4 + 5 + 6 + 7 + 8 + 9 + 10 + 11 = 66$ **12 people**

Blank line   blank line

Andrew scored 7 more points than Stuart at the Balloon Pop. Together they scored 51 points. How many points did Andrew score?

$(51+7)/2 = 58/2 = 29$

(sum+difference)/2 = bigger number

Blank line   blank line

Sam has more blocks than Melody. He gives Melody 4 blocks, and then they have the same number of blocks. They have 12 blocks all together. How many bocks did Sam start with?

The difference is 8 $(12+8)/2 = $ **10** blocks

(sum + difference)/2 = bigger number

(sum - difference)/2 = smaller number

Blank line   blank line

Fill in each box by a number.

☐ ✖ 5 + ☐ ✖ 10 = 60   4

Eric spent 20% of his money on a pair of shoes. He spent $\frac{3}{5}$ of the remainder of a book.

He had $72 left. How much money did he have at first?

$72 \div 2/5 = 72 \times 5/2 = 36 \times 5 = 180$

$180 \div 0.8 = $ **$225**

Blank line   blank line
Blank line   blank line
Blank line   blank line

Paired fractions

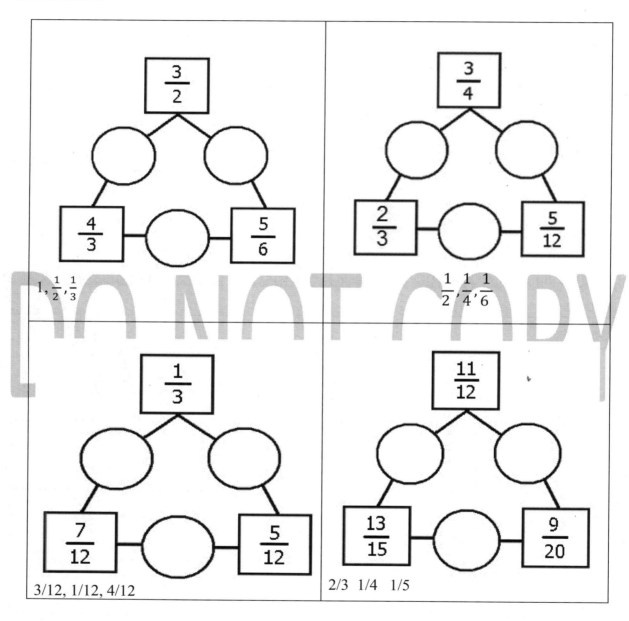

□ $+2, -2, \div 5, -4, \times 3 = 36$ **80**
Blank line   blank line

□ $\times 5, \times 0.2, \times 0.1\%, \times 1000 = 1000$ **1000**
Blank line   blank line

How many possible answers are there for A, B, and C?
    ABC
− CBA
   4 9 5   C must be less than A and A, C cannot be zeros. C can be 1, 2, 3, 4 and A is 5, 7,
                8, 9, respectively, with B from 0 to 9. So, the total possibility is 4 times 10 = **40.**

A number multiplied by itself 3 times is 343. What was the original number?
7
Blank line   blank line
Blank line   blank line

Write 64 as the product of primes.
64 = 2⁶
Blank line   blank line
Blank line   blank line
Blank line   blank line

Draw a diagram to illustrate $\frac{1}{3} \times \frac{1}{4}$.

answer

$4747474747 \div 47 = 101010101$
Blank line   blank line
Blank line   blank line

$87878787 \div 87 = 1010101$
Blank line   blank line
Blank line   blank line

$4.567 \times 1000000 \div 100 \div 0.001 = 45670000$
Blank line   blank line
Blank line   blank line

Math IQ fitness advanced level 3

Add each row to the right and each column to the bottom to have the same total. Replace each ?

4	-7	?6	3
-2	?5	0	?3
?1	5	-3	?3
?3	?3	?3	

Add each row to the right and each column to the bottom to have the same total. Replace each ?

-11	8	?-7	?-10
-8	?-19	?17	?-10
?9	1	?-20	?-10
?-10	-10	-10	

$- \boxed{} - (-3) = -2$ 5

$- (+4) - \boxed{} = -5$ 1

$+ (-7) + (- \boxed{}) = 13$ -20

$- (+9) - (- \boxed{}) = -13$ -4

It is 18^0C in Sunville with altitude 550m. The temperature decreases by 6.2 ^{0}C for every 1000m increase in altitude. If there is precipitation in an altitude of 2350m, what is the temperature, and will it be rain or snow?

Rain at 6.84^0C.

Calculate $- 2^2 - (-2)^2 - 2(4-6)(-1) + (-1)^3$ -13
Blank line   blank line
Calculate $- (-4^2) - (-3)(3-2)(-4-6)(-1)^2 + (-1)^3$ -15
Blank line   blank line
Calculate $- (-2+3)(2-3)(4-5)(6-2) - (3-4)(2-3)(5-7) + (-1)^3$ -3
Blank line   blank line

What is wrong with the following calculation?

$x = -3$

$x^2 = 9$

$\left(x^2\right)^{\frac{1}{2}} = 9^{\frac{1}{2}}$ When an equation has one side negative, you cannot just square both sides.

$x = 3$

It will produce an extraneous solution.

What is wrong with the following calculation?

$x^2 = 9$

$\left(x^2\right)^{\frac{1}{2}} = \sqrt{9}$ X on the left side could be negative so you cannot just take the

$x = 3$

square root of an equation, instead try to solve it. You will get 3 and –3.

What is wrong with the following calculation?

$(-3)^2 = 9$

$\sqrt{(-3)^2} = \sqrt{9}$ It is wrong to take a square root of a negative number.

$-3 = 3$

Find the value of ?

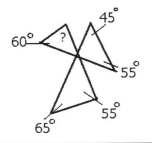

Fill in each same shape with the same number.

$\square + \square + \bigcirc + \triangle = 300$

$\square + \bigcirc + \triangle = 300$ $\square = 100$ $\bigcirc + \triangle = 100$ and answers

may vary

$x + 2y + z = 500$

$x + 3y + z = 600$

What is $x + z = ?$

$x - z = 100$

What is x?

What is z?

X=200, z=100

Eileen has 17 cents and is she doubles her pennies, and she will have 29 cents, how many pennies does she have?

6 pennies

What are the 2-digit numbers when dividing 135 with no remainder? 15, 27, 45

What are the 2-digit numbers when dividing 315 with no remainder? 15, 21, 35, 45

What are the 2-digit numbers when dividing 385 with no remainder? 11, 35, 55, 77

Student's name: _____ Assignment date: _____

$$2 \times \square + 2 \times \bigcirc = \square + \square + \bigcirc + \bigcirc$$

$$\underline{\quad} \times \square + \underline{\quad} \times \bigcirc = \square + \bigcirc$$

1, 1

Move only one number to make the following equation true.

$102 - 1 = 99$

Find the remainder of $\frac{3}{2}$.	$\frac{1}{2}$ answer
Find the remainder of $\frac{5}{3}$.	$\frac{2}{3}$ answer
Find the remainder of $\frac{1 \times 2 \times 3 \times 4 \times ... \times 7 \times 8 \times 9 \times 10 \times 11}{7}$.	0
Find the remainder of $\frac{1 \times 2 \times 3 \times 4 \times ... \times 7 \times 8 \times 9 \times 10 \times 11}{7} + \frac{9}{7}$.	2
Find the remainder of $\frac{1 \times 2 \times 3 \times 4 \times ... \times 7 \times 8 \times 9 \times 10 \times 11}{7} + \frac{11}{7}$.	4
Find the remainder of $\frac{1 \times 2 \times 3 \times 4 \times ... \times 7 \times 8 \times 9 \times 10 \times 11}{7} - \frac{2}{7}$.	5
Find the remainder of $\frac{1 \times 2 \times 3 \times 4 \times ... \times 7 \times 8 \times 9 \times 10 \times 11}{7} - \frac{5}{7}$.	2
Find the remainder of $\frac{1 \times 2 \times 3 \times 4 \times ... \times 7 \times 8 \times 9 \times 10 \times 11}{7} - \frac{9}{7}$.	5
Find the remainder of $\frac{1 \times 2 \times 3 \times 4 \times ... \times 7 \times 8 \times 9 \times 10 \times 11}{7} - \frac{11}{7}$.	3
Find the remainder of $\frac{1 \times 2 \times 3 \times 4 \times ... \times 7 \times 8 \times 9 \times 10 \times 11 \times 12 \times 13}{8} - \frac{13}{8}$.	3

No calculators are allowed — answer in the simplified or mixed fraction for fraction problems.

$3 + \dfrac{3}{2} = 4\dfrac{1}{2}$	$3 - \dfrac{3}{2} = 1\dfrac{1}{2}$	$3 \times \dfrac{3}{2} = 4\dfrac{1}{2}$	$3 \div \dfrac{3}{2} = 2$
$1.001 \div 0.1$ 10.01	$1.001 \div 0.01$ 100.1	$11.001 \div 0.001$ 11001	$111.001 \div 0.0001$ 1110010
$100 \times \dfrac{5}{2} =$ 250	$\dfrac{3}{5} \times 2.5 = 1\dfrac{1}{2}$	$100 \times \dfrac{1}{0.01} = 10000$	$24 \times \dfrac{a}{8} = 3a$
$\dfrac{0.01}{100} + \dfrac{0.1}{10} + 0.1 \times 1000$ 100.0101	$2 \div 0.1 + 3 \div 0.3 + 4 \div 0.4$ 40	$1 \times 0.1 + 2 \times 0.2 + 3 \times 0.3$ 1.4	$100 + \dfrac{100}{0.1} + \dfrac{10}{0.01}$ 2100

fraction	decimals	%
$\dfrac{3}{2}$	1.5	150
$\dfrac{31}{20}$	1.55	155
$22\dfrac{21}{200}$	2.105	210.5%
$2\dfrac{3}{4}$	2.75	275
$\dfrac{101}{100}$	1.00+0.01=1.01	101
$\dfrac{21}{10000}$	0.0021	0.21%

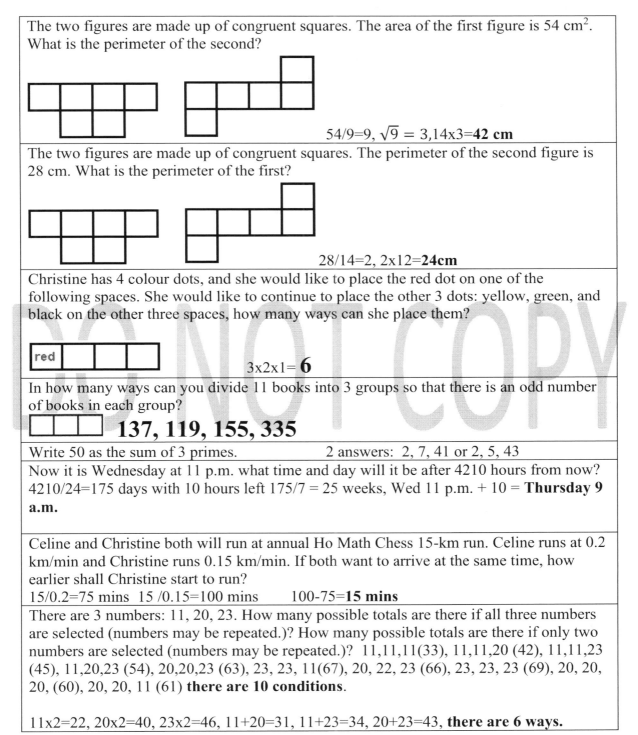

The two figures are made up of congruent squares. The area of the first figure is 54 cm². What is the perimeter of the second?

54/9=9, $\sqrt{9} = 3$, 14x3=**42 cm**

The two figures are made up of congruent squares. The perimeter of the second figure is 28 cm. What is the perimeter of the first?

28/14=2, 2x12=**24cm**

Christine has 4 colour dots, and she would like to place the red dot on one of the following spaces. She would like to continue to place the other 3 dots: yellow, green, and black on the other three spaces, how many ways can she place them?

3x2x1= **6**

In how many ways can you divide 11 books into 3 groups so that there is an odd number of books in each group?

137, 119, 155, 335

Write 50 as the sum of 3 primes.   2 answers: 2, 7, 41 or 2, 5, 43

Now it is Wednesday at 11 p.m. what time and day will it be after 4210 hours from now?
4210/24=175 days with 10 hours left 175/7 = 25 weeks, Wed 11 p.m. + 10 = **Thursday 9 a.m.**

Celine and Christine both will run at annual Ho Math Chess 15-km run. Celine runs at 0.2 km/min and Christine runs 0.15 km/min. If both want to arrive at the same time, how earlier shall Christine start to run?
15/0.2=75 mins 15 /0.15=100 mins   100-75=**15 mins**

There are 3 numbers: 11, 20, 23. How many possible totals are there if all three numbers are selected (numbers may be repeated.)? How many possible totals are there if only two numbers are selected (numbers may be repeated.)? 11,11,11(33), 11,11,20 (42), 11,11,23 (45), 11,20,23 (54), 20,20,23 (63), 23, 23, 11(67), 20, 22, 23 (66), 23, 23, 23 (69), 20, 20, 20, (60), 20, 20, 11 (61) **there are 10 conditions**.

11x2=22, 20x2=40, 23x2=46, 11+20=31, 11+23=34, 20+23=43, **there are 6 ways.**

The chessboard is in the shape of 60cm. Christian moved her room in the centre and then moved east 15 cm. Then she moved rook 13 due south, then 12 cm due west. At this point, she moved her rook 21 cm due south, how far was her rook from the western edge of the chessboard (assume the length or width of the rook is not a concern in this problem.)

45-12 = 33

Jack's school's musical (小品) starts at 7:30 p.m. He must be at Celine's home to pick her up a half-hour before the musical starts. The trip to school takes 23 minutes. Jack will participate in the musical, and the make-up will take 15 minutes. At what time should he start to leave his home?

6:22 p.m.

What is the sum of the first 2008 terms of the sequence 0, 1, 2, 0, 1, 2, 0, 1, 2, …?

2007

Find $1 + 2 + 4 + … + 8 + … + 1024 = ?$

1024x2-1=2047

$\Box + 1\frac{3}{5} \times 0.\overline{1} = \frac{8}{9}$

32/45

One gas pump fills 3 times as fast as another one. It takes 24 minutes for both pumps to work together to fill a tank. How fast does each pump fill the tank separately?

32 minutes and 96 minutes.

Celine gave Christine $100, but later Christine found out she only was supposed to receive $99, so she kept $2 and gave Celine $3 back to her.
Christine did the calculation on how much each one got is as follows.

Celine only gave $100 - $3 (refund) = $97 to Christine. Christine kept amount is $100 + $2 (kept) - $3 (refund) = $99
Celine in fact only gave $97 and yet Christine's calculation showed that she got $99, what happens to the missing $2?
Christine's calculation is illogical because she received $100, not $100 + $2, so the $2 should not be used in the computation.

$33 \times \dfrac{1}{3} =$ _____ $11

If $\dfrac{1}{3} = 0.33333...$ so $33 \times 0.3333 = \$10.9989$

The first calculation uses a fraction and the second calculation uses decimal, which one is more accurate? The fraction is more accurate because it provides the exact answer.

If a decimal is used to describe partial, then why we still need fractions?

_____

For computation, the fraction, sometimes, could provide more accurate answer such as $3 \times \dfrac{1}{3} = 1$.

For communication, sometimes, the decimal is much easier to say $0.33 instead of $\$\dfrac{1}{3}$.

We need both fractions and decimals, depending on the situation.

Ho Math Chess　何数棋谜 奥数,解题策略,及 IQ 思唯训练宝典

Student's name: _____ Assignment date: _____

Evaluate $3 \times 7 + 3 \times 3$.	30
Evaluate $2 \times 73 + 27 \times 2$.	200
Evaluate $3 \times 29 + 3 \times 21$.	150
Evaluate $4 \times 4 + 6 \times 4$.	40
Evaluate $4 \times 19 + 4 \times 1$.	80
Evaluate $5 \times 21 + 9 \times 5$.	150
Evaluate $6 \times 7 + 3 \times 6$.	60
Evaluate $8 \times 8 + 12 \times 8$.	160
Evaluate $15 \times 13 + 2 \times 15$.	225
Evaluate $35 \times 3 + 32 \times 35$.	1225
Evaluate $25 \times 23 + 25 \times 2$.	625
Evaluate $45 \times 8 + 45 \times 37$.	2025
Evaluate $50 \times 13 - 3 \times 50$.	500
Evaluate $60 \times 18 - 60 \times 8$.	600
Evaluate $70 \times 7 - 2 \times 70$.	350
Evaluate $80 \times 9 - 80 \times 4$.	400
Find the prime factorization for 128.	2^7
Find GCF and LCM for 14, 32, 24	GCF=2, LCM= 672
Cindy ate $\frac{4}{8}$ pizza, and later, she ate $\frac{2}{4}$. How much did she eat altogether?	1
Grace ate $1\frac{2}{4}$ pie and later, she ate $\frac{3}{6}$ pie. How much did she eat altogether?	2
Compare $\frac{27}{28}, \frac{25}{26}$.	$\frac{27}{28} > \frac{25}{26}$
Evaluate $\left(3 + \frac{1}{2}\right)\left(3 - \frac{1}{2}\right)$	$8\frac{3}{4}$
Evaluate $3\frac{2}{3} - \square = 1\frac{1}{2}$	$2\frac{1}{6}$
Evaluate $\frac{4}{8} \times \frac{4}{2} \times \frac{9}{3} \times \frac{6}{27}$.	$\frac{2}{3}$
Evaluate $\frac{4 \times 3 + 4 \times 2}{4}$.	5

Student's name: _____ Assignment date: _____

Evaluate $3\frac{2}{3} \div \dfrac{\square}{\square} = 1\frac{3}{4} \times 2\frac{2}{7}$ $1\frac{1}{11}$	
Simplify $\dfrac{1}{2\times2} \times \dfrac{2}{3} \times \dfrac{3\times3}{4} \times \dfrac{4}{5} \times \dfrac{5}{5\times6}$. $\dfrac{1}{20}$	

Calculate $0.3 \div 0.5 + 0.02 \div 0.05 + 0.5 \times 20$

2   Blank line   blank line

Calculate $(3 - 2) \div 1 \div \dfrac{3}{5} \div \dfrac{25}{9} + [2 + (-4)] \div 5 + \dfrac{4}{5}$

1

Blank line   blank line

Calculate $(2 \div 9) \times (27 \div 4) \times (2 \div 3)$

1   Blank line   blank line
Blank line   blank line

Which one is larger $(3.3)^{4.4}$ $(4.4)^{3.3}$? Show how to calculate without using a calculator.

4.4 is 4 times 1.1 and 3.3 is 3 times 1.1, so we can just compare 3.3^4 and 4.4^3.

$(3 \times 1.1)^4, (4 \times 1.1)^3, \dfrac{3.3^4}{4.4^3} = \dfrac{(1.1 \times 3)^4}{(1.1 \times 4)^3} = \dfrac{1.1 \times 3^4}{4^3} = 1.1 \times 0.3$ **So 4. $4^{3.3}$ is bigger.**

Blank line   blank line

At the post office, Cindy spent a total of $3.00 on buying some 13 cents stamps and some 16 cent stamps and received no change. How many stamps in total did Cindy buy?

12 of 13 cents and 9 of 16 cents. Total 21 stamps.

Arthur can drive his car at 100 km/ 5 L. At this rate, what will be the litres needed for driving per km?

0.05 L / km   Blank line   blank line
Blank line   blank line
Blank line   blank line

A movie ticket is $7.50 per adult and $5.50 per child. One day, 500 people went to the movie and paid a total of $3550 in tickets fee. How many children went to the movie on that day?
400 adults and **100** children.
Blank line   blank line
Blank line   blank line

The integer part of a positive decimal number is the part before the decimal point. The fractional part of a positive decimal number is the part from the decimal point on. For example, the integer part of 45.9 is 45, while its fractional part is 0.9. What is the largest number whose fractional part is equal to one-fifth of its integer part? Express answer in decimal notation.

4.8   Blank line   blank line
Blank line   blank line

Find the value of $\dfrac{a - b}{b - c}$ if $\dfrac{a}{b} = \dfrac{9}{4}$ and $\dfrac{b}{c} = \dfrac{5}{3}$. Express your answer in a common fraction.

Blank line   blank line

$\dfrac{25}{8}$ Divide the top and bottom by b. Method 2 is to use ratio to convert a:b:c = 36:20:12

Blank line   blank line
Blank line   blank line

Calculate using shortcut $4200 \div 200 =$
21

Blank line　　　　blank line

Calculate using shortcut $420 \div 20 =$ **21**

Blank line　　　　blank line

Calculate using shortcut $3000 \div 600 =$ **5**

Blank line　　　　blank line

Blank line　　　　blank line

Calculate using shortcut $6000 \div 500 =$ **12**

Blank line　　　　blank line

Blank line　　　　blank line

Calculate using shortcut $-0.84 \div (-1.4) =$ **0.6**

Blank line　　　　blank line

Blank line　　　　blank line

Calculate using shortcut $-0.42 \div (-0.3) =$ **1.4**

Blank line　　　　blank line

Blank line　　　　blank line

Calculate using shortcut $-3.36 \div (-0.4) =$ **8.4**

Blank line　　　　blank line

Blank line　　　　blank line

Alisa is 36 years old now. This is three times as old as Eileen was when Alisa was as old as Eileen is now. How old is Eileen now?

Blank line　　　　blank line

Back x years ago, this equation holds $36 - x = 12 + x$　= **12**

How many different rectangles are there in the diagram?

Blank line　　　　blank line

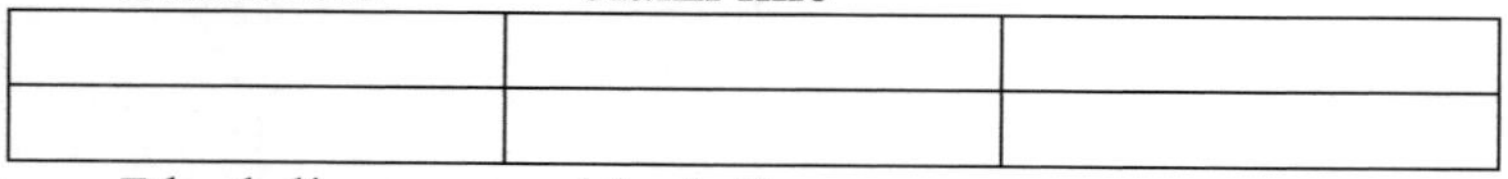

Blank line　　　　blank line

1 by 1 (2×3)

1 by 2 (2×2)

1 by 3 (2×1)

2 by 1 (1×3)

2 by 2 (1×2)

2 by 3 (1×1)

(1+2) (1 + 2 + 3) (**sum of rows times sum of columns**)

3 times 6 = 18

Blank line　　　　blank line

Student's name: _____ Assignment date: _____

Use shortcut to calculate $125 \times 25 \times 8 \times 4 \times 27 \times 2$ $125 \times 8 \times 25 \times 4 \times 27 \times 2 = 1000 \times 100 \times 54 = 5400000$	Blank line	blank line
Use shortcut to calculate $125 \times 16 \times 25$ $125 \times 16 \times 25 = 125 \times 8 \times 2 \times 25 = 1000 \times 50 = 50000$	Blank line	blank line
Use shortcut to calculate $119 \times 73 + 27 \times 119$ $119 \times (63+37) = 119 \times 100 = 11900$	Blank line	blank line
Use shortcut to calculate 14×199 $14 \times (200-1) = 2800 - 14 = 2786$	Blank line	blank line
Use the shortcut to calculate $75000 \div 4 \div 25$ $\dfrac{75000}{4 \times 25} = \dfrac{3000}{4} = 750$	Blank line	blank line
Use the shortcut to calculate $2500 \times 6 \div 25$ $\dfrac{2500 \times 6}{25} = 600$	Blank line	blank line
Use the shortcut to calculate $210 \div 42 \times 6$ $\dfrac{210 \times 6}{42} = 30$	Blank line	blank line
Use the shortcut to calculate $200.012 \div 25$ $2100.012 \div \dfrac{100}{4} = \dfrac{2100.012 \times 4}{100} = 84.00048$	Blank line	blank line
Use shortcut to calculate 333333×999999 $333333 \times (1000000-1) = 333333000000 - 333333 = \mathbf{333332666667}$	Blank line	blank line
Use the shortcut to calculate 333333×333333 $= 111111 \times 3 \times 333333 = 111111 \times 999999 = 111111 \times (1000000-1)$ Blank line blank line $= 111111000000 - 111111 = \mathbf{111110888889}$ Blank line blank line or use the answer of the above question. $333332666667 \div 3 = \mathbf{111110888889}$		
Use the shortcut to calculate $375375 \div 15015$ $\dfrac{375375}{15015} = \dfrac{375 \times 1000 + 375}{15 \times 1000 + 15} = \dfrac{375 \times (1000+1)}{15(1000+1)}$ $= \dfrac{375}{15} = 25$		

Use shortcut to calculate $36 \times 3737 - 37 \times 3636$
$36(3700+37) - 37(3600+36) = 36 \times 3700 + 36 \times 37 - 37 \times 3600 - 37 \times 36 = 0$
  Blank line   blank line
  Blank line blank line		

Student's name: _____   Assignment date: _____

Calculate $777777777^2 - 222222222^2$

$= (777777777 + 222222222)(777777777 - 222222222) = 999999999 \times 555555555$
$(1000000000 - 1)\,555555555 = 555555555000000000 - 555555555 =$
555555554999999995

There are 32 fruits and the ratio of apples to oranges to pineapples = 3:7:1. What is the ratio of all apples to all fruits?
$3 : (3+7+1) = 3:11$

Use mental math to subtract. Explain what you did.
$249 - 199 = 249 - 200 + 1 = 29 + 1 = 50$ Blank line   blank line

Use mental math to subtract. Explain what you did.
$1200 - 199 = 1200 - 200 + 1 = 1001$ Blank line   blank line

Use mental math to subtract. Explain what you did.   Blank line   blank line
$6900 - 698 = 6900 - 700 + 2 = 6200 + 2 = 6202$ Blank line   blank line
Blank line   blank line

Use mental math to subtract. Explain what you did.
$650 - 49 = 650 - 50 + 1 = 601$ Blank line   blank line

Estimate the answer.
$4981 - 372 = 5000 - 400 = 4600$ Blank line   blank line
$2261 - 650 = 2000 - 700 = 1300$ Blank line   blank line
$3789 - 786 = 4000 - 800 = 3200$ Blank line   blank line
$9108 - 1856 = 9000 - 2000 = 7000$ Blank line   blank line

Vanessa paints three times as fast as Samantha. If it took Samantha 6 hours to paint the room. How long would it take if both paint the room together?
$1 \div (\frac{1}{2} + \frac{1}{6}) = 1.5$ hours
Blank line   blank line   Blank line   blank line

If the average of 7 consecutive whole numbers is 11, what is the largest number?
Blank line   blank line

$19\overline{)A} = 21$ $17\overline{)B} = 13$ remainder is 3

$A - B = $ _____ 175

$A = 9 \times 21 = 399$, $B = 17 \times 13 + 3 = 224$, $399 - 224 = 175$

If 0.99 is about $\dfrac{n}{10}$, then n is closest to the whole number of _____.   10
Blank line   blank line

Student's name: _____ Assignment date: _____

15% of ☐ =$1.75, ☐ is closet to a whole number _____ $11.67, $12
    Blank line   blank line

For what price is 40% off the same as $40. _____ $100
    Blank line   blank line

If $m \otimes 3 = \dfrac{m}{3}$, which of the following is a whole number?

(1) $1 \otimes 3$
(2) $6 \otimes 3$
(3) $9 \otimes 2$
(4) $2 \otimes 4$
(2) and (3)
        Blank line   blank line
        Blank line   blank line
        Blank line   blank line

Circle the figure which cannot be drawn without lifting the pencil or retracing.

answer
        Blank line   blank line
        Blank line   blank line

If Howard, Jeff, and Joyce played in a chess tournament. Each person played one game with each of the others. How many games were played?
6
        Blank line   blank line
        Blank line   blank line

If Russell spent $5 more than half of his money and bought shoes. He then spent $5 more than half of the money that was left to buy a hat and then he had $5 left. How much did Russell have originally?
(5+5) x2= 20   Blank line   blank line
(20+5) x2 =**50**   Blank line   blank line

Divide 17 pennies into 4 groups. Each group has a different number of pennies. How many pennies can be in the largest group? What is the least number of pennies that can be in the least group?

11, 3, 2, 1 The largest number of pennies in the group is 11, and the least penny is 1.

56 students sit at 10 tables with no empty seats. There are small tables for 4 students and large tables for 6 students. How many small tables are there? How many large tables are there?

$$4x + 6y = 56$$

x	14	11	8	5	2
y	? 0	? 2	? 4	? 6	? 8

Evaluate $0.1\% \ of \left[\left[\dfrac{joyce}{joyce} \times 10 \div \dfrac{20 \oplus}{10 \oplus} - \left(1 \div \dfrac{1}{\frac{1}{4}} \right) \right] + 3\% \ of \left[\dfrac{tony}{tony} \times 100\% + \left(1\frac{1}{2} \div 2\frac{5}{3} \right) \right] \right]$

1129/44000

Evaluate $2.5\% \times 100 + 4.5 \times 1000 + \dfrac{\frac{2}{3} \times 6}{0.04}$ 4602.5

The sum of length and width of a rectangle is 196 cm, and the difference of length of width is 146 cm. What is its area?

L + w=196
L - w=146
2l = 342 L = 171
W = 196-171 = 25
171x25=**4275 cm²**

Blank line	blank line
Blank line	blank line
Blank line	blank line
Blank line	blank line

After a discount of 15%, the sale price of a pair of shoes is $85. What is the sale price after a 35% discount on its original price?
$85/0.85 = $100, 100 x 0.65=$65.

Blank line	blank line
Blank line	blank line
Blank line	blank line

Jimmie used her measuring tape to measure the length of a streamer and found the measuring tape is longer than the streamer by 1 metre. She folded her measuring tape into half and measured again and found the streamer is longer than the measuring tape by 1 metre. What is the length of her measuring tape, and what is the length of her streamer?

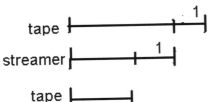

tape = 4 metres, streamer = 3 metres

| Blank line | blank line |
| Blank line | blank line |

Three people shared a bowl of rice, and four people shared a bowl of soup. How many people were there if 364 bowls are used?

Each person used 1/3 bowls of rice and a ¼ bowl of soup. Each person used 1/3+1/4 = 7/12 bowl

The number of people is $364 \div \dfrac{7}{12}$ =624 people.

Blank line　　　　　blank line
Blank line　　　　　blank line

Jonathan decorated the Christmas tree with LCD lights in 7 layers. The number of lights on the lower layer is always two times the number of lights on the higher layer. How many light bulbs are on the top layer if the total number of light bulbs is 381?
The ratio of number of lights from top to the bottom = 1:2:4:8;16:32:64
The total = 1+2+4+8+16+32+64 =127 so the number of lights on the top layer is 381 x (1/127)=**3**.

It takes 7 days for wildfowl flying from the south sea to the North Sea, and it takes goose 9 days from the North Sea to the south sea. If both fly from each end toward each other, and how long does it take for them to meet?
$1 \div (\dfrac{1}{7} + \dfrac{1}{9}) = 3\dfrac{15}{16}$ days.

Chickens and rabbits are in the same cage. There are 35 heads and 94 legs. How many chickens and how many rabbits are there?

Hint: Use "***chicken stands on one foot, and rabbits raise 2 legs***"(金雞獨立兔子舉手) method.
(Use the "heads" method which is fast to get an answer for chicken and rabbit problems.)
Try if you can use 3 methods (including the above), the system of equations, and "assume all heads are chicken method" to solve.
If the above is true, then the chicken will have 1 head with 1 foot, and the rabbit has 1 head with 2 legs.
Assume there are all chickens, so there will be 94/2=47 chickens. In fact, there are only 35 heads, so chicken must be exchanged for some rabbits. 47 – 35 = 12 rabbits. Chicken = 35 – 13 = 23.

The Kwan's went to a restaurant, and there will be an extra $3 if everyone pays $8; there will be short of $4 if everyone pays $7. How many people went to a restaurant, and how much is the total cost of the meal?

8s-t=3
t-7s=4　　7 people and the total cost is $53.

Student's name: _____ Assignment date: _____

There is a whole number A. If A is doubled and then its result adds half of A, adds a quarter of A, and then adds one, the final total is 100. What is A?

Hint: Use LCM and ratio to solve it. You can also use the algebraic method to solve it. The LCM is 8
$8 + 8 = 16$, half of 8 = 4, quarter of 8 = 2. $8 + 16 + 4 + 2 = 22$. So, if 8 becomes 22 then the number was 100 before adding 1 so x/8=99/22, x=**36**.
Method 2: $x (1+1+1/2+1/4) +1=100$, x=**36**

Blank line   blank line
Blank line   blank line
Blank line   blank line

100 buns are given to 100 people. It is known that every adult gets 3 buns, and every 3 children get one bun. How many adults and how many children are there? How many buns do adults get, and how many buns children get?

Hint: Use ratio (You can also use system of equations)
Adult: children = 1:3 $100 \times ¼ = 25$ number of adults, $100 = 25 = 75 =$ number of children.
Buns for adults = $25 \times 3 = 75$, buns for children = $75/3=25$
Blank line   blank line
Blank line   blank line
Blank line   blank line
Blank line   blank line

Part G – Math IQ Fitness Challenging 数学智商健腦挑战题

Every visitor to the oasis town of Dunhuang in northwestern China encounters a very unusual image of three rabbits that appear to be chasing each other in a never-ending circle. This motif is prominently displayed in marble at the entrance to the Dunhuang Museum (below) and is a popular decoration on the scarves, paintings, carpets and t-shirts sold in the local tourist markets.

While each individual rabbit has two ears, the three rabbits in the image together have a total of only three ears. So, in effect, 3 (rabbits) times 2 ears will result in 3 ears instead of 6 ears. Of course, the answer to this riddle lies in the fact that the three ears are arranged to form a triangle, with each pair of adjacent rabbits sharing an ear.

The problems in this section are a collection of school word problems, mathematical puzzles, arithmetic computation problems, math, chess, and puzzles integrated problems and some math contest problems. The purpose of this section is to raise student's brainpower and each student's critical thinking ability using fun math problems.

Evaluate and show your work.
$156 - 7 - 7 - 7 - 7 - 7 - 7 - 7 - 7$

$156 - 7 \times 8 = \mathbf{100}$

Blank line	blank line
Blank line	blank line
Blank line	blank line

Evaluate and show your work.
$9 + 99 + 999 + 9999 + 99999 + 999999$

$10 - 1 + 100 - 1 + 10000 - 1 + 100,000 - 1 + 1,000,000 - 1 = 1,111,110 - 6 = \mathbf{1,111,104}$

Blank line	blank line
Blank line	blank line
Blank line	blank line

Replace each ? with a number. (no same number can be repeated on the same row or column.).

♜	COLUMN 1	COLUMN 2	PRODUCT
ROW 1	?3	?4	12
ROW 2	?8	?2	16
PRODUCT	24	8	?192

Andy and Christie have 180 chess books altogether. Andy has three times of Christie's. How many does each one have?
It means there are 4 equal parts so $180 / 4 = \mathbf{45} \ldots \mathbf{Christie}$, $45 \times 3 = \mathbf{135} \ldots \mathbf{Andy}$

Blank line	blank line
Blank line	blank line
Blank line	blank line
Blank line	blank line
Blank line	blank line

Evaluate and show your work.
$100 + 99 - 98 + 97 - 96 + 95 - 94 + \ldots + 4 - 3 + 3 - 2 + 1$
100 + there are 49 of 1's + 1 = 150

Evaluate and show your work.
$199998 + 1 + 19998 + 1 + 1998 + 1 + 198 + 1 + 18 + 1$

$199,999 + 19,999 + 1,999 + 199 + 19 = 200,000 - 1 + 20,000 - 1 + 2000 - 1 +$
$200 - 1 + 20 - 1 = 222,220 - 5 =$ **222215**

Replace each ? with a number.

    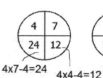

4x1-4=0　　4x7-4=24
4x5-4=16　　　4x4-4=12

answer
Use bishop moves to multiply the top by 4 and then minus 4 to get the bottom row. 4 x 9 – 4 = **32**

Harry went to a chess tournament, with 20 children participated altogether. If everyone plays against each other only once, how many games needed to finish the tournament?

Line up numbers in 2 rows and then add each pair to get 20 and there are 19 pairs. 19 + 18 + … + 3 + 2 + 1 and 1 + 2 + 3 …　+ 17 +18 + 19 = 20 x 19 but we only need one, so the total is divided by 2 = **190**

Replace each ? with a number.

3	2		4	
	3	2	1	
?	1	4		
		?	5	

The sum of 2 adjacent squares, vertically or horizontally, is 5, the sum of 3 adjacent squares is 6. **The answers are 1, 0.**

Student's name: _____   Assignment date: _____

Number puzzle and pattern 数字谜及规律

What is A?

```
    1 A 2
  ×     2
  ---------
   □□□
  − 2 A 1
  ---------
      2 3        A = 2
```

Blank line   blank line

$$\square = \bigcirc + \bigcirc + \bigcirc$$

$$\bigcirc \times \square = 48$$

$$\bigcirc = \underline{\quad} \quad 4$$

$$\square = \underline{\quad} \quad 12$$

Replace each ? by a number.

1	2	3
✗	4	⬦

✛	8	✳
?	?	?

7, 10, 11 Add 2 to get bottom.

If the number pattern (1, 1, 1) (2, 4, 8) (3, 9, 27) continues, then the sum of the 100th term is

(100, 10000, 1000000) 1000000+10000+100= **1010100**   Blank line

From 1 to 2008, there are _____ natural numbers. The sum of all even numbers subtracts
the sum of all odd numbers is _____. **2008, 1004**

From 1 to 2008, there are 1004 even numbers and 1004 odd numbers, but for every pair of even and odd, even − odd = 1, so the difference is 1004. The even sum is 1009020, and the odd sum is 1008016.

Student's name: _____   Assignment date: _____

Evaluate

$$\frac{1}{\frac{1}{1}} + \frac{1}{\frac{1}{2}} + \frac{1}{\frac{1}{3}} + \frac{1}{\frac{1}{4}} + \frac{1}{\frac{1}{5}} + \frac{1}{\frac{1}{6}} = \underline{\hspace{2cm}}$$

$1 + 2 + 3 + 4 + 5 + 6 = 3 \times 7 = 21$

$$\square = \bigcirc + \bigcirc + \bigcirc, \bigcirc \times \square = 147$$

$$\bigcirc = \underline{\hspace{2cm}}, \square = \underline{\hspace{2cm}}$$

$147 / 3 = 49, \sqrt{49} = 7 = \bigcirc, \square = 21$

Blank line   blank line

What are the possible answers?

$\frac{?}{4} + 3 = a\ natural\ number\ between\ 20\ to\ 30.$ **80, 96**

$\frac{?}{5} + 2 = a\ natural\ number\ between\ 20\ to\ 30.$ **110, 135**

Blank line   blank line

5689 is to 9865 as ▶ ✟ ■ ☺ is to ☺ ■ ✟ ▶

Blank line   blank line
Blank line   blank line
Blank line   blank line
Blank line   blank line

Student's name: _____ Assignment date: _____

Evaluate

$50 \times 0.5 =$ _____ $\times 5$ **5**

$100 \times 0.6 = 0.1 \times$ _____   **600**

$150 \times 100 = 15 \times$ _____   **1000**

$0.7 \times 150 = 7 \times$ _____   **15**

$\frac{1}{2} \times 0.1 = 500 \times$ _____   **0.0001**

If $\frac{1}{3} = 0.3 = \frac{3}{10}$ then $\frac{1}{3} = \frac{3}{10}$.

But $\frac{1}{3}$ is not an equivalent fraction of $\frac{3}{10}$, what is wrong with the "If " statement?

_____ **Because $\frac{1}{3}$ is 0,3333333, not**

just 0.3

Replace each ? by a number.

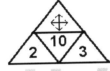  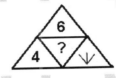

6 + 4 + 1 = 11

A number multiplied by itself and then added to the original number, and the result is 42. What is this number?

6 x 6 + 6 = 42, **the number is 6.**

A number multiplied by itself and then subtracted the original number from its product, and the result is 42. What is this number?

7 x 7 – 7 = 42, **the number is 7.**

What digit does A, B, C represent?

```
  BA
  BA
  BA
+ BA
----
  CB
```

23+23+23+23=92

Fraction 分数

Shade the following figures to represent corresponding fractions or equivalent fractions.

0.25

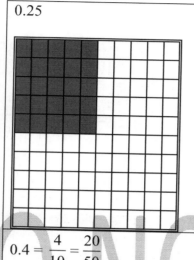

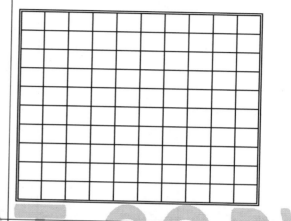

$0.4 = \dfrac{4}{10} = \dfrac{20}{50}$

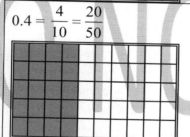

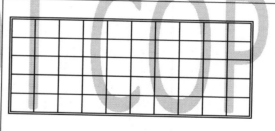

Match the equivalent fractions on the right to the left by connecting lines.

$1\dfrac{2}{5}$	$2\dfrac{6}{20}$
2.3	$\dfrac{9}{4}$
$2\dfrac{1}{4}$	$1\dfrac{4}{10}$
$3\dfrac{4}{3}$	$4\dfrac{1}{3}$

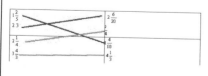

Student's name: _____ Assignment date: _____

Draw the model of 4.92.

Draw 4 of 10 by 10 and then shade 92 squares of another 10 by 10.

Draw the model of $\dfrac{4.92}{3}$.

Show that one of three 10 by 10 is shaded. The remaining is 192 squares and then divided by 3, and each is 64.

Show $2\dfrac{1}{4}$ and $\dfrac{9}{4}$ are equivalent on a number line.

The first one is marked at 2 and a quarter on a 0 to 3 number line. The second is shown that 9 of the quarter is accumulated.

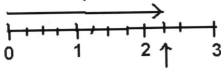

Draw 3 number lines to compare $\dfrac{2}{5}, \dfrac{1}{4}, \dfrac{5}{8}$ and rank them from the least to the largest.

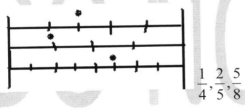

$\dfrac{1}{4}, \dfrac{2}{5}, \dfrac{5}{8}$

Repeat each number of 3.1, 2.8, $\dfrac{12}{4}, \dfrac{16}{10}$ on a number line. Draw a line with 1, 2, 3, and 4.

Between each mark, there should be 10 marks, so the order is 1.6, 2.8, 3, 3.1.

What is the sum of $x+y+z$? (45+60+51)/2=78

$x+y=45$
$y+z=60$
$x+z=51$

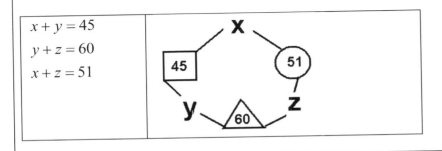

$13 \times 1999 + 13 \times 1 = 13(1999 + 1) = 13 \times 2000 = 26000$

Blank line   blank line

$17 \times 2002 - 17 \times 2 = 17(2002 - 2) = 17 \times 2000 = 34000$

Blank line   blank line

$0.00001 \times 1999900000 - 100000 \times 0.19999 = 19999 - 19999 = 0$

Blank line   blank line

$2 \times 98765 = 98765 \times 2 = 197530$

Blank line   blank line

$0.4 \times 2008 + 2008 \times 0.6 = 2008 \times (0.6 + 0.4) = 2008 \times 1 = 2008$

Blank line   blank line

Blank line   blank line

Circle one of the following figures, which does not belong to the group.

answer

Blank line   blank line

Circle one of the following numbers, which does not belong to the group.

2, 3, 6, 7, 8, 14, 15, 30   **8**, plus 1, times 2, plus 1, times 2

Blank line   blank line

Blank line   blank line

Circle one of the following figures, which does not belong to the group.

answer

Blank line   blank line

Blank line   blank line

Tammy bought 4.5 kg of roast beef. She kept 2 kg or herself and then divided the remaining amount equally among five friends. How many kilograms of roast beef did each friend get?

$(4.5 - 2)/5 = $ **0.5 kg**

Blank line   blank line

Blank line   blank line

Melody added 0.6 years to her age and then divided that result by 4. The final answer was 2.4. How old is Melody?

$2.4 \times 4 - 0.6 = 9$

Blank line   blank line

Blank line   blank line

Blank line   blank line

Student's name: _____ Assignment date: _____

Circle all equivalent decimals.

$$0.1,\ 0.10,\ 00.01,\ 0.100,\ \frac{1}{10},\frac{10}{100},\ 0.01\times 10,\ 100\times 0.001$$

~~0.1, 0.10~~, **00.01** , ~~0.100,~~ $\frac{1}{10},\frac{10}{100}$, ~~0.01×10, 100×0.001~~   answer

---

Find the numbers for the following pattern.

1, 4, 9, 61, 52, 63, _____, _____ **46, 18**
   Blank line   blank line

Use 0, 1, 2, 3 each digit once to make as many 4-digit numbers as you can.

3	3	2	1

3 x 3 x 2 x 1 = **18**

   Blank line   blank line

Replace each ? with a number.

answer
  Blank line   blank line
  Blank line   blank line

How many right angles, obtuse angles, or acute angles are there?

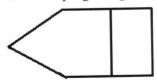

6 right angles, 2 obtuse angles, 1 acute angle
  Blank line   blank line
  Blank line   blank line

Evaluate $1000 \times 0.01 \div 10 \div 0.001$
$= 10 \div 10 \div 0.001 = 1 \div 0.001 = 1 \times 1000 = \textbf{1000}$

Evaluate $123400 \times 0.001 \div 0.1 \div 0.001$
$= 123.4 \div 0.1 \div 0.001 = 1234 \div 0.001 = 1234 \times 1000 = \textbf{1234000}$

How many ways can a bishop move top to down only from e8 to d1? **35**

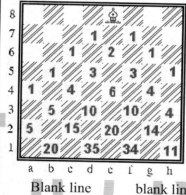

Blank line　　　blank line

How many numbers less than 1000 would round to 1000 when rounded to the nearest hundreds?
99X
98X
97X
96X
95X
Each X has from 0 to 9 possibilities so 5 x 10 = **50**

Continue the pattern.

720, 360, 240, 180, ___ **144**, 720 x by $\frac{1}{2}, \frac{1}{3}, \frac{1}{4}, \frac{1}{5}$

　　Blank line　　　blank line

60, 30, 20, 15, 12, ___ **10** $\frac{1}{2}, \frac{1}{3}, \frac{1}{4}, \frac{1}{5}, \frac{1}{6}$

　　Blank line　　　blank line
　　Blank line　　　blank line

Frank Ho, Amanda Ho © 1995 - 2020

Student's name: _____ Assignment date: _____

Find the next number 1, 5, 14, 30, _____ **55**

$1+4$, ,$1+4+9$, $1+4+9+16$, $1+4+9+26+25$

Evaluate

$2^2 + 2^2 + 2^2 + 2^2 =$ _____ 16

$2^2 \times 4 =$ _____ 16

$-2^2 \times 4 =$ _____ -16

Blank line · · · · blank line

When a digit 2 is placed in the following boxes to form 3-digit numbers, how many numbers are there altogether (digits can be repeated)?

8x1x9 + 1 x 9 x 10+ 10 = 180

Blank line · · · · blank line

Replace the ? by a number.

1, 111, ⬦, ⬦11, ✳, ? 11

Blank line · · · · blank line
Blank line · · · · blank line

When 3 is divided by a one-digit whole number, and the answer is just less than 2, what is the divisor?

Blank line · · · · blank line
Blank line · · · · blank line

5

Find two ways to divide the following isosceles trapezoid into 4 congruent parts.

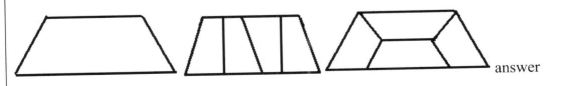

answer

Evaluate

$\dfrac{0.25}{1} + \dfrac{0.2}{50} + \dfrac{0.4}{10} - \dfrac{0.1}{0.5}$ = 0.25 + 0.004+0.04- 0.2 = 0.292-0.2 = **0.094 (47/500)**

Fill in each □ with a number.

$34 \text{ m} = \boxed{} \times 170 \text{ cm},$ **20**

$4 \times 34 \text{ m} = 10 \times 13 \text{ cm} + \boxed{} \text{ cm},$ **13470**

There are 5 colours of the same size beads with 1000 of each colour. What is the fewest number of beads you must pick to make sure that there are 5 beads of the same colour?

21 (1111, 2222, 3333, 4444, 5555 maximum 20 beads with no 5 of the same colour so far.)

When a 2-digit number is reversed, the difference between the original number and its reversed number is a factor of 3015. Find these 2 numbers. **83 and 38 or 61 and 16**

(83-38) x 67 = 3015
(61-16) x 67 = 3015

Fill in each blank box with a number.

31 + □ = ◯ × ◯
31+18=7x7

7 + □ = △ × △
7+18 = 5x5

Fill in each blank box with a number.

6 + □ = □ × □
6+3= 3x3

13 + □ = △ × △
13+3=4x4

Student's name: _____ Assignment date: _____

Fill in bank boxes with digits 1, 2, 3, 4, 5.

□□ = □ + □ + □   12 = 3 + 4 + 5

Fill in bank boxes with digits 2, 3, 4, 5, 6.

□ × □ = □ + □ + □   2 × 6 = 3 + 4 = 5

How many months of five weeks of Mondays are there if the first Thursday falls on January 1st of a year with 365 days?

365 days / 7 days = 52 weeks (or 52 Mondays) with one day extra.
On average, there are 4 weeks per month (even in February.), but for those months with 30 days or 31 days, the number of weeks varies. 28 days – 4 weeks. 31 days (Months of Jan, Mar, May, July, August, Oct, Dec) – 3 weekdays per month having 5 weeks. 30 days (April, June, Sept, Nov) – 2 weekdays have 5 weeks.
52 weeks (or 52 Mondays) – 48 weeks (or 48 Mondays) = 4 weeks (This is true for all other weekdays too.) (If the first Monday falls on Jan 1st, then there will be 5 months for Monday with 5 weeks.).

Observe the pattern and replace the ? by a number.

4	✚	✛
8	?	7
✛	2	6

All 4 adjacent numbers (4, 3, 8, 5; 3, 5, 7, 5; 8, 5, 2, 5; 5, 7, 6, 2) add up to 20, so the middle number is 5.

Calculate.

$$-\frac{9}{99}\times\frac{11^2}{1}\times\frac{5}{625}\times\frac{125}{1}\times\frac{33\frac{1}{3}}{1}\times\frac{1}{\frac{1}{3}}= \quad -11\times\frac{100}{3}\times 3=-1100$$

Calculate.

$$2^2\times5^2\times4^2\times25^2\times2^2\times50^2=10^2\times100^2\times$$
$$100^2=100000^2=10,000,000,000$$

Calculate.

$$\frac{3}{\oplus}+\frac{2}{\oplus}-\frac{2}{\boxplus}$$

$$1-\frac{2}{3}=\frac{1}{3}$$

There are three digits 5, 6, 9. Arrange 5, 6, 9 into A, B, C boxes such that the product is the largest. 56 x 9 = 524, **65 x 9 = 595**, 69 x 5 = 345, 96 x 5 = 470, 95 x6 = 370

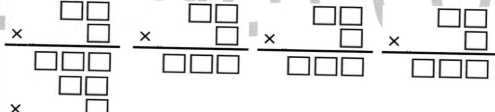

Harry bought 16 m of fencing to put up a rectangular garden. What dimensions might her garden be?

L+W=8

L	W
7	1
6	2
5	3
4	4

ANSWER

Student's name: _____   Assignment date: _____

The perimeter of an isosceles triangle is 10 cm. How long might its sides be (in natural number)?

The base length could be an even number 2, 4, 6, 8.

Suppose the area of your rectangular garden is 8 cm². What are its possible perimeters?

$9 \times 2 = 18 \ cm$
$6 \times 2 = 12 \ cm$

Student's name: _____ Assignment date: _____

Which figure in the following table will have a perimeter of 36 units and an area of 81 square units.

Figure number	Perimeter	Area
1	4	1
2	8	4
3	12	9
4	16	16
9th figure	36	81

Find 2 consecutive 2-digit numbers whose product is 812.
Use the repeated division method to find the answer 28, 29.

Two consecutive 4-digit numbers whose sum is 9173. What are these 2 numbers?
The problem is a Sum and Difference model problem. A+B=9173, A-B=1.
A=4587, B= 4586

Find a fraction that is neither close to $\frac{1}{2}$, nor close to 1. What happens if you round it to the tenth?
The fraction is $\frac{1}{2}$. When rounded to tenth, it is 1.

Find ☐.   9

$$\frac{☐ + 0.6}{4} = 2.4$$

Find ☐.

$$\frac{☐}{⊕} + \frac{2}{⊕} - \frac{2}{⊞} = 1$$

answer $\frac{x}{5} + \frac{2}{5} - \frac{2}{3} = 1$, $x = 5$

Student's name: _____ Assignment date: _____

A cube measuring 4-unit on each side is painted only on the outside and then cut into 1-unit cubes.
How many cubes have 3-side painted? _____ 8
How many cubes have 2-side painted? _____ 24
How many cubes have 1-side painted? _____ 24
How many cubes have no sides painted? _____ $8 = 64 - 8 - 24 - 24$

A rectangle has a perimeter of 60 units and an area of 81 square units. What could be its dimension?
 3 unit by 27 unit

Which number is just as far from 5 as it is from 13?

15+3=18, 18/2=9

Find a fraction that is neither close to $\frac{1}{2}$, nor close to 1. What happens if you round it to the tenth? 1 +1/2 divided by 2 is 3/4. 0.8

Replace ☐ by the same number.

$$11 + \square = 17 - \square \quad 3$$

How many triangles are in the following figures? **9**

Student's name: _____ Assignment date: _____

Convert the following improper fraction to $\frac{p}{q}$.

$3\dfrac{0.2}{0.5} =$

$-1\dfrac{0.1}{10} =$

$answer\ \dfrac{17}{5}, \dfrac{99}{100}$

Which of the following fractions are equivalent? Show by connecting lines.

answer

Ashley had some cookies. After eating one, she gave half of the remainder to Jacqueline. After eating another cookie, Ashley gave half of what was left to Christian. Ashley now had only 6 cookies left. How many cookies did she start with?

Replace each ? by a number.

                        answer 4+2+3=9

I am a 3-digit whole number that does not contain any 0, 1, 2, or 3. No digits are repeated, and I am between 400 and 600. What am I?
(456, 457, 458, 459), (465, 467, 468, 469), (475, 476, 478, 479), (485, 486, 487, 489), (495, 496, 497, 498) Repeated the same pattern and starts the first digit by 5, 6, 7, 8, 9. Each has 20 different numbers. **There are 20 x 6 = 120 different kinds of numbers.**

I am a 4-digit whole number, and each digit is even. All digits are different. What is the greatest possible number?

7 x 8 x 9 x 5= 63 x 40 = 2520

Fill in each box with a number. (Use the same number for the same box.)

$$\Box + \Box > \Box \times \Box$$ 1+1 > 1 x 1

Fill in each box with a number. (Use the same number for the same box.)

$$\Box + \Box = \Box \times \Box$$ 2+2 = 2x2

Replace ? by a number.

$$2^{20} = 32^? = (2^5)^4$$

Fill in each $\Box$ by a different number.

$$\Box^2 + \Box^2 + \Box^2 = 180$$ **10, 8, 4**

The following 14 squares are made of 24 matchsticks. Remove 6 sticks so that the remaining figure does not have any squares.

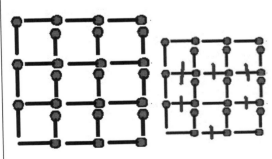

Answers may vary.

Fill in each box with a number.

$$23 \times 22 \times 21 \times \ldots 4 \times 3 \times 2 \times 1$$

$$= 24 \times 23 \times 22 \times \ldots \times 7 \times 6 \times 5 \times \square \times \triangle \times \bigcirc$$

1x1x1

Fill in each box with a number.

$$2 \times (2 + 6) = 4 \times \square \ 4$$

$$A + B + C + D = 10$$

$$A \times 10 + B \times 10 + \times 10 + D \times 10 = ? \ \textbf{100}$$

Fill in each $\square$ with a digit from 1 to 5.

$$\square\square \times \square = \square\square \quad \textbf{13x4=52}$$

Fill in each $\square$ with a digit from 1 to 6.

$$\square\square \times \square = \square\square\square \quad \textbf{54x3=162}$$

Fill in each $\square$ with a digit from 1 to 8.

$$\square\square\square \times \square = \square\square\square\square$$

453x6=2718

Student's name: _____ Assignment date: _____

Replace ? by a number.

2, 3	3, 6	3, 4	2, 9
6	6	12	? **18**

Find the next 2 terms.

ACB, BCA, C, CDE, EDC, D, EFG, _____, _____ **GFE, F**

Replace ? by a chess piece.

 2

2 3

4 5

 ? or ♟

Find the size of angle C.

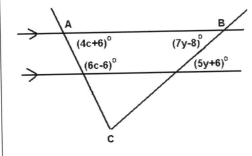

61⁰

Geometry and measurement 几何及测量

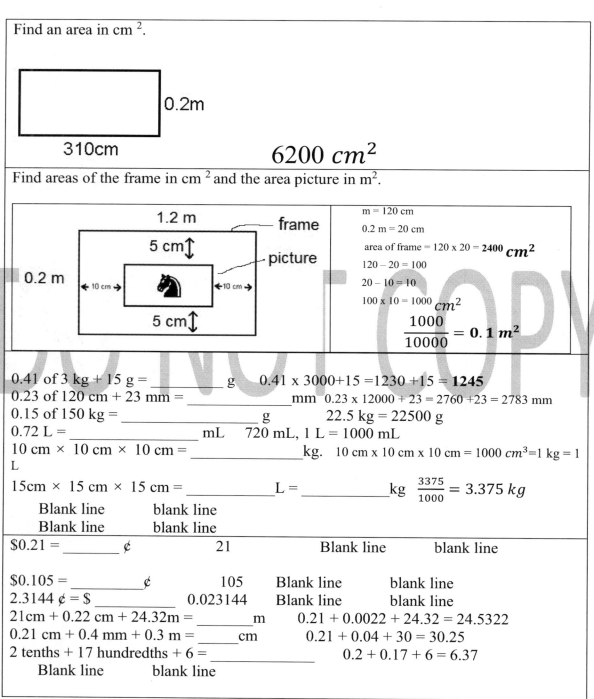

Find an area in cm ^{2}.

0.2m

310cm

$6200\ cm^2$

Find areas of the frame in cm ^{2} and the area picture in m ^{2}.

1.2 m — frame

5 cm

picture

0.2 m ←10 cm→ ←10 cm→

5 cm

m = 120 cm

0.2 m = 20 cm

area of frame = 120 x 20 = **2400** cm^2

120 − 20 = 100

20 − 10 = 10

100 x 10 = 1000 cm^2

$$\frac{1000}{10000} = \boldsymbol{0.1\ m^2}$$

0.41 of 3 kg + 15 g = _____ g　　0.41 x 3000+15 =1230 +15 = **1245**

0.23 of 120 cm + 23 mm = _____mm　0.23 x 12000 + 23 = 2760 +23 = 2783 mm

0.15 of 150 kg = _____ g　　　　22.5 kg = 22500 g

0.72 L = _____ mL　　720 mL, 1 L = 1000 mL

10 cm × 10 cm × 10 cm = _____kg.　10 cm x 10 cm x 10 cm = 1000 cm^3 =1 kg = 1 L

15cm × 15 cm × 15 cm = _____ L = _____ kg　$\frac{3375}{1000}$ = 3.375 kg

　Blank line　　　　blank line
　Blank line　　　　blank line

$0.21 = _____ ¢　　　21　　　Blank line　　　blank line

$0.105 = _____ ¢　　105　Blank line　　　blank line

2.3144 ¢ = $ _____　0.023144　Blank line　　　blank line

21cm + 0.22 cm + 24.32m = _____m　　0.21 + 0.0022 + 24.32 = 24.5322

0.21 cm + 0.4 mm + 0.3 m = _____cm　　0.21 + 0.04 + 30 = 30.25

2 tenths + 17 hundredths + 6 = _____　　0.2 + 0.17 + 6 = 6.37

　Blank line　　　　blank line

Student's name: _____ Assignment date: _____

$0.8 \times 240 = 192$

Blank line   blank line

Fill in each box by a number.

$80 \div 4 \times 3 = 80 \times \dfrac{\Box}{\Box}$ 3/4

Blank line   blank line

Replace each ? with a whole number.

Blank line   blank line

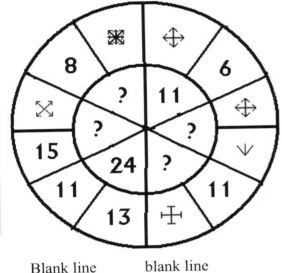

17, 6, 14, 18

Blank line   blank line
Blank line   blank line

What comes next?

124 81 6 32 641 2 ?

1, 2, 4, 8, 16, 32, 64, 12 8

Blank line   blank line
Blank line   blank line
Blank line   blank line
Blank line   blank line

Student's name: _____ Assignment date: _____

$$\square + \bigcirc = 21$$
$$\square - \bigcirc = 11, \quad \square = 16, \quad \bigcirc = 5$$
$$2\square + \bigcirc = 28$$
$$\square + 2\bigcirc = 36, \quad \square = 10, \quad \bigcirc = 8$$

What time will be 52 minutes past 11:20 A.M.?

Blank line   blank line

11:20 + 0:52 = 12:12 P.M.

Blank line   blank line

Julian has 5 coins, and only one of them is a penny. What is the least amount of money Julian can have?

1¢ + 5¢ + 5¢ + 5¢ + 5¢ = 21¢

Blank line   blank line

5	87	86	89	86	85
4	86	87	83	81	82
3	89	87	100	84	83
2	81	87	85	84	89
1	83	84	86	89	82
	a	b	c	d	e

You are at c2 = $\square$.

$\square = \boxed{+}$ (____) + ____ 100 = 82 + 18

$\square = \boxed{+}$ (____) + ____ 100 = 89 + 11

$\square = \boxed{\times}$ (____) + ____ 100 = 84 + 16

Draw a rectangle with perimeter 36 cm and the least possible area.

cm by 17 cm

Blank line   blank line
Blank line   blank line
Blank line   blank line
Blank line   blank line

Student's name: _____ Assignment date: _____

Fill in each box by a number, the same box has the same number.

$$2 \times \square + 2 \times \triangle = 38$$

$$\square + \triangle = 19$$

$$\square - \triangle = 3 \qquad \square = 11, \triangle = 8$$

Fill in each box by a number, and the same box has the same number.

$$\square + 2 \times \triangle = 32$$

$$2 \times \square + \triangle = 46 \qquad \square = 20, \triangle = 6$$

$$\square + \triangle = 9 \qquad 8+1=9$$

$$\bigcirc \times \square + \square \times \triangle = 21$$

$$2 \times 8 + 5 \times 1 = 21$$

Place an $\times$ on a square where all rooks can move to in the shortest distance. Trace the line for each rook to reach the $\times$ square.

5		⬌		⬌	
4	⬌				
3			×		
2	⬌				⬌
1			⬌		
	a	b	c	d	e

Find the next number

3, 2, 5, 4, 7, 6, _____ **9**

Fill in each box by a number, the same box has the same number.

$$\square + \triangle = 6 \qquad 2+4=6$$

$$4 \times \square + 2 \times \triangle = 16 \qquad 4\text{x}2+2\text{x}4=16$$

Fill in each box by a number, the same box has the same number.

$$\square + \triangle = 8 \qquad 2+6=8$$

$$5 \times \square + 2 \times \triangle = 22 \qquad 5\text{x}2+2\text{x}6=22$$

$$5 \times \square + 10 \times \triangle = 60 \qquad 5\text{x}2+10\text{x}5=60$$

$$\square + \triangle = 9 \qquad 7+2=9$$

$$\square + \bigcirc = 11 \qquad 4+7=11$$

$$\bigcirc = 7$$

$$\square + \triangle = 38 \qquad 22+16=38$$

$$\triangle + \bigcirc = 26 \qquad 4+22=26$$

$$\square = 22$$

Fill in each box by a number.

?	÷	2	×	3	=	9
+		×		+		÷
5	×	?	−	7	=	3
−		+		÷		×
7	−	3	−	?	=	2
‖		‖		‖		‖
4	+	?	−	5	=	6

6, 2, 2, 7

Fill in each box by a number.

?	×	2	−	6	=	?
+		×		+		−
4	÷	2	+	?	=	4
−		×		−		+
6	+	?	−	5	=	2
=		=		=		=
?	+	4	−	3	=	6

7, 8, 2, 1, 5

Fill in each box by a number.

$$\boxed{} + 4 - 7 + 6 - 2 = 28.$$ 27

A number added itself 5 times is 30. What was the original number?

6

Draw a diagram to illustrate 3 times 4.

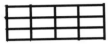

Find A, B, C.

$$\begin{array}{r} A\,B\,C \\ -\ C\,B\,A \\ \hline 9\ 9 \end{array}$$

C	1	2	3	4	5	6	7	8
A	2	3	4	5	6	7	8	9
B	0-9	0-9	0-9	0-9	0-9	0-9	0-9	0-9

8 times 10 = 80 ways of getting 99.

Fill in each box by a number.

$$\boxed{} + \triangle = \underline{\quad}$$
$$\boxed{} - \triangle = \underline{\quad}$$ >× 128

12, 4; 33, 31; 18, 14

Fill in each box by a number.

$$\boxed{} + \triangle = \underline{\quad}$$
$$\boxed{} - \triangle = \underline{\quad}$$ >× 72

9, 3; 19, 17; 11, 7

Multiplication puzzle 乘法数字谜

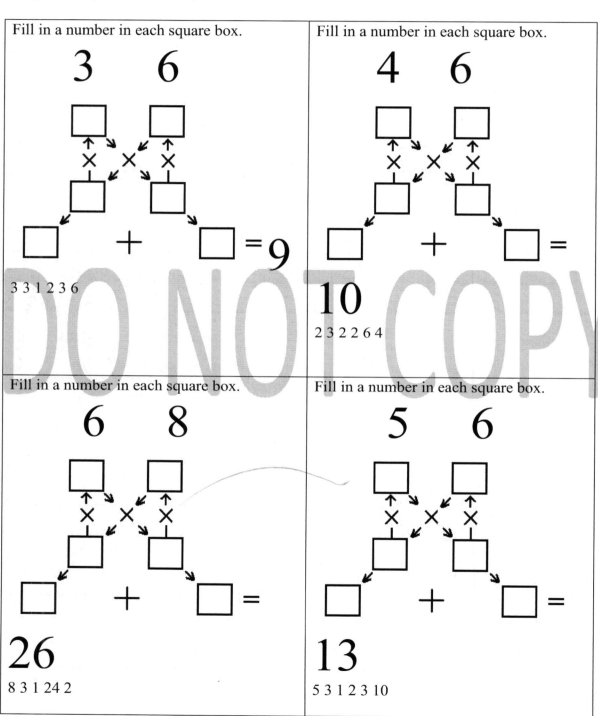

Fill in a number in each square box.

3   6

□ + □ = 9

3 3 1 2 3 6

Fill in a number in each square box.

4   6

□ + □ = 10

2 3 2 2 6 4

Fill in a number in each square box.

6   8

□ + □ = 26

8 3 1 24 2

Fill in a number in each square box.

5   6

□ + □ = 13

5 3 1 2 3 10

Student's name: _____   Assignment date: _____

Fill in the same shape with the same whole number.

$$\square + \bigcirc = 11 + 2$$

$$\square - \bigcirc = 9 \quad \square = 11, \quad \bigcirc = 2$$

Fill in the same shape with the same whole number.

$$\square + \triangle - 8 = 22$$

$$\square - \triangle = 4 \quad \square = 17, \quad \triangle = 13$$

Fill in the same shape with the same whole number.

$$\square - \triangle = 20 + \triangle$$

$$\square + \triangle = \triangle + \triangle + 20 \quad \square = 20, \quad \triangle = 0$$

Fill in the same shape with the same whole number.

$$\square \times \triangle = 300$$

$$\square = 15, \quad \square = 15, \quad \triangle = 20$$

Fill in the same shape with the same whole number.

$$5 \times \square + 20 \times \square = 700, \quad \square = 28$$

Fill in the same shape with the same whole number.

$$18 \times \square - 15 \times \square = 12, \quad \square = 4$$

Ho Math Chess 何数棋谜 奥数,解题策略,及 IQ 思唯训练宝典
Frank Ho, Amanda Ho © 1995 - 2020

Student's name: _____ Assignment date: _____

Fill in $\square$ by a number.

$$(\square + 8 - 1) + 6 - 3 = \frac{(9+3) + 7 - 4}{5}$$

What is the sum of 3 consecutive numbers when multiplied together is 120?

15

The sum of the ages of my parents now is 85. Seven years ago, the sum of their ages is _____.

85 -14=71

The total area of a cube is the same as the volume of the same cube. What is the length of the cube in cm?

$6s^2 = s^3$
S = 6 cm
6 cm

The total area of a cube is the same as the perimeter of the same cube. What is the length of the cube in cm?

$6s^2 = 12s$
S = 2 cm

Student's name: _____ Assignment date: _____

Fill in each box by a number.

$$\frac{2+4+\square}{3}=6 \qquad 12$$

Fill in each box by a number.

$$\frac{7+\square+10}{3}=7 \qquad 4$$

Fill in each same shape by a same number.

$$\square + \bigcirc - \triangle = 120 \qquad \text{From this equation, we know } \bigcirc - \triangle$$

=30.

90+45-15=120

$$\square - \bigcirc + \triangle = 60 \qquad 90, 45, 15$$

$$\square = ? \qquad 90$$

$$\bigcirc + \triangle = 60 \qquad 45+15 = 60$$

$$\bigcirc = ? \qquad 45$$

$$\triangle = ? \qquad 15$$

5					
4					
3					
2			✳		
1					
	a	b	c	d	e

How many squares can queen control? _____ 15

How many squares can rook control? _____ 8

How many squares can be controlled by either queen or rook or both? _____ 23 (15+8=23)

How many squares can only be controlled by both rook and queen? 23-17=6

This page is for advanced students because it might need Systems of Equations.

Fill in each box by a whole number.

$$\square \times 3 + \triangle \times 2 = 35$$

$$\square + \triangle = 5 \times \bigcirc$$

5, 10, 3

Fill in each box by a whole number.

$$\square \times 3 + \triangle \times 2 = 22$$

$$\square + \triangle = 2 \times \bigcirc$$

2, 8, 5

Fill in each box by a whole number.

$$\square \times 3 + \triangle \times 2 = 37$$

$$\square + \triangle = 2 \times \bigcirc$$

5, 11, 8

Fill in each box by a whole number.

$$\square \times 3 + \triangle \times 2 = 28$$

$$\square + \triangle = 11 \times \bigcirc$$

6, 5, 1

Student's name: _____ Assignment date: _____

$12 - \square = 4$ 8

$\square + 5 - 6 = \triangle$ 8, 7

$\bigcirc - 7 + 2 = \triangle$ 12, 7

$\bigcirc = \square + \square + \square$ 6, 2, 2, 2

$\bigcirc + \square + \square + \square = 12$ 6, 2, 2, 2

$\bigcirc = \square$ 6

$\bigcirc + \square + \square + \square = 24$ 6, 6, 6, 6

$\bigcirc = \square$ 9, 9

$\bigcirc + \square + \square = 27$ 9, 9, 9

$\bigcirc = \square$ 18, 18

$\bigcirc + \square + \square = 18 + 18 + 18$ 18, 18, 18

$\bigcirc = \square$ 98, 98

$\bigcirc + \square + \square = (100-1) + (100-2) + (100-3)$ 99, 98, 97

$\bigcirc = \square$ 101

$\square + \square + \square = 3 \times 101$ 101, 101, 101

$\bigcirc = \square$ 4, 4

$\square + \square + \square = 4 \times 3$ 4, 4, 4

Student's name: ______________________ Assignment date: ______________

For advanced students

$\bigcirc + \square = 10$ $2\times\bigcirc+4\times\square = 28$	6, 4
$\bigcirc + \square = 5$ $2\times\bigcirc+4\times\square = 14$	3, 2
$\bigcirc + \square = 5$ $2\times\bigcirc+4\times\square = 16$	2, 3
$\bigcirc + \square = 7$ $2\times\bigcirc+3\times\square = 17$	4, 3
$\bigcirc + \square = 11$ $3\times\bigcirc+4\times\square = 38$	6, 5
$\bigcirc + \square = 17$ $2\times\bigcirc+3\times\square = 47$	4, 13
$\bigcirc + \square = 19$ $2\times\bigcirc+3\times\square = 55$	2, 17
$\bigcirc + \square = 19$ $2\times\bigcirc+3\times\square = 48$	9, 10

Factor, LCM, GCF 因素, 最小公倍数, 最大公约数

Fill in each ? by a number. Each circle has a sum of 19. 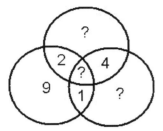 The 3-group intersection is 7. 6 , 7	Fill in each ? by a number. Each circle has a sum of 19. 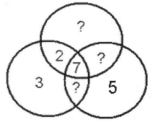 The 3-group intersection is 7. 16, 7, 0

Christine has no more than half as many marbles as Celine. Celine has 16 marbles. How many marbles could Christine have?

1, 2, 3, 4, 5, 6, 7

The number $N = 2 \times 2 \times 3 \times 3 \times 5 \times 11$. Is 4 a factor of N? Explain reason.

Yes, because 2 times 2 is 4.

Factorize 1870 to produce a product of primes.

$1870 = 2 \times 5 \times 11 \times 17$

Test if 167 a prime. Write the answer in steps.
Divide 167 by 2, 3, 5, 7, …, 37, 41, 47, the remainder is not 0, so 167 is a prime.

Find GCF and LCM of 41 and 2.

GCF=1, LCM = 82.

Find GCF and LCM of 13, 39, 2.
GCF =1, LCM = 78

Find GCF and LCM of $2^2 \times 3^2 \times 5$, $2^2 \times 3^3 \times 5^2$, $2 \times 3^2 \times 5$.
GCF = $2 \times 3^2 \times 5$
LCM= $2^2 \times 3^2 \times 5^2$

Cecilia gave Jonathan a gift, and she packaged it with ribbon, as shown below. The bow took 12 cm by itself. How much ribbon did she need to wrap the package, including the bow?

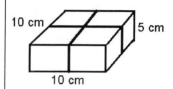

10 cm

10 cm

5 cm

(10+10)x2 = 20
5 x 2 = 10
5 x 2 = 10
bow 12
The total is 20 + 10 + 10 + 12 = 52 cm

Cindy is 3 kinds of trading toys: airplanes, dogs and cats. Which toy is worth more?

dog

List all possible answers. $\square \neq \bigcirc$

$\square + \square + \square + \bigcirc + \bigcirc + \bigcirc = 36$

$\square$	$\bigcirc$
0	12
1	11
2	10
3	9
4	8
5	7

0, 12; 1, 11; 2, 15; 3, 9; 4, 8; 5, 7

Student's name: _____   Assignment date: _____

Twice of 24 divided by one half of 8 half-dozen = 6 − ☐   4

How many pages are there in a book starting from page 19 (inclusive) and finishing on page 37 (inclusive)?

19

Circle the following product which has the smallest ones' digit.

(a) $222 \times 555 \times 111 \times 444 \times 333$

(b) $111 \times 221 \times 331 \times 441 \times 551 \times 661$

(c) $115 \times 225 \times 335 \times 445 \times 555 \times 665$

(d) $1 \times 2 \times 3 \times 4 \times 6 \times 5$ (d)

○ ☐ is a 2-digit number less than 40.

○ + ☐ = 7   2, 5

○ ☐ = 5 × ☐   2, 5, 5

If apples are only sold in a package of 5, what is the least number of packages I must buy to have 28 apples?

6

Fill in the same shape with the same number.

$\square = 5$

$\bigcirc = \square - 1$ 4, 5

$\square + \square + \bigcirc + \square = 21$ 6, 6, 4, 5

Fill in the same shape with the same number.

$\square = 6$

$\bigcirc = \square - 1$ 5, 6

$\square + \square + \bigcirc + \square = 31$ 10, 10, 5, 6

Fill in the same shape with the same number.

$\square = 11$

$\bigcirc = \square - 1$ 10, 11

$\square + \square + \bigcirc + \square = 33$ 6, 6, 10, 11

Fill in the same shape with the same number.

$\square = 16$

$\bigcirc = \square - 1$ 15, 16

$\square + \square + \bigcirc + \square = 41$ 5, 5, 15, 16

Student's name: _____ Assignment date: _____

Fill in the same shape with the same number.

□ =19

○ = □ + 1   20, 19

□ + □ − ○ − □ = 41   35, 35, 20, 19

Fill in the same shape with the same number.

□ =14

○ = □ + 1   15, 14

□ + □ − ○ − □ =51   40, 40, 15, 14

Fill in the same shape with the same number.

□ =23

○ = □ + 1   24, 23

□ + □ − ○ − □ = 65   9, 9, 24, 23

Fill in the same shape with the same number.

□ =29

○ = □ + 1   30, 29

□ + □ − ○ − □ = 47   53, 53, 30, 29

Student's name: _____ Assignment date: _____

Calculate the following area of triangle ABC.

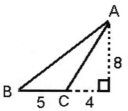

20 U²

Calculate the following area of triangle ABC.

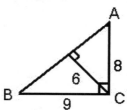

36U²

Write the following fractions as non-terminating but repeating decimals.

Calculate $\frac{1}{9}$ =	Calculate $\frac{11}{99}$ =	Calculate $\frac{1}{90}$ =
Calculate $\frac{1}{90}$ =	Calculate $\frac{10}{90}$ =	Calculate $\frac{1}{99}$ =
Calculate $\frac{10}{9}$ =	Calculate $\frac{100}{9}$ =	Calculate $\frac{11}{9}$ =
Calculate $\frac{11}{90}$ =	Calculate $\frac{100}{99}$ =	Calculate $\frac{100}{90}$ =
Calculate $\frac{1}{11}$ =	Calculate $\frac{1}{110}$ =	Calculate $\frac{10}{11}$ =

$0.\overline{1}$ 0.0 $1.\overline{1}$ $0.1\overline{2}$ $0.\overline{09}$ $0.\overline{1}$ $0.10\overline{1}$ $11.\overline{1}$ $1.\overline{1}$ $0.00\overline{9}$ $0.0\overline{1}$ $0.0\overline{1}$ $1.\overline{2}$ $1.\overline{1}$ $0.9\overline{09}$

Student's name: _____ Assignment date: _____

Calculate 400089 − 38998

361091

Calculate 410012 − 367898   42114

Calculate
3098×4109

12729682

Calculate
$31 \bullet 218$

868

Calculate
$213(987)$

210231

Student's name: _____ Assignment date: _____

$2 + 3 \times 3 \div 4$

17/4

Steven spent $30 after saving two-thirds of his money, and he had $20 left. How much did he have originally?

$150

Frankho ChessDoku™

Frankho ChessDoku™ is solved by using addition, subtraction, multiplication or division by following chess moves and logic.

Rule: All the digits 1 to 3 must appear in every row and column. The number appears in the bottom right-hand corner is the end result calculated according to the operator(s) and chess move(s).

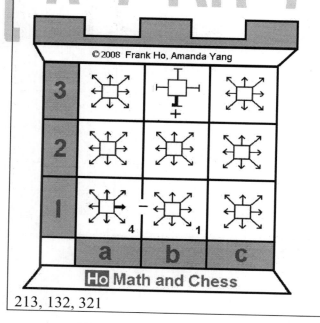

213, 132, 321

$1 = \dfrac{1}{a} + \dfrac{1}{b} + \dfrac{1}{c}$, a, b, c are unequal counting numbers. Find a, b, c.

Answers may vary, $\dfrac{1}{2} + \dfrac{1}{3} + \dfrac{1}{6}$

Find all possible answers.

Example The result of the left-most first equation is placed in the circle.	
$\square + 12 = \bigcirc - 8 = 20$	16, 28
$\square + 7 = \bigcirc - 9 = 30$	32, 39
$\square + 9 = \bigcirc - 10 = 40$	41, 50
$\square + 12 = \bigcirc - 18 = 50$	56, 68
$\square + 32 = \bigcirc - 17 = 60$	45, 77
$\square \times 12 + \bigcirc + 15 = 60$	2, 21
$\square \times 6 + \bigcirc + 9 = 29$	3, 2
$\square \times 13 + \bigcirc + 7 = 40$	2, 7
$\square \times 5 + \bigcirc + 4 = 50$	6, 16
$\square \times 4 + \bigcirc + 15 = 60$	10, 5

What is p?

$$P = 0.2 \times 1000 \times \left(0.1 \times 10^4 \times \frac{500 - 200}{5} \right)$$

12,000,000

Alex divided a basket of his apples into 2 equal parts and then divided one part into 3 equal parts. Alex gave away half of one of the 3 equal parts to his friends, and he had a total of 66 apples left in his basket. How many apples did he have in the basket originally?

72

Twenty-four squares each with 1 cm by 1 cm are put together, what is the largest perimeter?

50 cm

Replace each ? with a number.

Sequence	Value	
1	6	2x3
2	12	3x4
3	20	4x5
4	30	5x6
5	42	6x7
6	56	7x8
7	? 72	8x9
8	? 90	9x10
9	? 110	10x11

When throwing a die, what is the probability of getting an even number which is greater than 3?

2/6=1/3

What is the value of y?   **answer 2**

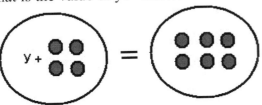

Andrew bought $100 stocks and sold at a loss of 15%. He then used the money which he sold stock to buy another stock and made a 25% gain. How much % did he gain or lose when compared to the original investment of $100?

6.25%

There are 99 squirrels, rabbits, and groundhogs. If adding as many as 18 times the number of squirrels, three times as many as rabbits, and a quarter of as many as the number of groundhogs, the total will be 100. Find the number of squirrels, rabbits, and groundhogs, respectively.

s=5, r=2, g=16

.

A basket of oranges is divided among Sam, Tom, and Mario. Sam took away one apple and then divided the rest into 3 piles with an equal number of apples in each pile and then he took away one pile. Tom took away one apple and then divided the rest into 3 piles with an equal number of apples in each pile and then he took away one pile. Mario took away one apple and then divided the rest into 3 piles with an equal number of apples in each pile. What was the minimum number of apples in the basket originally?

25

If Thomas gives Steven 5 cards, then Thomas will have as many as Steven has. If Steven gives Thomas 5 cards, then Steven will have twice as many as Thomas. How many does each one have?

Steven 35, Thomas 25

Use an estimating strategy to find $\sqrt{645}$.

The square root of 645 is about 25 since 25 x 25 = 625, so 645 is between 676 (square root is 26) and 625.

$$\frac{645 - 625}{676 - 625} = \frac{20}{51} = 0.39$$

The answer is 25.39

Find the answers to the next sequence.

Jenny wanted to phone Jasmine. She remembered that the first three digits were 604 but forgot the last four digits, but knew they were made of 3's and 4's. Show all the different possible telephone numbers Jenny could dial.

14 3344 3434 3443 3334 (4) 4334 4343 4433 4443 (4)

$2 - 3 = 2 + 0 - 3 = 2 + (1 - 1) - 3 = 2 + 1 - 3 - 1 =$

Can you explain the above operation by using diagrams?

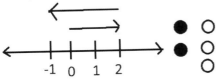

$2 - (+3) = 2 + 0 - (+3) = 2 + (+3) + (-3) - (+3) = 2 + (+3) - (+3) + (-3) = 2 + (-3) =$

Can you explain the above operation by using diagrams?
$+ 3 = 3, - (+3)$ means to go left on the number line 3 steps.

How to prove $-(+3) = +(-3)$?

- (+3):   ⇨   + (-3):

$-(+3) = -(+3) + 0 = -(+3) + (-3) + (+3) = +(+3) - (+3) + (-3) =$

Can you explain the above operation by using diagrams?

$(-(-9 - 3)) - (-(-8)) - (-7)(-1)$

-3

$(-(-9 - (-3))) - (-(-8)) - (-7)(-1) ÷ (-1)$

5

Student's name: ______________________ Assignment date: ________________

Fill in each box by a number.

$7 \times \bigcirc - 4 \times \bigcirc = 13.5$ 4.5
$50 \times \bigcirc - 42 \times \bigcirc = 48$ 6
$\bigcirc + 1.4 \times \bigcirc = 408$ 170
$\square - \bigcirc = 200$ $\square \div \bigcirc = 3$ 300-100=200
$\square + \bigcirc = 42.5$ $\square - \bigcirc = 5.5$ 24+18.5
$\square = 2\bigcirc + 95$ $\square - \bigcirc = 195$ 295-100=195

Arthur bought some stamps at $8 for every 12 stamps, and later, he sold for $8.00 for every 8 stamps. He sold all stamps and made a profit of $24. How many stamps did he buy and sell?

LCM for 12 and 8 is 24. 2x8=16, 8x3=24. 24-16=8, which is profit. To make 24, it means 24 times 3 = **72**

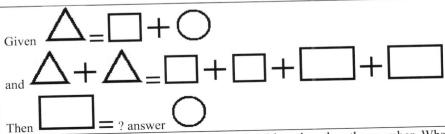

Given $\triangle = \square + \bigcirc$

and $\triangle + \triangle = \square + \square + \square + \square$

Then $\square = ?$ answer $\bigcirc$

The sum of two numbers is 32. One number is 14 less than the other number. What are the two numbers?

9, 23

The sum of two numbers is 40. One number is 4 times the other number. What are the two numbers?

8, 32

Solve C in terms of A, B for $\dfrac{1}{A} = \dfrac{1}{B} + \dfrac{1}{C}$

$C = \dfrac{AB}{B - A}$

What is the value of $1234567890a + 1234568b - 1234567890a - 1234567b$ if a = 1234567 and b = ?

1

A boy bought an equal number of apples, oranges, and pears for $84. He paid $3 for each of the apples, $4 for each of the oranges, and $5 for each of the pear. How many of each kind did he buy?
7

Solve $2\dfrac{2}{3} = \dfrac{4}{3x}$

$\dfrac{1}{2}$

Solve $0.1 = -\dfrac{3}{2}x + \dfrac{4}{5}$　　　$\dfrac{7}{15}$

Solve $2b = -b$　　　　　b=0

What are the last digits of perfect square numbers? If a number ends with digits 2, 3, 7, or 8, is it possible to be a perfect square?

All perfect squares end with 0, 1, 4, 5, 6, 9. So it is not possible.

The sum of the squares of the digits of a positive number is 50. All digits are in increasing order from left to right. Find these numbers.

17, 345, 1236

Find the 15th and the 56th element of the following number sequence.

0, 1, 0, 2, 1, 0, 3, 2, 1, 0, 4, 3, …15th …0, 56th ….3

Introducing Ho Math Chess™

Ho Math Chess™ = math + puzzles + chess

Frank Ho, a Canadian math teacher, intrigued by the relationships between math and chess after teaching his son chess, started **Ho Math Chess™** in 1995. His long-term devotion to research has led his son to become a FIDE chess master and Frank's publications of over 20 math workbooks. Today **Ho Math Chess™** is the world's largest and the only franchised scholastic math, chess and puzzles specialty learning centre with worldwide locations. **Ho Math Chess™** is a leading research organization in the field of math, chess, and puzzles integrated teaching methodology.

There are hundreds of articles already published showing chess benefits children and that math puzzles are a very good way of improving brain power. So, by integrating chess and mathematical chess puzzles, the learning effect is more significant.

Parents send their children to **Ho Math Chess™** because of they like **Ho Math Chess™** teaching philosophy – offering children problem-solving questions in a variety of formats. The questions could be pure chess, chess puzzles or mathematical chess puzzles in the nature of logic, pattern, tree structure, Venn diagram, probability and many more math concepts.

Ho Math Chess™ has developed a series of unique and high-quality math, chess, and puzzles integrated workbooks. **Ho Math Chess™** produced the world's first workbook **Learning Chess, to Improve Math.** This workbook is not only for learning chess but also for enriching math ability, and this sets **Ho Math Chess** apart from other math learning centres, chess club, or chess classes.

The teaching method at **Ho Math Chess™** is to use math, chess, and puzzles integrated workbooks to teach children fun math. The purposes of **Ho Math Chess™** teaching method and workbooks are to:

- Improve math marks.
- Develop problem-solving and critical thinking skills.
- Improve logic thinking ability.
- Boost brainpower.

Testimonials, sample worksheets, reports, and franchise information can be found at www.homathchess.com.

More information about **Ho Math Chess™** can also be found from the following publications:

1. Why Buy a **Ho Math Chess™** Learning Centre Franchise: A Unique Learning Centre?
2. **Ho Math Chess™** Sudoku Puzzles Sample Worksheets
3. Introduction to **Ho Math Chess™** and its Founder Frank Ho

The above publications can be purchased from www.amazon.com.

介紹何数棋谜 (Introducing Ho Math Chess)

何数棋谜 = 奧数棋谜 + 思唯腦力開發
英文教材, 中英双语教学

什麼是何数棋谜?

上百篇科學論文已發表國際象棋可以提高兒童問題解答能力.並且訓練他們的專心及耐力.所以我們已經知道下國際象棋對兒童有好處.但是因為國際象棋與計算能力並無直接開係,所以如何讓兒童能在一個歡樂的環境下也能利用下棋來提高數學的計算呢? 何老師首創並發明有版权的幾何棋藝符號並利用此符號發明了世界第一的独特結合數學与棋谜教材.何数棋谜讓兒童能利用幾何棋藝符號進行邏輯推理及數字的運算.棋藝與算術的綜合題含蓋了整數,幾何,集合,抽象數,對比異同,函數,座標,多空間圖形資料,及規則性數字分析.並且把棋藝的趣味性和數學的知識性結合在一起.

何数棋谜如何幫助兒童腦力思唯的開發?

很簡單的一個道理就是讓學生自願地同时去用左右腦.何数棋谜棋谜式数学即是專为当達到此目的而研發的教法及教材.
訓練右腦

何数棋谜首創独一無二的融合數學與棋谜的独特趣味寓教於樂教材,利用國際象棋訓練右腦的座標,空間分析及圖形及表的處理.

訓練左腦
何数棋谜發明了整合棋子與數學的圖形語言,讓兒童能利用抽象棋子符號圖形訓練左腦進行邏輯推理及數字的收集以創造題目並進行數字的運算.

國際象棋與算術的綜合題含蓋了整數,幾何,集合,抽象數,對比異同,函數,多空間圖形資料.所以枯燥無味的計算題變成了謎題,學生需要通過更多的思考.能讓腦去思考愈多則腦力也愈開發.處里訊息,分析資料才能發掘出題目.做這些謎題式數學時可以訓練學生比較會專心及有耐心.

何数棋谜教学结果有科研报告吗?

何数棋谜融合數學與國際象棋的教學理論已在 BC 省數學教師刊物上發表.科研報告已經證實何数棋谜教學法不但可以提高兒童數學解題及思維能力,還可以開發兒童的腦力,及分析問題的能力並且增加兒童學習的耐力,學生的探索創造精神及求知欲.判斷力,及自信心等,啓發思維訓練機警靈巧及加強手腦眼的靈活運用.

Made in the USA
Columbia, SC
17 June 2020